THE
ARTILLERY SERVICE
IN THE
WAR OF THE REBELLION

THE
ARTILLERY SERVICE
IN THE
WAR OF THE REBELLION
1861-65

John C. Tidball

Edited by Lawrence M. Kaplan

WESTHOLME
Yardley

Frontispiece: From left to right, Lt. Robert Clarke, Capt. John C. Tidball (with beard), Lt. William N. Dennison, and Capt. Alexander C. M. Pennington standing next to a Model 1861 wrought iron 3-inch rifled Ordnance gun in the vicinity of Fair Oaks, Virginia, June 1862. Tidball commanded Battery A, 2nd U.S. Artillery Regiment (Horse Artillery). (*Library of Congress*)

Westholme Publishing, LLC
904 Edgewood Road
Yardley, Pennsylvania 19067

ISBN: 978-1-59416-149-0

Printed in the United States of America.

Book Club Edition

CONTENTS

List of Maps

INTRODUCTION

JOHN C. TIDBALL (1825-1906) was a career army officer noted for his service as an artilleryman. He was born near Wheeling, West Virginia, and grew up in eastern Ohio. He graduated from the United States Military Academy in 1848 and entered the U.S. Army as a brevet second lieutenant in the 3rd U.S. Artillery Regiment. He received a commission in 1849 and transferred to the 2nd U.S. Artillery Regiment. He served in Florida from 1849 to 1850 during hostilities against the Seminoles. He spent three years in South Carolina before being assigned to frontier duty at Fort Defiance, New Mexico. Promoted to first lieutenant in 1853, he transferred to the 3rd U.S. Artillery Regiment and accompanied an exploring expedition to California from 1853 to 1854. He served on Coast Survey from 1854 to 1859 and was stationed at the Artillery School for Practice at Fort Monroe, Virginia, until 1860. During this period he was part of the expedition sent to suppress abolitionist John Brown's raid at Harper's Ferry, Virginia.

Tidball served all through the Civil War, being brevetted five times for gallant and meritorious conduct on the field. He also received a personal compliment from President Abraham Lincoln for his work at the battle of Gettysburg, where he was in command of the 2nd Brigade Horse Artillery under Major

General Alfred Pleasonton. He served in most of the major campaigns in the eastern theater, from the first battle of Bull Run through the siege of Petersburg.

At the outbreak of the war Tidball served in Captain William F. Barry's Battery A, 2nd U.S. Artillery Regiment. After Barry's promotion, Tidball received a promotion to captain in May 1861 and became the battery commander. His battery became the U.S. Army's first horse artillery battery, in which all the cannoneers were mounted. He served with this battery until June 1863 before accepting a commission in the U.S. Volunteers. He received an appointment as colonel of the 4th New York Heavy Artillery Regiment in August 1863. He commanded the Second Corps artillery of the Army of the Potomac during the Overland campaign, including the battle of the Wilderness. He was commandant of cadets at West Point from July through September 1864, and then returned to the field, leading the Ninth Corps artillery from October 1864 until April 1865 in the Appomattox campaign. He became a brigadier general of volunteers in 1864 and a brevet major general in 1865.

After the war Tidball resumed his position of captain in the 2nd U.S. Artillery Regiment. He served in the west, where he was promoted to major in 1867. While commanding the District of Alaska, he wrote the "Manual of Heavy Artillery Service," which later became a standard text at the Artillery School at Fort Monroe. He was the Superintendent of Artillery Instruction at the Artillery School from 1874 to 1881. He served as an aide-de-camp for General William T. Sherman, the Commanding General of the Army, from 1881 to 1884, and received promotion to lieutenant colonel during this assignment. He was commandant at the Artillery School at Fort Monroe from 1884 until his retirement in January 1889, and received promotion to colonel during this assignment.

When Tidball retired he was widely regarded as one of the U.S. Army's foremost artillerymen. No one was better suited

to examine and analyze the service
of field artillery in the Union forces
of the Civil War. He wrote a comprehensive study of the subject in a
series of essays titled "The Artillery
Service in the War of the Rebellion,
1861-65," which appeared in the
*Journal of the Military Service
Institution* from 1891 to 1893. These
essays are collected and edited here
for the first time since their original
publication. Tidball's work offers
new, important, and sometimes surprising insights and additions to our
understanding of the role of artillery
in many key battles of the Civil War.
Tidball divided his essays into examining the Army of the Potomac,
including the battles of Fair Oaks,

Colonel John C. Tidball,
circa 1884-1889, as com-
mandant of the Artillery
School at Fort Monroe,
Virginia. (*Companions of the
Military Order of the Loyal
Legion of the United States*)

Gaines' Mill, Mechanicsville, Malvern Hill, Antietam,
Fredericksburg, Chancellorsville, and Gettysburg; the Army of
the Tennessee, including the battles of Stones River and
Chickamauga; and finally the Army of the Ohio's battle of
Shiloh. He expertly presents the war through the eyes of an
artilleryman in describing the organization, equipping, and
manning of the artillery service. He also explains how the
improper use of artillery, particularly tying batteries down to
relatively small infantry commands that diluted their firepow-
er, seriously undermined the army's effectiveness until reforms
produced independent artillery commands that could properly mass artillery fire in battle. In 1905, he wrote an unpub-
lished study, "Remarks Upon the Organization, Command,
and Employment of Field Artillery During War, Based on
Experiences of the Civil War, 1861-1865," which included
additional insights into the artillery service, as well as a general overview of the Petersburg campaign. This edition has been

edited to include excerpts from this study, such as the artillery overview of the Petersburg campaign, a comparative analysis of artillery at Shiloh, Stones River, and Chickamauga, a section on Civil War battle reports, a section on artillery on the march, and a section on personal armament of batteries.

The narrative has been edited to standardize nomenclature and include full proper names of individuals and military units when appropriate. For example, independent batteries are cited first by their numerical designation and state, such as the 6th New York Independent Light Artillery Battery. Some modern word usage has been substituted, such as entrenchment replacing intrenchment. Spelling and name corrections also have been made where appropriate.

THE
ARTILLERY SERVICE
IN THE
WAR OF THE REBELLION

A portion of a Federal battery of 12-pounder "Napoleons" at Fredericksburg, Virginia, May 3, 1863. (*Library of Congress*)

ONE

ARTILLERY ORGANIZATION, MATERIEL, AND PERSONNEL

MAJOR GENERAL HENRY J. HUNT, in his able and interesting article entitled "Our Experience in Artillery Administration," published in the April 1891 number of the *Journal of the Military Service Institution*, mentions several vital defects that weighed heavily upon the artillery branch of the service during the late Civil War [see Appendix A]. As a mere matter of history it would be unprofitable to enlarge upon this topic; but as it is one of great importance in a professional point of view, and especially interesting to the artillery branch, some observations, supplementary to those of General Hunt, going into the details of that which he mentions only in a general way, are here proposed.

In order to fully to understand the character of the artillery branch of the service during the late Civil War, it is necessary to make some preliminary remarks on the organization of this branch during that period. These remarks will not, however, embrace the first Bull Run campaign, which taking place so soon after the opening of hostilities found everything military in a state of newness and without any systematic organization. The artillery serving with the Union armies was of two distinct kinds; heavy artillery and field artillery. The former, when not acting as infantry in the field, garrisoned fortified places such as Washington and Nashville and served the artillery with which the works were armed.

At the outbreak of the war, before volunteers were called to the field, all except eight of the 48 companies of artillery then in service were acting as foot artillery, either as infantry on the western frontier or as garrisons for forts along the seaboard. The eight excepted companies, two for each of the four regiments, were mounted as light field batteries. Soon, however, nearly all the remaining companies (they were then called companies) were converted into mounted batteries and took the field. About the same time the 5th Regiment of Artillery was raised, first as a provisional regiment authorized by the president, but subsequently confirmed by legislation as a permanent part of the regular military establishment. All of its batteries were mounted.

The heavy artillery of the war period was, therefore, almost exclusively from the volunteers and came from the several states, generally, as regiments or battalions, and served as such either with the active armies of the field or as garrisons and guards at fortified places and depots. Neither in its organization nor its service was there anything requiring comment, except that taken as a class it was a remarkably fine body of men and being well officered and but little subjected to the vicissitudes of campaign service, it was well instructed and disciplined. When the Army of the Potomac was so fearfully depleted by the battles from the Wilderness to Petersburg, a number of these regiments were called to the front from the works around Washington, and as infantry testified to their good fighting qualities. As garrisoning the works at Washington was considered a favored service, these regiments had no difficulty in obtaining recruits, and many of them took the field with upwards of 2,000 bayonets each.

The other branch of the artillery service, the field artillery, comprised all batteries of whatever denomination, operating

Henry J. Hunt, left, as a brevet major general of volunteers, commanded the Artillery Reserve of the Army of the Potomac in the 1862 Peninsula campaign before succeeding William F. Barry as its chief of artillery just prior to the Antietam campaign, which he occupied until the end of the war. William F. Barry, right, as a brevet major general of volunteers, was chief of artillery of the Army of the Potomac in the 1862 Peninsula campaign and occupied the same position in Major General William T. Sherman's campaign of 1864-65. He was Inspector General of Artillery between these periods for all the armies, with his headquarters in Washington, D.C. (*Library of Congress*)

with armies in campaigns. As before stated, nearly all of the 60 batteries of the regular service were mounted and equipped as light field batteries and were with the active armies in the field. But these did not constitute a tithe of the field artillery called into service; the other and greater portion came as volunteers from the states, some of which had fully organized regiments of 12 batteries each, in addition to which there was a very large number of independent batteries, *i.e.*, batteries belonging to state quotas, but not belonging to any regimental organization. This was the method of accepting volunteer batteries most favored by the War Department. Some of the volunteer batteries were equipped as horse batteries for service with cavalry. A proportionally large number of regular batteries were also thus equipped.

At the outbreak of secession, in the winter of 1860-1861, rifled guns had not been introduced into our service; but about this time Parrott began manufacturing in large numbers rifled guns of his model and the Army was speedily supplied with them. These were soon followed by the "Ordnance" 3-inch gun which eventually became the favorite. In the meanwhile great confusion as to kind and caliber existed. The arsenals of the North were ransacked and every piece, of whatever character, was placed in the hands of the troops then taking the field. This variety in guns caused great confusion and vexation in the supply of ammunition and material of all kinds. Many batteries were mixed as to their armament, having two and often three kinds of pieces.

Immediately after the Bull Run campaign a call was made for 500,000 volunteers, a call which was responded to with enthusiasm. About one-half of this force was designated for operations west of the Alleghenies, the remainder to the east, especially along the line of the Potomac. The latter embraced the Army of the Potomac proper, which was intended to be about 150,000 strong and organized for active campaigning.

Major General George B. McClellan, now in command, selected Major William F. Barry as his chief of artillery, and to him entrusted the organization of the artillery, and the following general principles were adopted with reference to it:

1. That the proportion of guns to other troops should be at least two-and-one-half pieces to 1000 men.

2. That the proportion of rifled guns should be restricted to the system of the U.S. Ordnance Department, and of Parrott, and the smooth-bores to be exclusively the 12-pounder bronze pieces commonly known as the "Napoleon" gun. Note: Neither mountain nor prairie howitzers were included in this scheme.

3. That each field battery be composed, if practicable, of six guns, and none to be less than four guns, and in all cases the guns of each battery to be of uniform caliber.

4. That the field batteries were to be assigned to divisions and not to brigades, and in the proportion of four to each division, of which one was to be a battery of regulars, the remainder of volunteers, the captain of the regular battery to be the commander of the artillery of the division. In the event of several divisions being united to form an army corps, at least one-half of the divisional artillery was to constitute the reserve of the corps.

5. The Artillery Reserve of the whole array to consist of one hundred pieces and to comprise besides the "light mounted batteries," all the horse batteries until such time as the cavalry might be massed as to its organization.

6. That the amount of ammunition to accompany field batteries should be not less than 400 rounds per gun—-that not being carried in the ammunition chests of the batteries to be carried in ordinary transportation wagons.

By the end of the first year of the war nearly all of the batteries of the Army of the Potomac were supplied either with rifles of uniform model or with smooth-bore 12-pounder "Napoleon" guns. In the armies of the West this reform was not so rapid and it was not until near the close of the war that anything like approximation to uniformity was effected.

Provision was also made in the scheme for a siege train of 50 pieces. Such a train was organized for the siege of Yorktown, Va. [see Appendix B], after which some of its batteries accompanied the Army of the Potomac through the Peninsula campaign. Two of the batteries of 4.5-inch rifles continued with the army in most of its campaigns and occasionally had opportunity to do good service; but being cumbersome on the march, unhandy to get into firing position, and difficult to supply with ammunition, they were kept very much to the rear and not available for duty when most needed—-as for instance, at Gettysburg.

A few batteries of the Army of the Potomac were armed with the 20-pounder Parrott, a gun between a light field piece and a siege gun. After trial this gun did not find favor with the army and gradually passed out of use. In addition there were a few batteries of siege rifles, 30-pounder Parrotts which accompanied some of the armies in the field.

Such, in brief, were the personnel and material of the artillery of the Union Army; an army that at one time had over a million men on its rolls and which was armed and equipped with an abundance, even a superabundance, of field artillery. The system of organization of this vast artillery was one of development. Some of the regiments of infantry responding to the first call for volunteers brought with them to the field sections of batteries. These, of course, proved of no service. But batteries were generally attached to brigades. This was but little better. Finally they were attached only to divisions. It will be remembered that army corps were not formed in the Army of the Potomac until March 1862 and in the other armies not until several months subsequent to this. Even after the establishment of army corps, batteries continued to be assigned to divisions; and in the Army of the Cumberland to brigades, until after the battle of Chickamauga. It was not until the spring of 1864 that the batteries of each corps were united into a brigade and made a separate command with its own staff and supply departments.

The development of the system of organization and management of the artillery was essentially the same in each of the Union armies and will be best understood by considering that of one of them separately; and as the Army of the Potomac was the first organized, the largest, the most compact and most symmetrical as to its various parts, it is selected by way of illustration.

At the commencement of its organization, soon after the battle of Bull Run, its artillery consisted of nine imperfectly equipped batteries of 39 guns, 650 men, and about 400 horses. By the following March these numbers had swelled to 92 batteries of 520 guns, 12,500 men and 11,000 horses, fully equipped and in readiness for active field service. Of this force 30 batteries were regulars and 62 volunteers.

The 1st Connecticut artillery park at Yorktown, Virginia, circa May 1862. (*Library of Congress*)

Nearly all of the batteries of the regular service were with the Army of the Potomac, but in consequence of the difficulty of obtaining men for them, owing to bounties and preference for the volunteer service, many of them were consolidated, making one battery out of two.

In the foregoing scheme, fixing the proportion of guns to other troops at two-and-one-half pieces to 1,000 men, proved eminently satisfactory, varying but little from beginning to end of the war; the number 1,000 meant those men actually present. Deducting the absent, the ratio averaged about three-and-one-half per thousand. While from various causes the infantry and cavalry strength present varied considerably from time to time, the number of guns continued practically constant. The ratio laid down included the guns of the Artillery Reserve as well as those attached to divisions, but did not include those of the siege train, employed on special occasions, as at Yorktown and Petersburg, Va. The armies of the West, following the lead of the Army of the Potomac, adopted the same artillery ratio.

This army was organized during the fall of 1862 into 11 divisions of infantry, to each of which were assigned four field batteries, one of which was a regular battery while the other three were volunteers. The purpose of this arrangement was that the regular battery should serve as an object lesson to the volunteers. The latter, both officers and men, coming fresh from civil life, had to learn everything of their new profession from the very alphabet up. They, however, proved themselves apt scholars and in an incredibly short time, favored by the protracted Indian summer of that year, most of this raw material was transformed into good serviceable batteries. The regular officers who were thus set before them as fuglemen, were as a rule of superior fitness for the work. Many of them had seen war service in Mexico and understood the requirements of campaigning; nearly all had, as subalterns, served tours of duty in light batteries, batteries then of unsurpassed excellence, and understood the internal economy of this complicated branch of the service. The senior captain of the four batteries of each division was styled, more through courtesy than anything else, chief of artillery for the division, and had a vague sort of supervision over the whole. Field officers of artillery found no place in this arrangement, for organization it can scarcely be called.

At first glance it may appear that this arrangement of batteries was all that could be required for their efficient service in the field, but subsequent campaigns developed its weakness. The batteries, well equipped and fairly well instructed, were as though a multitude of well-equipped and instructed companies of infantry had been assembled, and without higher organization sent to the field. There was no gradation of rank and command; all commenced and ended with the battery commanders, and the batteries were attached, like excrescences, to incongruous commands of infantry.

In addition to the batteries thus assigned to divisions, an Artillery Reserve was formed. This reserve was a complete organization in itself, with its own distinct commander, staff

Wrought and cast iron 20-pounder rifled Parrott guns of the 1st New York (Pettit's) Battery in the Peninsula Campaign, Virginia, 1862. (*Library of Congress*)

and supply departments. It consisted of 18 batteries of 100 guns. Of these batteries 14 were regulars and four of volunteers. All of the former had six guns each, about one-half being "Napoleons" and the remainder rifles. Three of the volunteer batteries were armed with the 20-pounder Parrott, while the fourth had six 32-pounder howitzers of the old bronze type. It was in fact the only complete artillery organization and command in that army until the assembling of the batteries of each corps into brigades in the winter of 1863-1864. The fact of its being thus organized conferred upon it the power of maintaining itself in the most complete state of efficiency, and it was therefore relied on with confidence. While the other and larger number of batteries was distributed to divisions, and necessarily restricted to a limited sphere of operations, and frequently, from the nature of the topography of the field, not able to act at all, the batteries of the reserve, being concentrated and well in hand, were always in readiness for service wherever most needed. They were, perforce, always in demand and did, especially the horse batter-

ies, a large share of the effective artillery work of the first period of the war.

It will be observed that the armament of the Artillery
Reserve was of several types; this for the purpose of meeting
any probable contingency. Four of the regular batteries were
horse batteries, attached to the Artillery Reserve, until the
cavalry (with which they were to serve) could be massed into
commands suitable for efficient service, a thing which was not
done until after the close of the Peninsula campaign of 1862.
In the meanwhile these batteries in addition to doing considerable duty with detachments of cavalry, took part in the principal battles of that campaign as also that of Antietam, where
they took a conspicuous and prominent part.

Being rapid of movement and always in condition they
were handy for any service. After the Chancellorsville campaign four additional batteries, all regulars, were equipped as
horse batteries, making eight in all. These were organized into
two brigades of four batteries each. For want of field officers
each of these brigades was commanded by its senior captain,
who was provided with a suitable staff for administrative purposes.

When divisions or brigades of cavalry were detached for
special service, one or more batteries were assigned to them
for the occasion; after the occasion had passed the batteries
returned to their brigade for rest and refitting. Service with the
cavalry was, especially after the introduction of the raiding
system, arduous and wearing upon batteries. The brigades of
horse batteries were now permanently attached to the cavalry corps, and ceased to be an attachment of the Artillery
Reserve.

The Artillery Reserve was organized into four brigades, one
of which consisted of the four horse batteries, and another of
the four volunteer batteries; the other 10 batteries constituted
two additional brigades, the whole being under command of
Major Henry J. Hunt, who being an additional aide-de-camp,
held the rank of colonel. He was assisted by a complete staff

consisting of an adjutant, a quartermaster, an ordnance officer (so styled), a chief medical officer, and a commissary. The quartermaster had charge of the train which, in addition to his own wagons, consisted of those carrying commissary supplies, medical supplies and ammunition. Each battery had two, or for horse batteries, three wagons for forage, rations and baggage. The Artillery Reserve was thus a complete and self-sustaining organization in itself.

The name "artillery reserve" was a misnomer; it was in reality an artillery division, and instead of being in reserve, in the ordinary acceptation of that term, was generally the first in the fight. Whenever a corps commander wanted batteries for any emergency, having no reserve of his own, he invariably sent for them to the reserve. The fact of batteries being assigned to divisions made division commanders chary of parting with them, and they gave them up, though but temporarily, only after many objections and often with delays fatal to the object in view. All who had comprehensive experience with artillery during the war will remember many instances of this kind within their own observation.

When the batteries of the corps were finally brigaded and thus rendered more efficient, less artillery was required to do the same amount of work. The reserve gradually diminished in importance until finally it became little more than a place for the recuperation of broken-down batteries.

The whole subject of artillery in the Army of the Potomac was under the general supervision of a chief of artillery, who with the rank of brigadier general was one of the staff of the general commanding. He was assisted in his duties by a sub-staff of his own, and in addition to purely administrative duties, exercised a certain degree of command until shortly before the battle of Chancellorsville, when even this was taken from him; but during the disasters of that battle he was reinvested with command for the purpose of gathering the scattered batteries together and with them affording cover for the withdrawal of the discomfited army.

The commanding general had, in addition, a chief ordnance officer, who was at first for a brief period a colonel, but subsequently a captain or lieutenant, who supervised requisitions for artillery supplies and was a sort of red tape channel for their procurement.

The senior officer of artillery in a division, nearly always a captain of one of the batteries, was its chief of artillery, but his functions as such were chiefly nominal. When a corps was created the senior artillery officer in it was by law its chief of artillery "in addition to his other duties"; but as batteries continued to be distributed to divisions, his duties, always uncertain and undefined, were principally administrative; and this continued until the consolidation of batteries into corps brigades, each a distinct and definite command. This latter was a long stride towards greater efficiency and was apparently all that could be desired towards maintaining the batteries in good fighting condition and using them efficiently on the field of battle. But the habit of having them assigned to divisions had now become so fixed and strong as to make it difficult to wean them away. It was a new departure and encountered opposition from many sources.

Division commanders had been so long accustomed to having them as part of their commands that they felt as though bereft of something really essential to them, and parted from them with as much reluctance as did old-time officers from their pig-tails and hair powder. So much was this the case that they still insisted on having batteries assigned to them for the march and for the battle, and upon one pretext or another generally managed to have them temporarily under their control, and this too at the very time they should have been free, under appropriate commanders, to render service where most needed.

The advantages of the new system were thus in a measure nullified and a great deal of the viciousness of the old system left still to plague the service. The war closed before prejudice against it was entirely overcome, but sufficient was accom-

"A squad of Capt. Smith's battery–Lieut. Woods in command." This battery is probably A Company, 1st Light Artillery (Illinois) at Camp Smith or Fort Prentiss, Cairo, Illinois, c. 1861. (*Library of Congress*)

plished in the way of reform to demonstrate the wisdom of the change. All of this will be more fully understood when we come to analyze certain battles and turn over, leaf by leaf, the records showing how the artillery was used and misused in each campaign, not only of the Army of the Potomac, but of the armies of the West also.

The old system of attaching batteries to small aggregations of infantry, belonging to the epoch of flint-locks and smooth-bores, had outlived its usefulness. The War of the Rebellion, following next after the Mexican War, naturally adopted the methods of the latter; but in the meanwhile, short as the interval was, a mighty change had taken place. The smoothbore musket, of short range and inferior accuracy, had given place to the rifle, of long range, great accuracy and wonderful power, while the efficacy of artillery had advanced in equal ratio. Thus new conditions of battle were imposed upon both arms. That most affecting the use of artillery was that it should have a corresponding freedom of action and ability to take positions where full advantage could be had from its improved arm, and this, it is obvious, could not obtain so long as batteries continued to be tied down to the narrow limits occupied by comparatively small bodies of infantry, so long as they were apportioned out, as it were, in equal quantities at regular intervals along a line of battle, regardless of all topographical considerations of the field.

Reason points out that artillery should occupy those positions, afforded more or less by every battlefield, where it can reach the enemy to best advantage with its fire, and thus give support and assistance to the infantry irrespective of any particular division. In other words the artillery should be used for the benefit of the whole and not for any especial part. Position is the chief factor in the use of artillery, and its importance increases in compound ratio with the range, accuracy and power of the arm. Often the positions most favorable for infantry, or at least where the necessities of battle require its employment, are the very worst possible for artillery. Under such conditions, and they occur in every battle, it is manifestly worse than folly to emasculate the artillery by unnatural attachments.

The straitened resources of the Confederacy forced the recognition of this fact upon its commanders much sooner than it was forced upon the Union commanders. The first campaigns in Virginia pointed out to Robert E. Lee the inadequacy of the obsolete system, and, before the year was out, he had all of his artillery organized into battalions of from four to six batteries each. To the command of each battalion was assigned a colonel or lieutenant colonel, and to each two batteries a major. Thus his artillery was always in hand and available for service whenever and wherever most needed; consequently a smaller amount of it was able to perform an amount of work equal to that performed by the much larger artillery force of his adversary.

Braxton Bragg's experience, up to and including the battle of Stones River, caused him to withdraw his batteries from brigades and adopt the battalion system. But it was not until after the disasters of Chickamauga that the batteries of the Army of the Cumberland were thus withdrawn and a more efficient arrangement adopted for the artillery of that noble army.

Batteries attached to small infantry commands (such as were brigades and divisions during the Rebellion) being deprived by such attachment of any higher function than simply to follow their divisions or brigades and in battle take whatever positions might offer, have but little use for officers of higher grade than battery commanders; but when organized into battalions for more efficient service, officers become necessary who have rank commensurate with the importance of the command, and who are thereby more upon an equality as to official influence with those of other arms cooperating with them.

This leads directly to the notice of another defect of our system during the war, most forcibly mentioned by General Hunt, who points out *ex cathedra*, that the War Department was from the beginning possessed with an idea that field officers of artillery were unnecessary for an army in the field. George B. McClellan and other commanders anxious to promote the efficiency of this arm by giving to it a proper system of command were hampered in their efforts by this incubus. As far as possible the War Department, influenced by this idea, suffered no army organization that required field officers of artillery, the consequence of which was that but few, even of the limited number who were mustered in as volunteers, had legitimate commands. They were, in the slang of the time, "sent a-fishing," and were assigned to this or that duty, it is difficult now to tell what; but certain it is they were not performing duty in their appropriate spheres as artillery commanders.

Of those of the regular service, the retired list, then recently established, took a few who were totally incapacitated, physically, for the performance of duty (this however did not diminish the number, for others were promoted in their places); quite a number became general officers of volunteers and were assigned to infantry commands; others were placed on duty in the various States as mustering and disbursing officers in connection with the enrollment of volunteers, positions demanding character and efficiency of the highest order. Not only were field officers of artillery thus employed, but those also of other branches of the service, who brought to the performance of the duties of these important positions not only experience, but that exactness in matters of detail and accountability which had become to them, through years of service, a second nature. Generally they were, it is true, "old fogies" of the Army, but in these positions their "fogyism" was a desirable quality. It was experience combined with integrity, and fortunate was the Government in having such a class of men upon whom to rely.

It is fitting here to mention that during the first period of the war captains of the regular artillery were not permitted to accept colonelcies of volunteer regiments, it being claimed at the War Office that their services were much more valuable as battery commanders than as regimental commanders; that while there was an abundance of good material elsewhere for colonels of volunteers, capable battery commanders were more rare. This prohibition, although advantageous to the formation of a good artillery, proved of great personal disadvantage to this class of officers. Their comrades in other branches of the service pushed ahead of them in rank, and gained a start that was not made up even after the embargo was raised.

It must, however, be said that as much as such officers were sought for to take volunteer regiments, captains of batteries were not so eager for the position as might be supposed. The brilliant services and reputation of batteries in the Mexican War, and the name and fame of such commanders as James Duncan, Samuel Ringgold, Braxton Bragg and others, had imbued them with the idea, true for the Mexican War, that the command of a battery was far superior to that of a regiment. As subalterns of artillery they had looked to the command of a battery as the *ne plus ultra* of all their hopes, and when they at last reached this position, they were for a time contented, and this contentment caused them to neglect to take the long look ahead which would have regarded a colonelcy of volunteers as but a stepping stone to higher rank and command. Even after the prohibition was removed, many, through preference for their own arm, or despairing to regain what they had lost, left their batteries with reluctance. The policy of the War Department, in preferring independent batteries without a proportional number of field officers, shut off promotion to captains of volunteer artillery, and forced them to serve without the stimulus of hope of advancement.

As a rule the captains of volunteer batteries were a superior class of men who entered the service with enthusiastic pride in their adopted profession. But service without hope of soldierly reward had its depressing influence, affecting each individually and the service collectively.

In the Army of the Tennessee, batteries were attached to divisions as in the Army of the Potomac, but there was no reserve artillery, consequently nothing to rely upon in case of disaster, as was illustrated by the battle of Shiloh. In the Army of the Cumberland the batteries were attached to brigades, one to each brigade, and this army, too, was without any reserve. The battles of Stones River and Chickamauga fully demonstrated the utter inefficiency of such an arrangement.

The Army of the Tennessee and of the Cumberland had artillery camps at their bases of operations upon which they could call for fresh batteries when needed. The Army of the Potomac had a similar camp at Washington where newly trained batteries were sent, generally without horses or guns, to be put in condition for field service. To this camp were sent from the field such batteries as required refitting or were to be discharged through expiration of service.

Recruits for batteries in the field received no instruction whatever in target practice or in the exercises leading to it. All their preliminary instruction previous to going into campaign was confined to the manual of the piece and to some battery maneuvers. Even under these adverse conditions many of the men, gifted with natural aptitude, became passably expert in using their guns and greatly assisted in making their batteries efficient. There was no military head to the War Department to direct in such matters, and suggestions coming from the field generally proved not to be happy experiences to the officers offering them.

The prescription of 400 rounds per gun of ammunition to be carried in the field proved to be approximately correct. It is certain that the army never suffered for want of ammunition. On a few occasions there was temporary scarcity; but this arose, not from lack of ammunition, but from mismanagement of trains carrying it. Notably was this the case at Chancellorsville and at Gettysburg. Up to the latter date the management of ammunition trains had not been entrusted to the artillery and ammunition, although abundant in the train, generally several, and often many miles away, could not be procured at the front when needed.

The custom obtaining throughout of carrying ammunition, whether for artillery or infantry, in ordinary transportation wagons was faulty, inasmuch as the wagons had glaring white covers making them most conspicuous objects for the enemy to trace the movements of the army by. While this was an objection adhering to any and all trains it was especially applicable to wagons carrying ammunition, which are frequently required to be as convenient as possible to the firing line, and should therefore be as little conspicuous as possible.

After the artillery of the Army of the Potomac was organized into brigades—one for each corps, each brigade had its own supply trains, that for ammunition being under an efficient artillery officer. This method obviated many blunders and uncertainties that vexed the original system. General Hunt who became chief of artillery of the Army of the Potomac just prior to the Antietam campaign, established very rigid rules about the lavish use of ammunition. One of these was that a battery should not withdraw from its firing position on account of having exhausted its ammunition. This was intended to prevent not only a too lavish expenditure of ammunition, but to counteract the bad moral affect upon our own troops of having batteries withdraw from the line of battle during the fight and also to deprive the enemy from deriving spirit and comfort by seeing batteries retiring from the firing line. The battery was to retain its position until relieved by another battery.

When corps artillery brigades were formed all of these matters were greatly simplified. When a battery in action found itself running short of ammunition the fact was made known to the artillery brigade commander who took means to have the battery supplied. Usually when a battle is imminent the brigade commander if alive to his duties, manages to have a few wagons from his ammunition train brought as close to the front as safety and other conditions will permit. The battery commander by judiciously arranging his ammunition, manages to have two or more of his caissons empty, and these are sent (if practicable with an officer) to the ammunition wagons to be refilled. Thus a battery can maintain its position on the firing line so long as ammunition can be brought up to it.

It is now proposed to follow the campaigns, or at least some of the campaigns, of the chief Union armies, and note the manner in which this magnificent artillery was employed. In doing this, it is necessary to mention the operations of other troops cooperating with the artillery, but this will be done only so far as may be required to elucidate the part taken by the latter.

Model 1861 wrought iron 3-inch rifled Ordnance guns of Horatio G. Gibson's C and G Batteries, 3rd U.S. Artillery Regiment, Fair Oaks, Virginia, 1862. (*Library of Congress*)

TWO

PENINSULA CAMPAIGN

C OMMENCING WITH THE ARMY OF THE POTOMAC; its first campaign was upon "The Peninsula of Virginia," that neck of land lying between the Chesapeake Bay and York River on the east, and the James River on the west, and extending from Fort Monroe to the city of Richmond, a distance of 84 miles. The troops landed on the Peninsula for the prosecution of this campaign, of which Richmond, the capital of the Southern Confederacy, was the objective, consisted originally of three army corps, soon reorganized into five, each of two divisions of infantry. Each division consisted of three brigades of four regiments. Prior to the battles near Richmond, Brigadier General George A. McCall's division of Pennsylvania Reserves was added, making a total of eleven divisions, averaging between nine and ten thousand men each. The corps were commanded respectively by major generals Edwin V. Sumner, the Second; Samuel P. Heintzelman, the Third; Erasmus D. Keyes, the Fourth; Fitz John Porter, the Fifth; and William B. Franklin, the Sixth.

To each division were attached four batteries of six guns each, in addition to which the Artillery Reserve contained 106 pieces, making a total of 346 guns. For the command and management of this large force of artillery the only general and field officers were one brigadier general; four colonels; three lieutenant colonels, and three majors, a number obviously insufficient. In number of men alone, it was equal to an ordinary division of infantry, which would have at least four times as many of each of the foregoing grades.

By the 3rd of April 1862, all of this army, except two divisions, had arrived from Alexandria, and disembarked at Fort Monroe and vicinity, and on that day started on its memorable but fruitless campaign towards Richmond. Two days marches brought it to a stand before the enemy's entrenchments at Yorktown. The Peninsula at this point is only about eight miles wide, and is almost cut in twain by Wormley's Creek, emptying into the York River, and Skiff Creek, into the James River. These two creeks almost interlock, and with their marshes, dams, and inundations form a formidable moat behind which the enemy was strongly entrenched.

The village of Yorktown, standing on a bluff overlooking the York River, was surrounded by an earthwork of extraordinary strength, constructed with great engineering skill by the labor of slaves gathered there for that purpose. This work was armed with about 70 pieces of artillery, many of which were of the heaviest caliber. Strong redoubts, armed in like manner, had been constructed, at intervals across to the James, all connected by infantry parapets well protected in front by abattis [an obstacle formed of trees or tree branches laid down in a row with their sharpened points towards the enemy] and [wire] entanglements. Altogether it was a most formidable obstacle to the further progress of the Army of the Potomac.

In front of Yorktown itself, the country was quite clear of forest, with a gentle undulating surface, a good deal cut up, however, by brambly ravines. Further towards the James, the country is more level, and was more wooded. Gloucester Point, across the river from Yorktown, was held and strongly entrenched by the enemy, and cooperated with the fortifica-

A naval gun in a Confederate battery at Yorktown, Virginia, July 1, 1862.
(*Library of Congress*)

tions at the latter place in blockading the river against turning operations by water.

Before the army was fairly in position in front of Yorktown a storm of rain and snow occurred of several days duration, and of such volume as to convert the whole region into a quagmire; to such an extent, in fact, as to preclude the movement of artillery or other wheeled vehicles. It was with difficulty that men and animals could get about. The whole bottom of the earth appeared to have fallen out, and prayers were offered up in the churches of the South for this seeming interposition of Divine Providence in behalf of its cause. Meanwhile, Major General McClellan, having decided that the lines were too strong for assault, settled down to a regular siege of the place, and for this purpose brought up his siege train of 50 guns, to which were added pieces of heavier calibers–guns and mortars–until the whole amounted to 101 pieces, some of which were 100- and 200-pounder rifles, the heaviest then in service. The 1st Connecticut Heavy Artillery Regiment of 1,400 men, under Colonel Robert O. Tyler, and the 5th New York Infantry Regiment, under Colonel Gouverneur K. Warren, were assigned to the management of this artillery, in the labor of which they were assisted by strong details from other regiments.

Siege operations were pushed forward with great diligence and energy. Parallels, bayeux, batteries, magazines, traverses, and all other operations known to military engineering were carried on in the most systematic manner. During this time–occupying a month–the light batteries had little to do, except to furnish officers to superintend work on the trenches; men to construct gabions and fascines, and teams to haul the siege pieces to their places on the line of investment, which latter had to be done at night, and over very bad roads. Occasionally a battery was called to the front to suppress some fire of the enemy troubling the working parties. This was a service of emulation among the batteries, and afforded them good instruction in practical gunnery.

Everything was in readiness for opening fire on the morning of May 4th. But the enemy, well informed of this fact, quietly evacuated his lines during the night, leaving behind 56 of his heaviest pieces of artillery together with much material in the way of ammunition and stores.

As soon as possible, the cavalry under Brigadier General George Stoneman and the four horse batteries under Major William Hays started in pursuit, overtaking the rear of the retreating column near Williamsburg, when a slight skirmish ensued, in which one piece of Captain Horatio B. Gibson's horse battery, Battery C, 3rd U.S. Artillery Regiment, fell into the hands of the enemy by reason of being left unsupported by the cavalry. It was subsequently recovered, being so deeply imbedded in the mud as to make it impracticable for the enemy to remove it. Late in the afternoon Brigadier General William F. Smith's division of infantry arrived; but as the country was wooded and entirely unknown to his troops, further operations were suspended until the following morning. The enemy encountered was merely the rear guard of General Joseph E. Johnston's army, consisting of only about 3,000 men; but Johnston, finding it necessary to hold the pursuing army in check until he could get his trains still further on their way to Richmond, called back other troops until almost his entire army took part in the battle.

The topography of the Confederate position at Williamsburg was very similar to that at Yorktown. Queen's Creek on the east, and College Creek on the west, almost interlock in the middle of the narrow peninsula, leaving space sufficient only for the main roads from Yorktown and Hampton. From these creeks to the town, distant about two miles, the country is a rich, almost open plain, slightly undulating near the creeks. Behind the creeks, the enemy had constructed a cordon of forts and redoubts, the principal one of which was Fort Magruder, near the center, covering the main roads. It was a regularly constructed, enclosed fort, of great strength. On the opposite side of the creeks from this cordon of forts, extended a belt of timber about a mile wide, beyond which, were open fields. The timber in front of Fort Magruder had been felled and formed into a powerful abattis. Rifle pits abounded everywhere. All of this line of works had been carefully prepared as a position upon which to fall back if forced from Yorktown. But Johnston, now in command on the Peninsula, having decided to withdraw entirely to other lines prepared nearer Richmond, did not stop to occupy that at Williamsburg until forced to do so to cover his retreat; and the resistance that he then made developed into a considerable battle, the first, thus far, of the Army of the Potomac. The troops of the latter actually engaged, consisted, however, only of the divisions of brigadier generals Joseph Hooker and Philip Kearny, and the brigades of brigadier generals Winfield Scott Hancock and John J. Peck.

A heavy rain during the night converted the peculiar soil of the country into mud without bottom. Hooker, by strenuous exertions, got his division up soon after daylight on the morning of the 5th, [the day he received a promotion to major general,] and immediately deploying it in the strip of woods before mentioned, led it forward through the fallen timber towards the enemy's rifle trenches near Fort Magruder. At the same time, with more zeal than judgment, he ordered forward his batteries into the quagmire among the stumps and fallen trees. Captain Charles H. Webber's Battery H of the 1st U.S. Artillery Regiment, and Captain Walter M. Bramhall's 6th New York Independent Light Artillery Battery, got in, and, notwithstanding the difficulty of the position, and the heavy musketry fire to which they were exposed, served their guns with excellent effect until the infantry was driven back. Their carriages, being hopelessly sunk in the mud and tangled up among the stumps and logs, had to be abandoned. Webber's pieces were carried off, but the enemy being unable to extricate Bramhall's contented himself with chopping the carriages to pieces. The other two batteries of the division, coming into position later, profited by the experience of the two preceding and were posted where they did equally good service with comparatively little loss.

Hooker made his attack at 7:30 A.M., and pressed it most vigorously until about 4:00 P.M., when his division was relieved by that of Kearny, together with the brigade of Peck. Kearny's troops made spirited dashes through the fallen timber and gained some of the rifle trenches beyond, but night coming on put a stop to further operations. Owing to the density of the woods and the miry condition of the ground, none of Kearny's batteries were placed in position. Hooker generously assumed all responsibility for the error in the misplacement of his batteries. It was his first experience in the management of artillery.

While the battle was in progress in the center, it was ascertained that one of the redoubts of the enemy, on the flank towards York River, was unoccupied, and Hancock was ordered to take possession of it with his brigade. Making a

Capt. Rufus D. Pettit's Battery B, 1st New York Light Artillery, in Fort Richardson, Virginia, June 1862. (*Library of Congress*)

detour to the right, he crossed the creek on the breast of a dam, and taking possession of the nearest redoubt, pushed on to another, also vacant. The one next in order to this he found occupied by infantry. The two batteries which accompanied him, Captain Charles C. Wheeler's Battery E, 1st New York Light Artillery Regiment, and Captain Andrew Cowan's 1st New York Independent Light Artillery Battery, were placed in position; and by the precision and rapidity of their fire soon dislodged the enemy, many of whom were shot down by Hancock's skirmishers as they fled from the works. The enemy had some pieces of artillery near by, but these were soon driven away by the batteries just named.

Hancock now halted to await reinforcements promised him, and immediately thereafter received peremptory orders to withdraw to the first redoubt. This he postponed doing as long as possible, sending to his superiors information of the advantage of the position gained by him. While awaiting replies by his messengers the fighting was most severe in front of Fort Magruder, upon which position Hancock now had a flank and somewhat reverse fire with his batteries. These also fired into all reinforcements going to the assistance of the enemy. It was now 5:00 P.M. and no reinforcements coming, and no information from his superiors, Hancock began preparations to retire as ordered. At this moment the enemy, appreciating the advantages he had gained, brought up a heavy force to dislodge him. Hancock, showing as stout a front as possible, withdrew, retiring his batteries piece by piece, to a second line which he was forming on a slight elevation in rear. The last piece delivered charges of canister into the ranks of the enemy before retiring. The infantry regiments, keeping themselves well covered with skirmishers, retired with like system and order; the whole operation was, in fact, a model, on a small scale, of battle tactics. When the enemy's line had approached to within a few yards of the crest on which Hancock had established his line, the latter moved forward and, delivering three volleys, charged down the slope upon the enemy, who fled leaving many dead and wounded besides 160 prisoners. No reinforcements arriving, Hancock was unable, as before, to reap the fruits of his victory by following it up. Shortly after this action was decided General Smith arrived with two other brigades and several batteries as reinforcements, but it was now dark and further operations were suspended for the night.

Sumner, then in command on the field, did not appreciate the very great advantage gained by Hancock's turning movement, and thus a rare opportunity of gaining prestige by giving the enemy a telling blow in this first battle was lost. Hancock's operations were the only redeeming features of the battle and for this reason have been given somewhat in detail.

During the night the enemy withdrew, following his trains, now well on their way towards Richmond. Owing to the condition of the roads he had to abandon a number of guns and caissons. For the same reason, little could have been accomplished by pursuit, if attempted, and McClellan therefore rested his troops at Williamsburg until the 8th, when he again resumed the march. Meanwhile the divisions of Franklin, Brigadier General John Sedgwick, Porter and Brigadier General Israel B. Richardson were sent by water from Yorktown to West Point, on the Pamunkey River, which brought them within about 25 miles of Richmond. Here, on the 16th, they reunited with that portion of the army that had marched by land. McClellan established his base of supplies at the "White House" on the Pamunkey, and by the 21st, had closed up his entire army and taken position on the Chickahominy River, distant seven to ten miles from Richmond.

Two of the horse batteries, Captain James M. Robertson's Battery B and Captain John C. Tidball's Battery A, 2nd U.S. Artillery Regiment, accompanied the cavalry, which, with some infantry, had been formed into a light command under Stoneman, for the purpose of closely following the enemy and of ascertaining the topography of this little known region, so that the bulk of the army could follow understandingly. In this duty these horse batteries demonstrated the ability of this kind of artillery to cooperate with cavalry under all vicissitudes of service.

This was the first campaigning epoch of the Army of the Potomac and, for this reason, has been given with more minuteness than it is practicable to bestow upon other events, although of much greater magnitude.

All the approaches to Richmond were fortified and the city itself surrounded by a strong line, in fact several lines of entrenchments. About eight miles to the eastward of the city, sweeping around to the southward, flows the Chickahominy, a tributary of the James River, which in this part of its course is but an insignificant stream, only about 40 feet wide; fringed by a dense growth of forest trees, and bounded by low marshy bottom lands varying from half a mile to a mile in width. It is subject to frequent, sudden and great variations in the volume of water and a rise of a few feet overflows the bottom lands on both sides. Such a rise occurred soon after the arrival of the Army of the Potomac, when a part of it had crossed to the farther side, placing it in a most critical position.

Before commencing operations on the Richmond side of the Chickahominy, McClellan cleared his right flank of a threatening force of the enemy, of about 9,000 men under Brigadier General Lawrence O'Bryan Branch, stationed in the vicinity of Hanover Court House, some 15 miles due north from Richmond. This duty was entrusted to Fitz John Porter, who had for the purpose a mixed command of infantry, cavalry and four batteries of artillery, one of which was Captain Henry M. Benson's horse battery, Battery M, 2nd U.S. Artillery Regiment. The enemy made stout resistance, but was finally forced back upon Richmond with considerable loss. This was a handsomely managed engagement and the artillery took a conspicuous part in it.

While this was transpiring on the extreme right, Heintzelman's Third, and Keyes' Fourth Corps, crossed the Chickahominy and took up a line eight miles south of Richmond, extending from the Chickahominy on the right to the eastern edge of White Oak Swamp on the left, a distance of some seven miles, with Seven Pines on the Williamsburg road as the center. The corps of Sumner, Porter, and Franklin remained on the other side of the stream opposite the right of Heintzelman's line. Heintzelman being the senior officer on that side commanded the whole. Brigadier General Silas Casey's division of Keyes' corps was at first stationed at Seven Pines, but was ordered to take position about three-fourths of a mile in front on the Williamsburg road, where it constructed a small redoubt for a battery for six field pieces. This redoubt was flanked to the right and left by incomplete rifle trenches.

Brigadier General Henry M. Naglee's brigade of this division extended to the right and front through Fair Oaks, a station on the West Point railroad, Brigadier General Henry W.

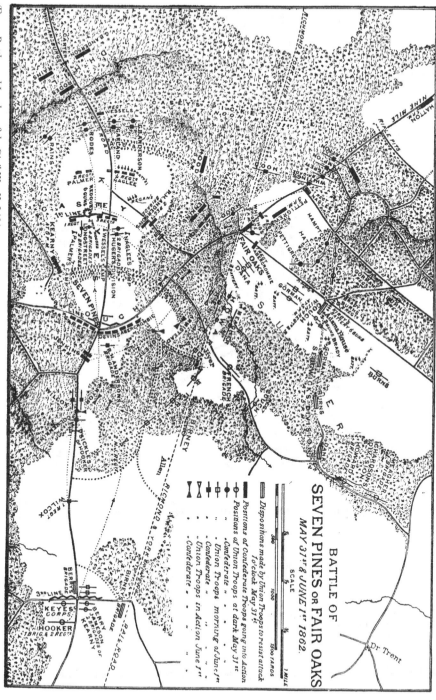

BATTLE OF
SEVEN PINES OR FAIR OAKS
MAY 31ST & JUNE 1ST 1862.

SCALE

Dispositions made by Union Troops to resist attack
10 o'clock May 31st
Positions of Confederate Troops going into action
" " Confederate "
" " Union Troops morning of June 1st
" " Confederate " " "
" " Union Troops in Action June 1st
" " Confederate " "

Wessels' brigade occupied the trenches on the left of the redoubt, while Brigadier General Innis N. Palmer's was in support in rear. Captain Thomas H. Bates' Battery A, 1st New York Light Artillery Regiment, occupied the redoubt with its six Napoleons, and nearby was Captain Joseph Spratt's Battery H of the same regiment. Captain Peter C. Regan's 7th and Captain Butler Fitch's 8th New York Independent Light Artillery batteries were near the trenches to the right and left respectively.

Casey's position was virtually that of an outpost, assailable not only in front, but on both flanks. Furthermore, it stood directly across the main road to Richmond and within a mile or so of the enemy's entrenched position.

The second or main line, running through Seven Pines, three-fourths of a mile in rear of Casey, was held by Brigadier General Darius N. Couch's division, also of Keyes' corps, with Hooker's division of Heintzelman's corps, far to the left, near the edge of White Oak Swamp, Kearny's division, also of Heintzelman's corps, was in support (or supposed to be), at Savage Station, some two miles back of Couch's position. The troops of these two corps, thus scattered, consisted of only about 25,000 men present for duty. Couch had with his division Captain Jeremiah McCarthy's Battery C, Captain Edward H. Flood's Battery D, Captain Theodore Miller's Battery E, and Captain James Brady's Battery F, 1st Pennsylvania Light Artillery Regiment, commanded by Major Robert M. West of the same regiment.

Hooker had batteries H and D, also of the 1st Pennsylvania, together with the 4th and 6th New York Independent Light Artillery batteries, all under command of Major Charles S. Wainwright of the 1st New York Light Artillery Regiment. Kearny had batteries B, New Jersey Light Artillery Regiment, E, 1st Rhode Island Light Artillery Regiment, and G, 2nd U.S. Artillery, all under Captain James Thompson of the last named battery. None of Kearny's batteries were, however, engaged; the miry nature of the ground, by reason of the constant rains, precluding the possibility of getting them to the front, except by the use often of more horses to each piece.

Constant skirmishing had been kept up between the pickets of Keyes and Heintzelman and those of the enemy; large bodies of whom were seen in front of Casey's position. The wooded nature of the country screened the movements of the opposing forces from each other's close observation.

Meanwhile, McClellan, to establish communication between the wings of his army, was vigorously pushing forward the construction of several bridges across the Chickahominy. But during the day and night of the 30th of May, a violent storm occurred; the rain falling in torrents, rendered work on the rifle trenches and bridges impracticable, made the roads almost impassable, and threatened the destruction of the bridges over the Chickahominy.

The enemy, perceiving the unfavorable position of the Army of the Potomac and the possibility of destroying that part of it cut off by the rising stream, threw an overwhelming force upon the isolated corps of Heintzelman and Keyes. His troops consisted of the grand divisions of major generals James Longstreet, Daniel H. Hill, Gustavus W. Smith and Benjamin Huger, numbering in all about 55,000 men present for duty and commanded by General Johnston in person.

Leaving the left wing of his army to guard against any counter attack that McClellan might attempt by crossing the Chickahominy further up, Johnston organized the troops just mentioned into three columns of attack. The center, or main column under Longstreet, consisted of two divisions of thirteen brigades. This column took the line of the Williamsburg road directly for Casey's position. The left column under G.W. Smith consisted of eight brigades, and taking the "Nine Mile Road," was intended to close in around the right flank of the Union position. The column of the right, consisting of five brigades under Huger, taking the Charles City road, was to sweep around upon the Union left. The central column was accompanied by six batteries. The other columns also had several batteries. Johnston had thus 26 brigades against 12 of his adversary. Sumner's arrival late in the afternoon of the 31st added six more. With this great disparity of numbers in his favor, the enemy was justly confident of success.

That portion of the Richmond and West Point railroad in front of Fair Oaks station was intact and the enemy used it to its fullest capacity during the night of the 30th in bringing troops to that part of his lines, which being but a mile or so in front of Casey's position made it not difficult for him to mass near it under cover of the woods.

Early in the morning of the 31st Casey's troops were set to work as usual on the rifle trenches, but about 10:00 A.M., the pickets in front reporting the advance of the enemy, preparations were at once made for his reception. The batteries, with the exception of the one in the redoubt, were hitched up. The real attack, however, was not made until about 2:00 P.M., when the enemy began shelling the position from guns stationed beyond the woods, from which his line of infantry soon emerged. Spratt's battery was sent as rapidly as the condition of the ground would permit to the right, to the support of Naglee near Fair Oaks. Here the musketry firing soon became intense, and Spratt and one of his lieutenants were wounded; but his battery continued to be skillfully and bravely handled by Lieutenant Charles E. Mink and held its position until the infantry was forced back, when it too retired to another position and continued the fight. In retiring, most of the horses of one of the pieces were disabled and the piece fell into the hands of the enemy. Regan's battery, stationed on the right of the redoubt and near the "Nine Mile Road," being behind some infantry that had been thrown forward to the woods, was unable to fire, but moving to the left opened with marked effect upon the masses of the enemy then near the redoubt. The latter, working around Regan's flank, caused him again to change his position, which in consequence of the mud, was done with great difficulty. It was while superintending the operations of this battery that Major David H. Van Valkenburg of the 1st New York Light Artillery Regiment was killed. Fitch's battery on the left of the redoubt fired with rapidity and effect until compelled to retire with the infantry. Bates' battery, in the redoubt, was splendidly served and held the position against the most determined attacks of the enemy. Owing to the miry condition of the ground the enemy was not able to bring his artillery to bear directly on it.

Some of Casey's regiments had not behaved well, and leaving the field in disorder caused an impression that his whole division acted in the same manner. Such was not the case; the majority of it fought well, and some of it heroically. The force of the enemy opposed to Casey, more than five times his number, struck him not only in front, but upon both flanks so as almost to envelop his position. His troops then fell back, but were soon rallied, some of them, however, not until it was too late to take further part in the battle of that day. The losses of this division in killed and wounded, not exceeded by any other division, is evidence of the fighting it did. A few regiments from Couch's division were sent forward to its assistance, but from some unaccountable reason neither Kearny nor Hooker arrived in time to render it any aid. When it became evident that the redoubt could no longer be held, Colonel Guilford D. Bailey, 1st New York Light Artillery Regiment, commanding Casey's batteries, entered it to superintend spiking the guns, and was there killed by a musket shot through his head. Bailey was a lieutenant of the 2nd U.S. Artillery Regiment, and was an officer of great merit and promise. About the same moment his adjutant, William Ramsey, was also killed.

When the redoubt was abandoned, all that remained of Casey's division fell back, some to Couch's line, but most of it to the vicinity of Savage Station. The whole force of the attack now fell upon the second line, held by Couch and such of Casey's regiments as had been rallied, together with portions of Kearny's division just up from the rear. When it looked as though the enemy would succeed in carrying the redoubt, Keyes posted the batteries of Flood and McCarthy of Couch's division on the right and left of the Williamsburg road and lined the rifle trenches near them with infantry. Miller's battery was posted farther to the right to resist the enemy coming against that flank. This battery, though forced to change position several times, did splendid service, as did also the other two batteries. So active were they in resisting several brigades of Smith's wing coming to the assistance of Longstreet that vigorous efforts were made to capture them, but without success. The official reports of the enemy testify to the efficacy of the Union artillery in this battle. It so happened that nearly all the field officers of artillery of the Army of the Potomac were with the corps of Keyes and Heintzelman, which accounts in a great measure for the efficient handling of the batteries.

Smith was to have made his attack simultaneously with that of Longstreet, but owing to some peculiar atmospheric cause the firing of the latter was not heard at Smith's position, and it was not until between four and five o'clock that Johnston, who was present with Smith, was informed by messenger of Longstreet's attack. Smith's brigades were at once advanced. Couch observing them approaching his right, hastened with part of Brigadier General John J. Abercrombie's brigade and Brady's battery to head them off, but being overpowered and cut off from the rest of his command he fell back towards the "Grapevine Bridge," a wobbly structure over the Chickahominy hastily constructed by Sumner's corps to reach the field of battle. Here he was joined soon after by Sumner with Sedgwick's division, accompanied by Lieutenant Edmund Kirby's Battery I of the 1st U.S. Artillery Regiment. The other batteries of the division were unable to follow on account of the miry condition of the ground. It was only by almost superhuman efforts that Kirby was able to get his battery through. His horses were useless in the mud and the guns had to be drawn by hand, a hundred or more men to a piece.

Sumner, anticipating the urgent necessity of sending his troops to the assistance of those across the stream, had made the most strenuous exertions to construct a practicable bridge. No sooner had Sedgwick joined Couch than the enemy came in strong force and opened a heavy fire along the whole line. He made several charges, but was each time repulsed with great loss by the steady fire of the infantry and the splendid practice of the battery. After sustaining the enemy's fire for a considerable time, Sumner ordered five regiments to advance and charge with the bayonet. This charge was executed in the most brilliant manner. The enemy was driven in confusion from this part of the field and darkness now ended the battle for the day. In this attack, which lasted not over an hour, Smith reports that he lost 164 killed, 1,010 wounded and 109 missing.

Just as this conflict was closing, Captain John A. Tompkins, commanding another of Sedgwick's batteries, Battery A, 1st Rhode Island Light Artillery Regiment, struggled into position by the side of Kirby, and about the same time Captain Walter O. Bartlett, Battery B, 1st Rhode Island Light Artillery Regiment, succeeded in getting up one of his pieces. The ground was in such condition that the wheels of the carriages sank to their hubs and horses mired to their girths. No number of horses that could be attached could move a piece without the assistance of men at ropes.

About sunset Richardson arrived with Sumner's other division and took position on the left of Sedgwick, extending his left towards Kearny's division near Seven Pines. Richardson had crossed also on the "Grapevine Bridge," but his batteries, together with the remainder of Sedgwick's, were unable to follow. The rising water had swept away the corduroy roadway at either end of the bridge and this could be replaced only by the greatest labor. Each piece and caisson had to be dragged over by hand. The entire night, dark and rainy, was consumed in this work, but the batteries were all in position before the enemy attacked in the morning. Seldom, perhaps never during the war, were batteries moved under such difficulties and with such untiring zeal and energy on the part of their officers and men.

During the night and early morning such dispositions were made along the entire line as were necessary to close up gaps and make connections. The divisions stood from right to left: Sedgwick, Richardson, Kearny, Couch, and Hooker, with the fragments of Casey's brigades between the two last. The batteries were disposed along the line with their divisions, but the miry condition of the ground precluded all maneuvering. Sumner, as senior officer, commanded the whole.

Soon after 6:00 o'clock on the morning of June 1st, the enemy approached and opened a rolling fire of musketry at short range along the right of Sumner's line, and at the same time moved heavy columns down the roads in front of Richardson's position. The batteries of the latter met these columns with a crushing fire. The infantry at the same time opened with a fire so hot and well sustained as to cause the enemy to fall back. Bringing up fresh troops he renewed the attack, and again was repulsed, and this time followed up by bayonet charges of Brigadier General William H. French's and Brigadier General Oliver O. Howard's brigades, which checked all further attempts at attack on that part of the field

Kearny's, Couch's, and other troops in front of Longstreet, did not wait for him to attack, but opened the action themselves. D. H. Hill, whose division was the head and front of the attacks upon Casey's position the day before, says of this: "[Brigadier General Lewis A.] Armistead's brigade fled early in the action, with the exception of a few heroic companies with which that gallant officer maintained his ground against an entire brigade. [Brigadier General William] Mahone withdrew his brigade without orders, I sent up [Brigadier General Raleigh E.] Colston's to replace him, but he did not engage the Yankees as I had expected him to do."

Hill then mentions a number of brigades that fought well, but for some reason a great deal of the spirit of fight had been taken out of Hill's troops in the battle of the previous day. After being driven back, Longstreet's column kept up a show of resistance until dark, when all silently withdrew. Hill, speaking of the withdrawal says: "The delicate operation of withdrawing 30,000 men in the presence of the enemy had to be performed before daylight. The artillery and wagons had to pass through slushes and mud-holes over the axle, and the whole road was almost impassable for infantry." The enemy left upon the field his dead and wounded, and many signs of his discomfiture and hasty retreat. But he had not far to go before being secure behind his impregnable entrenchments. It was simply out of the question for the Union troops to follow him up with any prospect of reaping the slightest advantage.

Thus ended the battle of Seven Pines, or of Fair Oaks as it is generally called, a battle probably less understood than any other of the war. The unprecedented rise of the Chickahominy, preventing almost the possibility of reinforcing that part of the army on the further side, practically assured success to the enemy. It enabled him to attack with a vastly superior force, over ground entirely familiar to him, and with all the advantages of the initiative.

The Union artillery, although so hampered by the condition of the ground, took no insignificant part in this victory. The redoubt that figured so conspicuously in the battle of the first day was constructed by Colonel Bailey for the artillery that so gallantly defended it, and it prevented the enemy from breaking the lines at his first onset and delayed him until Kearny and Sedgwick could arrive upon the field. The firmness of the other batteries was reassuring to the infantry, who held more firmly to their rifle trenches through the influence of good example.

We have seen with what pertinacious bravery the redoubt was held against the assaults of the enemy's main column. The artillery fire from this redoubt disorganized the enemy's efforts until reinforcements arrived. The delay of Smith's column to attack at the appointed time, and the non-arrival of

Huger's column on the right flank, all tended to make the success of Longstreet's column incomplete.

On the second day, owing to the arrival of Sumner, there was less disparity of numbers, but still, according to all rules of battle, the Confederates should have succeeded. Johnston was carried from the field, wounded. Late in the afternoon of the first day, Smith, as senior officer present, succeeded him in command, and he attributes the mishaps of the second day to the meddlesome interference of Jefferson Davis, who was present on the field. About 2:00 P.M. of that day the latter invested General R. E. Lee with command of this army, a command which he held until he surrendered it at Appomattox three years afterwards.

Seeing the hopelessness of driving this wing of McClellan's army into the swamps of the Chickahominy, as had been expected, Lee ordered his army to withdraw to their entrenchments. The losses in this battle were heavy. Those of the Army of the Potomac were 790 killed, 3,594 wounded, and 647 missing; making a total of 5,031. That of the Confederates was 7,997, nearly all of whom were either killed or wounded. The enemy carried off the six guns captured with the redoubt, together with the one taken from Spratt's battery; certainly a very moderate price for the Union cause to pay for a victory which prevented the greatest of disasters to that army.

The good fighting of those two days undoubtedly saved the Army of the Potomac from a most serious disaster, and disaster at that time meant something more than the mere loss of a battle. The losses sustained at Fair Oaks, by each side, were almost the same as at the great battle of Missionary Ridge, including Lookout Mountain and Orchard Knob, a battle that figures in history as one of the greatest of the war.

The rains that had so interfered with military operations at the time of the battle of Fair Oaks, continued until about the middle of the month, keeping the whole country in a condition of quagmire, entirely impracticable for artillery and almost so for infantry. This hot and damp June weather had developed the fatal Chickahominy fever, which together with other diseases incident to campaigning was reducing McClellan's army at a fearful rate. Reinforcements that had been promised him were withheld in consequence of Major General Thomas J. "Stonewall" Jackson's operations in the Valley of Virginia, which had a threatening look towards Washington.

As soon as the Chickahominy subsided and the ground had become firm enough for moving trains and artillery, Franklin's corps was crossed to the other side, leaving only that of Fitz John Porter to hold the right flank and guard the line of communication with the base on the Pamunkey. Porter was reinforced by McCall's division from Irvin McDowell's corps, which corps had been held back on the line of the Rappahannock River as a guard to Washington, but which later had been hastened to the Shenandoah Valley to assist major generals John C. Fremont and Nathaniel P. Banks in repulsing Jackson, who was then driving everything before him in that quarter.

The line occupied by the troops on the Richmond side of the Chickahominy was about the same as that established by Keyes and Heintzelman previous to the battle of Fair Oaks. By incessant labor it had grown into one of formidable breast-works with redoubts and emplacements for batteries at frequent intervals. Porter entrenched himself, in like manner, behind Beaver Dam Creek, a small tributary of the Chickahominy. His batteries occupied positions commanding the roads and open ground across the creek.

Jackson, having meanwhile cleared the Shenandoah Valley, was now approaching with mysterious rapidity to assist Lee in crushing the right flank of McClellan's army and destroying his connection with the White House base. Preparatory to this, Lee had constructed a powerful line of entrenchments confronting McClellan on the Richmond side of the Chickahominy. These he now proposed to hold with a comparatively thin line while he withdrew the bulk of his forces to the other side to crush Porter.

At this time Lee's army, including that of Jackson, then upon the point of junction with him, consisted of seven divisions of 35 brigades, containing 168 regiments. McClellan's army consisted of 11 divisions of 33 brigades, containing 132 regiments. As regiments in each army were about of equal strength, the foregoing numbers represent very closely the relative strength of the two armies. This is exclusive of cavalry, in which Lee had slightly the preponderance.

Lee had about 190 field guns; McClellan had 346, a very great preponderance in this arm. But the former had quite a number of seacoast guns in position on his works and besides had already adopted the battalion system for most of his artillery and therefore had greatly the advantage in its' management and use.

It may here be remarked that 10 guns of the siege train at Yorktown, five 4.5-inch ordnance and five 30-pounder Parrotts, followed up as soon as the roads became firm enough, and joining the army were placed in position on the left side of the Chickahominy opposite some heavy guns of the enemy on the other side. During the night before the battle of Gaines' Mill they were moved across to the other side and placed in battery to strike the enemy's columns as they advanced against Porter. From each position these guns fired a few shots, probably not over a hundred in all. These guns were in charge of two batteries of the 1st Connecticut Heavy Artillery Regiment.

Batteries B and M of this regiment, each serving four 4-inch siege rifled guns, continued with the Army of the Potomac through all of its campaigns from Fredericksburg, December 1862, to April 1864. Notwithstanding the weight and clumsiness of these siege guns they managed to get through and were always on hand, but were seldom used. In consequence of the limited amount of ammunition that could be carried for

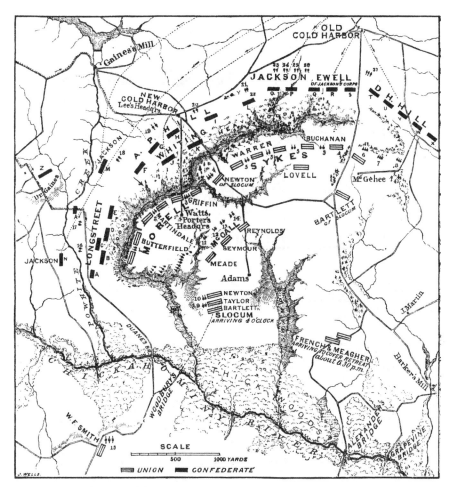

(From *Battles and Leaders of the Civil War*, II: 334.)

them, they were always reserved for the supreme crisis, and that seemingly never arrived.

On the morning of June 26th, Lee, leaving the divisions of Huger and Major General John B. Magruder in the entrenchments confronting McClellan, and withdrawing those of D.H. Hill, Longstreet and Major General Ambrose P. Hill, crossed the Chickahominy to make his junction with Jackson and together attack Porter. The divisions left behind consisted of nine brigades of 44 regiments and 15 field batteries of about

60 pieces. The three divisions which crossed to the left side consisted of 17 brigades of 81 regiments and 21 batteries of about 84 guns. These united to Jackson's force gave Lee 26 brigades of 124 regiments and about 120 guns, against Porter's force of nine brigades of 37 regiments and 96 guns. Towards the close of the battle of the 27th, Gaines' Mill, Brigadier General Henry W. Slocum's division of 12 regiments joined Porter, making his entire force engaged in that battle amount to 49 regiments as against Lee's 124. Very late in the afternoon the brigades of French and Brigadier General Thomas F. Meagher were crossed over also, but reached the field after the close of the battle. These brigades are not therefore counted in with Porter's fighting strength.

Huger and Magruder were to hold their positions against any assaults and to observe closely the movements of the troops opposed to them. Lee thought McClellan would probably withdraw to save his base at the White House; in this case Huger and Magruder were to follow closely. Brigadier General James Ewell Brown "JEB" Stuart's cavalry of 10 regiments with a horse battery was thrown out on Jackson's left to guard his flank and observe all movements of the Union Army.

Lee having crossed his three grand divisions, commenced about 3:00 P.M., an attack along Porter's whole line, making a determined effort to force the passage of the road on the right. This was successfully resisted by the brigade of Brigadier General John F. Reynolds and the artillery posted to sweep this approach. After a severe struggle he was forced to retire with heavy loss. A rapid artillery fire with desultory skirmishing was maintained along the whole front while the enemy massed his troops for another effort about two hours later at the lower road. This attack was likewise repulsed, the artillery taking a conspicuous part in it also. The firing ceased and the enemy retired about 9:00 A.M. This was the battle of Mechanicsville, the first of the "Seven Days Battles."

The position on Beaver Dam creek, although so successfully defended, had its right flank so far in the air as to be easily enveloped by Jackson's force. It was, therefore, determined that Porter should fall back and occupy the high ground near Gaines' Mill and there make a stand to gain time for the trains and other impedimenta to get on their way to a new base on James River, a change that McClellan had now decided upon deeming it impracticable to maintain the base on the Pamunkey.

After daylight on the morning of the 27th Porter withdrew and unmolested took up his new position. The enemy followed closely, but were delayed by the skillful maneuvering and excellent fire of two horse batteries, which unsupported by any other troops covered the rear. These batteries had been sent to Porter for this express duty.

Porter disposed his corps with his right and center on the hills and his left extending down to the low grounds. Part of the front was covered by the ravine of the Gaines' Mill stream, filled with underbrush. The ground occupied, as also that in its front, consisted of open fields, interspersed with strips of woodland. On the right and on the low ground towards the Chickahominy, the country was entirely wooded.

Although Porter's troops occupied the ground several hours, awaiting the appearance of the enemy, no attempt whatever was made to strengthen the position by temporary works. A few trees were felled on the extreme left as a barrier and that was all. This, further on in the war, would have been deemed culpable neglect. Two years after this date, when Lieutenant General Ulysses S. Grant fought over this same ground with the combined armies of the Potomac and James, and with a difference in numbers as great in his favor as it was now against Porter, the whole surface of the land was converted into entrenchments. Every command, large or small, entrenched itself as if by instinct.

Porter arranged his troops with the division of Brigadier General George Sykes on the right and that of Brigadier General George W. Morell on the left, each of three brigades. Each brigade had two of its regiments in reserve. Part of the artillery of these divisions was posted with the infantry at intervals along the front line, the rest was held in reserve. McCall's division formed a second line in rear of a strip of woods between it and the front line. Six additional batteries, two of which were horse batteries, had been sent over from the artillery reserve and were temporarily attached to the divisions. For all the 16 batteries that Porter had, there was no artillery commander, none but the battery commanders themselves, who fortunately proved themselves equal to the occasion. There was little or no judgment exercised by division commanders in posting their batteries. Sykes evidently thought he had fulfilled every condition when he divided Captain John Edwards' battery, composed of batteries L and M, 3rd U.S. Artillery Regiment, and sent two guns from it to each of his three brigades. Morell divided some of his batteries in the same manner, besides posting a couple of them, with little or no support, on the extreme left, where from the topography of the field they had little scope for their own defense and fell an easy prey to the enemy. As the battle progressed the batteries in reserve were thrown forward and took the best position available. The extreme simplicity of the battle favored this and enabled battery commanders to supplement by their own good judgment what was lacking in proper organization and command of the artillery.

Two regular batteries, almost entirely unsupported, were posted on the extreme right flank and by their united and well sustained fire were enabled to repel three powerful assaults and prevent Jackson from enveloping and crushing in that flank. Jackson, in his report says that he brought up parts of four battalions of batteries, in all about 30 pieces, to break this flank. The two batteries referred to, withstood a good portion of the firing of these pieces. Brigadier General Philip St. George Cooke, with a handful of cavalry, took position under the hill near the extreme left to observe that flank, and if opportunity offered, was to strike the enemy on the plain.

The march of Jackson's column having been somewhat delayed, he did not effect a junction with Lee until the forenoon of this day. For this reason Lee delayed his attack until about noon, when he began feeling with skirmishers for the weakest points of his adversary's line. Soon thereafter, large bodies of infantry, supported by a warm fire of artillery, engaged Porter's whole line. This first attack, made with great impetuosity, continued for about an hour, but was finally repulsed. Lee says his regiments were rallied and in time repelled the advance of the enemy. Some brigades were broken, others stubbornly maintained their positions, but it became apparent that the enemy was gradually gaining ground.

Lee readjusted his lines and massed his troops for another assault. Porter drew his infantry and artillery towards the center and prepared to receive the shock. In about an hour the enemy advanced and renewed the attack, more furiously than before. Lee says of this attack: "On the right the troops moved forward with steadiness, unchecked by the terrible fire from the triple lines of infantry on the hill, and the cannon, on both sides of the river, which burst upon them as they emerged upon the plain. The dead and the wounded marked the way of this intrepid advance." After about an hour of the most sanguinary struggle, this assault also was repulsed, followed by an hour of ominous silence; indicating that Lee was again massing for a still greater effort.

Porter, appreciating from the first the greatly superior numbers of his adversary, had sent repeated requests to McClellan for reinforcements from the corps disengaged on the opposite side of the Chickahominy. But so skillfully were Huger and Magruder keeping up their show of attack in that quarter that McClellan could be induced to part with but one division, that of Slocum, of Franklin's corps, which joined Porter in time to render invaluable assistance in repelling the third assault. This the enemy made about 6:00 P.M., advancing immense bodies of infantry under cover of a terrific fire of artillery. This furious attack was, likewise, successfully resisted and repulsed, but immediately renewed by fresh troops.

Porter pushed up his reserves as rapidly as possible to strengthen the front line, and again the enemy was repulsed. As each fresh regiment went in, the effect was shown by the enemy giving way on that part of the line. This continued until the last reserve regiment had been advanced. But those of the enemy appeared to be inexhaustible and, little by little, he gained ground. As if for a final effort, just as the sun was setting, the enemy massed all that he had on the right and left, and then threw them with overpowering force against Porter's thinned ranks. Porter says: "In anticipation of this our artillery, which until now had been well engaged at favorable points of the field in dealing destruction upon the enemy, or held in reserve, was now thrown to the front to cover the withdrawal of our own retiring troops. The batteries already engaged continued playing on the coming masses, while the others (in all about 80 guns) successively opened as our troops withdrew from in front of their fire, and checked in some places, in others drove back the advancing enemy."

The shortness of the line occupied by these 80 or more guns so concentrated them as to make of them virtually one battery and gave to their fire the effect of artillery in mass. The enemy, in their reports, gives full credit for the execution produced by this fire. On the extreme left the enemy had gained a strip of woods and was forcing back the infantry at that point. Cooke, fearful for the safety of the three batteries at that point, ordered a charge by the five small troops of the 5th U.S. Cavalry, during which the fire of the batteries became masked. While no impression whatever was made on the enemy by the charge, a volley of musketry broke it and sent the cavalrymen and many riderless horses in utter rout to the rear through the batteries. Before the latter could recover from the confusion into which they were thus thrown the enemy was upon them. This break caused the entire line to fall back, not, however, in confusion, but by contesting bravely every inch of the ground and showing such a stout front as to deter the enemy from following.

The object of the battle had been gained. McClellan was enabled by it to complete his arrangements for changing his base to the James River, an operation of the utmost delicacy as a military movement.

During the night following, Porter withdrew unmolested across the Chickahominy. McClellan, in not attacking the line in front of him on the south side, while the bulk of Lee's army was fighting Porter on the north side, committed the fatal mistake of his military career.

In this severe contest, one of the most remarkable of the war, from the disparity of numbers, the determination and persistency of the assaults and the pluck with which they were resisted, each battery played its own special part and did it nobly. In the aggregate their services were as valuable as brilliant. It is not probable; it is highly improbable, that the infantry, as bravely as it held its ground, could have withstood even the first assault without the support and confidence imparted to it by the artillery. This support and confidence was mutual, and never did two arms of the service cooperate to greater advantage. There were, it is true, 19 guns lost, but they were not lost when standing idle or when entangled in the woods endeavoring to escape, but while bravely doing their duty on the front line of battle. "It was not until the last successful charge of the enemy that the cannoneers were driven from their pieces or struck down that the guns were captured." The losses in killed and wounded were in proportion to the intensity and length of the engagement.

McClellan determined upon Harrison's Landing, a few miles below the confluence of the Appomattox River, as his new base. In a straight line this was about 25 miles almost due south of the right of his position on the Chickahominy. He had about 40 miles of trains, exclusive of the artillery carriages, and but one road over which to move, and this was intersected by several others leading from Richmond in such manner as to bring the enemy upon his right flank at dangerous points.

Lee, discerning the object of this movement, lost no time in following it up, and making use of the roads just mentioned, endeavored to cut in so as to engage the Union column in detail. He so far succeeded in this as to bring on several heavy engagements with portions of McClellan's army, in each of which he was, however, unsuccessful in breaking the column. The first of these was on June 28th, the day succeeding the battle of Gaines' Mill, when he attacked Franklin's corps as it was withdrawing from its entrenchments at Golding's farm. On the same day Sumner's corps had a sharp engagement at Allen's farm, near Savage Station. In both of these affairs the artillery was conspicuous for its efficiency.

On the following day, that is, June 29th, occurred the battle of Savage Station, in which both Sumner's and Franklin's corps were engaged, and in which their batteries did most excellent work. This engagement, although short, was sharp and decisive, resulting in a signal repulse of the enemy.

At the crossing of White Oak swamp, the enemy made another attempt to cut the column, but were handsomely repulsed after a severe fight by portions of Sumner's, Franklin's and Keyes' corps. Here the artillery was directed with great effect by Captain Romeyn B. Ayres, afterwards Major General Ayres. George W. Hazzard's Battery C of the 4th U.S. Artillery Regiment was heavily engaged and exposed to a very hot musketry fire in which Captain Hazzard was killed.

A few miles beyond White Oak swamp several roads from the direction of Richmond converge at a place known as Glendale or Nelson's farm. Here, on the morning of the 30th, McCall deployed his division, posting two of his own batteries and three from the Artillery Reserve in front of his infantry line in an open field surrounded by woods. He had no artillery officer other than the battery commanders to regulate and control these batteries and see that they were properly posted.

Some of the infantry, proving unsteady, communicated their panic to Captain Otto Diederichs' Battery A, 1st New York Light Artillery Regiment, and Captain John Knieriem's Battery C, 1st New York Light Artillery Regiment, which stampeded to the rear, leaving a number of their pieces with the enemy. A most determined charge, or repeated charges, were made upon Lieutenant Alanson M. Randol's Battery E of the 1st U.S. Artillery Regiment, which under that plucky officer stood its ground and for a time repelled with canister the furious onsets of the enemy. The latter, however, rushed on in perfect recklessness and captured the battery, mortally wounding one of Randol's lieutenants and killing and wounding the men while in the act of serving their pieces for the last discharge. A portion of the corps of Sumner, Heintzelman and Franklin now came up, as likewise did many reinforcements for the enemy, and a severe battle ensued, which resulted in the enemy being again repulsed.

In this conglomeration of commands there was no one in particular to supervise and give direction to the whole. The batteries of the various divisions, increased in number by several from the Artillery Reserve, took up the positions assigned them by division commanders, or such as they could find for themselves, some of which proved good, and the batteries occupying them did excellent service. Other batteries wasted ammunition by shelling woods and firing at unseen enemies. With inexperienced commanders "shelling woods" is always a favorite method of employing batteries and here the batteries being without appropriate officers of their own branch were at the mercy of any who chose to give them orders. Having repulsed the enemy at this point, the troops resumed the march during the night and on the following morning took position on Malvern Hill, where was fought the hotly contested battle of July 1st.

As there was now no force threatening Richmond at any point, Lee was enabled to withdraw every man from the defenses for the pursuit of McClellan, and in addition, he was joined by Major General Theophilus H. Holmes' command of 20 regiments and 10 batteries from the Department of North Carolina, bringing his army up to 188 regiments against the 132 of McClellan's army. Their field artillery was now about equal. McClellan had lost about 40 pieces and Lee had gained about the same number by the arrival of Holmes, as also some from other sources. Malvern Hill being the last point favorable for an attack, Lee put forth every effort to concentrate there his whole force and give McClellan a final and crushing blow.

Malvern Hill is an elevated plateau overlooking the James River, about a mile-and-a-half by three-fourths of a mile in area, well cleared of timber, and with several converging roads running over it. In front the ground slopes gradually, giving clear range for artillery to the woodland from which the enemy emerged. The left end of this ridge, the hill proper, slopes off abruptly to the bottom land of the James River, distant at this point about a mile. Upon this plateau the army took up its line of battle. Porter's corps was on the left or hill proper, then Heintzelman, Sumner, Franklin and Keyes in the order named, except that Couch's division of Keyes' corps was between Porter and Heintzelman.

From the position of the enemy his most obvious lines of approach would bring him first in contact with the left, and here the Union lines were strengthened by massing the troops and assembling batteries of the Artillery Reserve. The divisional batteries were posted with their divisions, together with some of the Reserve batteries. There were no entrenchments of any kind, all the fighting was done in the open fields.

A little before midday the enemy commenced feeling with artillery and infantry for a weak place along the front and soon thereafter commenced a series of assaults in force, each one more powerful than the preceding, but always repulsed. "At six o'clock the enemy suddenly opened upon Couch and Porter with the whole strength of his artillery, and at once began pushing forward his columns of attack to carry the hill. Brigade after brigade, formed under cover of the woods, start-

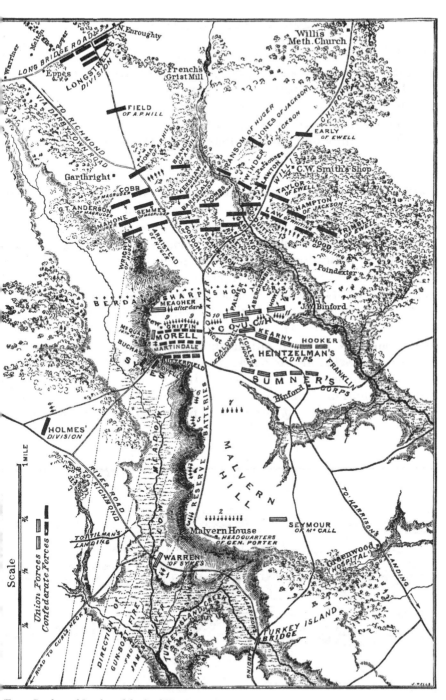

(From *Battles and Leaders of the Civil War*, II: 412.)

ed at a run to cross the open space and charge our batteries, but the heavy fire of our guns, with the cool and steady volleys of our infantry, in every case sent them reeling back to shelter, and covered the ground with their dead and wounded."

Lee, describing these assaults, says: "Several determined efforts were made to storm the hill at Crow's house. The brigades advanced bravely across the open field, raked by the fire of a hundred cannon and the musketry of large bodies of infantry, driving back the infantry, compelling the advanced batteries to retire to escape capture, and mingling their dead with those of the enemy. For want of concert among the attacking columns their assaults were too weak to break the Federal lines, and after struggling gallantly, sustaining and inflicting great loss, they were compelled successively to retire." He gives as a reason for the want of concert between his columns, the wooded and unknown nature of the country, the same difficulty experienced by the Union troops through-out the campaign. For the same cause he says he was unable to bring up his artillery in a concentrated form to oppose that of his adversary. His chief of artillery says: "Too little was thrown into action at once; too much was left in the rear unused. We needed more guns taking part, alike for our own protection and for crippling the enemy."

Just as the sun was setting, the enemy made his last and most determined assault in which he brought up his entire strength. This assault fell entirely upon Porter. The corps to his right was unable to afford him immediate assistance and it seemed as though he must give way to the overwhelming pressure against him. But at this critical moment the batteries of the Artillery Reserve were pushed forward by Colonel Henry J. Hunt, who opened with every piece for which he could find position. An almost continuous battery of about 60 guns was thus opened on the enemy, crushing him back into the woods, from which he did not again return.

This was the most marked instance during the war of the power and effect of artillery when brought in mass against the enemy at the crisis of a battle. There were many instances in which batteries were concentrated and demonstrated the effect of concentrated fire. At Shiloh, for instance, fragments of batteries were assembled and formed a cordon of guns behind which the discomfited divisions of the Army of the Tennessee took shelter for the night and awaited reinforcements. At Stones River the batteries, having through disaster to the infantry become shaken loose from the brigades to which they were attached, gathered themselves together and by their united fire held the ground and saved the Army of the Cumberland from further disaster. At Chancellorsville, batteries were united and stayed the enemy, who were in a fair way of pushing Hooker's army back into the Rappahannock. But in no instance were they brought up in mass, as at Malvern, to snatch victory from imminent defeat.

On the previous day, when the troops were first arriving upon the hill at Malvern, a heavy column of the enemy under Holmes, approaching unobserved by the river road, appeared on the low ground to the left and rear of the hill. When within easy range he opened with one of his batteries upon the troops visible on the hill. Almost instantly, several batteries of the Artillery Reserve, which happened to be there, opened fire on this battery and in a few minutes mashed it to pieces, compelling it to abandon two of its pieces and all of its caissons, with nearly all of its horses killed or disabled. The fire upon the column caused it to retire hastily, not again to be heard from in that quarter.

Not more than one-third of McClellan's force was actually engaged in the battle of Malvern Hill, and notwithstanding the decisive repulse that had been given to the enemy he immediately commenced withdrawing his corps, continuing his march to Harrison's Landing, 11 miles further down the river. The enemy as hastily withdrew in the opposite direction, both sides leaving their dead and wounded on the field. This, it may be remarked, was the only battle of the Peninsula campaign in which the entire army was drawn up in continuous line of battle and here only about one-third of it was engaged.

By the evening of the 3rd of July the whole army had arrived at Harrison's Landing, and taking a strong position about Westover, secured itself by formidable entrenchments. Lee withdrew to his fortifications about Richmond, and thus ended the Peninsula campaign of the Army of the Potomac, of which the foregoing were among the most prominent incidents in which the artillery took part. There were scores of minor occasions in which batteries took active part, but they are too numerous for mention in an overview of this kind.

The losses of the Army of the Potomac from the 26th of June to the 2nd of July were 1,734 killed, 8,062 wounded, and 6,053 missing; making a total of 15,849. Many of those reported as missing were wounded and left on the field and should be included among the wounded. Lee's losses, as compiled from the official reports of his subordinates, were for the same period 2,836 killed and 12,946 wounded; in all 15,882. His missing were not nearly so numerous as were those of McClellan.

The loss by sickness in the Army of the Potomac was great, and altogether it was very much reduced in numbers. At Harrison's Landing it was joined by Major General James Shields' division from Banks' corps, making 12 divisions in all, numbering not above 80,000 men, a force manifestly inadequate to the task of capturing Richmond.

McClellan continued to plead with the Washington authorities for additional troops, still harboring a plan for advancing on Richmond via Malvern, and on August 5th, he actually did reoccupy this position with Hooker's and Sedgwick's divisions, preparatory to a general advance of his whole army. But events happening on the Rappahannock, with an army under Major General John Pope, demanded the presence of the Army of the Potomac in that quarter and it was withdrawn from the Peninsula. By the middle of August the whole of it had left Harrison's Landing.

At about this time Lee detached Jackson on a campaign against Pope, who, with an army of about 45,000 men, had commenced a movement on Richmond by the direct route from Washington. Pope's army, called the "Army of Virginia," was made up of the troops that had been operating separately under Fremont, Banks and McDowell in the Shenandoah Valley and along the Rappahannock. Pope had been called from the West to command it and in the early part of August began to concentrate on the Rappahannock preparatory to his advance. Here, about the 6th of August, he was joined by Major General Ambrose E. Burnside from North Carolina with about 10,000 men. The Army of the Potomac was also to be united to it as soon as it could be withdrawn from the Peninsula.

Burnside had no artillery and the deficiency was supplied with all dispatch from the Army of the Potomac. The rapidity of Jackson's movements, and the blows that he was giving Pope, called for the presence of the Army of the Potomac without delay, and its transfer down the Peninsula and up the Chesapeake was made as expeditiously as possible. In the meanwhile, Lee had joined Jackson with Longstreet's corps. This campaign, called the second Bull Run campaign, proved highly disastrous to the Union cause, and by the 3rd of September Pope's entire force, including the Army of the Potomac, had taken refuge under the guns of the defenses of Washington.

Although this campaign was one in which there were some heavy battles and much desultory fighting, the general character of it was such as to afford but few lessons as to either the proper or improper use of artillery, therefore this period will be passed over and the thread of the narrative resumed with the opening of the Antietam campaign, which commenced immediately after the close of Pope's campaign.

Lt. Rufus King, Lt. Alonzo Cushing, Lt. Evan Thomas, and three other artillery officers in front of a tent at Antietam, Maryland, Autumn 1862. (*Library of Congress*)

THREE

ANTIETAM

L EE, IN ORDER TO PROFIT by a state of affairs in every way desirable to the Confederate cause, and not to permit the season for active operations to pass without endeavoring to inflict further injury, projected a campaign north of the Potomac River. By this, he says, he thought he might detain the Federal Army until the approach of winter should render another advance into Virginia difficult, if not impracticable. He furthermore thought that by entering Maryland he would encourage the secession feeling that already existed among many people of that State. He furthermore knew that such an invasion would arouse just fears for the safety of the capital and that efforts to secure that city would paralyze all other operations of the armies defending it.

Between the 4th and 7th of September, Lee crossed the Potomac at fords near Leesburg and encamped in the vicinity of Frederick, Maryland. He hoped by this movement, so threatening to Washington and Baltimore, to induce, as he says, the Federal Army to follow him, after which he would fall back to western Maryland, and establishing his line of communication with Richmond back through the

Shenandoah Valley, so maneuver as to keep the Federal Army from reentering Virginia. He had thought that his movement to Frederick would have led to the evacuation of Martinsburg and Harper's Ferry, thus opening his line of communication through the valley. This not having resulted, it became necessary for him to detach Jackson with a part of his corps to Martinsburg, and, after securing that place, sweep down the south side of the Potomac to the rear of Harper's Ferry. At the same time he detached Major General Lafayette McLaws' division of Longstreet's corps to attack the Federal position on Maryland Heights, directly opposite and commanding the heights of Harper's Ferry. After reducing the latter place, Jackson and McLaws were to rejoin him at Boonsboro or Hagerstown.

Harper's Ferry capitulated on the morning of September 15th, before McClellan could reach it with a relieving force. By this capitulation the enemy secured 11,000 prisoners, together with 73 pieces of artillery, some of which were field guns, which he immediately incorporated into his batteries.

Jackson, leaving A.P. Hill to dispose of the prisoners and property, hastened with the remainder of his troops to rejoin Lee, who, having resisted the advance of the Federal Army at Turner's and Crampton's passes of the South Mountain, was now, September 15th, taking position at Sharpsburg on the ridge between the Potomac and Antietam Creek; Longstreet on the right, and D.H. Hill, whose division belonged to Jackson's corps, upon the left. Jackson, with Major General Richard S. Ewell's division, arrived on the morning of the 16th, and joining D.H. Hill on the left, took command of that wing.

As soon as it was discovered that Lee was crossing the Potomac, McClellan was restored to command with instructions to use all the troops lately under Pope for the purpose of driving him back into Virginia. McClellan lost no time in gathering together this demoralized mass and starting in search of the enemy, whose exact whereabouts was unknown to the

War Department. The Army of Virginia was merged into the Army of the Potomac, thus passing out of existence after a career of less than two months. The numerical designations of corps in the Army of the Potomac, of which they had been deprived and which had been given to corps in Pope's army, were restored.

By September 7th, McClellan had his corps well under way, heading in the direction of Frederick. As the march progressed, the process of reorganization went on. The troops were rapidly regaining confidence and their former soldierly bearing and discipline were fast returning. In this respect there was not in the artillery so much change as in the infantry. The batteries, although suffering from the general depression of the late campaign under Pope, were still intact as units and in good condition. The Artillery Reserve, that solid rock of dependence, had not been meddled with and was still complete in its organization.

After having absorbed Pope's Army of Virginia, the Army of the Potomac consisted of nine corps, namely; the First, under Hooker; Second, under Sumner; Third, under Heintzelman; Fourth, under Keyes; Fifth, under Porter; Sixth under Franklin; Ninth, under Burnside; Eleventh, under Major General Franz Sigel; and Twelfth, under Major General Joseph K.F. Mansfield. Of these, the Third and Eleventh remained for the immediate protection of Washington, while all of the Fourth, except Couch's division, was left at Yorktown to hold the Peninsula; so that McClellan's moving force consisted of but seven corps and one division of another. These corps were necessarily small, numbering in reality, but little more than the divisions in the Confederate service. Divisions were, likewise, proportionally small.

As a rule the artillery was attached to these small divisions, two or three batteries to each, except that in the First Corps they were attached to brigades, one to each brigade. As the brigades were very small, averaging only from 1,200 to 1,500 men in line, the margin left for efficient service of the batteries of this corps was reduced to a minimum, as was demonstrated in the battle soon to follow. In the Twelfth Corps the batteries were attached to neither divisions nor brigades, but were merely a group, nominally under the direction of the senior captain.

McClellan first encountered Lee at the passes of South Mountain, through which the latter was withdrawing from Frederick. After some severe fighting these passes were forced on the 14th, and during the succeeding night Lee fell back through Boonsboro and took position as before stated on the Sharpsburg ridge, between Antietam Creek and the Potomac. Early on the following morning the cavalry under Brigadier General Alfred Pleasanton, and Tidball's horse battery, started in pursuit, coming upon the rear guard of the enemy at Boonsboro. Here a spirited encounter took place with the cavalry of the enemy, resulting in a chase of several miles towards Hagerstown and thence around to the front of Lee's position behind the Antietam. Here the horse battery, coming into position, caused the enemy to disclose the extent and nature of his line by the opening of a number of his batteries. Richardson's division of Sumner's corps soon made its appearance with its batteries, and during the afternoon a brisk artillery duel was maintained between the opposing forces.

The position taken up by Lee was one of great strength, being across a horseshoe bend of the Potomac and along a ridge, which, while giving him the command of the ground in his immediate front, afforded protection to his troops and a screen behind which he could maneuver free from observation by his opponent. In his rear were two fords across the Potomac, securing to him means of communication with his base and his supply trains already on the opposite side, they also enabled the troops not yet arrived from Harper's Ferry to join him with facility. In front, and at a distance of about a mile from the crest occupied by him, runs the Antietam Creek, a sluggish stream, winding among hills, fordable at numerous places, but with steep and rugged banks. Although it constituted something of an impediment all along, it was only at that part of it in front of Lee's right that it proved to be really an obstacle in his favor. This creek, flowing almost parallel to the ridge, empties into the Potomac a couple of miles below the horseshoe bend. About half a mile behind the center of Lee's front stands the village of Sharpsburg, from which two turnpike roads diverge to the eastward, one to Boonsboro across the Antietam at what became known in connection with the battle as the "Center Bridge," the other at Rohrersville, crosses the Antietam at a bridge about three-fourths of a mile below the former. These two bridges were under the enemy's fire and figured among the events of the battle. A third bridge, about two miles above the center bridge, afforded some facilities to McClellan in crossing his right wing. Owing to the hills on both sides of the creek, the roads across these bridges have a winding and tortuous course.

Another road, the main highway to Hagerstown leaving Sharpsburg, follows in a northerly direction the crest of the ridge upon which Lee had taken position, and on it, distant about a mile from the village, stands the Dunker church, a small white building situated in an open grove of oak and other forest trees. Lee's left wing was originally some distance in front of this church, but when during the battle of the following day, September 17th, it was forced back this position became La Haye Sainte of the field. The road leading by this church may be considered the axis of the ground over which the attack of the right was made, the most furious part of the battle of the day. There were numerous crossroads and lanes leading in various directions to farm houses, but as the country, although hilly, was generally open and tilled land, affording freedom of movement to troops, these played no special part in the battle, with the exception of one, which from washing and use, had become sunken, thus affording a sheltered position for the enemy, and which from the slaughter that took place therein, is known as the "bloody lane."

Between Lee's crest and the Antietam are smaller ridges and undulations, affording McClellan good positions for his artillery and some little shelter for infantry. Along the east side of the creek extends a ridge, a portion of which, near the center bridge, was occupied by batteries of the Reserve operating chiefly against Jackson's left about the Dunker church. But Lee's position, which was eminently favorable for artillery, dominated more or less all these positions.

With the exception of a few rails and stones hastily thrown together by the rebel detachments defending the lower bridge, there were no entrenchments whatever upon either side, but some stone fences and outcropping ledges of rock in the vicinity of the Dunker church afforded good cover for Jackson's troops and were liberally taken advantage of by them. Excepting the woods in which Jackson's left rested, and a few strips and clumps of trees here and there in other places, the battlefield was quite open, and most of it visible from the ridges on the east side of the Antietam, on one of which McClellan had his headquarters.

The extreme left of Lee's army, Jackson's wing, rested on the upper end of the horseshoe bend of the river, from which point, following the crest of the ridge, somewhat convex towards the enemy, it extended a distance of about three miles and terminated on the hills to the south of Sharpsburg. At favorable points along this line the enemy had his batteries and its shortness enabled him rapidly to reinforce any point of it from another. The ground in front of it to the Antietam consisted of rolling hills, each commanded by those in rear. Such, in brief, were the principal features of the battlefield of Antietam, which considering the vital issues at stake, was one of the most important of the war.

Lee had present on the field two corps of nine divisions comprising 40 brigades of 185 regiments of infantry. McClellan had present six corps of 15 divisions comprising 44 brigades of 186 regiments of infantry.

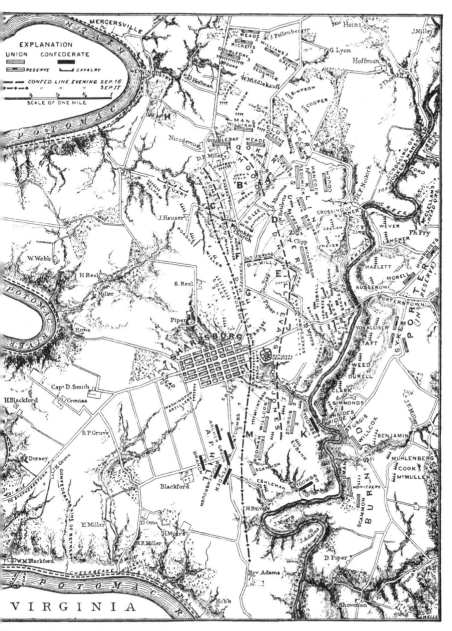

(From *Battles and Leaders of the Civil War*, II: 636.)

The former was slightly superior to the latter in cavalry, but as there was no opportunity for this arm on the field, it did not count on either side. The horse batteries of both sides were, however, actively engaged.

While the infantry of the two opposing armies was almost identical in point of numbers, McClellan was greatly superior in artillery. Lee had on the field 73 batteries of 288 guns; McClellan had 55 batteries of 322 guns, a difference in favor of the latter of 34 pieces. But this disparity was more than compensated for by Lee's superiority of organization, which was that of the battalion system. Each of his infantry divisions, which in strength were about double those of McClellan, had attached to it a battalion of from four to seven batteries. These battalions were commanded by colonels or lieutenant colonels, seldom by majors, and never by captains taken from their batteries. All of Jackson's 22 batteries were thus assigned, but of Longstreet's 29, eight constituted a battalion of reserve. In addition to all of which, Lee had a reserve of 22 batteries organized into four battalions, commanded by a brigadier general. This system of organization and command enabled the batteries to be used when and where most needed.

McClellan's artillery, with the exception of the Artillery Reserve, had no higher organization whatever than the individual battery, and these were attached, as before stated, in Hooker's corps to brigades, one battery to each brigade, in the other corps to divisions without any commanders other than the individual battery commanders. In the entire army, outside of the Artillery Reserve, there was but one field officer of artillery, a major on duty with the artillery. The consequence was that although all the batteries were engaged at some time or other during the battle, they were as a rule employed in such a desultory manner as greatly to weaken their effect as a whole. In only one or two instances were batteries massed so as to give decisive blows. The fact of their being tied down to the narrow limits of small infantry commands rendered their employment, other than in a scattered and feeble manner, impracticable. This was notably the case on the right, where the chief attack was on Jackson's left along the Hagerstown road.

The Artillery Reserve was organized into three battalions with three field officers for the whole, one of whom, Major Albert F.R. Arndt, 1st Battalion, New York Light Artillery Regiment, was killed on the first day of the battle. Most of the batteries of the Reserve were, however, detached temporarily to supplement the batteries of the divisions, and even this, the only artillery organization worthy of the name, was thus, to a degree, emasculated.

During the 15th, all of McClellan's forces, except Franklin's corps and Couch's odd division of the Fourth Corps, came up and temporarily occupied positions near the center and lower bridges. Four of the long-range batteries of the Reserve were put in position on the crest of a ridge overlooking the Antietam to the right of the center bridge, from which they had a good field of fire over the left of the enemy's position, particularly so upon Jackson's line towards the Dunker church, which they either enfiladed or took in flank. Jackson and other commanders mention the damaging effect of this fire.

Early on the morning of the 16th the enemy opened a sharp fire of artillery on this position, which was soon silenced by the batteries just referred to. Major Arndt, commanding these batteries, was killed at this time.

The whole of the 16th was consumed in getting the troops into position and in getting up ammunition and supply trains. This delay enabled Lee to get up the troops that had been detached to reduce Harper's Ferry, and this neutralized about the only advantage McClellan had.

About 2:00 P.M. Hooker, with the First Corps, crossed the Antietam at a ford and the upper bridge to attack, and if possible, turn the left of the enemy. A sharp contest took place, resulting in Jackson's advance being driven from a strip of woods several hundred yards to the rear. Here Hooker rested for the night in readiness to make an early attack in the morning. In this affair, several of Hooker's batteries took a spirited part, so much so as to call for special remark by Jackson as being very damaging to him.

While this combat was going on, Brigadier General John B. Hood's division of Longstreet's corps was sent from the right to reinforce Jackson, A.P. Hill's division of his own corps having not yet arrived from Harper's Ferry. Hood took position with his left on the Hagerstown road. Brigadier General John R. Jones' division (Jackson's old division) took position on Hood's left, while D.H. Hill's division was on Hood's right, extending along towards the center of Lee's line. J.R. Jones' left, resting near the bend of the river, was strengthened by "Jeb" Stuart's horse batteries. Stuart's cavalry was sheltered under the hills towards the river. During the night Ewell's division of Jackson's corps arrived and relieved Hood, but next morning, when Jackson was again hard pressed, he returned to his former position and assisted Jackson throughout the battle.

Mansfield, commanding the Twelfth Corps, crossed the creek during the night and bivouacked about a mile in rear of Hooker. Sumner was ordered to hold his corps, the Second, ready to cross early the next morning (the 17th) to support Hooker and Mansfield, who were to attack at an early hour. Porter's corps, the Fifth, was held to defend the center bridge and support the batteries near it. Burnside's corps, the Ninth, was behind the ridges near the lower bridge. Franklin's corps, the Sixth, had not yet arrived from Pleasant Valley, where it had been sent with Couch's division to endeavor to save Harper's Ferry. Couch's division was sent to reoccupy Maryland Heights and was therefore not present at the battle.

McClellan's plan for the impending general engagement was to attack the enemy's left with the corps of Hooker and Mansfield supported by Sumner's, and if necessary, by Franklin's, and as soon as matters looked favorable there, to move Burnside's corps against the enemy's extreme right, upon the ridge south and in rear of Sharpsburg, and having carried this position, to press along the crest towards the left of the enemy, and whenever either of these flank movements should be successful, to advance the whole center with all the forces there disposable. This was a very simple, and withal a reasonably good plan, but was but feebly executed. Its success involved one vital condition, that is, precision of cooperation between the two wings to prevent the enemy from concentrating first upon one and afterwards upon the other, a thing which actually did occur.

The attack on the right was really a succession of attacks, each made just after the preceding had failed, first by Hooker, then by Mansfield, each with a corps, then by Sumner with Sedgwick's division, and finally by Colonel William H. Irwin's brigade of Franklin's corps. Meanwhile, Burnside did nothing on the left to prevent troops from being sent from Longstreet's wing to reinforce that of Jackson. Finally, when in the afternoon Burnside did make his attack, the attack upon Jackson was not renewed to prevent him from sparing troops to reinforce Longstreet against Burnside. The attack of French's and Richardson's divisions of Sumner's corps upon Lee's left center was too late to serve as support to Hooker and Mansfield. The trouble upon this wing seems to have been the want of a commander actually present. Until the arrival of Sumner, which was not until after both Hooker and Mansfield had failed, Hooker was the senior officer, but he was fighting his own corps and gave no attention to Mansfield's until it came up to his assistance. In consequence of some delay in transmitting orders, Sumner did not start for the battlefield until an hour or more after the appointed time, and consequently was not present at the supreme moment to insure promptness and precision of cooperation.

Hooker was to commence the attack soon after daylight, striking directly for Jackson, whose left stood across the Hagerstown road about a mile in front of the Dunker church. On the right of the road, extending to the bend of the river, the land was chiefly wooded, while on the left strips of wood alternated with corn and other fields. Through the woods, parallel with Jackson's lines, limestone ledges cropped out affording natural rifle trenches for his troops. His right, composed of troops from Longstreet's corps together with D.H. Hill's division, extended off along the ridge, or rather in front of the main ridge, towards the Boonsboro road, which was the center of Lee's position. Owing to the delay of Sumner's attack with French's and Richardson's divisions, Hill was enabled to strengthen Jackson with three of his brigades, which together with the divisions of Ewell and Major General David R. Jones, gave him 57 regiments of his own corps alone, to say nothing of Hood's division and other troops from Longstreet, against which Hooker had but 43 regiments. Jackson had between 20 and 30 batteries, containing more guns than he could find room for. Hooker had but nine batteries of 54 pieces, many more than he made good use of.

Notwithstanding this great disparity of force in favor of Jackson, Hooker at first drove him back, seeing which, Lee reinforced him from Longstreet's wing, which was then idle in consequence of Burnside's delay in making his attack. Hood's division of 14 regiments was first sent, soon followed by 31 regiments from Longstreet's other three divisions, making a grand total of 103 regiments that Jackson had in the fight around the Dunker church.

Mansfield brought up to the support of Hooker his two divisions of 22 regiments and seven batteries, followed by Sedgwick's division of 13 regiments and two batteries, and, still later, by Irwin's brigade of five regiments, in all 40 regiments and nine batteries which, added to Hooker's corps, gave a grand total of 83 regiments and 18 batteries of Federal troops against the foregoing enumerated force of Jackson. By thus reinforcing Jackson, Lee had at this point of contact about 20 percent more troops than McClellan had, and when later in the day Burnside finally made his attack on Lee's right, the latter managed to have a still greater percentage against him at that point of contact. It will be remembered that the two armies were almost identical in infantry strength and that McClellan's plan of battle contemplated a simultaneous attack upon both wings of the enemy. As they were not made simultaneously, Lee was enabled, by the shortness of his line, so to maneuver as always to have a superior force at the point of actual contact.

At dawn of day on the 17th, the enemy opened the battle by a spirited fire from his numerous batteries, which was replied to by some of Hooker's batteries, and also by the batteries of long-range guns on the ridge on the further side of the Antietam. As soon as possible Hooker advanced his lines over the fields and through the strips of wood heretofore mentioned, and soon came upon the enemy in position, extending across a large cornfield and into woods upon each side of it. To dislodge him from this field, Hooker says: "Instructions were immediately given for the assemblage of all my spare batteries near at hand, of which I think there were five or six, to spring into battery on the right of the field, and to open with canister at once. In the time I am writing every stalk of corn in the north and greater part of this field was cut as closely as could have been done with a knife, and the slain lay in rows precisely as they had stood in the ranks a few moments before."

This somewhat iridescent description is sustained in substance by Confederate reports. Gradually, but by the most desperate fighting, the enemy were forced back about a mile into the woods in which stands the Dunker church, around which occurred the fiercest conflicts of the day. The ground over which Hooker had driven Jackson were the open field and bodies of wood interspersed with the limestone ledges before mentioned, as being so admirably adapted as natural rifle trenches. Over this ground the opposing forces literally tore each other to pieces. But Jackson's superiority of numbers soon told in his favor and Hooker was driven back in disorder.

Jackson, who was not given to exaggeration or florid descriptions, in describing this conflict, says: "Batteries were opened in front from the wood with shell and canister, and our troops became exposed for near an hour to a terrific storm of shell, canister and musketry. With heroic spirit our lines advanced to the conflict, and maintained their position in the face of superior numbers with stubborn resolution, sometimes driving the enemy before them and sometimes compelled to fall back before their well sustained and destructive fire. The carnage on both sides was terrific."

While this was going on in Jackson's immediate front, the batteries of long-range rifles posted beyond the Antietam on the ridge near the center bridge were active. Of these Jackson says: "At the dawn of day skirmishing commenced in front, and in a short time the Federal batteries, so posted on the opposite side of the Antietam as to enfilade my line, opened a severe and damaging fire."

To silence these batteries Lee directed his chief of artillery to post his most powerful batteries along the crest in front of Sharpsburg, but before this could be effected the four horse batteries of Pleasanton's cavalry pushed across the center bridge, and amid a shower of shot, shell and musketry, took position on an intermediate crest between Lee's line and the batteries on the opposite side of the Antietam. The fire from the 24 pieces of these horse batteries was so spirited as not only to prevent the establishment of other batteries in their front, but to drive away those already there. In the course of a couple of hours these batteries expended all their ammunition and while absent for a short time replenishing their chests, the position was held by other batteries sent there from the Reserve temporarily for that purpose. The horse batteries continued to hold the position until withdrawn at dark. In addition to attending to their immediate front they, as occasion offered, directed their fire to the right upon Jackson's masses and to the left upon the troops confronting Burnside.

A Federal artillery battery at rest can be seen in the far background of a photograph entitled, "Antietam, Md. Battlefield on the day of the battle." (*Library of Congress*)

As previously stated, Hooker's 10 batteries were attached, one to each of his 10 brigades, each brigade numbering about 1,000 men actually in line. The ground over which Hooker was to advance, and did advance, was less than half a mile wide and was mostly covered with woods. As he had about 10,000 men in line it is readily seen that he had but little room left for batteries. Some of the batteries, however, managed to get in and did heroic service, but most of them were unable to follow their brigades and were of but little real service in the action. The same thing obtained with the seven batteries of the Twelfth Corps, when the latter advanced under Mansfield over the same ground a little while afterwards. Most of the batteries of these two corps were unemployed at the most critical period of the battle and while the infantry to which they were attached was engaged in a life and death struggle in their front.

On the left of the ground then being fought over, between it and the Antietam, were knolls and secondary ridges, admirably adapted to artillery, and in such positions that batteries occupying them could have taken Jackson in flank, enfiladed his lines, and disorganized his masses about the Dunker church. The advantages of these positions did not probably come under Hooker's own observation and he had no chief of artillery to point them out to him. It was certainly not the province of his battery commanders, in fact, it would have been highly improper for them, to have left their commands to search the battlefield for positions for their batteries. Had the batteries been organized into brigades or battalions, the commanders of these could have thrown out to this position a dozen or so of batteries, the fire from which on Jackson's flank would probably have enabled Hooker not only to hold that which he at first gained, but to gain still more. But the system of tying down batteries to the narrow limits of small infantry commands did not admit of this freedom, consequently Jackson was unmolested on his flank by Hooker's batteries, many of which were in enforced idleness while his infantry was being beaten and driven back.

Hooker in his advance got as far as the edge of the woods in which stands the Dunker church, but no further. At the far side of this strip of timber, towards Jackson's left, is an eminence upon which Stuart posted his horse batteries and some other artillery. This proved of the greatest service to Jackson, as it gave the left of his line a firm point of rest, and enabled him to use his artillery upon any troops advancing beyond the Dunker church. In the same manner Hooker's batteries could have served him if they had been stationed a little to the left of the ground over which he was forging his way against Jackson.

Hooker had now been engaged about two hours and the enemy had already commenced to force back his shattered brigades when Mansfield came to his relief with the Twelfth Corps. This veteran officer was killed while examining the ground over which his corps was to advance and the command devolved upon Brigadier General Alpheus S. Williams. This corps went into action with about 7,000 men, to which was attached seven batteries under one of the captains as chief of artillery. The batteries were not attached to either divisions or brigades, but were supposed to be directed by the corps commander through his chief of artillery. The facts were that the batteries received but little direction from anyone. The infantry pushed forward into the woods to struggle with the enemy and was lost to view, while most of the batteries remained behind. The Twelfth Corps, with some assistance from fragments of the First, forced the enemy back again to the Dunker church wood and partly beyond. Here the Union troops became exposed to Stuart's artillery and other batteries judiciously posted, and Jackson, having by this time been greatly reinforced from Longstreet's wing, making his numbers more than two to one of his opponents, the Twelfth Corps was in turn driven back.

About this period Hooker was wounded and the command of his corps devolved upon Brigadier General George G. Meade, one of his division commanders, who caused the batteries to assemble on some eminence slightly in rear where their fire became useful in preventing the enemy from establishing batteries in the openings of the wood. They also formed points of rest for the assembling of the discomfited infantry.

At this time Sumner appeared upon the scene with Sedgwick's division, and being senior officer on that part of the field, assumed command. It will be remembered that he had been ordered to cross the Antietam early in the morning with his entire corps, which he did, but owing to some delay in transmitting orders to him he did not move to the attack until the morning was well advanced, and then did not reach the point of contact until about 8:30 A.M. Sedgwick marched his division straight to the front, which brought him to where the First and Twelfth Corps were engaged. French, with his division, was on the left of Sedgwick, but in moving forward a considerable interval occurred between these divisions and the fight that French subsequently had was entirely distinct from that in which Sedgwick engaged. Richardson's division was on the left of French, and from Richardson to Burnside on the extreme left was an interval of over a mile, occupied only by the four horse batteries before mentioned, and a few companies of Sykes' regular infantry holding back the skirmishers of the enemy in the cornfield in front of these batteries.

The cavalry that had crossed the bridge in company with these batteries, finding itself greatly exposed, and without power of acting, took shelter in hollows and under the banks of the creek. At this period of the war the cavalry had not yet fallen into the hands of those who knew the proper use to make of it. Sedgwick marched his division, numbering about 5,000 muskets, into battle over the same ground that had proved so disastrous to the corps of Hooker and Mansfield. He, however, got farther than either of the former, so far in fact, that his troops came under a flank fire from the batteries established by Stuart on the eminence before mentioned, and also a fire from the other direction; in other words his division was exposed to the heaviest possible fire of both musketry and artillery upon not only its front, but both flanks, and partly in rear also. This doubled it up, causing portions of it to break and retire several hundred yards before being rallied. Meanwhile, however, it did some of the most stubborn fighting of the day and lost heavily in killed and wounded.

Sedgwick himself was wounded and the command of the division devolved upon Howard. Jackson, at this epoch, bringing forward heavy reinforcements, forced Sedgwick's division, together with the remnants of the First and Twelfth Corps, back to within 1,000 yards of the line occupied by the enemy when the battle commenced in the morning. In thus falling back, the batteries in rear were unmasked and their fire, together with that of the infantry, caused the enemy to stay his pursuit and take shelter in the woods and behind the ledges of outcropping rocks.

This repulse of the enemy gave opportunity for rearranging the lines and reorganizing the commands, now in considerable confusion. The batteries became united more or less into groups on ground suitable for their fire. Howard in his report, speaking of one of these groups, says: "The batteries opened fire, and checked several attempts of the enemy to establish batteries in front of our right, and to turn our right flank. About an hour before sundown the enemy succeeded in getting four pieces in position and opened fire upon us, somewhat enfilading my lines. General Sumner ordered me to change front, placing the infantry in rear of the batteries, while the batteries, in a semicircular order, brought a concentrated fire from twenty-six pieces upon the enemy's guns just established, and in less than ten minutes the enemy was driven back and did not appear again in that quarter."

Brigadier General Abner Doubleday, in his report, speaking of another group, says:

> Thirty guns had been concentrated on the right flank of the general line of battle, and my division (First, of Hooker's corps) was directed to join the remains of General Sumner's corps as a support to these guns. General Sumner assumed command in person, and I was directed by General Meade to receive the orders of General Sumner, to assume the command of these thirty guns in addition to the command of my division. About 5:30 P.M. the enemy massed his infantry and opened fire with his artillery to force our position, but my thirty guns replied with such vigor and effect that the column of attack melted away and the rebels gave up the attempt. After this we were not disturbed.

This was the flank movement alluded to by Jackson in his report, and of which he says: "In the afternoon, in obedience to instructions from the commanding general, I moved to the left with a view of turning the Federal right, but I found his numerous artillery so judiciously established in their front and extending so near the Potomac, which here makes a remarkable bend, as to render it inexpedient to make the attempt." Jackson here mentions the judiciously posted artillery. If it had been as judiciously posted for assisting in the fight as for covering the retreat, the latter would not probably have occurred. The reasons why this did not obtain have already been stated. It seems that for want of artillery officers of proper rank to exercise command over the batteries, a division commander had to be assigned to the duty of collecting the batteries and placing them in position. It was not until the following year that these glaring defects of organization and command of artillery were corrected.

About the time of Sedgwick's repulse and the formation of the line just mentioned, that is, about noon, Franklin arrived from Pleasant Valley with the Sixth Corps, which he at once pushed forward to the support of, not only the sorely distressed right, but also the divisions of French and Richardson now pushing the enemy in their front. One brigade of the Sixth became heavily engaged. Of this McClellan says:

> Finding the enemy still advancing, the Third Brigade of Smith's division; commanded by Colonel Irwin, 49th Pennsylvania Volunteers, was ordered up, and passing through Lieutenant Edward Thomas' battery, 4th U.S. Artillery Regiment, charged upon the enemy and drove back the advance until abreast of the Dunker church. As the right of the brigade came opposite the woods it received a destructive fire, which checked the advance and threw the brigade somewhat into confusion. It formed again behind a rise of ground, in the open space in advance of the batteries.

The fact was that this brigade was pretty well cut up. Out of only 1,300 men present, it lost 71 killed, 335 wounded and 33 missing. Irwin went in a little to the left of the ground over which the other troops had been fighting. It was in fact over the ground upon which the surplus batteries of Hooker and

Mansfield should have been posted and from which they could have had an admirable fire upon Jackson's flank. Franklin brought with him seven batteries, but none of them were much engaged. By this time both sides were greatly exhausted by the struggle around and in front of the Dunker church, and neither being disposed to renew it, each rested on the ground held by it, which was virtually the same as that held in the morning when the battle commenced. The battle had raged for about six hours and on an area of ground less than one square mile.

Hooker, with the First Corps numbering about 10,000 muskets, first went in and was repulsed with a loss of 417 officers and men killed and 2,051 wounded. Then Mansfield with the Twelfth Corps, numbering about 7,000 muskets, went in and was repulsed with a loss of 275 officers and men killed and 1,386 wounded. Sedgwick, with his division of about 5,000 men, then went in and was repulsed with a loss of 373 officers and men killed and 1,593 wounded. Finally, Irwin with his brigade of not over 1,200 men went in and was repulsed with a loss of 71 officers and men killed and 335 wounded. In all, there were about 23,300 men engaged with a total loss of 1,136 killed and 5,385 wounded, or 6,521 killed and wounded. The loss of the enemy was presumably about the same, making a grand total of 13,042.

No other equal area upon the American continent has been so drenched with human blood. There were but few prisoners taken, about 500 upon each side. The attacks were made successively by the Union troops with sufficient interval of time between each to allow of their repulse being complete before the next attack. In this there was no generalship whatever displayed, and in the fight itself there was none exercised, further than that each commander held his command together as much as possible and dealt his heaviest blows. That the troops were well led is attested by the fact that no less than seven general officers were struck down, together with a number of colonels commanding brigades.

Captain Joseph M. Knap's wrought and cast iron 10-pounder rifled Parrott guns of Battery E, Pennsylvania Light Artillery Regiment, at Antietam, Maryland, 1862. (*Library of Congress*)

While the artillery had but little opportunity, for reasons heretofore stated, to show what it was capable of doing, it nevertheless did invaluable service in repulsing the enemy and establishing a new line for the infantry. Under the circumstances it is astonishing that the batteries did so much in the battle. Some of them, pushing their way forward, fought with the enemy at the muzzle of their pieces, and although often tangled up in the woods, lost but one gun, and the battery from which it was lost was so fortunate as to bring from the field one of the enemy's pieces in its stead.

While the battle still raged in and about the woods of the Dunker church, French and Richardson were instructed to press the enemy in front of them, which they did most vigorously. The "Sunken Road," and other positions from which they forced the enemy, became historic from the carnage

enacted there. The five or six batteries on this part of the line did gallant service, attending not only to the enemy in their immediate front, but occasionally to that part of the field towards the Dunker church. It was here that the surplus batteries of Hooker and Mansfield should have been posted.

Jackson's position at the Dunker church was prolonged to his right by D.H. Hill's division of his own corps and Brigadier General John G. Walker's division of Longstreet's corps. The division of Major General Richard H. Anderson of Longstreet's corps came to the assistance of those of Walker and Hill, but all were unable to regain the ground lost. Lee says of this: "The heavy masses of the enemy again moved forward, being opposed only by a few pieces of artillery, supported by a few hundred men belonging to different brigades rallied by General D.H. Hill and other officers, and parts of Walker's and Anderson's commands." The truth was that these troops, outnumbering French and Richardson perhaps three to one, were so badly demoralized that it was with the greatest difficulty a sufficient number of them could be rallied to make a show of holding the line.

The battle in front of Jackson having now ceased, that upon this part of the line also came to an end, and Sumner's divisions bivouacked for the night upon the ground they had so gallantly won. This was the only permanent gain during the day.

A little to the left of Richardson, who, by the way, was mortally wounded at this place, were the horse batteries before mentioned, which having crossed at the center bridge, took position close under Lee's line directly in front of Sharpsburg. These batteries, together with the long-range guns beyond the creek, did most excellent service. Still further to the left is the bridge over which Burnside was to have crossed early in the day.

The bridge is a stone structure of three arches. The road from it on the side held by the rebels curved up through a ravine and over rolling hills to Sharpsburg, distant about one and a quarter miles. The approach to the bridge on Burnside's side was somewhat exposed, but the ridges in rear afforded excellent positions for batteries to sweep the further side. Along these crests and knolls were stationed 10 batteries, two of which were 20-pounders. The opposite side was held by a detachment of Brigadier General Robert Toombs' Georgia Brigade, numbering in all 403 muskets and one battery of four pieces. A little in rear was another battery, also of his command. This little command was strung out, covering the stream for about half a mile, with orders to prevent the enemy from crossing as long as possible and then to fall back to a hill about 400 yards in rear of the bridge, which it was to hold as long as practicable, after which it was to fall back and take position in the line of battle about six or eight hundred yards in rear of the bridge. This line of battle was on a continuation of the crest of the main ridge occupied by Lee, and which extended on around to the Dunker church, distant about two miles. The right of this line was held by D.R. Jones' division of Longstreet's corps. The remainder of this corps was on the left assisting Jackson. Along and near the stream was a fringe of timber, beyond that the ground, ascending rapidly, was open farm land intersected by strong stone walls and fences of which the enemy took every advantage for cover. Toombs sheltered his men as much as possible behind trees, inequalities of the ground, and by some very slight breastworks of rails, stones, etc.

About the time that Hooker was making his assault on Jackson, Burnside received orders to force his way over the stream and attack vigorously the right of the enemy, but his attempts to cross the bridge were dilatory and feeble. As things were beginning to assume a very unfavorable aspect on the right, McClellan sent him other and still more imperative orders to cross. Still, he wasted the time until one o'clock, when a couple of his small regiments charged over the bridge, while at the same time Brigadier General Isaac P. Rodman's division forded the creek a few hundred yards below and marching up, routed Toombs' men from their cover. Slowly his entire corps filed over the bridge and formed in line on the opposite side. Four of his batteries crossed likewise, the other six remained, occupying positions from which they could render service by covering his flanks and reaching the enemy upon the crest. In this operation of crossing, the batteries do not seem to have been used as vigorously as they might have been, otherwise a concentrated fire from so many pieces would have soon cleared the way.

It was not until about 3:00 o'clock that Burnside was induced to advance. This his corps did with alacrity, and moving steadily up the hill broke through Jones' line and into the outskirts of the village. Burnside was in a fair way to double up and roll back Lee's right, when at this critical moment A.P. Hill, with his powerful division of Jackson's corps arrived, and at once attacked and crumbled up the left of Burnside's line, causing the whole of it to retire to the banks of the Antietam under cover of the batteries upon the opposite side. Although Burnside lost but a score or so of men in forcing the bridge, he lost very heavily, 2,220 killed and wounded, in the desperate fighting that took place on the ridge. Hill and Jones together lost but 1,024. They had greatly the advantage in position. Hill had marched that morning from Harper's Ferry, distant 15 miles, had forded the Potomac at Shepardstown, and came in, like Blucher, to make Antietam a Waterloo for McClellan.

At sundown on the day of the battle, Lee, owing to the arrival of Hill, was probably in better condition to meet assaults than in the morning and could have resisted indefinitely had McClellan continued to assault by piecemeal. But matters in other respects had not developed as he had expected and it was clearly his best policy to place the Potomac between his army and that of his adversary as speedily as possible. He remained, however, the whole of the next day before commencing this movement. To have left the field at once would have been to acknowledge defeat.

Two of McClellan's corps, those of Porter and Franklin, were quite intact as they had been but very slightly engaged on the 17th. During the following day, Couch's division joined from Maryland Heights as did also Brigadier General Andre A. Humphreys' division of new troops from Frederick, making altogether two-thirds as many fresh troops as McClellan had engaged on the 17th.

But McClellan was cautious, perhaps over cautious. Nothing but his army stood between Lee and the National capital. A decided repulse would be an immeasurable misfortune and there was no certainty that he could fight his army better on any other day than he had on the 17th. He therefore allowed the 18th to pass without attacking, and during that night, commencing immediately after dark, Lee silently and successfully withdrew across the river, leaving his dead and wounded on the field, an acknowledgment, in popular estimate, of defeat. It was in reality a drawn battle. But a drawn battle to an invading army is little less than defeat.

As soon as Lee's movements were discovered on the morning of the 18th, the cavalry and horse batteries, following in pursuit, came upon the tail of his column as it was leaving the ford on the opposite side of the river. A few shots from the batteries developed the fact that Lee had taken the precaution to line that side with batteries covering the ford. It was therefore deemed not advisable to attempt to cross in pursuit. Porter now arrived with his corps, and posting his batteries, as also some from the Reserve, on the ridges along the river, a hot artillery duel ensued in which the fire of the opposite batteries was so much subdued as to permit Brigadier General Charles Griffin to cross with a brigade of infantry. Lee's batteries had been strangely left without much support and Griffin was enabled to secure five or six of the pieces, after which he withdrew.

On the following morning Porter sent over the divisions of Morell and Sykes to make a forced reconnaissance. A.P. Hill was sent to meet them and a fierce engagement ensued. Hill says: "The enemy had lined the opposite hills with some 70 pieces of artillery, and the infantry who had crossed lined the crests of the high banks on the Virginia shore. My lines advanced simultaneously and soon encountered the enemy. This advance was made in the face of the most tremendous fire of artillery I ever saw, and too much praise cannot be awarded my regiments for their steady maneuvering step."

Hill's numbers were too much for Porter's small divisions and they were forced to retire. The enemy, following and screening themselves from the effects of the artillery fire behind trees and inequalities of the ground, and in some lime kilns along the banks, opened a most deadly fire on Porter's troops as they forded the river, a most difficult crossing even without such a fire. The slaughter was pitiless, the men were shot down by scores as they waded the river and were swept away by the swift flowing current. In this affair Hill reports his loss at 30 killed and 231 wounded, total 261. Porter's loss was 68 killed, 136 wounded and 123 missing, total 327.

This closed the fighting connected with the Antietam campaign, in which the Federal losses were 2,082 killed and 9,582 wounded, a total of 11,664, or more than 25 per cent, of the force actually engaged. The reported loss of the Confederates was 10,691 killed and wounded.

Up to this time Antietam was the heaviest battle of the war and remained to the end, the heaviest single day contest. It demonstrated the great difficulty of securing exact cooperation between troops acting disconnectedly on a field, and conveys the moral that a general should not attempt important operations requiring prompt and unhesitating action without knowing the personal equation of the generals upon whom he is to rely for carrying out his plans.

In this entire campaign not a gun was lost save one, and the battery losing it was so fortunate as to secure one from the enemy on the field in place of it. The enemy lost 14 pieces in all.

The position occupied by Lee was decidedly more favorable for artillery than that held by McClellan, but owing to scarcity of ammunition his batteries did not do so much firing as those of the latter. They were held in hand back of the ridge and were brought forward when and where needed. His battalion system enabled him to do this, and thus while economizing ammunition, always to have a superior force at the point most requiring it.

Owing to the defective system of the Army of the Potomac, the quantity of ammunition expended was generally out of proportion to the good accomplished. Brigade and division commanders always wanted their batteries to fire whether their positions enabled them to do so with effect or not, and battery commanders themselves, desirous of not being backward, accepted the situation without question.

At the commencement of the Antietam campaign General Hunt was appointed chief of artillery for the Army of the

Potomac, a position which he ably and satisfactorily filled until the close of the war. Up to this time he had commanded the Artillery Reserve, which gave him the experience which enabled him to perceive the glaring defects of the artillery system in vogue. From this time on he was untiring in his efforts to secure an organization of greater efficiency, but the system had already worn a groove from which it was difficult to extricate it, and it was not until after the disastrous Chancellorsville campaign that he succeeded in effecting a change from the dispersed system to one of concentration by uniting the batteries of each corps into one brigade under commanders with appropriate rank and official influence.

Brigadier General William F. Barry, the former chief of artillery, was assigned to duty in Washington as inspector of artillery, a new office, the functions of which comprised supervision over artillery matters pertaining to all the armies. Up to this time there had been no one to collect and systematize data upon this branch and make it available for use in the War Office. The consequence was that things went a great deal at haphazard, resulting often in grave blunders, as for instance upon one occasion some batteries were required without delay for a certain expedition. The official in the War Office, looking over the returns, found batteries here and there at places in the North, apparently available for service at the front, and these were accordingly ordered to join the expedition forthwith. But, when they reported it was discovered that they had neither guns, horses, nor other equipments of batteries ready for the field, only the officers and men; batteries only in name. There was no chief of artillery with a bureau in Washington to regulate such matters and it was partly to supply this deficiency that the temporary office of inspector was created.

An artillery camp of instruction was established at Washington where the newly raised batteries were received, equipped, instructed and prepared for the field. Other such camps were established for the Western armies.

It was during the Antietam campaign that the horse batteries of the Army of the Potomac began to become identified with the cavalry service, and it was during this campaign that the latter service began to *walk alone*. In the original organization of that army, the cavalry, with the exception of a small reserve of a few regiments, was attached by regiments or squadrons to divisions, after corps were formed, to corps, a regiment or so to each corps, and there was no head to it anywhere, not even a nominal chief at headquarters. Thus dispersed, its services amounted to almost nothing. Its range of operations extended scarcely beyond the infantry pickets of the corps to which it was attached.

Colonel Benjamin W. Crowninshield admirably describes its status at this period when in his article "Cavalry during the Rebellion," in the May 1891 number of the *Military Service Journal*, he says:

> Until 1862, in the summer, in the Federal Army the cavalry was groping about for its place in the field, while learning the elements of its duty. During the Peninsular campaign it did nothing to gain a reputation, being hardly mentioned in dispatches; while Stuart won a brilliant reputation by his raid around McClellan's army, and originated the "raid" which afterwards became such a feature in every campaign. Pope, in his campaign, exhausted the mounted troops by hurrying them hither and thither, . . . Lee used his intelligently, and, with half the work, it did not only good service but gained a brilliant reputation.

Lee, when crossing the Potomac, covered his movements by a well organized cavalry under that energetic leader, "Jeb" Stuart, and to penetrate his intentions and discover his whereabouts, McClellan was forced to concentrate his cavalry and give it an organization enabling it to act independently of infantry commands. He accordingly formed it into a division of two brigades, under Pleasanton and Colonel William W.

Averill, both of whom were active and soon demonstrated the proper use to be made of this arm of service. At the same time Brigadier General John Buford was made chief of cavalry.

Up to this time the four batteries of horse artillery had divided their services between the cavalry and infantry. When advancing up the Peninsula they were with the cavalry in the advance and in retiring down the Peninsula assisted it to cover the rear. They accompanied it when endeavoring to discover Lee's intentions and movements prior to the battle of Antietam, but in that, as well as in most of the principal battles of both campaigns, they fought with the infantry and established for themselves a distinguished reputation. After the Antietam campaign they began to serve exclusively with the cavalry brigades, but it was not until after the Chancellorsville campaign in the following year that they became a permanent fixture to the cavalry, which by this time had become greatly increased in numbers. The Antietam and Chancellorsville campaigns had so developed the functions and use of horse artillery as to call for an additional number of batteries. Accordingly, immediately after Chancellorsville, four additional batteries were so equipped and placed in readiness for the Gettysburg campaign, and still another battery came in by absorption with the cavalry division of Brigadier General Julius H. Stahl from the valley of Virginia. These nine batteries were organized into two brigades, each under its senior captain who was assisted in his duties by a suitable staff, and with supply departments necessary for independent and efficient service.

It may here be remarked that these two brigades were the first properly organized artillery commands, except the Artillery Reserve, in the Army of the Potomac, or for that matter, in any of the Federal armies. The long marches and wearing service required of batteries serving with cavalry suggested that, ordinarily, the brigades should alternate in the performance of it, thus affording them time and opportunity between terms of duty to refit and recuperate.

It is not out of place here to remark that the service of field batteries differs essentially from any other branch of the service. While it has the ordinary duties of both infantry and cavalry, it has in addition that which belongs to artillery as a specialty. A battery, to be efficient, must be complete in all its parts, in its personnel, its horses, its guns and carriages, its ammunition and its means of repair. It moves and operates as a whole, the strength of which is measured by its weakest part. An infantry or cavalry regiment may become greatly reduced in numbers, but that which remains is proportionally as effective as before. Not so with a battery, which, to be efficient, must be complete in all its parts, in officers, men, horses and material. Preeminently is this the case with batteries of horse artillery, the service of which, with cavalry, frequently requires them to be remote for indefinite periods from sources of supply.

The nature of cavalry service requires it to act more or less as detached brigades. In this the service differs essentially from that of infantry, which, except for special purposes, operates more in masses by divisions and corps and with the combat as its objective rather than raids and reconnaissance. The cavalry acting more or less as detached brigades, each requiring the service of artillery, calls for an assignment of batteries differing from that of those serving with infantry. While it is detrimental to the efficiency of batteries to be attached to brigades of infantry, or even to small divisions, it is entirely proper that they should be attached to brigades of cavalry. The reasons for this are too obvious to require extended explanation. The horse batteries of the Army of the Potomac were organized, as before stated, into battalions (brigades they were called), and when the cavalry moved a battery was generally assigned temporarily to each brigade. When the duty was ended, the batteries reunited, and recuperating, prepared for the next move. The duty was necessarily arduous and exhausting to both men and horses. Days and nights of marching, in all kinds of weather and over the most difficult roads, it mattered not what was the occasion, the batteries always managed to pull through and were equal at all times to their comrades of the cavalry in capability of overcoming difficulties. And in this duty they had their full share too in the engagements, combats and skirmishes of the cavalry, which in the aggregate were equal to great battles and were far more trying.

After the battle of Antietam, McClellan distributed his army in camps so as to guard the Potomac from Williamsport to Harper's Ferry, waiting for the river to rise so as to make it impossible for the enemy to ford it again, after which he proposed to concentrate somewhere near Harper's Ferry and then move upon the enemy in whatever direction it might best be determined. Meanwhile, Lee had his army distributed from Martinsburg to Winchester. Both commanders were exerting themselves to their utmost in recuperating their armies from the exhaustion caused by the three arduous campaigns through which both had passed since the beginning of April. Lee had the advantage of the conscript system, which enabled him to fill up the companies of his old regiments, while the additions received by McClellan were chiefly new recruits with fresh officers, all of whom had to be instructed from the alphabet up. The veteran regiments, with their experienced officers, were allowed to dwindle away, many of them to almost nothing.

While the two opposing armies were thus engaged in recruiting and refitting, Lee projected a cavalry "raid" into Pennsylvania, for the purpose, as he says, of ascertaining the position and intention of McClellan's army, of destroying depots of supplies and lines of communication, and of capturing from the farming districts as many horses as possible. He hoped, in addition, greatly to benefit the Confederate cause by the moral and political effect that such an enterprise would produce both at home and abroad. He felt that his army had lost greatly in prestige by being driven back across the Potomac and he thought that a raid of this kind would indicate that he was still master of the situation.

He entrusted the raid to his active lieutenant "Jeb" Stuart, but before starting him he caused the partisan leader, Colonel John D. Imboden, to make threatening demonstrations against Cumberland, Maryland, which had the desired effect of drawing off in that direction a large part of McClellan's cavalry under Averill. The latter, accompanied by a horse battery, left the vicinity of Hagerstown on the morning of October 9th, and arrived at Green Spring, near Cumberland, on the following morning, a distance of 58 miles through the Allegheny Mountains, in 24 hours. Averill being thus out of the way, Stuart crossed the Potomac in his rear with a picked body of 1,800 cavalry and a battery of horse artillery. Guided by sympathizing citizens of Maryland, he pushed forward to Chambersburg, Pennsylvania, where he found hospitals filled with sick and wounded, and large quantities of clothing and other supplies for the Army of the Potomac. Such of these supplies as he could not make use of he destroyed. He had appointed Brigadier General Wade Hampton his provost marshal and the latter was not slow in burning the depot, store houses and other property. From Chambersburg, Stuart struck southward for the mouth of the Monocacy River, near which he hoped to find some ford of the Potomac unguarded. He arrived at this point on the morning of the 12th, having traveled a distance of 90 miles in 48 hours, gathering on the way about 800 good cavalry horses, besides destroying an immense amount of public and private property, as well as cutting and interrupting all lines of communication.

Following close after this raid, an epidemic broke out among the horses, almost paralyzing for a time the cavalry and artillery service of both armies. The disease had the form of sore tongue, which prevented the horses from eating. It also affected the feet, in some cases to such an extent that the hoofs sloughed off.

This and other reasons prevented McClellan from making any movement until October 26th, when he commenced crossing the Potomac at and below Harper's Ferry, with the intention of concentrating at Warrenton, from whence he could move against the enemy according to circumstances. This movement caused Lee to make a parallel movement up the Shenandoah Valley, with the Blue Ridge between the two armies. The cavalry and horse batteries, skirting along the east side of the mountains, guarded the right flank of the Federal army. At nearly all the passes they encountered the enemy in greater or less force, and daily, almost hourly, skirmishes took place in most of which the batteries alone were sufficient to dislodge the enemy from the positions held by him. It was expected that the two armies would come together for a decisive battle somewhere in the vicinity of Orange Court House.

Meanwhile, the army had moved unmolested to Warrenton, where on the 7th of November 1862, McClellan was relieved from the command and Burnside appointed to it. This therefore may be assumed as the termination of the Antietam campaign.

View of Fredericksburg, Virginia, from Col. Tyler's battery of the "left center" division of the Federal artillery reserve. (*Library of Congress*)

FOUR

FREDERICKSBURG

$\mathbf{T}$HE ARMY OF THE POTOMAC, now commanded by
Burnside, consisted of eight corps: First, commanded by
Reynolds; Second, by Couch; Third, by Stoneman; Fifth,
Brigadier General Daniel Butterfield; Sixth by William F.
"Baldy" Smith; Ninth, by Brigadier General Orlando B.
Willcox; Eleventh, by Sigel; and Twelfth, by Slocum.

The Eleventh Corps had been left to guard the approaches to Washington from the direction of the passes through the
Blue Ridge from the Shenandoah Valley, and the Twelfth to
guard the Upper Potomac at and near Harper's Ferry. The
remaining six were organized into three "Grand Divisions,"
the Right, the Left and the Center, commanded respectively
by Sumner, Franklin, and Hooker. The Right consisted of the
Second and Ninth Corps; the Left, of the First and Sixth; and
the Center of the Third and Fifth.

The artillery consisted of 373 pieces, including 24 of the
horse batteries and eight siege pieces. The Artillery Reserve,
which had received fostering care from McClellan, and which
had done him such good service, was now under command of
Colonel William Hays and consisted of 18 batteries of 88

guns, including the eight siege pieces and the four batteries of horse artillery. This left 51 batteries of 285 guns distributed in the usual manner to infantry divisions, from two to four batteries to each division. For the command of all this artillery, equal in magnitude and importance to an army corps, there were but one brigadier general (the chief of artillery of the Army), three colonels, two lieutenant colonels, and two majors.

The cavalry, consisting of 15 small regiments, was organized into three brigades and constituted a division under Pleasanton. Mention was made previously of the activity and of the gallant service of the cavalry and horse batteries in guarding the right flank of the army as it skirted along the Blue Ridge, and until the main body took position opposite Fredericksburg. After this, until the opening of the following spring campaign, the cavalry had little other than outpost and picket duty to perform, which, however, was extremely harassing. In this the horse batteries fortunately had no share. Artillery in the Federal Army was seldom employed in outpost duty, not so much in fact as it should have been.

Burnside, upon taking command of the Army of the Potomac, was instructed by the War Department to continue the program laid out for McClellan, and which the latter was pursuing when relieved, which was to hug closely to the Blue Ridge with a view of forcing the enemy to battle by intervening between him and Richmond. Burnside, however, favored the more direct route to Richmond via Fredericksburg, and submitting his views to the President received from him a reluctant assent to try it. On the following day (November 15, 1862) he put his army in motion for Fredericksburg, opposite which Sumner arrived on the 17th. Burnside expected a pontoon train to arrive at the same time, to enable Sumner to cross without delay and seize upon the heights behind the town. But, owing to awkward delays, the pontoon train was not there and in fact did not arrive until the 25th. In the meanwhile, Lee, divining Burnside's intentions, moved rapidly and occupied the opposite side of the Rappahannock but a few hours after the arrival of Sumner. Thus, the opportunity was lost which Burnside had relied upon for success. Still adhering to his purpose of moving through Fredericksburg, he conceived the project of crossing the river directly in front of the enemy and of driving him from the strong position he now held on the heights immediately in rear of the town. Burnside's method, or rather want of method, of carrying out this project was so faulty, and as it turned out so uselessly bloody, that it is refreshing to refer to any part of it not subject to adverse criticisms. This was the part enacted by the artillery.

Fredericksburg, a substantially built town of about 5,000 inhabitants, is situated at the head of tidewater on the Rappahannock, at the point where it emerges from a ridge of hills which runs back of the town almost parallel with the course of the river. This ridge is terminated about five miles below the town by the narrow valley of the Massaponax Creek, a tributary of the Rappahannock. Between the river and the foot of the ridge the land is slightly undulating and ascending. The town stretches along the bank of the river for about a mile-and-a-half and back toward the ridge for about half a mile. Between the town and the ridge, and parallel with the river, is a canal, crossed by three wooden bridges. This canal formed a troublesome obstacle to the troops as they advanced to storm the ridge. Beyond the canal, at the foot of the ridge, runs a road, which for some distance has a stone wall on either side of it, that next the hill being a sustaining wall for the sloping grounds in front of the Marye mansion, which stands back upon the ridge, giving to this part of it the name of Marye's Heights. The wall upon the other side of the road had been strengthened by earth and formed a secure parapet for infantry, over the heads of which successive lines in rear, one above the other in rifle trenches on the ascending slope of the heights, could fire with safety. These walls proved an insuperable obstacle to the advance of the Federal troops.

None got beyond them. All the valley, from the town down to the Massaponax, is open farm land, with here and there a group of farm buildings with orchards about them. The upper end of the ridge, or that directly back of the town, is cleared, but towards the Massaponax it is wooded, with the woods extending somewhat into the valley. This wooded part of the ridge and valley was occupied by Jackson's corps, which was attacked by the left wing under Franklin.

The Confederate Army occupied the entire ridge from the river above the town to the Massaponax, a distance of about five miles. The valley of the Massaponax from the ridge to the Rappahannock, a distance of about two miles, was held by Stuart's cavalry and his horse batteries. Longstreet's corps held the left of Lee's line, that portion of the ridge behind the town embracing Marye's Heights. Under the diligent labor of the Confederate troops the ridge grew into a formidable line of redoubts, batteries, and infantry epaulments [small parapets giving soldiers cover], covered in front by abattis and every device known to engineering skill. Lee had 66 batteries of about 264 guns, of which not less than 200 were in position on the ridge, while the remainder were near at hand for such service as might be required of them. In support of this formidable artillery he had upwards of 78,000 infantry present for duty. It was across this river and over this low ground, and against this formidable rampart that Burnside decided to hurl his brave army. The river at this part of its course is about 200 yards wide and being unfordable was to be crossed only by pontoon bridges. On the northern side of the river, occupied by Burnside, the land is high and rolling and is known as the Heights of Stafford. The undulating brows of these heights along the river afforded many excellent positions for artillery, commanding with its fire the entire ground in front of the ridge upon which Lee was posted. With rifles, most of the ridge could be reached also. The chief portion of Burnside's army was far enough back upon the Heights to be out of view from the enemy. Lee had most of his infantry encamped at convenient points several miles distant and so situated as to guard against flanking movements of his adversary, but all within easy supporting distance of each other.

While many changes had taken place among commanders in the Army of the Potomac, including the head of it, but few had been made in the Army of Northern Virginia. Lee still commanded it, with lieutenant generals Longstreet and Jackson, as his trusty lieutenants, and Major General Stuart, as his commander of cavalry. There was no change in his system of organization, which was that of two large corps, with heavy divisions and moderate sized brigades. His regiments averaged in number of men about the same as in the Army of the Potomac. His artillery system was the same as at Antietam, that is, it was organized into battalions of from four to six batteries to a battalion, each of which was commanded by a colonel or lieutenant colonel, while each two or three batteries were under majors. Each division of infantry had one of these battalions attached to it and each corps had a reserve of two battalions. In addition to all this there was an army reserve of four battalions. The chief of artillery was a brigadier general. It will thus be seen that the principle of rank somewhat commensurate with command was recognized as much for artillery as for other arms of service. In the Army of the Potomac there was, with the exception of the Artillery Reserve, no organization of artillery higher than that of the battery, these, however, were of the highest excellence and individually made up in a measure for what was lost for want of proper organization.

Burnside's army on the morning of the battle (December 13th) numbered 113,000 for duty, of which about 80,000 crossed the river. When it was determined to make the attack directly across the river against the front of Lee's position, all of the available artillery was posted upon the projecting bluffs of the Heights of Stafford in order, as stated by Brigadier General Hunt, chief of artillery: "to control the enemy's movements on the plain; to reply to and silence his batteries along the crest of his ridge; to command the town; to cover and protect the throwing of the bridges and crossing the troops, and to protect the left flank of the army from attacks in the direction of Massaponax Creek. For this it was necessary to cover the entire length with artillery posted in such positions as were favorable for these purposes." All the artillery, except one battery for each division, was withdrawn from the corps and temporarily attached to the Artillery Reserve, and all arranged into four divisions. The right division, under Colonel Hays, consisted of 40 rifles, including six 20-pounders. The right center, under Colonel Tompkins, consisted of 24 rifles and 12-pounder Napoleons. The left center, under Colonel Tyler, consisted of 27 rifles, of which seven were 4.5-inch and eight were 20-pounders, the rest being 3-inch guns. The left division, under Captain Gustavus A. DeRussy, consisted of 44 rifles, of which eight were 20-pounders and the remainder 3-inch. Altogether there were about 149 guns thus posted. Eighteen batteries, about 100 guns, chiefly Napoleons, remained with the infantry divisions, and in addition there were four horse batteries of six guns each for cavalry service, making a grand total of 273 pieces thus disposed of. Hunt's instructions for the operations of each of these divisions of batteries, so full, clear and practical as to be a model for all such operations, were carried out to the letter.

The batteries of each division were stationed near their respective places, but kept out of view of the enemy until the night preceding the laying of the bridges, when they were brought forward and each posted in its appropriate place. The crossing was to be effected at three bridges: two in front of the town and the other about two miles still further down the river. Subsequently, a fourth was placed near this last. The enemy occupied the town in considerable force and resisted the laying of the two upper bridges until six batteries of Napoleons were brought down and so riddled the houses as to drive out all except a few sharpshooters, who, screening themselves in cellars and behind strong walls, still prevented

A Model 1857 bronze 12-pounder smooth-bore "Napoleon" gun, location and date unknown. (*Library of Congress*)

the laying of the bridges. Finally, the pontoons were filled with infantry, who, rowing across, soon silenced the fire of the sharpshooters, and the bridges were laid without further delay. At the lower crossing five batteries were brought down to the river and speedily drove away the enemy, thus permitting the bridge to be put down without further trouble. It was not the policy of Lee to resist the Federal troops at the crossing, or upon the plain in front of his fortified ridge where his troops would be exposed to the fire of the numerous artillery from the Heights of Stafford. The slight resistance was, as he states, merely to gain time until he could get his troops into position behind his entrenchments on the ridge.

The bridges were laid on the forenoon of the 11th of December. On the following morning, covered by a dense fog, the Right Grand Division under Sumner, crossing at the upper bridges, occupied the town, filling its streets with infantry, artillery and ambulances. Franklin crossed his Left Grand Division at the lower bridges and formed line a short distance in front of the river. As the infantry divisions crossed the bridges they were rejoined by the batteries borrowed from them for the purposes before stated. In this way, 19 batteries of 104 guns passed over with Sumner's command, but it being manifest that so many could not find space there for employment, all except seven were recalled. Those remaining took a prominent part in the struggle of the next day.

Twenty-three batteries of 106 pieces crossed with Franklin, and this being in open ground there was ample space for all of them. The development of the attacks on this flank was such as to give active employment to all, and some of them were severely engaged.

Hooker's Grand Division, the center, was used as a feeder for the other two. To Franklin was given Major General David B. Birney's and Major General Daniel E. Sickles' divisions of the Third Corps. Brigadier General George D. Bayard's cavalry brigade also crossed with Franklin.

As the battle progressed, and it was found that Sumner was making no headway against the formidable obstacles in front of him, Brigadier General Amiel W. Whipple's division of the Third and Griffin's, Sykes', and Humphreys' of the Fifth Corps were sent to him. These detachments absorbed about the whole of Hooker's Grand Division. One of Sumner's divisions, that of Brigadier General William W. Burns of the Ninth Corps, was with Franklin, making the total force of the latter amount to about 45,000 men; that of Sumner numbered about 35,000.

The crossing was effected without much annoyance from the enemy until about noon when the fog cleared away and the enemy opened a spirited though rather harmless fire of artillery. By the time the crossing was completed the day was too far advanced for further operations and the attack postponed until the following morning. The troops bivouacked for the night on Lee's side of the river, Sumner's in and around the town, and Franklin's on the plain below. The latter established his line of battle, extending from Hazel Run, a small tributary of the Rappahannock near Lee's center, to within a

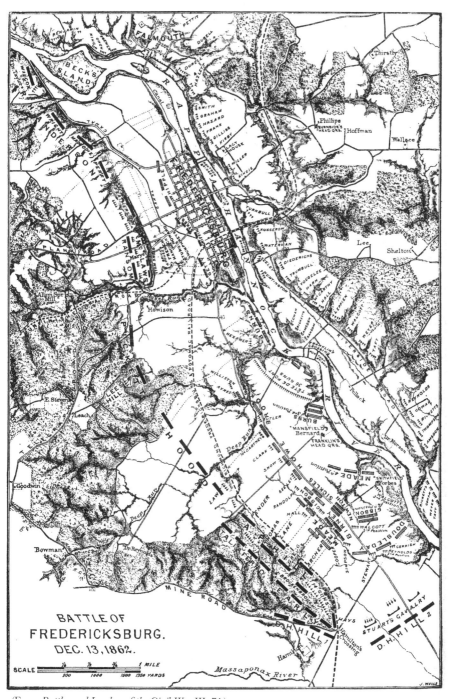

BATTLE OF
FREDERICKSBURG.
DEC. 13, 1862.

SCALE

(From *Battles and Leaders of the Civil War*, III: 74.)

few hundred yards of the Massaponax Creek, a distance of nearly three miles. The right of his line was held by the Sixth Corps, the left by the First. Birney's and Sickles' divisions of the Third Corps, and Bayard's cavalry brigade were massed in rear of the First Corps. Burns' division of the Ninth was nearer the river, guarding the crossing.

Franklin says: "The enemy had artillery on the hills and in the valley of Deep Creek, in the wood near Reynolds' right and on the Massaponax, so that the whole field was surrounded by it except on the right flank. His infantry appeared in all directions around the position."

A space of a mile or more intervened between Franklin's right and Sumner's left. For the security of this flank Captain Ayres, chief of artillery of Major General Smith's corps, posted 28 guns, which battery was prolonged by other groups of guns to the extreme left of Franklin's line where a number of batteries were stationed by Colonel Wainwright, chief of artillery of the First Corps. Although the batteries of Franklin's command were attached in the usual way to divisions, the management of them in this battle was entrusted to Colonel Wainwright and Captain Ayres, the chiefs of artillery of his two corps, and were thus enabled to perform such excellent service as to elicit praise even from the enemy. They were held well in hand and time and opportunity was not lost in hunting them scattered about with divisions or brigades. They were always available where most needed. Jackson in his report says: "The artillery of the enemy was so judiciously posted as to make an advance of our troops across the plain very hazardous." This he gives as a reason for not having followed up the repulse which he gave to part of Franklin's command. Jackson confronted Franklin with the 94 regiments of his own corps together with major generals Hood and George E. Pickett's divisions of Longstreet's corps, altogether 137 regiments.

Franklin had the 94 regiments of his own Grand Division, together with the divisions of Birney, Sickles and Burns of

Sumner's and Hooker's Grand Divisions, in all 143 regiments. Franklin had a few regiments of cavalry under Bayard, but Jackson had a much greater number under Stuart, so that in number of regiments, which is a pretty fair gauge of the number of men, the two forces were about equal. In artillery, too, Franklin and Jackson were about equal, the former took over with him 23 batteries of 106 pieces, the latter had about 50 pieces acting with his troops, together with a group of 24 pieces near Deep Run on his left, another of 15 pieces near his center, and another of 14 pieces under Colonel Walker on his extreme right. These latter performed excellent work in repelling Franklin's attack. Stuart had a dozen or more pieces with his cavalry and was exceedingly active with them against Franklin's left. In all, Jackson had about 115 guns.

That portion of the ridge occupied by Jackson was more broken and wooded than that held by Longstreet. The woods were dense and tangled and extended a considerable distance into the plain in front of Franklin's left. It was in every respect most favorable for the Confederates, giving them not only the advantage of command from the ridge, but cover from the woods. Confederate soldiers were better bushwhackers than those of the Federal Army and were therefore superior to them, man to man, in the woods.

Burnside had now, on the evening of the 12th, nearly all of his fighting strength safely in position on Lee's side of the river, but was evidently undecided as to what next to do. He apparently understood the hopelessness of attempting to carry Longstreet's part of the ridge by direct assault, but he did not seem to comprehend the advantage that might be gained by moving Sumner during the night, to the left, and there, joining him with Franklin, making a powerful attack upon Lee's right with a view to crushing it in before it could be reinforced from the left. He, however, decided to assault Marye's Heights, and also attack Lee's right, and about 7:00 o'clock on the eventful morning of the 13th sent Franklin an order to attack without delay.

The order was ambiguous and confusing, but as well as Franklin could interpret it, he was to attack with one division to be supported by another. He accordingly sent in Meade's division, but to be on the safe side, supported it by the other two of Major General Reynolds' divisions, those of Doubleday and Brigadier General John Gibbon. Preliminary to the attack a heavy fire of artillery was opened upon the woods in hopes of developing the position of the enemy, but without effect. Meade's division moved steadily to the assault. Jackson says of this advance: "Walker (commanding the fourteen-gun battery on a knoll on his extreme right) reserved his fire until the enemy's lines came within less than 800 yards, when the fourteen guns opened, pouring such a storm of shot and shell into his ranks as to cause him first to halt, then to waver, and at last seek shelter by flight."

The division thus forced to retire was soon rallied and again advanced, this time with the division of Gibbon on its right. Of this second advance, Jackson says:

> About 10:00 o'clock the main attack was made by a rapid and heavy discharge of artillery. Under the protection of this warm and well directed fire, his infantry in heavy force advanced, seeking the partial protection of a piece of woods extending beyond the railroad. The batteries on the right played on their ranks with destructive effect. The advancing force was visibly staggered by our rapid and well directed artillery, but soon recovering from the shock, the Federal troops, consisting of Franklin's Grand Division, supported by Hooker's Grand Division, continued to press forward. Advancing within pointblank range of our infantry and thus exposed to the murderous fire of musketry and artillery, the struggle became fierce and sanguinary.

He then describes with minuteness how his own lines, were broken at certain points, and how restored, and how

Franklin's lines were finally repulsed after a struggle so severe and sanguinary, as to call for nearly all of his troops.

The divisions of Meade and Gibbon, becoming somewhat separated as they advanced through the thick wood, left a weak place in the line. The enemy discovering this, immediately took advantage of it and forced back these divisions. At this moment Birney's division of the Third Corps was put in "and drove the enemy from the front of the wood, where he had appeared in strong force. This division, with the aid of the artillery, soon drove the enemy back to shelter, and he did not again appear." Sickles came up with his division and assisted to hold the enemy back.

All of this time Smith's Sixth Corps was deployed in line of battle on the right of where the fighting was going on, and with the exception of its batteries, was comparatively idle. The batteries engaged those on the ridge in front of them.

While the battle was in progress in the woods, in front, the enemy made a serious demonstration on Franklin's left. This was met by Doubleday's division and the batteries Wainwright had assembled on that flank, greatly assisted by DeRussy's artillery on the opposite side of the Rappahannock.

Nothing further was done on this part of the line. Burnside appears to have had no plan for Franklin to carry out, and he carried out none. Not one-half of his troops were engaged to amount to anything. On Jackson's side the division of D.H. Hill did not, in the language of Hill, "pull a trigger." But the troops of both sides that were engaged were engaged fiercely. Franklin lost 528 killed, 3,525 wounded and 811 missing, chiefly captured, for a total of 4,864. Jackson reported his loss at 344 killed, 2,545 wounded and 526 missing, for a total of 3,415. His more advantageous position accounts for the difference in loss.

The fighting upon the right, where Sumner attacked Longstreet, was altogether of a different nature. Scarcely a man of the troops of the latter left the cover of his entrenchments and the attacks of Sumner were confined to the most desperate efforts to scale the ridge and get possession of the formidable earthworks lining its crests. Burnside's orders to Sumner were so confusing that it was not until about noon that he moved forward to attack. He too, like Franklin, was ordered to attack with one division supported closely by another. French's division of the Second Corps was selected as the leading column and boldly debouched from the town by the three streets leading to the bridges over the canal before mentioned. This canal proved a great and unexpected obstacle, causing the division to defile slowly over the bridges, from one of which the planking had been removed, thus forcing the men to cross on the string pieces, all the while exposed to a concentrated fire from the artillery on the ridge and musketry from the rifle pits and sunken roads. Major General French deployed his division and most gallantly moved forward to the assault. The fire, now concentrated on it, literally tore it to pieces, but sheltering themselves as much as possible behind slight inequalities of the ground, the regiments doggedly held what they had gained. French's division was closely followed by that of Major General Hancock, which underwent the same experience. The attacks from both were made by brigades with a view chiefly to get possession of the wall skirting the road. Hancock says: "Each brigade advanced in succession, under a most murderous fire of artillery and musketry; the artillery fire reaching the troops in a destructive manner in the town even before they had commenced the movement." The distance to overcome, by the way the troops were obliged to march before reaching the enemy's works, was probably 1,700 yards, and it took an unusually long time to advance that distance in consequence of the canal, fences, and other obstacles.

The divisions of French and Hancock were then formed into one line, which they continued to maintain until after dark, and after the troops had exhausted their ammunition, and after the ammunition of the killed and wounded within reach had been expended. Howard's division of the same corps then followed Hancock's, but met with like fate. Then those of Whipple of the Third, and Griffin and Humphreys of the Fifth Corps, were sent in, in the same manner, but without advancing the attack a pace beyond the ground gained by French and Hancock. Humphreys' was the last attack made. When all before it had failed, Burnside ordered Hooker to lead in his two last divisions, those of Sykes and Humphreys. Hooker remonstrated against this as being useless slaughter, but being ordered peremptorily to do so, he first brought to bear upon the enemy as much artillery fire as possible in hopes of shaking the enemy at that point and then sent Humphreys forward to attack with the bayonet. This attack was made with a spirit and determination seldom, if ever, equaled in war. Humphreys, himself, was simply heroic. But the impregnable position of the enemy gave such great advantage that the attack was almost immediately repulsed. Humphreys' charge was made about sundown, after which the troops remained, holding the ground under the murderous fire of the enemy until recalled a few hours later.

Longstreet, in his report, describing these attacks says: "The batteries had hardly opened when the enemy's infantry began to move towards my line. Our pickets in front of the Marye house were soon driven in, and the enemy began to display his forces in front of that point. Our artillery being in position, opened fire as the masses became dense enough to warrant it. This fire was very destructive and demoralizing in its effect, and frequently made gaps in the enemy's ranks that could be seen at the distance of a mile." It was evident that the defenses of the enemy were too powerful to be taken by an assault of infantry.

The seven batteries that took part in these assaults boldly followed up the infantry, and while doing their utmost, shared the same fate. Some of them met with unprecedented loss in men and horses. The nature of the ground was such that the artillery could give but little assistance to the infantry.

Of this attack by Sumner, Lee in his report says:

> All the batteries on the Stafford Heights directed their fire upon the positions occupied by our artillery, with a view to silence it and cover the movements of the infantry. Without replying to this furious cannonade, our batteries poured a rapid and destructive fire into the dense lines of the enemy as they advanced to the attack, frequently breaking the ranks and forcing them to retreat to the shelter of the houses. Six times did the enemy, notwithstanding the havoc caused by our batteries, press on with great determination to within 100 yards of the foot of the hill, but here encountering the deadly fire of our infantry, his columns were broken and fled in confusion to the town.

The two divisions of the Ninth Corps remaining with Sumner and forming the left of his line were not idle. These divisions were commanded by brigadier generals Samuel D. Sturgis and George W. Getty, and were sent forward to storm the ridge, but with the same result as the others just mentioned.

Sumner's loss was 743 officers and men killed, 5,368 wounded and 958 captured, making a total of 7,069, which added to that of Franklin gives a grand total of 11,933. Lee lost 595 killed, 4,061 wounded and 653 missing, many of whom were captured, making a grand total of 5,309.

The chief part of Lee's loss occurred in Jackson's command; that of Longstreet was comparatively slight by reason of his troops being covered by entrenchments. Lee's ordnance officer reports that 9,091 muskets were collected from the field of battle. Comparing this with Burnside's loss, it appears that but few of these could have been thrown uselessly aside by the Federal troops.

The attacks of Sumner and Franklin were entirely independent of each other; their troops did not unite towards the center by half a mile or more. The attack of one did not serve even as a diversion in favor of the other.

It now became evident to Burnside that he could not succeed by proceeding in this manner, and having no other plan, his troops remained idle during the following day and until after nightfall on the 15th, when they were all withdrawn, without molestation, to the north side of the river. Nothing was left behind but the dead and those too severely wounded to be moved. The artillery brought away every gun and caisson. The batteries posted to cover the crossings remained in position until the bridges were taken up. The troops returned to their former camps and thus ended the "Fredericksburg Campaign," the only creditable thing about which was the sterling soldierly qualities evinced by the troops, and the only useful thing, the excellent practical lesson given them in crossing a river in presence of an enemy, and in this the artillery was preeminent.

Burnside was relieved from the command of the Army of the Potomac soon after this, and Hooker assigned to it. The latter, during the winter, was energetic in bringing the army up to a high degree of efficiency, and towards spring began planning a campaign which culminated in his defeat at Chancellorsville on the three first days of the following May.

Trees shattered by artillery fire on the south side of Plank Road at the Chancellorsville battlefield. (*Library of Congress*)

FIVE

CHANCELLORSVILLE

A FTER THE BATTLE OF FREDERICKSBURG, the Army of the Potomac remained encamped on the Heights of Stafford, facing Lee's army, which continued to occupy the heights and country in rear of Fredericksburg. A number of important changes took place during the winter in the former army. Burnside, upon being relieved, was assigned to the command of the Department of the Ohio, and took with him his old corps, the Ninth. This was replaced by the Eleventh, composed largely of German troops, who idolized Sigel, their former commander, but who, being relieved, was now succeeded by Howard. The Twelfth Corps, which after the battle of Antietam, had been left behind to guard the Upper Potomac, now rejoined, and was commanded by Major General Slocum. The other corps remained as before, but some changes took place among their commanders. Reynolds remained in command of the First, and Major General Couch of the Second. Sickles was assigned to command the Third, vice Major General Stoneman placed in command of the cavalry, now organized into a corps. Meade was assigned to command the Fifth, vice Butterfield made chief of staff of the new commander of the Army of the Potomac.

Sedgwick was assigned to the Sixth, vice "Baldy" Smith, who, together with Franklin, had been relieved from duty with this army in consequence of the dissatisfaction found with them by Burnside concerning the battle of Fredericksburg. Sedgwick continued the reliable commander of the Sixth until he was killed at its head at Spottsylvania two years afterwards. Reynolds was killed at the head of the First, at Gettysburg, in the following July. Sumner, the veteran commander of the Second Corps from the date of its organization until he was assigned to the command of the Right Grand Division at the battle of Fredericksburg, had died. Hunt continued as the able chief of artillery.

The organization of the artillery continued as before, i.e., the batteries, except those of the Artillery Reserve, remained assigned to divisions, and as a rule, without other than their own captains to command them. The Artillery Reserve was reduced to 12 batteries. Its former excellent commander, Colonel Hays, had received well deserved promotion to a brigadier generalcy, and was assigned to an infantry command. The Reserve was now under a captain.

General Hunt, in his report of the operations of the artillery in the Chancellorsville campaign, says: "It will, perhaps, hardly be believed that for the command and management in their operations of the artillery of this army, consisting of 412 guns, 980 artillery carriages, 9,543 men and officers, and 8,544 horses, besides their large ammunition trains, there were but five field officers of artillery in the army, and from the scarcity of officers of inferior grades these officers had miserably insufficient staffs."

In number of officers and men alone this command was equal to an ordinary division of infantry with a major general for its commander, together with three brigadiers and about 35 colonels and other regimental field officers. The grand division organization of Burnside was abandoned and the army returned to the *corps d'armée* as its highest unit.

The Army of the Potomac thus organized was recruited up to about 124,000 men, present and absent, or about 100,000 actually for battle, all armed, equipped, clothed, and in every way supplied to the fullest completeness. Hooker was not far wrong when he boastfully remarked that it was "the finest army on this planet." This was on the eve of still another disastrous campaign, that of Chancellorsville, a campaign in which it is safe to say that the artillery, despite the many disadvantages imposed upon it, saved this noble army from utter disaster.

The Army of Northern Virginia, still commanded by Lee, with his two reliable lieutenants, Longstreet and "Stonewall" Jackson, continued to hold the heights behind Fredericksburg, and on each side of it from Port Royal, 12 miles below, to the United States Ford about the same distance above. This entire distance was covered by an almost continuous line of infantry parapets, interspersed with which were battery epaulments advantageously located for sweeping the hill slopes and bottom lands over which the Federal troops would have to march to the assault, and which effectually protected the artillery with which they were abundantly supplied. Abattis, entanglements, and rifle pits covered the entire front. Lee's troops were so disposed along this line as to be readily concentrated at any threatened point. So secure, indeed, did Lee feel in his position, that he detached Longstreet with half of his corps to operate beyond the James River in the direction of Suffolk. Longstreet did not return until after the battle of Chancellorsville.

The experience of Burnside had demonstrated the futility of crossing and attempting to carry the enemy's position by a front attack. For various reasons it was impracticable to attempt to turn his right. Hooker therefore decided to make demonstrations at Fredericksburg with a portion of his army, as if to repeat the operations of Burnside, and with the remainder and larger part, march up the river to Kelley's Ford, distant about 25 miles, cross over, and sweeping down in rear of Lee, force him to come out of his entrenchments and either give battle or retreat. The First and Sixth Corps, under Reynolds and Sedgwick respectively, together with Gibbon's division of the Second Corps, were left behind to make the demonstrations, while the Third, Fifth, Eleventh and Twelfth, and the remainder of the Second, engaged in the turning movement. The cavalry, with the exception of one small brigade, had been started a few days previously on a raid under Stoneman and Averill to cut Lee's lines of communication. A couple of horse batteries accompanied these raiding parties.

Kelley's Ford is several miles above the confluence of the Rapidan River with the Rappahannock, and this involved the crossing of the former after crossing the latter stream. It enters the Rappahannock on the south, or Fredericksburg side, and the tract of country included in the angle after crossing the Rapidan is known as the Wilderness, a most appropriate name. It was here that Grant first met Lee in the spring of the following year and it was here, partly on the same ground, that Hooker was now to meet the same enemy. It is a slightly rolling country, covered with pine and oak forest, thickly interspersed with blackjack and other scrub growths. The clayey soil is so barren as to have induced but few settlements, and they of the poorest sort.

Chancellorsville, one of these settlements consisting of but one house, owes its importance to the meeting here of two or three roads. Around this house is an irregular cleared space of about one hundred acres. From here to Fredericksburg, distant about ten miles, are two good roads, which, some four miles from Chancellorsville, emerge into a more open country around and about Salem Church, soon to become famous as the place where Sedgwick with his Sixth Corps made such a stout resistance to an overwhelming force of Lee's army. One of these roads, known as the Fredericksburg and Orange plank road, after passing the Chancellor house continues on westward towards the Rapidan. About two miles from the Chancellor house, it again branches, and at this point is another cleared space of about a hundred acres, with several houses near by, one of which was known as Melzi Chancellor's, or "Dowdell's Tavern." It was here that the Eleventh Corps was stationed on the evening of May 2nd, when Jackson made his flank attack and sent it flying to the rear. This was the turning point of the battle and of the campaign.

Through the forest, in various directions, are country roads with here and there a clearing and a house. The Fredericksburg and Orange plank road, running by the Chancellor house, follows, in quite a straight east and west course, the undulating crest of a low, almost imperceptible ridge. As the principal part of the battle was fought along this road, or within a short distance of it on either side, for a distance of about three miles, it may be taken as the axis of the field and everything referred to it as an ordinate.

On this road about three-fourths of a mile west of the Chancellor house, is a slight eminence known as Fairview, beyond which, at about the same distance, another slight eminence and opening called Hazel Grove. In the depression between these eminences is a small brook, running southwardly, a tributary of Mine Run. On another swell of ground, a mile or so beyond Hazel Grove is Dowdell's Tavern, and half a mile beyond this, on still another rise of ground, is the Tully farmhouse, beyond which the right of the Eleventh Corps extended about half a mile and rested in the depths of the forest. This was the extreme right of Hooker's line; beyond it he did not have even a picket guard.

Hazel Grove became a place of great importance as a position for the Confederate artillery, while that of Fairview was of equal importance for the Federal batteries. The position at the Chancellor house was all important to Hooker because of the roads converging to it. With this position in the hands of the enemy, he would be cut off in every direction except towards the United States Ford about three miles in rear of Chancellorsville, between which two places was a common country road running through dense forest. This ford was guarded by Mahone's brigade, with another nearby in support. Upon the approach of Hooker's turning column, these brigades, after slight resistance, withdrew, thus uncovering the ford. Here a pontoon bridge was at once laid, establishing communication directly with the position opposite Fredericksburg and uniting in a measure the two wings of Hooker's army. The Second Corps (excepting Gibbon's division) being near at hand, at once crossed at this bridge and joined those already at Chancellorsville.

To the eastward of the Chancellor house, and within easy artillery range, was slightly higher ground, and also some in front, all of which the enemy took advantage of to assail the position. Dense forest surrounded the fields at the Chancellor house. The distance from wood to wood across these fields in every direction was less than easy musket range, thus affording the enemy the advantage of that kind of cover so congenial to him. Every road and path through this wilderness was familiar to the enemy, while they were entirely unknown to Hooker's troops.

About halfway between the United States Ford and Fredericksburg is Banks' Ford, which, owing to a bend in the river, is only about four miles in a straight line from the latter place. The steep bluffs about this ford were covered with rifle pits held by Brigadier General Cadmus M. Wilcox's brigade of Major General Richard H. Anderson's division. It was expected that Hooker's advance from Chancellorsville would cause Wilcox to withdraw, when another bridge would be laid, thus virtually connecting both wings of the army. For the purpose of assisting in this operation, and also of guarding against the contingency of the ford being used by the enemy in giving a counter blow, a battery of 36 pieces, chiefly batteries of the Reserve under Captain Archibald Graham, were posted here and did good service. Wilcox was driven away and a bridge constructed, to which Sedgwick fought his way and made good his retreat to the north side.

The Chancellorsville campaign opened on the morning of April 27, 1863, when the troops of the Army of the Potomac were put in motion for the various operations just indicated. The turning movement was so skillfully made that by the afternoon of the 30th, Hooker had assembled at and near Chancellorsville the Second, Fifth, Eleventh, and Twelfth Corps, while the Third was near at hand and could reach the place within a few hours. While these movements were being executed, others were in progress at Fredericksburg, where it will be remembered, Hooker had left Sedgwick and Reynolds to attract Lee's attention, and by misleading him hold him in his entrenchments until the flanking movement could be got well under way.

The arrangements for crossing these two corps were very similar to those employed by Burnside for crossing a few months before. At one of the bridges, below the town, was posted a battery of 34 pieces, chiefly rifles under Colonel Wainwright, chief of artillery of the First Corps. It is proper here to mention that this corps was left behind for the purpose of making demonstrations or of assisting Sedgwick in a real attack, as the case might require. One of its divisions crossed over, but was soon recalled, and the whole corps hastened to Chancellorsville where things were assuming a very unfavorable aspect. At the other bridge, where Sedgwick was to cross, another battery of 46 pieces, chiefly rifles also, was posted under Colonel Tompkins, chief of artillery of the Sixth Corps.

In laying the bridges at both of these crossings, considerable opposition was met with from the enemy sheltered in rifle pits on the opposite side. A well directed fire from some of the guns soon, however, cleared him away.

Still further down the river, nearly opposite the mouth of the Massaponax, another battery of 16 rifles was posted under Colonel Edward R. Warner, inspector of artillery. These guns were to command the bridge over the Massaponax, and the valley of that stream, to prevent the enemy from turning that flank and taking Sedgwick in reverse. As he advanced towards the town these guns followed up the movement along the opposite shore. In addition to the foregoing groups of guns, five batteries of Napoleons were stationed near Falmouth, in readiness for service at any point required.

The batteries posted at the several crossings had numerous duels with the enemy's artillery, in which but little good resulted, except as affording excellent lessons in practical gunnery. All of these admirable dispositions of batteries were made under the supervision of General Hunt, whose functions as chief of artillery had been curtailed almost exclusively to this duty. As the operations at the crossings near Fredericksburg ceased to require their presence, many of the batteries were hastened up to assist at Chancellorsville.

Hooker's flanking movement would, of necessity, call Lee from his entrenchments, seeing which, Sedgwick was to force his way through whatever force might be left on the heights back of the town and attack Lee in rear, while the latter should be engaged with Hooker. Sedgwick carried out his part of this program most successfully up to the point where Hooker was to engage Lee. Here Hooker failed him, and Lee, turning an overwhelming force against Sedgwick, forced the latter to retire across the river at Banks' Ford.

As has already been stated, Hooker's turning column arrived at Chancellorsville on the afternoon of April 30th. Hooker was with it in person. At this time Lee had not moved from his position at Fredericksburg, and Hooker's great mistake was in not continuing to move forward to gain possession of the open ground about Salem Church, where his artillery would have had a better chance, and which would have uncovered the position at Banks' Ford for the laying of a bridge. An advance of four miles that afternoon or early next morning would have put him in possession of all these advantages. As it was, he made no movement until late in the forenoon of the following day, by which time Lee had taken possession of the ground and was able to hold it. At the time referred to, Hooker sent, or rather started, a reconnaissance in

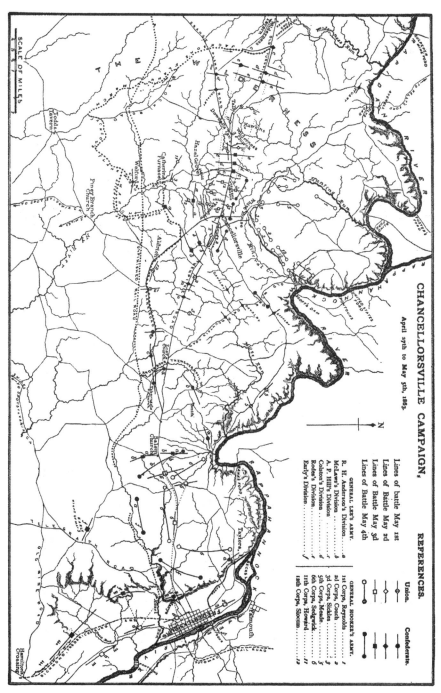

(From *Battles and Leaders of the Civil War*, III: 158.)

force down the three roads leading to Fredericksburg, which movement was to be preparatory to a simultaneous advance in that direction by his entire force about 2:00 P.M.

The troops for this reconnaissance consisted of the entire infantry of two corps, the Fifth and Twelfth, but, strange to say, of all the 13 batteries then present with these corps only four were to accompany the expedition.

The object of a reconnaissance in force is to push the enemy to a degree just short of a general engagement with a view to determine his strength and dispositions. It is manifest that artillery is preeminently the arm best adapted for this purpose.

In this instance the reconnaissance was recalled before becoming seriously engaged, except as to Sykes' division of the Fifth Corps, which was on the "Old Turnpike," a road intermediate between the Plank Road upon which was the Twelfth Corps and the River Road where marched the other two divisions of the Fifth. On gaining the ridge, about a mile from Chancellorsville, Sykes discovered the enemy advancing in force. Deploying rapidly and thinking himself supported on both flanks by the troops on the other roads, he pushed forward his line and gained the next ridge in advance, which he stubbornly held until recalled about two hours afterwards. While doing this he could hear nothing of his supports on the other roads. His flanks were becoming enveloped by the enemy and he was in truly a critical condition when Hancock, with his division of the Second Corps, was sent to assist him in retiring with safety.

Hooker had learned through other sources of the advance of the enemy and had recalled the reconnaissance, but by some blunder Sykes had not been informed of it. Blunders, from this time on, came thick and fast. Up to this point everything had gone well. Hooker's plan for flanking Lee out of his strong position was admirably conceived and the execution of it up to this period was skillfully managed. But Hooker now seems to have been greatly astonished that Lee should confront him so boldly, and at once decided to abandon the initiative and stand upon the defensive, a decision that threw every advantage into the hands of his adversary, and these advantages were numerous.

Sykes, in the sharp affair just mentioned, was ably supported by Captain Stephen H. Weed's battery of the 5th U.S. Artillery Regiment. In fact it is doubtful, taking the enemy's account, if he could have held the position as he did, until the arrival of Hancock, without the efficient service of this battery.

The enemy advanced and immediately commenced feeling Hooker's position, during which operation there was considerable desultory artillery practice. "Jeb" Stuart, with his cavalry, closely reconnoitered the whole of Hooker's line from left to right and reported to Lee the vulnerable condition of Hooker's right flank; that it was entirely in the air and easily reached.

Hooker had established his line with the left resting on the Rappahannock, about a mile below the United States Ford, at which ford were his pontoon bridges connecting him with his base which was still at Falmouth opposite Fredericksburg. The left was held by the Fifth Corps, which, extending out perpendicularly to the river, joined on to the Second, which, crossing the Orange Plank Road, curved around in front of the Chancellor house almost to the same road on the other side where its right connected with the left of the Twelfth. This latter corps, extending along in front of the road and passing over the Fairview elevation, joined the left of the Eleventh near Hazel Grove, from which point the latter corps extended past Dowdell's Tavern, over the rise at the Tully house, and into the depths of the forest beyond. This attenuated line was necessarily very thin, but was supported by the Third Corps, which, arriving by the United States Ford on the evening of the 1st, took an active part in repulsing the enemy when feeling Hooker's position on the following day. Birney's and Whipple's divisions of this corps took position between the Eleventh and Twelfth. The other division rested in support of a thin part of the line between the Second and Twelfth Corps.

Five batteries of 30 guns of the Fifth Corps were massed under Captain Randol on a knoll near the river to cover the approach to the United States Ford by the River Road. When the Twelfth Corps returned from the reconnaissance before mentioned, its batteries were grouped in position near the Chancellor house by Captain Clermont Best, chief of artillery of this corps. Hooker had upon the field at this time 35 batteries of about 200 guns, but with the exception of the two groups just mentioned, about 60 pieces, all the other batteries were scattered, distributed in the usual manner to divisions. "The woods seemed full of batteries." Hancock, who with his division of the Second Corps stood across the main road to Fredericksburg, the most exposed position on the field, says: "A section (two pieces) of artillery was placed on the turnpike, where my line of battle crossed it, and one piece in a wood road nearly parallel to it and about 200 yards to the left." This was all that was at this important point. What he reports was very good for an advanced guard, but entirely inadequate as against the ponderous blows soon to be dealt by the enemy, and which pulverized this part of the Union line.

On the extreme right where Jackson made his furious onslaught, the commanding general of the Eleventh Corps, after describing in his report the positions of his infantry, says:

The artillery was disposed as follows: Two pieces near [Brigadier] General [Charles] Devens's right, enfilading the old turnpike; the rest of [Captain Julius] Dieckmann's battery [13th New York Independent Light Artillery Battery] on the left of General Devens, covering approaches along the Plank Road. Four guns of [Captain Michael] Wiedrich's battery [Battery I, 1st New York Light Artillery Regiment] were placed near [Brigadier General Adolph Von] Steinwehr's right, and two guns near his left, covering the approaches from the front. [Captain Hubert] Dilger's battery [Battery I, 1st Ohio Light Artillery Regiment] was posted near the intersection of the turnpike and the plank road.

Three batteries were in reserve and so placed as to be used on any of the approaches.

The right of the Eleventh Corps, which was Hooker's extreme right, rested on no natural object to prevent it from being readily turned and broken by even the slightest attack. It should therefore have been strengthened by the formation of an artificial object. The batteries, lying idle in the woods, furnished means for this. The right of the Eleventh, instead of losing itself in the woods, should have been drawn back to cover the flank and rear, and the angle thus formed strengthened by a mass of guns. Devens, who commanded the right division of the Eleventh, permitted Colonel Leopold Von Gilsa, commanding his right brigade, to draw back two of his small regiments, but the angle was strengthened by only the two pieces mentioned in the report of the corps commander. The sequel showed how utterly inadequate was this preparation for such an attack as Jackson was about to make.

Hooker had dispensed with the services of his chief of artillery and there was no one upon the field to make proper disposition of the batteries. The senior battery commander in each corps was its chief of artillery and exercised a nominal control over its batteries, but there was no one to take a comprehensive view of the entire field and distribute the batteries where most needed. As a rule, the batteries stuck as closely as possible to their divisions, but in a country so wooded this necessarily threw many of them into positions where they could be of but little service, often of no service whatever. The line of battle thus formed, extending from the Rappahannock on the left around in front of the Chancellor house, and thence on along the Orange Plank Road to the woods beyond the Tully house, was strengthened as rapidly as possible by each division, brigade or regiment according to its own ideas of military engineering.

While this was going on at Chancellorsville, bridges had been laid below Fredericksburg and the Sixth Corps and part of the First crossed over to make demonstrations. These had the desired effect of confusing Lee and diverting his attention until after the turning column had crossed the Rapidan and was well on its way to Chancellorsville. Lee in his report says:

The enemy in our front near Fredericksburg continued inactive, and it was now apparent that the main attack would be made upon our flank and rear. It was, therefore, determined to leave sufficient troops to hold our lines, and with the main body of the army to give battle to the approaching columns. [Major General Jubal A.] Early's division of Jackson's corps, and [Brigadier General William] Barksdale's brigade of [Major General Lafayette] McLaws' division, with part of the reserve artillery under [Brigadier] General [William N.] Pendleton, were intrusted with the defense of our position at Fredericksburg, and, at midnight on the 30th, General McLaws marched with the rest of his command toward Chancellorsville. General Jackson followed at dawn next morning with the remaining divisions of his corps. He reached the position occupied by General Anderson (where Sykes met him) at 8 A.M., and immediately began preparations to advance.

It was knowledge of this advance and preparation for attack that caused Hooker to decide to stand upon the defensive.

Lee, after describing the resistance received from Sykes, goes on to say:

Here (at Chancellorsville) the enemy had assumed a position of great natural strength, surrounded on all sides by a dense forest filled with tangled undergrowth, in the midst of which breastworks of logs had been constructed, with trees felled in front, so as to form an almost impenetrable abattis. His artillery swept the few narrow roads by which his position could be approached from the front, and commanded the adjacent woods. . . . Darkness was approaching before the strength and extent of his line could be ascertained, and as the nature of the country rendered it hazardous to attack by night, our troops were halted and formed in line of battle in front of Chancellorsville at right angles to the Plank Road. . . . It was evident that a direct attack upon the enemy would be attended with great difficulty and loss, in view of the strength of his position and his superiority of numbers. It was, therefore, resolved to endeavor to turn his right flank and gain his rear, leaving a force in front to hold him in check and conceal the movement. The execution of this plan was intrusted to Lieutenant General Jackson with his three divisions. . . . Early on the morning of the 2d, General Jackson marched by the Furnace and Brock roads, his movement being effectually covered by [Brigadier General] Fitzhugh Lee's cavalry, under General Stuart in person.

Lee here speaks of Hooker's artillery being posted to sweep the roads and command the adjacent woods. He was in a measure mistaken in this, misled no doubt, by the fact that such should have been the case, and would have been had the Federal artillery been under the same system of command that existed in his army. As a preliminary to this unfortunate campaign, Hooker had deprived his faithful and skillful chief of artillery, General Hunt, of all except administrative control over the artillery, and had placed no one in the actual command. Hooker had assigned his chief of artillery the comparatively unimportant duty of assisting in laying the bridges at Fredericksburg; thus causing his absence from Chancellorsville at the very time when his services were most urgently needed on that complicated field. The artillery on that field was literally without a head, and it was too, a field which, on account of its peculiar topographical features, preeminently demanded a head; and not only a head, but from the head down to the individual battery, a proper gradation of command and supervision.

There was no one upon the field whose special business it was to look for eligible positions for batteries, and having found them, with authority to post them there, and to command them when so posted, to select rifle batteries for positions requiring such pieces and smooth-bores for service adapted to their kind. It was not until after disaster had befallen his army and everything was in confusion that Hooker recalled his chief of artillery and invested him with authority to restore order. If what was then done as a restorative had before been done as a preventive, the probabilities are that Chancellorsville would have had another and entirely different history.

Jackson, to reach Hooker's right flank, had to pass across the entire front of the latter. At one point, near "The Furnace" where there was an opening through the woods, his column was distinctly visible, passing in an uninterrupted flow for three hours and more. Birney, commanding one of the divisions of the Third Corps, sent a battery to an open space in his front, where, opening fire, it produced considerable confusion in the enemy's ranks by its excellent practice. The column, however, continued to move on, and about noon, Sickles, obtaining permission from Hooker, moved out with the divisions of Birney and Whipple of his corps and Brigadier General Francis C. Barlow's brigade from the Eleventh to ascertain the nature of it. Williams' division of the Twelfth Corps supported Sickles' movement on the left. Altogether, a force of 42 regiments took part in this movement, but strange to say, not a piece of artillery. Three batteries of Whipple's division were left behind in an open field at Hazel Grove. Here, subsequently, they were joined by Lieutenant Joseph W. Martin's horse battery, the 6th New York Independent Light Artillery Battery, in all 22 pieces. A collection of forges, battery wagons, and ambulances were left on a cart road through the woods a little to the westward of the field in which stood the batteries.

In approaching the road upon which Jackson's column was passing, Sickles' force met the flankers of the column, with whom it commenced a brisk skirmish and captured 200 or 300 prisoners. But the enemy, opening with artillery, checked further operations until a battery could be sent for and brought up from those left behind. By this time the rear of the column had passed and the opportunity of cutting it off or seriously damaging it was lost. This was another instance of service, the nature of which preeminently demanded the presence of artillery.

Jackson, pursuing his westerly course until beyond the right flank of Hooker's line, turned sharp to his right and continued this course until he was squarely across and considerably in rear of the right flank of the Eleventh Corps, and about a mile from its extreme end. Here, in an opening in the forest, he formed his three heavy divisions into a powerful column of attack. In the front line was Brigadier General Robert E. Rodes' division, in the second Colston's, and in the third that of A.P. Hill, with about one hundred yards distance between the lines. The artillery took such positions on the flanks as the wooded nature of the country permitted. This column was to move ahead, driving everything before it, and the position at Talley's house was to be carried at all hazards. After taking the high ground at this point, overlooking that further, on about the Dowdell Tavern, should determined resistance be met with, the column was to halt until artillery could be brought up to force the way for further advance.

The troops thus to be struck were those of the Eleventh Corps, commanded by Howard; an organization that had experienced considerable desultory service under Sigel, but, as yet, was unfamiliar with the solid fighting of the Army of the Potomac. It consisted of three divisions of two brigades each, comprising in all 26 regiments, or about 10,000 men actually present for duty. The corps occupied a front of nearly two miles, making the line necessarily thin and weak. Along this entire distance but 16 guns were in position. Three other batteries, of 18 pieces, were in park near at hand, but as it turned out, only a few shots were fired from these before they joined the fugitives to the rear.

As the failure of the campaign seems to hinge upon what took place in this corps, it is pardonable to particularize. The right division was commanded by Devens, whose right brigade, that of Von Gilsa, had its two right regiments (consisting of only about 700 muskets) thrown back at right angles to the main line, and covered by slight breastworks. In the angle thus formed two pieces of artillery were posted to enfilade the road, here passing through dense woods. This short line of Von Gilsa was the first encountered by Jackson's column and figures in the Confederate reports as something formidable. The two guns in the angle fell into the hands of the enemy. On the left of Devens' division, about half a mile from the angle just mentioned, were the other four guns of the same battery. These pieces did not fire at all, but withdrew early.

Next to Devens' division came that of Major General Carl Schurz, a few of whose regiments were in line connecting properly with Devens' left. Schurz, being convinced from what he could see and hear of the enemy's movements towards the right, that an attack was to be apprehended, placed some of his regiments so as to face in that direction, and these, covering themselves with slight entrenchments, formed another obstacle which figures in the reports of the enemy as a formidable line. Near where the right of Schurz's line rested, the Orange Plank Road branches off towards the southwest, and here Dilger's battery was posted, commanding this road and some open ground around it. When the attack was opened Dilger withdrew his battery to some higher ground, a short distance to his rear, where he could have a better field of fire to resist the enemy, now pouring in from the right. As soon as his front was clear of fugitives he opened on the advancing enemy with canister, and did good execution until the enemy was almost among his pieces. Owing to the killing of many of his horses he lost several of his pieces. Near him were four guns of Wiedrich's battery; these stood their ground also, but lost some pieces from the same cause.

On the left of Schurz was one brigade of Steinwehr's division. The other brigade, that of Barlow, had been sent to the front to assist the divisions of the Third Corps in cutting the tail of Jackson's column. Steinwehr's brigade had two regiments deployed to the front; the other two were in rear undeployed. Directly in rear of this brigade the three spare batteries of the corps were parked in a line perpendicular to the main line of battle. Some scattering entrenchments had been thrown up in front of these batteries and along their flanks. Behind these entrenchments quite a number of fugitives were rallied and for a short time made some resistance, and the batteries also did some firing. This line also is mentioned in the Confederate reports as constituting a formidable obstacle.

From the left of the Eleventh Corps to the right of the Twelfth was an interval of about three-fourths of a mile, intended to be occupied by the two divisions of the Third Corps now in front, in pursuit of Jackson's column. As has been stated, these divisions left their batteries behind when they moved to the front. Some of those of Birney's division were in the way of the fugitives of the Eleventh Corps, and being overrun and thrown into confusion, lost much of their material. The three batteries of Whipple's division, left in the open ground about Hazel Grove, were in position to do invaluable service in checking the enemy at the moment when in full tide of success.

Jackson's three divisions numbered 70 regiments, against which Howard had but 22. Barlow's brigade of four regiments, it will be remembered, had been sent out with Sickles. At this time the Confederate regiments were numerically stronger than those of the Federals, owing to the fact that their system of conscription was now in force in all its rigor by which the old regiments were filled up, as was not the case with their opponents. Jackson had 65 guns, Howard but 34. It will thus be seen that with this great disparity of force against him, Howard, unsupported as he was, had but slender chance of making a successful resistance. Even with the preparations that should have been made to meet the attack the chances were largely against him.

At about 5:30 P.M. Jackson set his column of attack in motion, and brushing aside the few pickets met with, soon came upon Von Gilsa's two regiments forming the short line in rear of Devens' right. Rodes, commanding Jackson's leading division, says of this:

> At once the line of battle moved forward with a yell, and [Brigadier General George] Doles' Brigade at this moment debouched from the woods and encountered a force of the enemy and a battery of two guns intrenched. Detaching two regiments to flank the position, he charged without halting, sweeping every-thing before him, and, passing on to Talley's, gallantly carried the works there, and captured five guns by a similar flank movement of a portion of his command. So complete was the whole manoeuvre, and such was the surprise of the enemy, that scarcely any organized resistance was met with after the first volley was fired. . . . The larger portion of his force, as well as his intrenchments, were drawn up at right angles to our line, and, being thus taken in the flank and rear, they did not wait for the attack. On reaching the ridge at Melzi Chancellor's (Dowdell's Tavern), which had an extended line of works facing in our direction, (those by the spare batteries, before mentioned) an effort was made to check the fleeing columns. For a few moments they held this position, but once more my gallant troops dashed at them with a wild shout, and, firing a hasty volley, they continued their headlong flight to Chancellorsville. It was at this point that Colston's line, which had followed closely on my rear,

went over the works with my men, and from this time until the close of the engagement the two divisions were mingled together in inextricable confusion.

A short distance beyond this Jackson's troops entered a thick wood and his right flank came opposite the open ground at Hazel Grove in which were the three batteries of Whipple's division of the Third Corps and Martin's horse battery.

Howard, in describing this attack, says: "At about 6 P.M. I was at my headquarters, at Dowdell's Tavern, when the attack commenced. I sent my chief of staff to the front when firing was heard. General Schurz, who was with me, at once left to take command of his line. It was not three minutes before I followed. When I reached General Schurz's command I saw that the enemy had enveloped my right and that the First Division was giving way."

A spirited resistance was made by some portions of this corps, but soon a great part of it gave way in blind panic and confusion, infantry and artillery overrunning everything in their flight. These fugitives, rushing through a battery and some caissons of another battery of Birney's division then at the front, threw them into such confusion as to cause them to fall into the hands of the enemy. The battery wagons, forges and ambulance, standing as before mentioned, in the cart road through the woods to the westward of Hazel Grove, stamped-ed, and rushing through the batteries in that field threw these likewise into temporary confusion, but through the exertions of the battery officers and the steadiness and discipline of the men, the stampede was not communicated to the batteries. As soon as the torrent of fugitives had passed, the guns of these batteries opened with canister on the enemy, now making his way into the field. This fire, evidently unexpected, caused the enemy to retire hastily to the cover of the woods from which they had just emerged, and from which they at once opened a heavy fire of musketry. The enemy, advancing through the woods between the field and the plank road, enfiladed the batteries, causing some of them to change the direction of their fire to that quarter and thus enfilade the line of the enemy. In this manner these batteries, entirely alone and unsupported, maintained their position, holding the enemy in check until the arrival, a considerable time afterwards, of Birney's and Whipple's divisions from the front.

It was the unexpected shock of this artillery fire that staggered the enemy. Nothing but the timely and gallant conduct of these batteries prevented the enemy from gaining the flank and rear of the Twelfth Corps as he had done that of the Eleventh. The batteries that did this invaluable service were Captain James F. Huntington's "H," 1st Ohio Light Artillery Regiment, and the 10th and 11th New York Independent Light Artillery batteries, commanded on this occasion by lieutenants Samuel Lewis and John E. Burton, respectively. Captain Huntington, as senior officer, exercised general supervision over the whole. Lieutenant Martin's horse battery, of four pieces, acted in conjunction with the others. It had been left there by the cavalry, which had gone by detachments for duty in other parts of the field. One of these detachments was from the 8th Pennsylvania Cavalry Regiment under command of Major Pennock Huey, which being ordered to report to General Howard ran unexpectedly into the enemy whom it charged with a vim and gallantry not excelled even by the charge of "The Six Hundred."

The enemy was completely and thoroughly checked by these batteries. Sickles, being informed of Jackson's attack and of the rout of the Eleventh Corps, hastily returned with his two divisions and took position with them at Hazel Grove, and assisted in holding this important position until withdrawn next morning.

The two front lines of the enemy had become intermingled by the time they had reached the point opposite Hazel Grove, and great confusion now existed in their ranks. Hill's division, comparatively intact, constituting the rear line, was now advanced to the front and the other two withdrawn, to reform in the open fields about Dowdell's Tavern.

While this was going on Jackson, with a numerous retinue of staff officers and orderlies, rode down the road towards Chancellorsville to examine the position in that direction. When returning, his own troops, mistaking his party in the obscurity of the evening for a body of Federal cavalry, poured into it a heavy volley of musketry, mortally wounding Jackson and tearing his escort to fragments. This firing caused the Federal troops to open with full force and for a time the musketry and cannonade was terrific, most of which came from the Twelfth Corps, which with other troops had now taken position to resist further advance of Jackson's column. Rodes says of this: "At this time the enemy opened a similar terrific fire of artillery to that which had taken place just before my withdrawal, which caused much confusion and disorder, rendering it necessary for me to place guards across the road to stop stragglers." In this fire General A.P. Hill was wounded. He had just succeeded Jackson in command, after the wounding of the latter. After Hill, the command devolved upon "Jeb" Stuart, who with a portion of his cavalry had gone to one of the fords of the Rapidan to meet Averill's cavalry approaching in that direction.

Up to this period the enemy, owing to the wooded nature of the country, had had but little opportunity of using his artillery. Lieutenant Colonel Thomas H. Carter, commanding Rodes' battalion of batteries says: "My artillery followed rapidly down the turnpike having no occasion to take position. After reaching Dowdell's, several pieces were put in position on both sides of the road in the intrenchments there formed, to repel an attack of the enemy should our lines be driven back at the woods just ahead." From here he advanced some pieces along the road and in openings to assist the infantry. He describes the artillery firing that occurred at the time Jackson and Hill were wounded as being very destructive upon his artillery near Dowdell's. During the night the enemy's other artillery battalions came up and joined that of Carter.

Hill, who had advanced his division to the front, says of the fire which opened at the time Jackson was wounded: "The enemy during this time had concentrated a most terrible fire of artillery on the head of my division from 24 pieces of artillery." It was during this fire that A.P. Hill was wounded. These 24 guns were in reality 34, a battery assembled under Captain Clermont L. Best, chief of artillery of the Twelfth Corps, who on the previous day had collected the five batteries of his corps in a position near the Chancellor house and thus had them in hand for this emergency.

Best, seeing what had happened to the Eleventh Corps on his right, says: "Having no doubt the enemy would follow in force, I gathered all our batteries, save [Captain Joseph M.] Knap's [Battery E, Pennsylvania Light Artillery Regiment] and Lieut. [Edward D.] Muhlenberg's section [Battery F, 4th U.S. Artillery Regiment], massing them on the ridge in rear of our First Division, and posting in position with them some of the fragments of the Eleventh Corps batteries, until I had 34 guns in what may be termed the key point of the battlefield." The infantry in front of him was on lower ground, enabling him to fire successfully over their heads. "Up to near 10 o'clock at night," he continues, "the cannonading at intervals was terrific, and, in my opinion, contributed much to checking the bold and elated enemy. That night I intrenched all my guns, the digging subsequently proving much protection."

Two divisions of the Twelfth and one of the Third Corps were formed in line across the plank road in the low ground in front of Best's batteries. This formed a new line facing westward, the direction from which Jackson's column was approaching. This made a right angle with the part facing south and continued in an irregular curve around in front of the Chancellor house, and thence on to the river about a mile below the United States Ford. At the angle was the high ground known as Fairview, and here was where Best had his batteries. Hazel Grove was to the left and front of this and during the night Sickles, occupying the latter position, thought himself entirely cut off from the main body. Close in front of Hazel Grove the enemy occupied the breastworks from which the Eleventh Corps had been driven. About midnight Sickles made a bold attack, resulting in a good deal of consternation to the enemy and the recovery of some of the artillery and debris of the battle of the evening before. After this everything remained quiet until early morning.

While these things were transpiring on the right of Hooker's line, Lee, in person, was directing vigorous attacks on that part of the line around the Chancellor house. Of this, Lee says:

> As soon as the sound of cannon gave notice of Jackson's attack on the enemy's right, our troops in front of Chancellorsville were ordered to press him strongly on the left, to prevent reinforcements being sent to the point assailed. They were directed not to attack in force unless a favorable opportunity should present itself, and while continuing to cover the roads leading from their respective positions towards Chancellorsville, to incline to the left so as to connect with Jackson's right as he closed in upon the centre. These orders were well executed, our troops advancing up to the enemy's intrenchments, while several batteries played with good effect upon his lines until prevented by the increasing darkness.

This part of Hooker's line was held chiefly by Hancock's and French's divisions of the Second Corps. Although the fighting was sharp the position remained unchanged. Hays' brigade of French's division was sent to the right of the new position of the Twelfth Corps, to strengthen that part of the line and prevent the enemy from getting in rear to the pontoon bridge at the United States Ford. Here it became severely engaged and Hays himself was captured. Up to within a short time before this he had, as lieutenant colonel, ably commanded the artillery reserve.

The Eleventh Corps was thoroughly broken up and scattered through the woods in every direction. As fast as its fragments could be collected they were transferred to the extreme left to replace Meade's Corps, the Fifth, Sykes' division, of which was now brought over to the right flank to prevent the enemy from gaining possession of the road leading back to the pontoon bridge, which, once in the hands of the enemy, would have cut Hooker off entirely. During the night the other two divisions of the Fifth were moved over in the same direction, thus forming the commencement of a new line near the "White House," about a mile in rear of the Chancellor house. Captain Randol's 30 guns of the Fifth Corps remained in position to cover the approaches to the pontoon bridge from the direction of Fredericksburg. As there was no attack made on this part of the line, these guns took no active part in the battle. The very fact of their being so favorably posted perhaps deterred the enemy from making an attack.

It will be observed from the foregoing that after the rout of the Eleventh Corps, when the enemy was in full pursuit, and upon the verge of taking the Twelfth in flank and rear, as he had done the Eleventh, the firm stand made by Huntington's 22 guns held him in check and enabled the Twelfth to make such arrangements as to hold him at bay until morning. After the wounding of Jackson and Hill, Stuart was called from a distant part of the field to command, and being unfamiliar with the condition of things, deemed it imprudent to continue operations in the dark.

As heretofore stated, the First Corps under Reynolds had been left at the crossing below Fredericksburg to assist Sedgwick, and had already one of its divisions over the river. On the morning of May 2nd, Reynolds received orders to withdraw, take up the bridges and proceed, forthwith, to Chancellorsville. By daylight of the 3rd, he had his corps in position as directed, occupying the right of the new line established by the Fifth. The extreme right of the First was broken to the rear, and at the angle thus formed were posted six 3-

inch and 12 Napoleon guns. The enemy, not attacking at this point, these guns were not engaged. The other six batteries of this corps were hastened forward to assist the troops now heavily engaged near the Chancellor house. Most of them soon became hotly engaged also, and although scattered about here and there, did excellent service. Some of them met with unprecedented losses in officers and men.

This was the general arrangement of Hooker's line when the battle was resumed on the morning of the 3rd. There was, however, much in detail about it that required rectifying and putting in shape for the coming contest, matters so numerous that it was physically impossible for Hooker to attend to them all personally. He had left his chief of staff, General Butterfield, back at headquarters on Stafford Heights, and was of course without his valuable assistance. General Warren, his chief engineer officer, had gone to join Sedgwick at Fredericksburg and there was no one but a captain left to fill his place, who, however active and accomplished, could have but little weight and official influence on a field swarming with general and other officers of rank and position. His chief artillery officer, General Hunt, was absent by his order, attending to other business, and there was not even the shadow of any one else to fill that important position. The consequence of all this was that when day dawned on the morning of the eventful 3rd, the army had a general crazy quilt appearance, little in accordance with the serious work before it, and in this the artillery had more than its proper share.

The key point of the whole position, that at the Chancellor house, was held by the Second Corps under Couch. Hancock still retained in position the three pieces previously mentioned, in addition to which two batteries were placed during the previous evening on his right. So little appreciation did Couch have of the value of artillery for holding such a position, that during the night he sent all his other batteries back to join his wagon train at the ford. Here it is not out of place to mention that one of the other corps commanders, when marching to Chancellorsville expecting every moment to meet the enemy, caused his batteries to accompany his wagon train as part of the impedimenta instead of as a part of his fighting force, the *élan* and soldierly spirit of which it was important to maintain, although he might not perhaps want its service at the time. The control of artillery matters by its own officers was rendered so feeble by the vicious system of dispersion, whereby the command was vested in others, that such like occurrences were not at all unusual.

With the exception of the 34 guns which Best still held intact, there were none others that could be said to be fairly in position on any part of the line threatened with attack. Of the nine batteries of the Third Corps, a few were posted here and there as if on picket, but without concert or unity of action those of the Eleventh, stampeded on the previous evening, were chiefly scattered through the woods.

The most important part of the line was the position at Hazel Grove where Sickles still remained with the divisions of Birney and Whipple and the 22 guns that had done such good service on the preceding afternoon. This position, slightly elevated, commanded that held by the enemy towards Dowdell's and that also of the Federals at Fairview and beyond towards Chancellorsville. In possession of the enemy it would enable Jackson's, now Stuart's, corps to connect with the remainder of Lee's forces in front of the Chancellor house. Sickles represented to Hooker the importance of holding it, but the latter, thinking differently, ordered him to fall back from it early in the morning of the 3rd. This was effected in good order, although not without some sharp fighting in which Huntington lost four of his pieces by having his horses disabled. The enemy at once crowned the position with artillery, which enfiladed the Federal front toward Chancellorsville, and had an oblique fire on the front running towards the river.

Stuart was busy during the night in putting his command in order to renew the attack at daylight. He says: "I sent Colonel E.P. Alexander, senior officer of artillery, to select and occupy with artillery, positions along the line bearing upon the enemy's positions, with which duty he was engaged all night." Certainly a strong contrast to what was not being done within Hooker's lines.

Owing to the wilderness nature of the country and the few avenues of approach, Alexander was able to find positions for but 17 pieces. The remaining 48, in four battalions of batteries, were held in readiness to advance and take up positions where opportunity offered. In all, he had 65 pieces.

When Stuart made his attack on the morning of the 3rd with his 70 regiments of infantry and the artillery just mentioned, he was confronted by the Third and Twelfth Corps and Hays' brigade of the Second, in all 74 regiments. But, for the reasons before stated, Stuart's regiments were stronger than those of his opponents and it is therefore probable that he had the superiority in numbers; besides, Anderson soon made a junction with him, thus very considerably adding to his strength.

When the Third Corps united with the Twelfth at Fairview, six of its batteries were put in position to the right and left of Best's 34-gun battery, making in all 70 pieces. The Third Corps batteries were, however, somewhat scattered and operated without concert of action. When Sickles withdrew his divisions and batteries from Hazel Grove, he took position with the Twelfth Corps at Fairview. Here, some of the hottest fighting of the day took place. The skirmish which occurred when Sickles withdrew from Hazel Grove now grew into a furious battle. The attack of the enemy became general, not only on this part of the field, but also on that part surrounding the Chancellor house. Lee sent in his entire force and soon his separated corps joined hands in front of Fairview.

Stuart pushing forward his command against the Third and Twelfth Corps, the battle became close and sanguinary. Although his attack, as a whole, was general, it was made more or less by subdivisions. To meet such attacks required considerable changing of positions by the divisions and brigades of his opponents; all of which were made in good order, although under a most murderous fire from the enemy. Each division and brigade stood its ground nobly and fought with stubborn firmness. Several times the Federal lines were forced back for a short distance, but advancing, regained the lost ground, the lines of the opposing forces often commingling.

Stuart, in his report, says of this attack: "As soon as the sun lifted the mist that shrouded the field, it was discovered that the ridge over the extreme right was a fine position for concentrating artillery. I immediately ordered thirty pieces to that point, and under the happy effects of the battalion system it was done quickly. The effect of this fire upon the enemy's batteries was superb."

The ridge which he refers to was that of Hazel Grove, just vacated by Sickles. He subsequently established there many more guns. And the battalion system so thankfully mentioned by him, was that so often referred to in these papers, wherein the Confederate batteries were organized into battalions, each commanded by an artillery officer of appropriate rank, who exercised positive, as well as administrative control over it. It was a system of concentration and efficiency, in contradistinction to that of dispersion; and, furthermore, one which relieved division and brigade commanders from the necessity of having their attention diverted from their own appropriate duties to attend to artillery matters, so much better attended to by officers especially appointed for the purpose. The celerity with which Jackson formed his column of attack, in the wilderness, on the flank of the Eleventh Corps, could not have obtained had the infantry commanders been burdened with the care and responsibilities of batteries.

The Third and Twelfth Corps held their ground at Fairview as long as it was possible for troops to do so under such circumstances. The junction of Anderson with Stuart gave the latter great superiority in numbers and his position enabled him to enfilade one face of the Federal angle while Stuart enfiladed the other. The Third and Twelfth yielded the ground inch by inch and withdrew in good order to the new line behind the "White House."

The battle had now raged for four hours and the batteries had exhausted their ammunition, and as they could not get a fresh supply they were successively withdrawn. Best conducted his to the United States Ford, there to replenish his chests. A portion of the Third Corps, when forced to retire, joined the right of Hancock's division nearer the Chancellor house, and there continued the fight until this part of the line also was forced back. Such of the batteries of the Third as still had ammunition took position with the infantry towards the Chancellor house and were exposed to a terrible fire from the enemy, now rapidly closing in upon that position, notwithstanding which, they continued to be most gallantly and effectively served until every round was expended. Their losses in men and horses were unusually severe.

Captain Best, reporting the part taken by his batteries, says: "Early Sunday morning (May 3rd) the enemy commenced the attack, evidently determined to carry that point, and all my batteries again opened on their masses. . . . My line of guns kept to its work manfully, until about 9 A.M., when, finding our infantry withdrawing, our right and left exposed, and the enemy's musketry already so advanced as to pick off our men and horses I was compelled to withdraw my guns to save them." He lost heavily in both men and horses.

Lee, in his report (following Stuart's account of the battle, but omitting the details) says:

> The second and third lines soon advanced to the support of the first, and the whole became hotly engaged. The breastworks at which the attack was suspended the preceding evening were carried by assault under a terrible fire of musketry and artillery. In rear of these breastworks was a barricade, from which the enemy was quickly driven. The troops on the left of the plank

road, pushing through the woods, attacked and broke the next line, while those on the right bravely assailed the extensive earthworks, behind which the enemy's artillery was posted (Best's 34 guns). Three times were these works carried, and as often were the brave assailants compelled to abandon them—twice by the retirement of the troops on their left, who fell back after a gallant struggle with superior numbers, and once by a movement of the enemy on their right, caused by the advance of General Anderson. The left, being reinforced, finally succeeded in driving back the enemy, and the artillery, under Lieutenant-Colonels Carter and [Hilary P.] Jones, (one battalion of batteries each) being thrown forward to occupy favorable positions—secured by the advance of the infantry, began to play with great precision and effect.

Simultaneously with the attack of Stuart on the right, Lee attacked the salient position around the Chancellor house with the divisions of McLaws and Anderson. This position was held by French's and Hancock's divisions of the Second Corps. These two divisions had six batteries, but as before stated, Couch, commanding this corps, had sent all except nine pieces back to the river as useless impedimenta. In the fury of the fight a battery was borrowed from another corps, making in all 15 pieces. It was a position demanding all that Couch had and all that could be borrowed besides. These 15 pieces did noble service, but drawing as they did both the artillery and infantry fire of the enemy, now assailing this position in overwhelming numbers, they were very roughly handled.

Lee had retained only about 22 pieces for his operations about the Chancellor house, but when Stuart got possession of Fairview and closed in towards Lee, the whole of his artillery too was brought in play against it, soon rendering it untenable. The Federal troops were forced back to the new line, which line also had a salient, the apex of which, pointing in the direction of the Chancellor house, was about three-fourths of a mile in its rear.

General Meade, commanding the Fifth Corps, directed Captain Weed, his chief of artillery, to collect all the batteries that he could find and place them in position in this salient. This order was subsequently confirmed by Hooker, and thus armed with proper authority, that energetic officer soon had 56 pieces in position, representing nearly, if not quite, every corps on the field. This salient was a commanding position, looking in the two most exposed directions. On the right face Weed established 28 guns, and on the other 24, with four in the angle. These guns occupied about 500 yards on each side of the angle. During that and the following day the enemy made demonstrations on this position, but no formidable attack. In a professional point of view it is almost to be regretted that he did not do so in order that the efficiency of the fire of batteries thus massed should have been still further demonstrated.

Weed's services on this occasion were recognized by his promotion to a brigadier generalcy of volunteers; not, however, to command artillery, for which he had proved himself so well qualified, but to command a brigade of infantry, with which arm he had had no experience whatever. Of the 28 officers of artillery upon whom were conferred the star of a brigadier, only Barry, Hunt, and for a time John M. Brannan, were continued upon artillery duties; all the rest were assigned to infantry commands, and this too when material for such commands was as plentiful as autumn leaves. Most of these artillery officers, Griffin, William R. Terrill, Ayres and others, had won their spurs in command of artillery and nothing else.

Captain Best was not as fortunate as Weed. He commenced his war service as a captain and the close of the war found him still a captain, in which grade he continued until, by regular promotion, he became a major two years thereafter.

The batteries of the Federal artillery were armed and equipped to perfection, and to a fair extent were well instructed also, but here all that was good about the organization ended. The brilliant service of batteries was due to their own excellent qualities, and was in spite of the defects attending the method of using them.

The official reports of the battle of Chancellorsville are laden with complaints that batteries could not have their chests replenished with ammunition. This was a direct result of attaching batteries to divisions, where they had to depend for their supplies upon division supply trains under quartermasters who knew little or nothing of artillery needs, particularly so as regards ammunition. It was not until the batteries of each corps were united into one brigade, with its own ammunition train under its own officers, that this glaring defect was remedied.

While the batteries were crying out for ammunition at Chancellorsville there was an abundance of it with the division trains near by, but the batteries could not obtain it, so defective was the system. There seemed to be a jealous feeling towards the artillery, apparently on the ground that it was desirous of aggrandizing itself by getting control of its own affairs.

While the battle of the forenoon of the 3rd was in progress, the First Corps arrived as heretofore stated. Colonel Wainwright, its chief of artillery, arrived with it and was the first, and in fact the only field officer of artillery on that field. He was at once assigned by Hooker to the task of collecting the batteries and assigning them to proper positions, and to supervising their supply of ammunition. He had scarcely commenced this duty when General Hunt arrived and relieved him of it. While the battle was raging and matters were becoming tangled, Hooker began to appreciate the importance of having a head for the artillery, and sending for Hunt, reinvested him with that control over the batteries of which he had deprived him at the opening of the campaign.

Such, in brief, were the operations of the artillery at the battle of Chancellorsville, which contest terminated abruptly about 10:00 A.M. on May 3rd. This abrupt termination was because of information received by Lee of Sedgwick's operations at Fredericksburg; which were at first so successful, as to threaten the rear of Lee's army at Chancellorsville and cause him to desist from further attack, and turn to meet the danger now threatening him from that quarter. It will be observed that of Hooker's six corps at Chancellorsville, but three of them, the Second, Third and Twelfth, were much engaged. The Eleventh stampeded; the Fifth, guarding the left flank, was not attacked; and the First did not arrive in time to take part in the battle. Portions of the Fifth were, it is true, engaged and suffered loss, but as a whole the corps was intact.

Lee, had present, engaged, 98 regiments: Jackson's three divisions, 70 regiments; McLaws' division, omitting Barksdale's brigade left at Fredericksburg, 15 regiments; Anderson's division, omitting Wilcox's brigade at Bank's Ford, 13 regiments. Hooker had in the two divisions present of the Second Corps, 31 regiments; in the Third Corps, 40 regiments; and in the Twelfth Corps, 24 regiments, for a grand total of 95 regiments. Besides having more of them, Lee's regiments were on an average considerably stronger in numbers than Hooker's.

Their losses were as follows. Hooker suffered 1,082 killed, 6,849 wounded, for a total of 7,931. Lee suffered 1,366 killed, 7,409 wounded, for a total of 8,775. The former lost 4,080 missing, most of whom were captured. Lee did not lose so many prisoners, perhaps not more than half as many.

The operations of Lee in this campaign was a marked instance of an inferior force beating a superior one, by taking it in detail, thereby always having a superior number at the actual point of contact. Jackson was sent around to the extreme right with 70 regiments to attack the Eleventh Corps of 22 regiments. This corps out of the way, Jackson's corps then attacked and defeated the Third and Twelfth, both together of 64 regiments. In this Jackson's force was materially assisted by Anderson's division, which gave it still greater superiority in numbers. Lee then concentrated his entire force upon Hancock's division of 18 regiments, assisted in a measure by French's division and a portion of the Third Corps; and of these he made short work. By 10:00 o'clock of the forenoon of the 3rd, not a man of Hooker's entire force at Chancellorsville occupied the ground upon which he stood when the battle commenced, excepting only the five batteries under Captain Randol, still holding their position on the extreme left.

The battle of the forenoon of the 3rd resulted in the formation of a new and shorter line in rear of the First Corps, still covering the United States Ford. This line was hastily entrenched. Lee, leaving Stuart with his 70 regiments to hold Hooker by frequent attacks and threatening demonstrations, withdrew the divisions of McLaws and Anderson, and turned upon Sedgwick, who in the meanwhile had stormed the Marye Heights, and broken through the thin line left by Lee to guard his entrenchments in rear of Fredericksburg. Sedgwick now had Lee in front of him and a large force under Early in his rear, both closing in to cut him off and crush him. But by consummate generalship and the bravery of his troops he was enabled to withdraw across the river at Bank's Ford. The demonstrations made by Stuart held Hooker from giving any assistance whatever to Sedgwick, who fought the battle of Salem Heights alone, against overwhelming odds.

Lee, having driven Sedgwick across the river, was now at liberty to unite his entire force against Hooker at Chancellorsville. But the latter prudently withdrew, crossing the river upon the pontoon bridge in his rear during the night of the 5th; and thus ended the Chancellorsville campaign which started out under such fine auspices, but which had such an inglorious ending. The conduct of the Eleventh Corps was eagerly seized upon as an excuse for the failure. This corps being struck, as by a cyclone, in flank and rear, the entire line was doubled up and rolled back upon itself, and there being no line or position in rear upon which the broken troops could rally, they scattered in confusion through the woods, conveying to all an exaggerated impression of panic. Obloquy was heaped upon these troops, unrestrictedly giving this corps a reputation for unsteadiness from which it never recovered, notwithstanding its subsequent good conduct at Gettysburg and afterwards in the Western Army under Major General William T. Sherman. The fact was that no opportunity was given them, on this occasion, to test their reliability. Struck as they were, unexpectedly, in flank and rear, no troops whatever could have withstood such a blow. It was a case in all essential respects similar to that of Stones River, where the veteran troops of the Army of the Cumberland gave way under even less aggravating circumstances. At the time the enemy burst, "with a yell," from the woods upon the exposed flank, those least surprised formed, as well as they could, and opposed a resistance that caused the enemy to consume more than an hour in overrunning the ground occupied by the corps. The enemy reports a sharp resistance at the short and feeble line occupied by Von Gilsa's two regiments on the extreme right; then a still shorter resistance by some of Schurz's regiments which happened to be in rear of the main line, and which had thrown up slight breastworks facing in the direction from which the enemy were approaching, and finally at the line occupied by the spare batteries facing in the same direction. Here, Rodes says, the second line joined with the first, and both were thrown into "inextricable confusion." This shows that all of the Eleventh did not flee, panic stricken, in the manner generally supposed. These facts were not known at the time to the other portions of the army, and all took up the cry of denunciation against the Eleventh.

There was never any question raised as to the steadiness of the Second, Third and Twelfth Corps in this battle. On the contrary, they were greatly extolled for their superior fighting. Yet, the records show that in proportion to the numbers engaged, the loss in killed and wounded of the Eleventh was very much greater than that of the Second, about the same as in the Twelfth, and only a little less than in the Third. These corps were not surprised and taken in flank and rear as was the Eleventh, but were attacked squarely in front, where they had good opportunity of showing their good soldierly qualities.

Had it not been for the timely and gallant resistance offered by Huntington's 22 guns at Hazel Grove, which held the enemy in check until the Twelfth changed position, this corps too would have been taken in flank and rear, and would probably have shared the same fate as the Eleventh. This would have cut off the two divisions of the Third, then detached looking after Jackson's column, and would have enabled Lee to have concentrated the whole of his force upon the Fifth Corps and the two divisions of the Second occupying the salient at the Chancellor house, and to have crushed the whole back, in confusion, upon the river. It is difficult to estimate the value of the services of the guns at Hazel Grove.

After this inglorious campaign both armies returned to their former positions, Hooker's to its camps on the Heights at Stafford, and Lee's behind Fredericksburg. Shortly after the battle, Longstreet rejoined with his absent divisions, and this, together with the new levies brought in by the rigidly enforced draft, brought Lee's force up to nearly 100,000 men. The next meeting of the Army of the Potomac and of the Army of Northern Virginia would be upon the field of Gettysburg.

The Army of the Potomac after the battle of Chancellorsville returned to its former camps opposite Fredericksburg, where it rested until June 9th, when it commenced the movements incident to the memorable Gettysburg campaign. During the month included between these two campaigns, a very important change was effected, or rather inaugurated, in the organization of its artillery. All battles and campaigns up to this time had so forcibly demonstrated the defects and weaknesses of the former system as to convince all, except the most stolid, of the necessity of a change. General Hunt, still the able chief of artillery of that army, had given the subject careful study from the beginning and had been persistent in his efforts for a reform.

Hooker's ideas connected with the management of artillery underwent a radical change through his lessons at Chancellorsville. In taking a broad view of the case he could not avoid seeing that the main secret of success of the enemy lay in the ability of the latter to maneuver his troops on such a field with promptness and celerity; thus enabling him to attack first at one point and then at another, as the phases of the battle demanded. Reasoning still further, Hooker became convinced that this celerity and certainty of movement arose from the fact that the infantry and artillery of Lee's army, although operating conjointly for a common end, were kept so distinct in method of management as not to hamper each other in their movements. He had no difficulty in seeing that it would have been impossible for Jackson to have made the march which he did and to have formed his divisions into column of attack with such phenomenal celerity, had his divisions or brigades been encumbered by batteries attached to them. And he furthermore saw that Jackson's batteries were, notwithstanding the difficulties of the forest, up and in hand for the battle with a celerity and promptness entirely impossible to a system permitting their assignment to subordinate infantry commands. Nor did he fail to note that the same conditions obtained with the troops over which Lee exercised personal command, and which he formed into line of battle in the dense woods directly in front of the Chancellor house, simultaneously with Jackson's movements against the Federal right flank. Here, too, Lee had an abundance of batteries which, under his battalion system, were brought up through the jungle and placed into such positions as the nature of the field afforded without interfering with the movements of his infantry. And, lastly, when in the midst of fierce battle at

Salem Heights, he took up this wing of the army and hastened away before Hooker became aware of the movement; a thing that could not have happened had subordinate commanders been hampered by the care of batteries.

Hooker made no such masterly movements at Chancellorsville. The nearest approximation to it was his forced reconnaissance towards Lee's position on May 1st, which turned out to be a total failure because he left his artillery behind him, and then again, on the following day, when Sickles went out to meet Jackson's column then passing to attack the Eleventh corps. This, too, resulted in a ridiculous fizzle because the artillery of Sickles force had been left behind.

As Lee subsequently marched and fought over the same grounds using his infantry and artillery most successfully in harmonious cooperation, Hooker could not fail to see a difference between the loose organization of his own artillery and the more business-like organization of that of his adversary.

Every defect of the former system was made manifest during the Chancellorsville campaign, and Hooker, still commanding the Army of the Potomac, and now willing to listen to the suggestions and advice of his artillery chief, consented that the artillery should be formed into brigades of batteries, one for each army corps, two for the cavalry, and four for the Artillery Reserve; each to be under its own distinct commander who received his orders direct from his corps commander. This was a long stride in advance, but for reasons heretofore stated there were at first but few officers on duty with the army who were of suitable rank to command these brigades. General Hunt, in his report of the battle of Gettysburg, animadverting upon this defect, says:

In my report of the battle of Chancellorsville, I took occasion to call attention to the great evils arising from want of field officers for the artillery. The operations of this campaign, and especially the battle of Gettysburg, offered further proof, if such were necessary, of the mistaken policy of depriving so important an arm of the officers necessary for managing it. In this campaign, for the command of 67 batteries (372 guns), with over 8,000 men and 7,000 horses, and all the material and large ammunition trains, I had one general officer commanding the Reserve, and but four field officers, two colonels, one lieutenant-colonel, and one major. In the seven corps, the artillery of two were commanded by colonels, of one by a major, of three by captains, and one by a lieutenant, taken from their batteries for the purpose. The two brigades of horse artillery attached to the cavalry were commanded by captains, and there was one field officer in the Reserve. The most of these commands in any other army would have been considered proper ones for a general officer. In no army, would the command of the artillery of a corps be considered of less importance, to say the least, than that of a brigade of infantry. In none of our corps ought the artillery commander to have been of less rank than a colonel, and in all there should have been a proper proportion of field officers, with the necessary staffs. . . . Not only does the service suffer, necessarily, from the great deficiency of officers of rank, but a policy which closes the doors of promotion to battery officers, and places them and the arm itself under a ban, and degrades them in comparison with other arms of service, induces discontent, and has caused many of our best officers to seek positions, wherever they can find them, which will remove them from this branch of the service.

Horses and materiel of the 9th Massachusetts Light Artillery destroyed outside of Abraham Trossel's house in Gettysburg. (*Library of Congress*)

SIX

GETTYSBURG

G ETTYSBURG WAS THE FIRST BATTLE of the Army of the
Potomac in which the artillery as a whole was brought
to the front, a fact due to the more efficient organization
which it had just received. If the same thing had occurred at
some of the other battles it is more than probable history
would have had a different story to record. One of the main
features of this battle was the grouping of batteries, thus giving to their fire the effect of concentration and mass. The history of this battle, like that of other battles, has been compiled
chiefly from the reports of corps, division, and brigade commanders, which as a matter of course, do not enter into the
reasons why the artillery was more efficient upon this than
other occasions. It is a question so purely professional as not
to belong to the popular or more ordinary accounts of the
battle, and therefore the valuable lessons so forcibly demonstrated by this, the most momentous battle of the war, have
been almost entirely overlooked. Gettysburg has been thoroughly discussed from every point of view except that of the
artillery, yet every account of the battle refers to the effectiveness of this arm. Scarcely any one of them omits to mention

the distinguished part which it performed, but how this was brought about, and wherein the management of batteries in this battle differed from that at Chancellorsville or other preceding battles, has been passed by as a mere tactical or administrative question quite overshadowed by the magnitude of the conflict as a whole.

The artillery of the Army of the Potomac had at last received the same efficient organization as that long in use in Lee's army, and at this battle the whole of the artillery of both armies was fought up to its fullest capacity, and fully demonstrated the great power and influence in battle of this arm when properly managed. The adoption of the new system in the Army of the Potomac was so recent as not to be entirely complete in its details at the time of the battle, but notwithstanding this, the advantages flowing from it were so numerous as to convince all of its utility except the few still wedded to old ideas.

With the exception of the artillery there was no other important change in the organization of the Army of the Potomac. The corps were identically the same as in the Chancellorsville campaign and were under the same commanders; with the exception of the Second, now commanded by Hancock, vice Couch, transferred to another field of duty; and the Fifth, now commanded by Sykes, vice Meade, now commanding the army. Stoneman had been relieved from the command of the cavalry by Pleasanton. This arm had received some increase by the incorporation of Stahl's division from the Valley of the Shenandoah, and with it a volunteer battery of horse artillery, making in all 10 batteries of this arm.

Immediately after Chancellorsville, Lee organized his army into three instead of two corps, thus giving to his command the natural function of a *right*, *left* and *center*. Ewell had been assigned to the command of Jackson's corps. Longstreet remained in command of his former corps, while A.P. Hill was assigned to the new corps, composed partly from the two original corps, together with some new troops. Stuart continued in command of his cavalry, which had been considerably increased since Chancellorsville.

On June 7, 1863, Lee began the campaign for the invasion of Pennsylvania, following in a general way the same route pursued by him in the Antietam campaign of the previous summer. Leaving A.P. Hill to maintain with his corps a show of occupancy, and thus retain Hooker as long as possible in his position on the opposite side of the Rappahannock, he quietly withdrew the corps of Longstreet and Ewell and started them, via Culpepper, on their way to the Shenandoah Valley, down which was to be his route, and thence across the Potomac into Maryland, and on into Pennsylvania, with Harrisburg, and perhaps Philadelphia, as his ultimate objective. Many reasons impelled him to make this invasion, chief among which was the influence that the occupancy, though but temporary, of so much Northern territory would have upon the foreign nations which the Confederacy was so very desirous of having recognize its belligerent rights.

As soon as Hooker discovered the nature of Lee's movements he withdrew his army from its camps in front of Fredericksburg, and started it (June 13th) for the Potomac, keeping between Lee and Washington. Lee marched his corps up the right bank of the Rappahannock, thence through passes in the Blue Ridge into the Shenandoah Valley. Using the mountains to screen his movements, he pushed down the valley and crossed the Potomac at fords above Harper's Ferry. This advance crossed the river on the 14th and reached Chambersburg on the following day. Stuart, with his cavalry and horse batteries, covered the right flank of Lee's army as it marched up the Rappahannock, and then guarded the passes of the mountains as it proceeded down the valley.

Hooker, following up Lee's movements, with the mountains intervening, covered his left flank with his cavalry and horse batteries. These two opposing cavalry forces were in constant collision, resulting in many skirmishes and combats, some of which, as those of Beverly Ford, Aldie and Upperville, approximated the dignity of battles, in fact were cavalry battles, in all of which the horse batteries performed as usual important services.

Stuart had been directed by Lee to hold the mountain passes with part of his force as long as any of the Federal army remained on the south side of the Potomac, and with the remainder to cross into Maryland and place himself on the right flank of the Confederate army to guard it as it proceeded into Pennsylvania. Stuart, however, adopting a different plan, started on a raid around the Federal army, passing between it and Washington, intending to join the main army in the vicinity of Harrisburg, which he knew to be Lee's objective. In pursuance of this scheme he crossed the Potomac near Drainsville on the 27th, and bearing off towards Washington, caused great consternation at the Capitol. Near Rockville he captured a large train of wagons loaded with supplies for Hooker's army. Retaining about 100 of these wagons he destroyed the rest, but secured the horses and mules. After doing considerable damage to the canal and railroads, and temporarily interrupting communication with Hooker's army, he struck northward toward York, Pennsylvania, where he expected to find part of Ewell's corps. On his way, he was, however, intercepted by Brigadier General Hugh J. Kilpatrick's cavalry, with which he had a series of skirmishes. His long train of captured wagons was a great encumbrance to him. Arriving at York, he found that Ewell's troops had left for Carlisle, whither he followed them. Here he ascertained that Lee was concentrating at Gettysburg, to which point he now hastened his march, but arrived there too late for the battle of the first day, but in time to have on the following day a sharp skirmish with Brigadier General David M. Gregg's cavalry division near Hunterstown. Here he was joined by a fresh brigade and on the following day had, near the same place, a heavy engagement with Gregg's force. In all of these engagements the horse batteries took an active part and came in for a full share of the fighting.

Stuart's absence from Lee proved a very great embarrassment to the latter, leaving him without means of discovering the movements and intentions of his adversary. Ewell's corps had proceeded to York and Carlisle, with detachments as far north as to the Susquehanna River, threatening Harrisburg. Hill and Longstreet were moving their corps northward, still on the western side of the Blue Mountain, near the Fairfield and Cashtown passes, west of Gettysburg. On the night of the 28th Lee obtained information through his scouts that the Federal army had crossed the Potomac and was now in the vicinity of Frederick, Maryland, moving towards South Mountain and threatening his long line of communication. This caused him to abandon his movement on Harrisburg and to direct his corps to concentrate on Cashtown, a central point between Chambersburg and Gettysburg, distant from the latter place about 12 miles.

Longstreet and Hill crossed the Potomac near Williamsport on the 24th. Hooker, being now satisfied of the intentions of the enemy, crossed on pontoon bridges at Edward's Ferry on the 25th. Sending the Twelfth Corps to reinforce the position at Harper's Ferry, deemed by the military authorities in the War Department of primary importance, he concentrated his other corps at or near Frederick. It was this concentration that caused Lee to abandon the project of carrying his campaign beyond the Susquehanna River.

At this critical moment, June 28th, Hooker was relieved from the command of the Army of the Potomac and Meade, then commanding the Fifth Corps, was appointed in his place. Hooker and Major General Henry W. Halleck, then general-in-chief and military advisor at Washington, had differed upon many points regarding the management of the campaign, notably upon that of retaining a large force guarding Harper's Ferry, which Hooker, as did McClellan under similar circumstances in the Antietam campaign of the preceding year, regarded as an unwise absorption of troops, and a weakening of the active force with which he was expected to meet and defeat the enemy.

This assignment to the command of the army was entirely unexpected to Meade, and as a battle was then imminent, the shortness of time allowed him no opportunity for maturing plans of his own for the movement of his troops. He therefore continued, without material change, the program of marches for the various corps designated by his predecessor. It may, however, be mentioned that one of his first acts was to withdraw the troops from Harper's Ferry, thus making available some 10,000 men for active work in the field, without which Lee would have had superiority in numbers, leaving to conjecture what might have been the result of the battle of Gettysburg under such conditions. The battle took place before Meade's action could be interfered with.

From Frederick, Meade started his various corps northward in the direction of Harrisburg, towards which he now knew the enemy was making his way. In the meanwhile, Hill had reached Cashtown, from which place Brigadier General James J. Pettigrew's brigade of Major General Henry Heth's division was sent forward on the 30th to Gettysburg to secure such supplies as the country stores of that place could furnish his needy soldiers. But before reaching the place, Pettigrew encountered the Federal cavalry and halted. On the following morning Hill, joining him with Major General William Dorsey Pender's division and two battalions of batteries, moved forward to ascertain the strength of the enemy whose force was then supposed to consist chiefly of cavalry. Hill encountered Buford's vedettes about three miles west of Gettysburg and continued to advance until within about two miles of the town when his leading brigade came upon the enemy in considerable force. This was Buford's division of cavalry, the battery with which, A, 2nd U.S. Artillery Regiment, under command of Lieutenant John H. Calef, had the honor of firing the opening gun of this sanguinary and momentous battle.

Buford having reported to Meade that the enemy was in force on the Cashtown road, near Gettysburg, the latter ordered Reynolds, then (June 30th) at Emmitsburg, 10 miles south of Gettysburg, to proceed with his own First Corps and Howard's Eleventh Corps, also near the same place, to the assistance of Buford. Upon reaching Gettysburg on the forenoon of the following day, July 1st, Reynolds found Buford's cavalry and Calef's battery hotly engaged with Hill's troops which they were holding in check in the most gallant manner. Reynolds deployed his leading division and attacked without delay, at the same time sending orders to Howard to advance his corps as promptly as possible. Soon after making his dispositions for attack, Reynolds fell, mortally wounded, and the command of his corps devolved upon Major General Doubleday, the senior division commander, while Howard succeeded to the command of the whole. The latter had arrived about this time, 11:30 A.M., with the Eleventh Corps, which for the time being fell to the command of Schurz.

Howard pushed forward two divisions of the Eleventh to the support of the First, now hotly engaged with Hill's corps on the ridge to the westward of the town. The remaining division of the Eleventh took position on Cemetery Hill, adjoining the town to the southward. Here Howard established his headquarters. The two divisions of the Eleventh moved through the town with a view to strengthening the right of the First, but soon after emerging from the town they encountered Ewell's corps then arriving from the direction of Carlisle. The arrival of Ewell gave the enemy such a preponderance in numbers as to cause both the First and Eleventh to yield to the pressure and fall back through the town to Cemetery Hill, where they took position about 4:00 P.M.

Upon learning of the death of Reynolds, Meade, whose headquarters were at this time at Taneytown, some eight miles distant, dispatched Hancock to the field to assume the management of affairs. In conjunction with Howard, Hancock proceeded to post the troops on Cemetery Ridge and to repel an attack made by the enemy on the right flank of that position. This attack being repulsed, the enemy rested satisfied with the ground he had gained earlier in the day and made no further attack that afternoon.

These, in general, were the operations of the battle of the first day, in which Lee had about one-half of his army engaged against two-sevenths of that of Meade. His facilities for concentrating at that point were superior to those of his opponent.

About 7:00 P.M. Slocum with the Twelfth, and Sickles with part of the Third Corps, arrived and took position on the left of that occupied by the First and Eleventh. Meade, being informed that it was evident Lee was concentrating his whole force at Gettysburg for the purpose of offering battle, ordered up his three remaining corps, and sent back to Westminster, about 20 miles distant, all unnecessary impedimenta, in which, strange to say, was included two batteries of long-range siege rifles; guns which would have found most useful employment had they been present on that field.

As soon as he had made these dispositions, Meade himself hastened forward and arrived on the field early in the morning of the 2nd. The two armies now about to meet, to continue as a whole the battle of the first day, consisted of the following corps, divisions, brigades and batteries, actually present on the field:

FEDERAL ARMY

	Div.	Brig.	Reg.	Batteries
First Corps	3	7	33	5
Second Corps	3	10	44	5
Third Corps	2	6	37	5
Fifth Corps	3	8	32	5
Sixth Corps	3	8	36	8
Eleventh Corps	3	6	26	5
Twelfth Corps	2	6	28	4
Cavalry Corps	3	8	35	9
Artillery Reserve	3		17	
	22	59	271	63 = 356 guns

CONFEDERATE ARMY

	Div.	Brig.	Reg.	Batteries
Longstreet's Corps	3	11	52	22
Ewell's Corps	3	12	61	20
Hill's Corps	3	13	57	20
Cavalry Corps	1	7	30	7
	10	43	200	69 = about 300 guns

The field returns of the Army of the Potomac for June 30th give the strength of that army, present, equipped for duty, as 5,286 officers and 71,922 enlisted men of infantry. The artillery and cavalry together, aggregated about 16,600, making a grand total of 88,522. Taking the regiments of the two armies as a common unit would make the strength of the Confederates a fraction over 65,000. But as the Confederate conscription was now in full operation and being inexorably enforced, filling up the regiments in the field, it is more than probable that Lee's regiments were much stronger than those of Meade, thus largely reducing the apparent disparity of numbers.

It will be observed from the foregoing table that the divisions in Lee's army were almost equal in strength to corps in Meade's army. To each of his nine divisions of infantry was attached a battalion of batteries, a battalion being synonymous with brigade in the Federal army. The battalions of Lee's artillery reserve were for this campaign distributed to the three infantry corps, two battalions to each corps. The cavalry had one battalion of seven batteries. Remembering that divisions in Lee's army were but little less than corps in that of his opponent, it will be perceived that the artillery organization and assignments in the two armies were quite similar.

Gettysburg, as the world now knows, was at that time, 1863, a country town of some 4,000 inhabitants, and a center from which radiated in every direction a number of roads. It is rather remarkable in this respect, and it was owing to this fact that it became the field upon which was decided, more than upon any other of the war, the integrity of the Union. The Confederates approaching from the north and west concentrated upon it by the Carlisle and Cashtown roads, while the Federals concentrated by the Emmitsburg and Taneytown roads converging from the southward and eastward.

Lee, as previously mentioned, was pushing his way towards Harrisburg when he got information that his adversary had crossed the Potomac and was threatening his communications from the direction of Frederick. He then turned about to give battle and this naturally brought his troops more promptly together than those of Meade, which were necessarily somewhat spread out to guard against any turn that Lee might make in the direction of Baltimore or Washington; and it was for this reason that he had more troops present on the first day of the battle than Meade had.

The town of Gettysburg is picturesquely situated about 12 miles from the Blue Ridge, in this part called the South Mountain. From the mountain eastward is a series of parallel undulations or ridges, the most important one of which, so far as the battle was concerned, is Cemetery Ridge, extending between Cemetery Hill on the outskirts of the town on its southern side, to a small mountain or butte called Little Round Top, standing about two miles south of Cemetery Hill. Beyond Little Round Top is another and larger butte called Round Top, separated from the former by a narrow, rocky and wooded valley. These two buttes are in fact one mountain with a narrow pass between, and both are but rugged piles of stones covered with trees and a thick entanglement of underbrush. Little Round Top, as the *point d'appui* of the Federal left, was a position of great military importance; and in the rocky gorges in front of it took place, for its possession, some of the most desperate fighting of the battle.

Cemetery Hill was, however, the key point of the situation. Overlooking, as it does, all the country round within battle range, it had a decisive influence upon the progress and final result of the contest. Its southern and western faces are gentle slopes, while towards the north it looks over the town and fields beyond, to ranges of hills, then in possession of the enemy, but too distant for the effective use of artillery. The two miles of fields between Cemetery Hill and Little Round Top is more an undulating plateau than a ridge, and is, as it were, a curtain connecting the eminences at its extremities as bastions. It was this curtain that received and resisted the heaviest attacks of Lee, made by the corps of Longstreet and Hill, on the 2nd and 3rd.

From the eastern side of Cemetery Hill, a spur known as Culp's Hill, extends around for about half a mile when it terminates precipitously at Rock Creek, a fordable stream running in a southeasterly direction and to the rear of Little Round Top, but at some distance from it. Culp's Hill was the scene of the determined assaults made by Ewell's corps for the purposes of breaking and turning the Federal right. This hill extends beyond the narrow, marshy valley of Rock Creek under the name of Wolf's Hill, a rocky and wooded ridge which played no further part in the events of the battle than as an obstruction to the enemy in his attempts at turning the right flank.

The first day's battle took place chiefly on Seminary Ridge, which lies about a mile to the westward of Cemetery Ridge and runs approximately parallel to it. The buildings of a Lutheran Theological Seminary, from which the ridge takes its name, are located on it due west of the town. The main building has a commanding position, the belfry of which, the building, Lee made use of as a point of observation during the battle. On the far side of these buildings from the town is a grove of trees, in the outskirts of which Reynolds was killed in the forenoon of the first day. About a third of a mile still farther to the westward is another undulation or ridge, between which and still another ridge further on, is a small brook called Willoughby's Run. All of these ridges and their intervening valleys or depressions constitute simply an undulating country, the unevenness of which, while sufficient to screen from view the movements of troops, was insufficient to afford them much protection from the artillery fire of the opposing forces. The slopes of the ridges were so gentle as to have about the same curvature as the descending branches of the trajectories of the projectiles, making their reverse sides more dangerous, if anything, than their fronts.

With the exception of a few open clumps of trees here and there along Cemetery Ridge, the whole of it, almost to Little Round Top, as well as the valley or depression in front to Seminary Ridge, were open fields of ripening grain. The Seminary Ridge was more wooded, especially on that part of it from near the Seminary buildings around to Little Round Top. The woods immediately in front of that mountain cover a rocky ravine known as the Devil's Den, in and about which took place some of the most desperate fighting of the contest. The woods on Seminary Ridge formed an excellent screen behind which Lee made his movements, and from which he launched his columns for the attack of the Federal position on Cemetery Ridge.

The Cashtown road coming in from the westward crosses the Seminary Ridge and the ridge beyond at right angles. It was by this road that Hill's corps, followed by that of Longstreet, reached the field. Ewell's corps, approaching from the northward, arrived simultaneously by the Carlisle and York roads.

Descending from Cemetery Hill through the town, to the northward, the country is more flat and level until some low ridges are reached a mile or so beyond. Here is where the Eleventh Corps encountered Ewell's troops when about to strike the rear and right of the First Corps, on Seminary Ridge, while sorely pressed by Hill's troops in front. Such, in general, were the topographical features of this celebrated field, a somewhat protracted mention of which is necessary for a more complete understanding of the events and operations of the battle now to follow.

It has already been stated that on June 30th, Buford held, with his cavalry, the road leading from Cashtown, and picket-

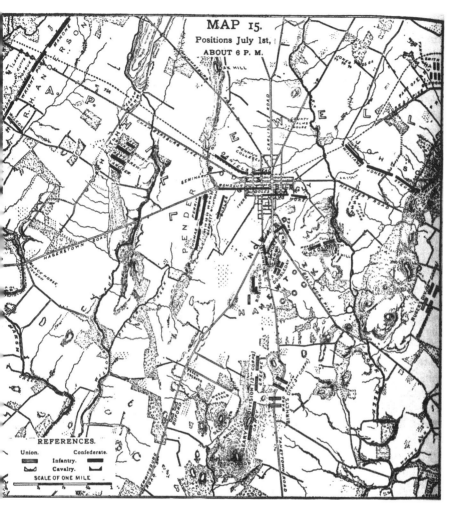

From *Battles and Leaders of the Civil War*, III: 282.)

ing around northward to the York road, gave information that the enemy was advancing in force from both of these directions. Buford in his report says:

> By daylight on July 1st, I had gained positive information of the enemy's position and movements, and my arrangements were made for entertaining him until General Reynolds could reach the scene. Colonel [William] Gamble formed an admirable line with his

brigade, and moved off proudly to meet him. The two lines soon became hotly engaged, we having the advantage of the ground, he of numbers (which were infantry). This brigade held its own for more than two hours, when it was withdrawn to a position more secure and better sheltered. Tidball's battery, commanded by Lieutenant Calef, Second U.S. Artillery, fought on this occasion as is seldom witnessed. At one time the enemy had a concentrated fire upon this battery from twelve guns, all at short range. Calef held his own gloriously, worked his guns deliberately, with great judgment and skill, and with wonderful effect upon the enemy. The First Brigade maintained this unequal contest until the leading division of General Reynolds' corps came up to its assistance, and then most reluctantly did it give up the front. While the left of my line was thus engaged, Devin's brigade, on the right, had its hands full. The enemy (Ewell's corps) advanced upon Devin by four roads, and on each was checked, and held until the leading division of the Eleventh Corps came to his relief.

It was now about 10:00 A.M. Buford, in withdrawing, took position on the left of the First Corps, where his cavalry continued aggressively active throughout the day in preventing the enemy from extending his forces around in the direction of Little Round Top. All reports of the enemy mention his operations on this flank as being exceedingly troublesome to them.

The advance of the First Corps, consisting of two brigades of Brigadier General James S. Wadsworth's division, was immediately deployed across the Cashtown road on the next ridge west of Seminary Ridge. Captain James A. Hall's Battery B, 2nd Maine Light Artillery Regiment, was posted on the road. The enemy soon advanced in greatly superior numbers and swept the right of this line back to Seminary Ridge. Hall, having his horses shot down, was forced to abandon one of his pieces. General Reynolds, who was with that part of the line still intact, was killed while superintending the progress of the action and anxiously awaiting the arrival of his approaching troops, some of whom were soon arriving. The enemy's advance was pushed back across Willoughby's Run and the ridge temporarily regained. Calef, whose battery was loaned to Wadsworth by Buford, was ordered into position on the ground lately held by Hall's battery, and here, as described by Buford, meeting the fire of three rebel batteries, suffered greatly in men and horses. When the enemy were forced back over Willoughby's Run, the Confederate Brigadier General James J. Archer, and a goodly number of his command were taken prisoners.

About 11:00 A.M. the other two divisions of the First Corps, those of Doubleday and Brigadier General John C. Robinson, arrived, and with them the remaining four batteries of the corps under Colonel Wainwright of the 1st New York Light Artillery Regiment. Some of these troops, with a couple of the batteries, were pushed forward into the severe contest now raging on the ridge just mentioned, while the remainder took position on Seminary Ridge. One of the batteries sent forward, that of Captain Gilbert H. Reynolds' Battery L, 1st New York Light Artillery Regiment, joined Calef's horse battery which was now contending against heavy odds of both infantry and artillery. These two batteries held their ground until the enemy, posting batteries upon their right, secured a heavy cross-fire upon their position, forcing them to retire from the unequal contest. Captain Reynolds was wounded and many men and horses of both batteries placed *hors de combat*. Calef then rejoined the cavalry to which he belonged.

Two divisions, Heth's and Pender's, of Hill's corps, were now up and formed on the ridge beyond Willoughby's Run. Together, these divisions numbered 36 regiments, with eight batteries of about 35 guns, against the First Corps of 29 regiments and five batteries of 28 guns. Notwithstanding this disparity of force in favor of the Confederates, the Federals were holding their own until the arrival of Rodes' division of Ewell's corps upon their right flank, when they were forced to fall back through sheer superiority of numbers.

The Eleventh Corps, having started from Emmitsburg at 8:00 A.M., reached Gettysburg about noon, and Howard, learning that Doubleday, now commanding the First Corps, was hard pressed on his right, hastened forward Schurz's and Barlow's divisions to take position on Seminary Ridge on the right of the First. Each of these divisions was accompanied by a battery. The other three batteries, supported by Steinwehr's division, were placed in position on Cemetery Hill. While these two divisions of the Eleventh were passing through the town on their way to the assistance of the First, Rodes' division of Ewell's corps arrived from the north by the Carlisle road, and screened from view by a strip of woods, was deploying to attack the flank and rear of the First, still holding on to Seminary Ridge. But before it got fully into position to effect this object, the divisions of Schurz and Barlow deployed and advanced to meet it. Rodes had already established batteries on high ground to the right of the First from whence they obtained an enfilading fire along Seminary Ridge. Dilger's Ohio battery of Napoleons, accompanying Schurz's division, engaged two of these batteries, and being soon afterwards joined by Wheeler's New York battery of 3-inch rifles, a spirited contest ensued, in which the Federal batteries were successful in driving their adversaries from their position, inflicting on them heavy loss in men and horses. Some of their guns had to be drawn off by hand, so much were the batteries used up.

Schurz's division was deployed on the left and Barlow's on the right, but in deploying, the latter extended so far to the right as to be in a measure detached. Rodes left Doles' brigade to hold Barlow until the arrival of Early's division, known to be near at hand on the York road, and in such position as to strike Barlow in the flank. Doles was suffering severely when

Early arrived to his assistance. Early says of his attack: "I immediately ordered my troops to the front, and formed my line across the Heidlersburg road. . . . Jones' battalion of batteries was posted in a field on the left of the road, immediately in front of [Brigadier General Robert F.] Hoke's Brigade, so as to fire on the enemy's flank, and, as soon as these dispositions could be made, a fire was opened upon the enemy's infantry, and artillery with considerable effect." The artillery he here refers to was Lieutenant Bayard Wilkinson's Battery G, 4th U.S. Artillery Regiment, which had accompanied Barlow to the front. Early goes on to say: "[Brigadier General John B.] Gordon's Brigade was then ordered forward to the support of Doles' Brigade, which was on Rodes' left and was hardly pressed by a considerable force of the enemy, which had advanced from the direction of the town. After a short but hot contest, Gordon succeeded in routing the forces opposed to him, consisting of a division of the Eleventh Corps, commanded by Brigadier General Barlow of the Federal army, and drove it back with great slaughter, capturing among a number of prisoners, General Barlow himself, who was severely wounded." Although Early seems to claim all the credit of this for the brigade of Gordon, the facts were that Doles attacked Barlow at the same time in front, thus bringing against Barlow's two diminutive brigades two of the Confederate heavy brigades, and in addition, a far superior number of guns.

Wilkinson's battery suffered severely from the hot infantry and artillery fire to which it was exposed. Wilkinson was himself mortally wounded, devolving the command of the battery on Lieutenant Eugene A. Bancroft, who handled it with skill, and by changing position several times was enabled to hold the enemy in check and finally got off with his guns. This battery was exposed to the fire of three batteries sent especially to subdue its fire. Barlow's division, thus driven back, retired through the town and took position on Cemetery Hill. It was the same division, which under Devens occupied the right of the Eleventh Corps at Chancellorsville, where it was struck in flank by the whole of Jackson's corps without an opportunity of making a stand.

The falling back of Barlow's brigade uncovered the right of Schurz's line to attack from the whole of Early's division. This too, while it was engaged in front by the other three brigades of Rodes' division, those of Colonel Edward A. O'Neal, Brigadier General Alfred Iverson, Jr., and Brigadier General Stephen D. Ramseur; the first of which was driven back in disorder, a large part of the second captured, while the third suffered severely. Rodes, in his report says:

> All the troops were in the woods excepting Doles' and O'Neal's brigades, but all were subject to some loss or annoyance from the enemy's artillery. This artillery fire became so annoying that I ordered the Alabama brigade (O'Neal's) from the line it had occupied to fall back abreast with Iverson, so as to obtain some shelter for the troops. Finding that the enemy was rash enough to come out from the woods to attack me, I determined to meet him when he got to the foot of the hill occupied. . . . Carter's whole battalion of batteries was by this time engaged hotly–a portion from the right, the remainder from the left of the hill–and was subjected to a heavy artillery fire in return.

The heavy artillery fire he refers to was that before mentioned from Dilger's and Wheeler's batteries. Rodes, proceeding in his description of the battle and of how his troops fell into disorder, says: "Iverson's left being thus exposed, heavy loss was inflicted upon his brigade, his men fought and died like heroes. His dead lay in distinctly marked lines of battle. His left was overpowered, and many of his men, being surrounded, were captured." Rodes describes the fight he had with the Eleventh Corps as being very severe. But Schurz's division, being attacked like Barlow's in both flank and front by overwhelming numbers, was forced also to give way and withdraw through the town to Cemetery Hill. To assist in doing this with safety, Captain Lewis Heckman's Battery K, 1st Ohio Light Artillery Regiment, was sent forward to the further edge of the town, where the guns were served with good effect until the enemy was among them. Heckman then retired, but with the loss of one gun, and with his battery so much crippled that it was sent to the rear and not again called into action. The other battery of this corps, retaining its position on Cemetery Hill, was engaged several times during the day at long range and did excellent service in holding the enemy in check until the troops could reach the hill.

The two divisions present of Ewell's corps consisted of 39 regiments and eight batteries of about 36 pieces. The Eleventh Corps, including the division held in reserve on Cemetery Hill, consisted of 26 regiments with five batteries of 26 pieces. It may be remarked that while most Federal batteries had each six pieces, but few of those of the Confederates had so many. A few even had only two pieces. The average was about four-and-one-half. While the precise number is ascertainable only in a few cases, that of the Federal batteries is known with precision from the records.

The reputation overshadowing the Eleventh Corps from its misfortunes at Chancellorsville was made still more somber by the hasty judgment formed by its falling back on this occasion. The facts were that so long as its two small divisions were opposed only by Rodes with about equal numbers, it not only held its ground but was making some headway when taken in flank by the arrival of Early's troops, which gave the enemy great superiority in numbers as well as in position; it was forced to give way. Its arrival at an opportune moment, and its fighting, prevented Ewell's corps from coming in at the back door, as it were, and seizing Cemetery Hill while the First Corps, engaged with Hill's corps on Seminary Ridge, was defending the front entrance. While the chief part of Rodes' division was engaged against the Eleventh Corps, a portion of it worked around further towards its right and became engaged with the right of the First Corps, now heavily pressed by Hill in front; and after the arrival of Early to hold in check the Eleventh, Rodes turned his entire attention to the First.

It will be remembered that when Wadsworth's division first arrived at the Cashtown road it repulsed an attack of the enemy, driving him back across Willoughby's Run, capturing General Archer and many other prisoners. This was but a reconnaissance in force by Hill to ascertain the strength and position of the Federal troops. Finding them to be somewhat numerous, he formed Heth's division in line of battle, supported by Pender's in a second line, and about 3:00 P.M., moved forward, and crossing Willoughby's Run, drove the advance of the First Corps steadily back to Seminary Ridge, where the entire corps took position with Robinson's division on the right, Wadsworth's in the center, and Brigadier General Thomas A. Rowley's (Doubleday's) on the left, about the Seminary premises, at which place some of this last division erected slight barricades with fence rails, which subsequently proved of great service to them. The batteries were posted upon this line, which was somewhat straggling and irregular, in the following order: Lieutenant James Stewart's Battery B, 4th U.S. Artillery Regiment, on Robinson's right; Captain Greenleaf T. Stevens' Battery E, 5th Maine Light Artillery Regiment, a little further to the left, while Reynolds' battery and Captain James H. Cooper's Battery B, 1st Pennsylvania Light Artillery Regiment, were near each other on the right of the Seminary. Hall's Maine battery had been so badly cut up in the fight earlier in the day as to require to be sent to the rear.

The enemy continued to advance steadily across the space between the two crests, but when the first line was within about 100 yards of the Seminary, a portion of Stewart's battery was swung around so as to enfilade it. This, with the fire of the other batteries, checked the enemy for a moment, but it was only for a moment, for the second line under Pender pushed on and now took the lead. The pressure of this fresh division in front and that of Rodes' now on the right flank, in

number of men as well as in guns about three times that of the
First Corps, was too great for it to stand, and it was forced to
retire to Cemetery Ridge, which was done without hurry or
confusion; the regiments turning from time to time to check
the enemy's advance by volleys of musketry. A few of the regiments, however, became confused by meeting with the
Eleventh Corps in the streets of the town and lost thereby
heavily in prisoners. The batteries, although they had suffered
severe loss in both men and horses were able to bring off
everything except one piece, which, while retiring, had its
horses disabled and was of necessity abandoned. The enemy
pressed hard after the retiring troops, and by ascending the
slopes to the northeast of the town endeavored to turn the
right of the Eleventh Corps, but his line was quickly broken
by the fire of Wiedrich's battery in position on Cemetery Hill.
The Eleventh Corps took position on the northwest face of
the hill, while Wadsworth's division of the First was sent to
hold a smaller hill or ridge on the right connecting with
Culp's Hill, which latter was a short time afterwards occupied
by part of the Twelfth Corps. The other two divisions of the
First were massed near the left of the Eleventh, in readiness to
move to any point threatened. The batteries of this corps were
posted by Wainwright on the right of the gateway of the
Cemetery, covering all approaches from the northeast and
also commanding the town. Those of the Eleventh Corps
were posted by Major Thomas W. Osborne, chief of artillery
of that corps, on the left of the gateway, commanding the
ground looking towards the Seminary and also the town. All
the pieces were put in battery and each protected from sharpshooters by a slight gun pit. The enemy, seeing the strength of
the position occupied by his adversary, seemed to be satisfied
with the success he had already accomplished and desisted
from further attack for the present.

The contest of this day would have been considered a great
battle of itself, had it not been for the overshadowing magnitude of those of the next two days. The First and Eleventh

Corps threw themselves boldly across the roads by which the enemy was concentrating in Gettysburg, and by stout resistance held him in check until it was too late in the day for him to seize upon Cemetery Hill and the ridge to Round Top. The advantages of this position were decisive of the campaign. Holding it from the enemy, as did the First and Eleventh, gave time for the arrival of the other corps, after which it proved secure against every assault.

The management of the artillery in this day's contest, that of the First Corps by Colonel Wainwright, and that of the Eleventh by Major Osborne, was skillful and effective, the only drawback being that they were without other field officers to assist them in locating batteries, which the conditions of the battle required to be widely separated. They were also badly off for the necessary staff. Batteries had no officers to spare for this purpose. The battery brigade system was of such recent origin as not yet to be in full completeness in these respects. But it will be observed that all the batteries of both corps were fully engaged and almost invariably on the front line where they could do the best work. There were none standing in idleness because of being attached to divisions or brigades occupying positions where they could not operate, but all were put in where they could do the most good for the whole. There was no frittering away of infantry commands by the detail of regiments to act as supports to batteries. The whole infantry line was the support. All of the infantry was engaged and every piece of artillery, and they formed mutual supports.

The guns of the enemy, greatly superior in number, being skillfully handled and vigorously worked, caused some loss to the material of the Federal batteries, which, however, inflicted equal loss upon their adversaries. There were but two pieces lost to the enemy, one from each corps.

About sundown of this day, the 1st, Slocum arrived with the Twelfth Corps, one division of which was placed on Culp's Hill in prolongation of Wadsworth's division of the First, which as before stated, occupied a short connecting ridge between this and Cemetery Hill. The other division took position on the left of Cemetery Hill, but early on the following day was moved over and stationed with the division already on Culp's Hill where they both covered themselves as speedily as possible with rude breastworks and abattis overlooking the steep declivity of the hill and the narrow, marshy valley of Rock Creek at its base. This entrenching subsequently proved of great service, as it enabled a small portion of the troops to hold the line, or at least a part of it, while the remainder were absent at a most critical moment assisting to repel an assault of the enemy on Cemetery Ridge. The line thus occupied by the Twelfth, being both rocky and wooded, afforded no available position for batteries, which, four in number, were massed in rear ready for any service. Later in the day, however, one battery was moved up on the line to suppress the annoyance given by a couple of the enemy's batteries on the high ground beyond the creek. A spirited artillery duel ensued in which the Federal battery came out victorious. About the time of Slocum's arrival, in the evening, Birney came up with his division of the Third Corps and took position on Cemetery Ridge on the left of the troops already there, and during the night was joined by the other division of this corps under Humphreys.

Meade, who was still back at Taneytown, being advised that the position at Gettysburg was favorable, determined to give battle there, and early in the evening of the 1st issued orders for all the corps to concentrate there with the utmost dispatch, at the same time directing all indispensable trains and other impedimenta to be sent to the rear to Westminster. The two batteries of 4.5-inch rifles were, as previously stated, strangely included in this, and thus the valuable services of these long-range guns were lost upon a field most eminently adapted to them.

Meade arrived on the field early in the morning of the 2nd, and as soon as it was sufficiently light made an inspection of the position and gave directions as to the posting of troops.

About 7:00 A.M. the Second and Fifth Corps arrived, the former taking position on Cemetery Ridge near the hill, while the latter was held in reserve pending the arrival of the Sixth, which having a march of over 30 miles to make, could not arrive until much later in the day. It did not in fact arrive until 2:00 P.M., about which time Lee was commencing his attack on the angle at the Peach Orchard. The Fifth then moved to the base of Little Round Top and soon took an important part in repulsing the attack.

The whole of the Federal army was now up and ready for battle. All of Lee's army was up also, excepting Pickett's division of Longstreet's corps, which did not arrive in time for the battle of this, the 2nd of July.

Lee says it was not his intention to deliver a general battle so far from his base, unless attacked, but coming unexpectedly upon the whole Federal army, to withdraw through the mountains with his extensive trains would be both difficult and dangerous. At the same time he says he was unable to await an attack on account of the state of his supplies. A battle had therefore become, in a measure, unavoidable, and the success already gained, alluding to the battle of the first day, gave hopes he says, of a favorable issue, whereupon he ordered up Longstreet's corps and the two absent divisions of Ewell's and Hill's corps. Ewell's corps continued upon the north side of the town, threatening Cemetery and Culp's hills, while Hill's corps continued on Seminary Ridge threatening Cemetery Hill and Ridge from the westward. Thus the two corps formed a right angle with each other, with the town and Cemetery Hill within the angle. When Longstreet's corps arrived, which was early in the afternoon of the 2nd, he took position on the right of Hill, inclining his right through the woods towards Little Round Top. The numerous artillery of these corps was posted on the hills and ridges occupied by the infantry.

Lee determined to make his principal attack on Meade's left near Little Round Top, for the purpose of gaining a position from which it was thought his artillery could be brought to bear with greater effect, by an oblique or enfilading fire along Cemetery Ridge. While Longstreet was making this attack, Ewell was to make demonstrations on Cemetery and Culp's hills to be converted into a real attack should a favorable opportunity offer. Hill was ordered to threaten the Federal center, to prevent reinforcements being drawn from either wing, and to give assistance, as occasion required, to both Longstreet and Ewell.

The Federal position upon Culp's and Cemetery hills was that of a crescent with the convex side towards the enemy. Culp's Hill formed the right cusp of the crescent, while the others, extending in a straight line along the Cemetery Ridge, terminated at Little Round Top. The extreme right of the line, on Culp's Hill, was therefore almost in rear of the center upon Cemetery Ridge, and distant there from only about half a mile. It was therefore not difficult, owing to the form and shortness of the line, to reinforce one part of it from another.

The enemy was forced to occupy an extensive line, necessarily of much greater extent, so great in fact as to make it impracticable in an emergency to reinforce either wing from the other. Even the communication of orders and information was so much delayed by the distance as to make abortive the simultaneous movements attempted by Lee. As a partial offset to this very great disadvantage, his artillery had a concentrated fire upon the Federal position, and not only this, but a reverse fire to some extent also; many of his shots passing over Cemetery Ridge reached Culp's Hill in rear, while Cemetery Hill had a crossfire directed upon it from every direction.

Early in the morning of the 2nd, as soon as it was daylight, General Hunt, chief of artillery, made an examination of the field, respecting the arrangement of the artillery for the coming battle. Commencing on the right, he found the batteries of the Twelfth, First and Eleventh Corps as before stated; those of the Twelfth, four in number under Lieutenant Muhlenberg, the corps chief of artillery, in support of the infantry line on Culp's Hill, but not directly in position; those of the First Corps, likewise four in number under Colonel Wainwright, on the northern side of the Cemetery crowning the hill; and those of the Eleventh, four in number, together with what remained of Hall's battery from the battle of the day before, under Major Osborne, on the west side of the Cemetery. Still further to strengthen this position, five additional batteries were ordered to Osborne from the Reserve, thus placing at his disposal six 20-pounder Parrotts, 22 light rifles, and 18 Napoleons; altogether 46 pieces, in addition to the 24 under Wainwright for the crowning of this hill. This arrangement of guns brought under a commanding fire all the positions lying within range that the enemy could occupy with his artillery. At various periods during the progress of the battle all of these guns were brought into requisition and did most effective service, in fact prevented this all important point from falling into the hands of the enemy. The eight long-range rifles sent back to Westminster as impedimenta, contrary to the advice of the chief of artillery, would have found if brought up, a rare opportunity for keeping at a distance batteries of the enemy that did considerable damage during certain periods of the battle. As it was, the guns upon this hill compelled the enemy to make a long detour from one wing to the other of his army, one of the results attending the great range of modern artillery.

The five batteries of the Second Corps were on the line of battle of that corps on Cemetery Ridge. None of the other corps, the Third, Fifth and Sixth, had yet taken position on the line, but their batteries were on hand in readiness for it.

Meade, after an inspection of the situation, gave directions as to where the arriving troops should be posted, but made no material change with reference to those occupying Cemetery and Culp's hills. The Second Corps, Hancock commanding, was directed to occupy that portion of Cemetery Ridge next to Hill and to connect with the left of the Eleventh, which

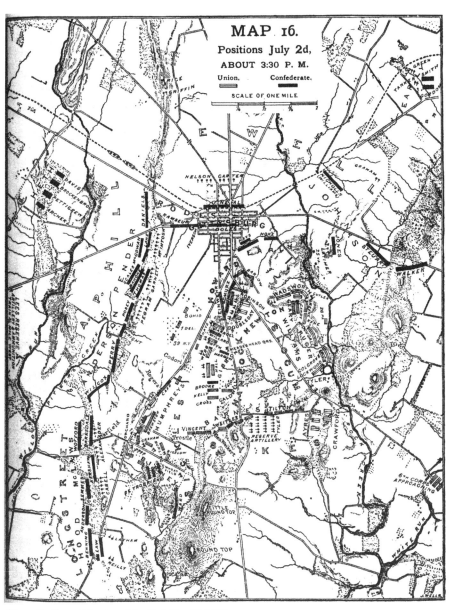

MAP 16.

Positions July 2d,
ABOUT 3:30 P. M.

Union.   Confederate.

SCALE OF ONE MILE

(From *Battles and Leaders of the Civil War*, III: 299.)

continued to occupy the western face of the hill. The Third Corps, Sickles commanding, connecting with the left of the Second, was to prolong the line towards Little Round Top. The Fifth, Sykes commanding, to be held in reserve near the latter place pending the arrival of the Sixth under Sedgwick. Upon the arrival of the latter corps, the Fifth moved to the assistance of the Third, now heavily engaged with the enemy, and became itself deeply involved in the battle raging for the possession of Little Round Top and the left of Cemetery Ridge.

Sickles, not fully apprehending his instructions, moved his corps to the front of Cemetery Ridge, to the line of the Emmitsburg road, which crossing from the town, skirts the western face of Cemetery Hill, and diverging at an acute angle from Cemetery Ridge, follows a secondary ridge or swell of ground lying between Cemetery and Seminary ridges. Along, or near this road, Sickles posted Humphreys' division with its right some distance from the left of the Second, while its left rested at a peach orchard about a mile in front and a little to the right of Little Round Top, and but a few hundred yards from that part of Seminary Ridge upon which the enemy was then taking position for the purpose of carrying out his plan of attacking the Federal left. Birney's division was posted at right angles to that of Humphreys', with its right resting in the Peach Orchard and its left on a rocky knoll in front of the base of Little Round Top, and overlooking a gloomy pedregal known as the "Devil's Den." Birney's small division had to cover about three-fourths of a mile of battle front and was consequently thin and weak; and while it had in its rear some open fields, its immediate front was covered by the dense woods surrounding the "Devil's Den," and by strips of timber in front of its right. Beyond these strips of timber were open fields screened from view and advantageous to the enemy for his formations and the posting of his batteries.

The advanced position of the angle at the Peach Orchard enabled Lee to envelop it and to enfilade both of its faces, that occupied by Birney from Seminary Ridge, and that by Humphreys' from the positions Longstreet was then taking up on and near the prolongation of the Emmitsburg road. Not only were these faces enfiladed, but they were each taken somewhat in reverse. It was a position too that could not be reinforced without exposing the assisting troops to the same disadvantages, and this without hope of successfully maintaining the position.

Meade had the disadvantage of having an army divided up into small corps, most of which were but little larger than divisions should have been; each of which was an independent command, without any intermediate command between him and the corps. Under such conditions it is physically impossible for a general to exercise such supervision over the entire field as will prevent mistakes similar to that which now befell the Third Corps.

The artillery of this corps was disposed of by Captain George E. Randolph, its chief of artillery, by posting Smith's New York battery of six rifles on the rocky knoll, before mentioned as situated on the edge of the "Devil's Den" and in front of Little Round Top, where it was supported by Brigadier General J.H. Hobart Ward's brigade of Birney's division. Somewhat to the right and rear of this knoll was Captain George B. Winslow's Battery B, 1st New York Artillery Regiment, of six Napoleons posted in a wheat field, but separated from Smith's position by a strip of woods. Captain A. Judson Clark's Battery B, 1st New Jersey Light Artillery Regiment, of six rifles was still farther to the right, near the Peach Orchard, while Captain Nelson Ames' Battery G, 1st New York Light Artillery Regiment, of six Napoleons, from the Artillery Reserve, was in the orchard. All of these batteries were on Birney's front to fire to the southward and were greatly obstructed in the field of fire by the woods and strips of timber before mentioned, while at the same time they were exposed to a heavy flank fire from the batteries of the enemy posted on Seminary Ridge.

On Humphreys' front, to fire to the westward, were posted Randolph's Battery C, 1st Rhode Island Light Artillery Regiment, of six Napoleons and Lieutenant Francis W. Seeley's Battery K, 4th U.S. Artillery Regiment, also of six Napoleons. About the time this disposition of the Third Corps was made General Hunt reached the locality, and seeing the weakness of the position and the danger threatening it, ordered up with all haste Lieutenant Colonel Freeman McGilvery's brigade of five batteries from the Artillery Reserve, which was fortunately near at hand. Fourteen of the 26 guns composing this brigade took position on Birney's front while the remainder were sent to strengthen that of Humphreys.

At the same time, Captain Dunbar R. Ransom was ordered up with three batteries of 18 guns from the brigade of regular batteries of the Reserve. On this front were therefore assembled seven batteries of 42 pieces, 14 rifles and 28 Napoleons. On Birney's front were an equal number of batteries, consisting of 38 pieces, 18 rifles and 20 Napoleons; in all 80 pieces, 50 of which were from the Artillery Reserve. The ground in front of Birney was, as just described, unfavorable for artillery. The strips of woods covering the rough ground in front screened the enemy from view and it was only through a few openings that the batteries were enabled to obtain a good fire; and when, during the hottest period of the fighting, the infantry pushed forward to meet the enemy in the woods, the batteries could not follow by reason of the rocky and woody obstructions.

In front of Humphreys' position, and around the Peach Orchard and through the woods, among the boulders and around the base, and upon the sides and crest of Little Round Top, took place during this afternoon (July 2nd) the hardest and fiercest struggle of this eventful battle. Lee's attack of the following day usually termed "Pickett's Charge" made across open fields and in full view, is better known to the world, and is generally taken as the high-water mark of the rebellion, as that point from which its military power and hopes began to recede and grow less to the end. As grand as was Pickett's charge it was but a reckless dash compared with the prolonged and persistent efforts put forth by Lee to crush Meade's left and secure the vital advantages of Little Round Top. The closeness with which he came to reaching this end made the battle of this day the real turning point of the battle and of the war.

The movement which Sickles made to the front with his corps broke its connection with the Second Corps on its right. To fill up as much as possible this gap, two regiments of Harrison's brigade of the Second were sent forward on the Emmitsburg road near to a brick house at which rested Humphreys' right. Here they hastily constructed a slight breastwork of fence rails, which a short time afterwards served them an excellent purpose. Lieutenant Thomas F. Brown's Battery B, 1st Rhode Island Light Artillery Regiment, and Captain James M. Rorty's New York batteries, the 14th New York Independent Battery and Battery B, 1st New York Light Artillery Regiment, that were also pushed forward to this point, and during the attack on this part of the line, following the break of the angle at the Peach Orchard, did splendid service, but with heavy loss in men and horses. Brown himself was wounded and his battery so much cut up that it was reduced to four pieces. The other three batteries of the Second Corps retained their position on Cemetery Ridge to the right of the two just mentioned, and although not so closely engaged, were nevertheless able to do a good part in assisting to repulse the enemy who, after forcing back Sickles' corps, was now following up the advantage of his onset and upon the point of breaking the more natural position of Cemetery Ridge.

While Sickles was establishing his corps in the manner just described, Longstreet, quite unaware of such disposition, was moving two of his heavy divisions around towards Little Round Top to feel for the Federal left flank and thus unconsciously enveloped the salient at the Peach Orchard. This movement brought one of his divisions, that of Hood, in front of Birney and the other against the Peach Orchard. Humphreys' division was confronted by Anderson's division of Hill's corps. Pender's division of the same corps, on the left of Anderson, confronted that part of Cemetery Ridge held by the Second Corps.

Hood, McLaws, and Anderson had together 59 regiments; opposed to these Sickles had but 37 regiments; so that in point of numbers alone, to say nothing of the disadvantages of his faulty position, the latter had but little showing for successful resistance. After the battle had commenced, division after division from other corps were sent in to the assistance of the Third, but all fighting under the same disadvantages, were finally forced back and a new line established on Cemetery Ridge, where it should have been in the first place.

The enemy recognized in Little Round Top the key of the position on that flank. Hood was therefore directed to work around in that direction and gain possession of it. McLaws was to move upon the Peach Orchard and attack Birney's right and Humphreys' left, while Anderson was to hold his division in readiness and attack Humphreys in front as soon as Longstreet's attack was fully developed. Anderson was supported by several battalions of batteries, while other battalions extended still further towards Hill's left, thus bringing about two-thirds of Lee's entire artillery force against the ridge between Cemetery Hill and Little Round Top.

Hood's division was accompanied by Major Mathias W. Henry's and Colonel E. Porter Alexander's battalions of batteries; McLaw's by Colonel Henry C. Cabell's battalion. The batteries of these battalions were posted in such manner as to enfilade both sides of Sickles' angle and to have a concentrated fire upon the whole of his position. The exact positions of most of these batteries were screened from view of the Federal batteries by intervening trees, but Sickles' position was such that wherever the shots of the enemy fell they were pretty certain of doing damage. In this the Federal batteries were at great disadvantage. It was only occasionally that those on Birney's front got a fair chance at the batteries opposed to them, but when they did they made the enemy suffer.

About 3:30 P.M. Hood's columns, until now sheltered from view by keeping in rear of Seminary Ridge, were observed moving to their right across the Emmitsburg road towards Little Round Top. Clark's battery in the Peach Orchard at once opened on them. This fire was promptly returned by batteries in the open fields near the road and from other points, and soon the cannonade became furious. The Confederate reports represent their batteries as suffering severely from it, but their suffering was little compared with that of their opponents, whose batteries were being enfiladed. As fast as the latter were disabled they were retired and replaced by others from the Reserve.

About 5:00 P.M. the enemy moved forward his infantry *en masse*, making his first attack on Birney's left, which was held by Ward's brigade, a portion of which, a mere skirmish line, rested on the knoll held by Smith's battery. Smith, seeing the danger confronting him and appreciating the advantages of the position, requested additional infantry support, but before this could arrive, the enemy, sheltered by the rocks, made their way to the knoll and captured three of his guns. The enemy, overlapping this flank by his superior numbers, worked his way among the rocks and bushes to the wooded depression or pass between Little Round Top and its neighbor, Round Top, with a view to gaining possession of the former, unoccupied as yet by the Federals. At this critical moment, General Warren, chief engineer on General Meade's staff, having ascended Little Round Top for the purpose of observation, perceived Hood's long line of infantry approaching and overlapping Birney's left in front of the mountain, and knowing that unless prompt measures were taken this vital point must soon fall into the hands of the enemy, he hastened to the first troops within reach, which happened to be James Barnes' division of the Fifth Corps, then just going into action to the assistance of Birney's yielding line, and from it obtained Colonel Strong Vincent's brigade, with which he hurried back to the crest of the mountain, which was reached just in time to meet, with the bayonet, the enemy who by this time was gaining the summit from the other side. The contest here soon became furious and the rocks alive with musketry. Lieutenant Charles E. Hazlett's Battery D of the 5th U.S. Artillery Regiment, supported by O'Rorke's regiment of Weed's brigade, was sent to the support of Vincent, who was now exposed to a severe fire from the batteries of the enemy. Hazlett's guns were dragged by hand, with great labor, through the rocks and bushes to the crest of the mountain, from which position they opened a fire represented by the enemy as being exceedingly damaging to them, taking them, as it did, in flank. Several of their batteries were turned upon the hill to subdue Hazlett's fire, which they failed to accomplish. A section of Captain Frank C. Gibbs' Battery L, 1st Ohio Light Artillery Regiment, took position on Hazlett's right and did excellent work. The other guns of the same battery were on a projecting spur still further to the right and lower down.

It was Brigadier General Evander M. Law's brigade of Hood's division that made this bold attempt to secure Little Round Top. Being repulsed, Law renewed the attempt at several places. The contest was among rocks and bushes and often hand to hand. It was not a momentary dash, but one prolonged until the assailants were finally beaten back at every point, and with a percentage of loss seldom met with in battle. Hazlett, who had displayed such energy in getting his battery to the top of the butte, was killed, as was likewise Weed, who had accompanied O'Rorke's regiment, and who too was killed. Weed, it will be remembered, had won his star only two months before by his energy in collecting the scattered batteries at Chancellorsville and by his judgment and skill in posting them so as to hold a new line and restore order on that unfortunate field. It being supposed at the War

Department that general officers were not needed for artillery commands, he was assigned to a small brigade of infantry. Vincent, who so gallantly led his brigade to the top of the hill and fought it with unsurpassed vigor, was also killed, as were many others of lesser note. As severe as was the Federal loss on this hill that of the Confederates was much greater.

But the heaviest fighting of the day, both in point of numbers engaged and in the prolonged intensity of the contest, took place among the rocks and woods in front of Birney's position, between Little Round Top and the Peach Orchard. The Federals, bringing up fresh divisions, pressed back for a time the enemy through the rocky recesses of the "Devil's Den" and the surrounding woods, where the battle surged back and forth with bloody fury. This ground was, however, too rough for batteries, which were forced to remain on the line as originally formed. But from this line they did excellent work according to the reports of the enemy, not only during the preliminary cannonading, but at opportune intervals during the battle. When the Federal infantry was finally driven back, some of these batteries were ordered to hold their ground to the bitter end, and to hold the enemy in check until the remainder could withdraw and establish a new line. Conspicuous in this forlorn hope duty was Captain John Bigelow's 9th Massachusetts Independent Light Artillery Battery and Captain Charles A. Phillips' 5th Massachusetts Independent Light Artillery Battery, both of which lost heavily in men and horses. Bigelow's had three officers out of the four present placed *hors de combat.*

When it became evident that Birney could not withstand the force in front of him, Barnes' division of the Fifth Corps and then Brigadier General John C. Caldwell's of the Second Corps were sent in and the fight waxed fiercer than ever. But the farther these supporting divisions advanced against Hood the more were their right flanks exposed to the attacks of McLaws, and they suffered accordingly. Caldwell, under cover of the artillery, extricated his division only after heavy loss. He had penetrated through the strips of woods to the fields beyond and only needed support to have made a permanent lodgment against the enemy. Ayres' division of the Fifth Corps, composed chiefly of regulars well commanded, followed closely upon Caldwell, but this division too was struck in flank and although fighting desperately, had to fall back with a loss of about 50 percent in killed and wounded. Ayres' withdrawal was likewise covered by the artillery and by the advance of some of the Sixth Corps which had arrived after a long forced march only a short time previous. The last advance to hold the enemy in check was made by the Pennsylvania Reserves, a division of the Fifth Corps commanded by Brigadier General Samuel W. Crawford. The charges made by the two brigades of this body were exceedingly gallant and resulted in retrieving, for a time, some of the lost ground. As a rule the Federal divisions had entered the fight in succession and were driven back in detail, a result always following when there is no wing or other common commander present to insure cooperation and unity of action between parts of various corps engaged at the same work.

But the inherent weakness of the Peach Orchard position was such that no amount of fighting could have held it against the forces Lee was bringing against it. Birney's face of the angle was completely broken and driven back to a new line, the line of Cemetery Ridge. The infantry was much confused by the severe work it had gone through among the rocks and thickets of the ground over which the battle had surged. But the batteries, or remnants of batteries, by being promptly established upon the new line, afforded divisions, brigades, and regiments a firm and well marked line upon which to form, and their fire held the enemy in check until the line could be well established, after which there was no further danger.

While the fighting was going on against Birney's line, that of Humphreys' was not seriously attacked in front, but suffered greatly from flank and reverse fire from the left. Lee's

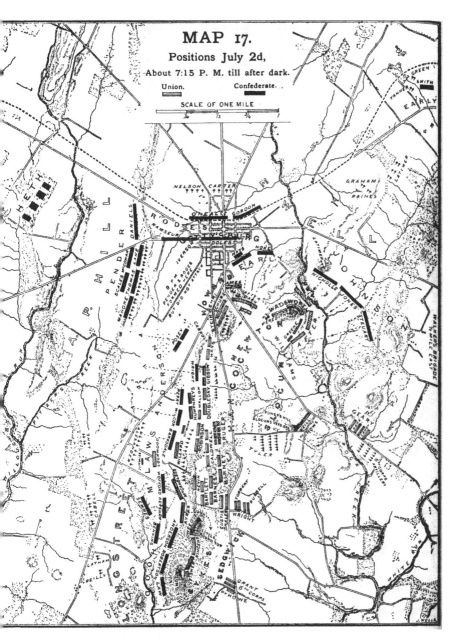

MAP 17.

Positions July 2d,
About 7:15 P. M. till after dark.

Union.   Confederate.

SCALE OF ONE MILE

(From *Battles and Leaders of the Civil War*, III: 308.)

plan of battle was for Anderson, of Hill's corps, to take up the attack as soon as Longstreet should break the left. Accordingly, when the Peach Orchard fell, Anderson made his assault upon Humphreys, who was still holding on to his position on the Emmitsburg road. Humphreys was now called upon to resist, with his small division, Longstreet upon his left and Anderson in front. Hancock, now in temporary command of that part of the line, threw in four regiments to support Humphreys' right, but the attack of the enemy was so sudden and violent as to afford them time for but a few volleys before Humphreys received orders to give up his advanced position and fall back to the new line. The batteries on Humphreys' line held the ground as long as possible to cover the with-drawal of the infantry, but the enemy, pressing on closely, got temporary possession of most of the pieces of several of the batteries. The fire from the new line became, however, so hot the enemy was forced to hastily abandon pursuit and leave his captures behind. During the night the guns were brought in, all except one, which the enemy succeeded in carrying off.

Three of Anderson's brigades fought their way up almost or quite to the new line, but being unsupported by the rest of the division, were driven back. Brigadier General Ambrose R. Wright's brigade, the one most in advance, was met by Brigadier General Alexander S. Webb's and Hall's brigades of the Second Corps, which not only repulsed it, but followed it up for some distance, recapturing from it a gun that was being used with effect upon the Federal troops, together with sever-al hundred prisoners.

The left brigades of Anderson's division having failed to advance, the adjoining division, that of Pender of Hill's corps, did not move to the attack according to the plan of battle pre-scribed by Lee, which was that the attack should be taken up successively from right to left until his entire line should become engaged. This break in the plan of attack occurred at the most critical period and undoubtedly had a most decided influence upon the fortunes of the day.

At this period of the battle not only the Third Corps had been driven back from its unfortunate position at the Peach Orchard, but likewise all the troops sent to its assistance. All had made their best fight and found themselves unable to hold a long stretch of line now in possession of the enemy. This gave to the Federal troops the appearance and feeling of defeat, and it was difficult for them to realize upon the spur of the moment that in their new position they were in fact stronger than before. On the other hand, the enemy was proportionally elated and confident and was following up his success with vigor when he met with such resistance as to check his efforts. The most critical moment of this period was when Hood's and McLaws' troops, flushed with the success they had met with, were pressing forward to make victory complete by a clean and permanent break through the left of the Federal position on Cemetery Ridge. But here they encountered the fire of the guns that the artillery commanders were putting in position for the establishment of a new line, and being arrested by it, the check thus given became the turning point of the battle, and perforce of the rebellion.

When matters were looking so very ominous on this part of the field, troops from every available part were ordered up to assist in repulsing the enemy. Among these was Brigadier George J. Stannard's brigade of the First Corps, which made a gallant charge driving the enemy back and recapturing several pieces of artillery. This brigade remained upon this part of the line and took an active part in repulsing the great charge of the following day. At the same time a division of the Twelfth Corps was withdrawn from the extreme right on Culp's Hill and sent over to the left. Owing to the curve in the line of battle around Cemetery Hill this distance was not very great, and one brigade, that of Brigadier General Henry H. Lockwood, arrived in time to take part in the fight. During the absence of this division from Culp's Hill, Ewell's troops took possession of its entrenchments and held them until driven out on the following morning.

It was quite dark when the battle closed upon the left. The enemy withdrew to Seminary Ridge, but bending his extreme right forward, still threatened Little Round Top. The battle of the day had been extremely sanguinary and exhausting. It was, in fact, Lee's supreme effort, and in it he put as much force as he could command. The energy thus expended weakened his power for attack on the following day. Upon the Federal side it had the effect of demonstrating the natural advantages of the position for a defensive battle. It clearly defined the line of greatest strength and brought the troops upon it in readiness for the contest of the next day.

The guns that had fallen into the hands of the enemy temporarily were restored to their batteries, and all the batteries that had suffered in the fight were made as whole as possible. The system of brigading the batteries enabled this to be done with promptness and thoroughness. The batteries of the Sixth Corps, eight in number, the corps being supposed to be in reserve, were temporarily attached to the Artillery Reserve thus making them more available for general service, and they came in very conveniently to replace batteries damaged by the fire of the enemy.

Lee's plan of battle contemplated, as before stated, that while Longstreet made the principal attack on Meade's left, Ewell should make a simultaneous demonstration on his right, to be converted into a real attack should opportunity offer. Hill, whose corps was between Longstreet and Ewell, was to support both of them as soon as occasion might offer. We have just seen that Anderson's division, or rather a portion of it, gave prompt and decided assistance to Longstreet, and that it was only by the laggardness of one of his brigade commanders that the attack was not continued along the line, and to include Pender's division also. Heth's division, on the left of Pender, was to assist Ewell.

Ewell's plan of attack was for Rodes' division to advance through the town directly upon Cemetery Hill. Early was to advance his division upon Rodes' left, while Major General

Edward A. Johnson's division, extending still further round to the eastward, was to attack the position held by the Twelfth Corps on Culp's Hill. It will be remembered, at this point that all of the Twelfth Corps except Brigadier General George S. Greene's brigade had been withdrawn to assist in the repulse of Longstreet from the left, a fact, however, not known at the time to Ewell, or even to Johnson. The latter, preparatory to his attack on Culp's Hill, posted Major Joseph W. Latimer's battalion of batteries on a hill further to the eastward and beyond Rock Creek, from which a spirited fire was opened from all the guns, and was replied to by the Federal batteries on Cemetery and Culp's Hills. Johnson says of this: "The terrible fire of the enemy's artillery, rendered his [Latimer's] position untenable, and he was ordered to cease firing and withdraw all of his pieces except four, which were left in position to cover the advance of my infantry. I then advanced my infantry to the assault of the enemy's strong position—a rugged and rocky mountain, heavily timbered and difficult of ascent; a natural fortification, rendered more formidable by deep intrenchments, and thick abattis."

Before his brigades had crossed the creek it was dark, nevertheless he attacked with vigor and spirit. Greene's brigade, the only one left when the Twelfth Corps withdrew, made a stout resistance and held fast that portion of the line occupied by it, but the enemy took possession of the remainder without much opposition. While Johnson was advancing to the assault, his troops suffered greatly from the artillery fire from the batteries on Cemetery Hill. One of his brigades was broken by it and sent in disorder to the rear. A portion of his attack fell upon Wadsworth's division of the First Corps, entrenched on Greene's left. This attack was repulsed without much loss to the defenders, but with great slaughter to the assailants. During this engagement, which lasted about three hours, well up into the night, Greene was reinforced by several regiments from the First and Eleventh Corps, all of which did valuable service in assisting to prevent the enemy from gaining the whole of Culp's Hill. Immediately after the repulse of Longstreet, that portion of the Twelfth that had been withdrawn from Culp's Hill returned and preparations were made to rout Johnson from that part of the line which he had taken possession of during its absence. This, however, was not to be done until daylight next morning, and therefore properly belongs to the operations of the 3rd.

Early, whose division was on the right of Johnson's, was ordered to advance on Cemetery Hill as soon as Johnson should be fairly engaged, and this he did with punctuality, preceding his movement by a fire from all the batteries of his division. His guns were, however, soon silenced by the greater number on Cemetery Hill. Brigadier General Harry T. Hays, who commanded Early's leading brigades, says:

> A little before 8 P.M. I was ordered to advance with my own and Hoke's Brigade on my left, which had been placed for the time under my command. I immediately moved forward, and had gone but a short distance when my whole line became exposed to a most terrific fire from the enemy's batteries from the entire range of hills in front and to the right and left; still, both brigades advanced steadily up and over the first hill, and into a bottom at the foot of Cemetery Hill. Here we came upon a considerable body of the enemy, and a brisk musketry fire ensued; at the same time his artillery, of which we were now within canister range, opened upon us, but owing to the darkness of the evening, now verging into night, and the deep obscurity afforded by the smoke of the firing, our exact locality could not be discovered by the enemy's gunners, and we thus escaped what in full day could have been nothing else than horrible slaughter.

The considerable body of the enemy mentioned by him was Von Gilsa's brigade of the Eleventh Corps, stationed in front as an advanced picket. Directly in its rear was a knoll, projecting from the main hill, upon which were posted Wiedrich's New York and Ricketts' Pennsylvania batteries. Von Gilsa's thin line made but slight resistance to Hays' brigades, and passing rapidly to the rear, opened the way to the two batteries, into which the enemy rushed. Ricketts says of this: "The cannoneers fought the enemy hand to hand with handspikes [,a wooden spike fixed to the trail for moving the gun horizontally,] rammers, and pistols, and succeeded in checking them for a moment, when a part of the Second Corps charged in and drove them back. During the charge I expended every round of canister in the battery, and fired case shot without the fuses." The other battery had the same experience. While the enemy was among the guns of these batteries, those upon the hill above and back were compelled to withhold their fire otherwise Hays' brigades would have been torn to pieces. As it was they suffered terribly. Early's other brigades shrunk back from the artillery fire, and getting but little way up the hill, did not come within musketry range. The repulse of this formidable assault was almost entirely by the artillery. The part of the Second Corps mentioned by Ricketts was Colonel Samuel S. Carroll's brigade, sent from the other side of the field. It continued in this position and did not therefore participate in the repulse of Pickett's charge of the next day.

Rodes was to have advanced his division simultaneously on the right of Early's, but as he was obliged to march out of the town before forming line, did not get fairly started up the hill before Early's attack had been repulsed. Rodes was to have been supported on his right by one of Hill's divisions, but it did not come into action because of Rodes' inability to do so.

Ewell's assault, although intended to have been simultaneous with Longstreet's attack, was not even commenced until the latter had been repulsed. This was caused in a great measure by the failure of Ewell's artillery to shake that upon Cemetery Hill and open the way for the advance of his infantry columns. About the time that Longstreet was to attack, Ewell had a battery of 10 guns (four 20-pounder rifles and six rifles of lesser caliber) established in a field to the north and east of Cemetery Hill, and within easy range, from which was opened a remarkably accurate fire upon that position. In a short time these 10 pieces, having suffered severely in men and horses from an equally accurate fire from the batteries on the hill, were forced to withdraw. Attempts were made to establish other batteries further to their right, but these, exposed to a still greater number of guns, were soon driven off, not however without having inflicted considerable injury to the batteries on the hill. This manifestation of the strength of the position on the hill evidently caused Ewell's troops to look upon its assault in the light of a forlorn hope, and caused his commanders to substitute desperation for alacrity. When finally about sundown his troops were ready to advance, his batteries again opened, but while inflicting considerable damage, were unable to impair the deadly effect of the artillery fire from the hill. The assaults were then made with the results just described.

Ewell's operations of this afternoon go to show most forcibly the difficulty of securing synchronous action on an extended field of battle. An apparently trifling circumstance prevented Rodes from assaulting the hill at the same time with Early, thus losing what was hoped to have been gained by simultaneous action.

This was the last assault made upon Cemetery and Culp's hills. The troops occupying these were, however, exposed throughout the following day to frequent outbursts from the batteries of the enemy, while a spiteful skirmish firing was indulged in all the while by the infantry.

While these events were happening on the flanks of the two armies, the center was by no means idle. The Second Corps under Hancock occupied that part of Cemetery Ridge adjoining the hill, extending along the ridge towards Little Round Top, where its left was to connect with the right of the Third. But when the latter was moved to the front, to the

Peach Orchard, an interval occurred which was partly filled by stretching out the left of the Second. When Caldwell's division was sent to assist the Third, a still greater gap was created, which was subsequently partly filled by Stannard's brigade of Doubleday's division, and the remnant of Robinson's division of the First Corps put in at intervals. Along this attenuated line of the Second its five batteries were distributed by Captain John G. Hazard, chief of artillery of the corps, to which were added two other batteries from the Artillery Reserve. While the battle was raging about the Peach Orchard and Ewell was assaulting the right, the batteries of Hill's corps maintained a furious cannonade upon this part of the line, to which Hazard's batteries made good reply. All day a brisk skirmish firing was kept up, occasionally swelling with volleys of musketry, approximating to a battle, and when Humphreys was forced from his position on the Emmitsburg road with the enemy following close after, it was Hall's and Webb's brigades of the Second that met and thrust back his foremost brigades when they were upon the very point of breaking through the Federal line.

The foregoing are the general features of the battle of the second day, which taken as a whole, was by far the heaviest fighting of either of the three days and the most critical to the Union cause. In it, a large part of the Federal artillery had been engaged and did work the nature and value of which has been but faintly portrayed in the foregoing. Neither the infantry nor the artillery, if alone, could have saved the field. It was only by their happy cooperation that this was done, and it is but fair that the artillery should receive due share of credit for its part.

The brigade system, notwithstanding its newness, worked admirably. By it the batteries were kept in hand and brought to their work to the best advantage. Division and brigade commanders were not hampered by the care of them, but were enabled to give their undivided attention to their more legitimate duties; and it is but logical to presume that the good fighting done by the infantry was largely due to this fact.

Many of the batteries had suffered severely during the day's battle and the night following was devoted in great part to repairing damages, replenishing ammunition chests, and reducing and reorganizing such batteries as had lost so many men and horses as to be unable to work efficiently the full number of guns. Batteries too much disabled were withdrawn and replaced by others from the Artillery Reserve. Otherwise there was no material change in the position of the artillery.

Lee's net gain by his ponderous and sanguinary assaults of this day was the line of entrenchments on Culp's Hill, taken possession of by Johnson's division when the Twelfth Corps withdrew to assist on the left. The Peach Orchard position, it is true, fell into Lee's possession, but as this was a false position from the beginning, its loss was not a gain to Lee, but in reality an advantage to Meade. Lee, mistaking this for a real gain and overestimating the value of the line of entrenchments captured by Johnson, was encouraged to make similar assaults on the following day, and so ordered. In this, however, he was opposed in judgment by Longstreet, his chief lieutenant, who probably had better opportunities of knowing the exact condition of things on Lee's extreme right and how they affected the center and other parts of the field.

Daylight of the morning of the 3rd found the Federal artillery disposed as follows. Lieutenant Edward D. Muhlenburg, chief of artillery of the Twelfth Corps, had 20 pieces in position ready to assist his corps in ousting Johnson from the position he had gained the evening before on Culp's Hill. Wainwright of the First Corps had 24 pieces on Cemetery Hill on the right of the cemetery gate, while Osborne of the Eleventh Corps had 46 pieces on the left of the gate. Hazard of the Second Corps had 38 pieces on that part of Cemetery Ridge occupied by his corps. On the left of these McGilvery had some 40 guns of the Artillery Reserve, and on the left of these were several batteries of the Fifth and Third corps, while 12 pieces still crowned Little Round Top; making altogether about 200 pieces in position along the line. All surplus batteries were with the Reserve, which was at a central point behind Cemetery Ridge in readiness to afford assistance to any point endangered. Near it was the Sixth Corps, held in like manner as a support to any point of the line.

The question of artillery ammunition was now giving Hunt and others great concern. The management of artillery ammunition trains was not yet under control of the artillery and many of the wagons carrying ammunition had been sent back as impedimenta to Westminster. The ammunition train of the Artillery Reserve, so frequently before called upon to supply deficiencies arising from similar causes, had already been drawn upon until the supply was becoming alarmingly low. There was, however, sufficient to replenish fully all the batteries, and all artillery commanders were cautioned to be as economical as possible in the use of it.

Lee in his report says of his plan of battle for this day (July 3rd): "The results of this day's operation [July 2nd] induced the belief that with proper concert of action and with the increased support that the position gained on the right [the Peach Orchard] would enable the artillery to render the assaulting columns, we should ultimately succeed; and it was accordingly decided to continue the attack." His general plan remained unchanged. Longstreet was to attack, as before, on the extreme right, Ewell on the left, while Hill, in the center, assisted both.

In pursuance of this plan Longstreet made arrangements to conduct the attack in such direction as would enable him to work his way around the Round Tops and thus gain a position in rear of Meade's left. This, if carried out, would have given the field to the Confederates, but other things were now happening to change this program. Ewell, in renewing his attack of the previous day, was expected not only to hold that which Johnson had already gained on Culp's Hill, but to break up the whole of Meade's right, and then cutting across the rear of the Federal position on Cemetery Ridge, to cooperate with Longstreet and Hill in making a clean sweep of the whole position.

Johnson had been strongly reinforced during the night, and at daylight attempted to move forward so as to gain a position for his artillery, but was met by Slocum with the Twelfth Corps, assisted by Wadsworth's division of the First Corps, when a severe contest ensued, lasting until about 10:30 A.M., when the enemy was driven from the hill, across the creek and to the position occupied by him before he commenced his attack of the day before, and with a heavy loss in killed and wounded, together with about 500 captured, in addition to the large number of wounded left on the field. Johnson's division was the one formerly commanded by "Stonewall" Jackson and as it had not been accustomed heretofore to reverses, its well known bravery took on this occasion the form of desperation. The four batteries of the Twelfth Corps, together with one from the Reserve, being advantageously posted, contributed largely to this repulse of the enemy. The reports of the latter all make special mention of the damage done them by the artillery fire.

Walker's brigade of Johnson's division was detained away from the attack of the evening before by the presence of Gregg's cavalry, then stationed well around on the right towards Hunterstown to prevent Stuart with his cavalry from raiding on that flank of the army. The demonstrations made by Gregg caused Johnson to detach Walker to hold Gregg's cavalry in check, resulting in a spirited contest between a portion of Walker's infantry and some of Gregg's cavalry dismounted and acting as infantry. This skirmish was of little moment *per se*, but it served to withhold an important part of Johnson's command at a moment when he most needed it.

Gregg, remaining near this position during the night, was in position next morning (July 3rd) to meet and drive back the Confederate cavalry under Stuart, which made a bold push to get around Meade's extreme right for the purpose of raiding his ammunition trains and of harassing his rear. An obstinate fight between the opposing cavalries here took place, not of such magnitude perhaps as some other cavalry battles, but certainly of great moment to the welfare of the Union cause. In it the horse batteries of Randol and Lieutenant Alexander C. M. Pennington, Jr., (Battery M, 2nd U.S. Artillery Regiment) took an unusually important part; in fact, so much so that without them Stuart would probably have gained his object.

While Johnson was being driven from Culp's Hill, Longstreet was making his best efforts against Meade's left, but at every step was meeting with such opposition as to convince him of the futility of such an attempt. Failing on both flanks to make the impression he had expected, Lee suddenly changed his plan to a concentrated attack upon the center of Cemetery Ridge, and directing Longstreet to suspend his operations against the flank, made preparations for carrying out his new scheme.

The assault was to be made by Pickett's division of Longstreet's corps, a division that had arrived too late in the evening before to be engaged in the battle of that day, and was therefore entirely fresh. It was moreover a veteran division and one of the best in the army. Pickett was to be supported on his left by Heth's division of Hill's corps, now commanded by Pettigrew; Heth having been wounded in the fight of the first day. Pettigrew was in turn to be supported by two brigades of Pender's division, also of Hill's corps.

Pickett's division was to stand the brunt of the assault, or rather to be the head and front of it. Anderson's division of Longstreet's corps was held in readiness to support Pickett. The division of the latter consisted of 15 regiments containing about 8,000 men, all Virginia troops of the first quality. Pettigrew had 17 regiments, all greatly depleted by the battle of the first day and by subsequent skirmishing. His command did not therefore number over 6,000 men. Brigadier General James H. Lane's and Brigadier General Alfred M. Scales'

brigades of Pender's division had together 10 regiments containing about 4,000 men, making a grand total of about 18,000
men present in ranks to move forward to the assault; certainly a mighty mass of force, but yet a very great tapering down
from the still mightier efforts made by Lee on the previous
day. This, however, had the advantage of being an attack of
one mass, while that of the day before was by different parts
of his army at various points and not entirely simultaneous.
Against this advantage was the very great disadvantage of
having to move this large mass of men nearly a mile over open
ground, exposed the whole distance to the direct, cross, and
enfilading fire of a numerous artillery, and then to the musketry of a strong line of infantry.

Longstreet, upon the right of the attacking line, and Hill
upon the left, were to hold the remainder of their corps in
readiness to take advantage of the break which was expected
to be made in the Federal line, and by pressing forward their
troops were to rend asunder the wings of Meade's army. In
execution of this bold project, Pendleton, Lee's chief of
artillery, posted the battalions of batteries of Longstreet's and
Hill's corps in the edge of the woods along Seminary Ridge
and towards the Peach Orchard in such manner as to have a
converging fire upon that part of Cemetery Hill to be assaulted. At the same time, "orders were given," says Longstreet, "to
Major General Pickett to form his line under the best cover
that he could get from the enemy's batteries, and so that the
centre of his assaulting column would arrive at the salient of
the enemy's position. General Pickett's line to be the guide
and to attack the line of the enemy's defenses, and General
Pettigrew, moving on the same line as General Pickett, was to
assault the salient at the same moment." The salient here
referred to was really no salient at all, but a part of Cemetery
Ridge, which in consequence of a swell of the ground,
appeared to the Confederates as such. The line from
Cemetery Hill to Little Round Top was virtually a straight line

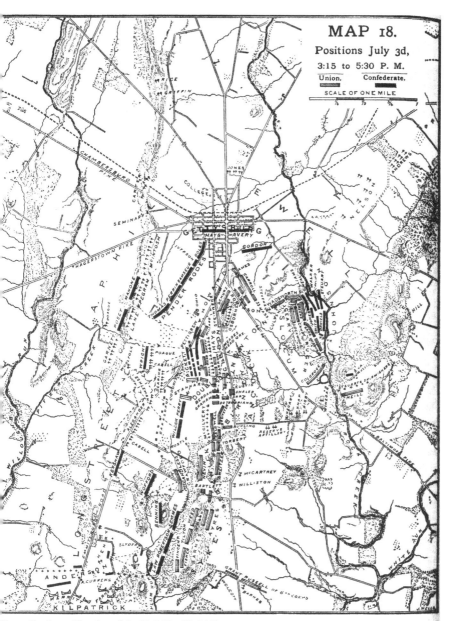

MAP 18.

Positions July 3d,
3:15 to 5:30 P. M.
Union. Confederate.

SCALE OF ONE MILE

From *Battles and Leaders of the Civil War*, III: 344.)

with but slight irregularities. Pickett and Pettigrew formed their divisions in two lines with a front of two brigades each.

Lee's battalion system enabled his chief of artillery to assemble his batteries and post them with promptness. The same system, although so new to the Army of the Potomac, enabled Meade's chief of artillery to handle his artillery with a promptness and efficiency before unknown to that army. Under the old system of having batteries distributed to infantry divisions without any special commander, the decisive blows given by the artillery to the assaulting column would have been quite out of the question and the final result of the battle extremely doubtful. It would probably have been, as many previous battles of the Army of the Potomac had been, either an out-and-out defeat, or at best but a Cadmean victory.

While these preparations were in progress, Kilpatrick, with Brigadier General Wesley Merritt's and Brigadier General Elon J. Farnsworth's brigades of cavalry and Captain William H. Graham's Battery K, 1st U.S. Artillery Regiment, and Lieutenant Samuel S. Elder's Battery E, 4th U.S. Artillery Regiment, horse batteries, was working his way around Longstreet's right, with a view of reaching the ammunition trains of the enemy which were in that vicinity, a counterpart of Stuart's operations so handsomely checked by Gregg as has just been mentioned. Kilpatrick's movements diverted a large part of Longstreet's force from either supporting Pickett or attacking Little Round Top, which he hoped to carry while the Federal troops had their attention turned towards Pickett's attack. Kilpatrick, although making a gallant fight in which Farnsworth was killed, was unable to make headway against the heavy force of infantry and Major Mathis W. Henry's battalion of batteries sent against him and was obliged to fall back without having damaged the ammunition train further than to cause its hasty removal, thus greatly inconveniencing the enemy in distributing the ammunition to the troops. "At length," says Pendleton, about 1 P.M., on the concerted signal, our guns in position, nearly one hundred and fifty, opened fire along the entire line from right to left, salvos by battery being much practiced, as directed, to secure greater deliberation and power. The enemy replied with their full force. So mighty an artillery contest has perhaps never been waged, estimating together the number and character of the guns, and the duration of the conflict. The average distance between contestants was about fourteen hundred yards, and the effect was necessarily serious on both sides. With the enemy, there was advantage of elevation; but his fire was unavoidably more or less divergent, while ours was convergent. His troops were massed, ours diffused. We, therefore, suffered apparently much less.

Hancock, in describing this cannonade, is even more graphic. He says:

From 11 A.M. until 1 P.M. there was an ominous stillness. About 1 o'clock, apparently at a given signal, the enemy opened upon our front with the heaviest artillery fire I have ever known. Their guns were in position at an average distance of fourteen hundred yards from my line and ran in a semicircle from the town of Gettysburg to a point opposite Round Top Mountain. Their number is variously estimated from one hundred and fifteen to one hundred and fifty. The air was filled with projectiles, there being scarcely an instant but that several were seen bursting at once. No irregularity of ground afforded much protection, and the plain in rear of the line of battle was swept of everything movable. The infantry troops maintained their position with great steadiness, covering themselves as best they might by the temporary but trifling defenses they had erected, and the accidents of the ground. Scarcely a straggler was seen, but all awaited the cessation of the fierce cannonade, knowing well what it foreshadowed.

In the meanwhile, the batteries along the Federal line worked their guns steadily and resolutely with scarcely any cover from the torrent of missiles poured upon them. Their conduct was the admiration of all who beheld them. As their cannoneers were reduced in numbers by those who fell, volunteers from the infantry took their places with alacrity.

General Hunt in his report says:

> To oppose these [the batteries of the enemy] we could not, from our restricted position, bring more than eighty guns to reply effectively. Our fire was well withheld until the first burst was over, excepting from the extreme right and left of our position. It was then opened deliberately and with excellent effect. As soon as the nature of the enemy's attack was made clear, and I could form an opinion as to the number of his guns, I ordered from the park of the Artillery Reserve, all the batteries to move at a moment's notice, and then proceeded along the line, to observe the effect of the cannonade, and to replace such batteries as should become disabled. About 2.30 P.M., finding our ammunition running low and that it was very unsafe to bring up loads of it, a number of limbers and caissons having been exploded, I directed that the fire should be gradually stopped, which was done, and the enemy soon slackened his also.
>
> About 3 P.M., soon after the enemy's fire had ceased, he formed a column of attack in the edge of the woods in front of the Second Corps. At this time four batteries from the Reserve reached this point, and were put in a position in front of the advancing enemy. I rode down to McGilvery's batteries, and directed them to take the enemy in flank as they approached. The enemy advanced magnificently. The batteries of

the Second Corps on our right, having nearly exhausted their ammunition, except canister, were compelled to withhold their fire until the enemy, who approached in three lines, came within canister range. When our canister fire and musketry were opened upon them, it caused disorder, but still they advanced gallantly until they reached the stone wall behind which our troops lay. Here ensued a desperate conflict, the enemy succeeding in passing the wall and entering our lines, causing great destruction of life especially among the batteries. Infantry troops were, however, advanced from our right; the rear line of the enemy broke, and the others, who had fought with a gallantry that excited the admiration of our troops, found themselves cut off and compelled to surrender. As soon as their fate was evident, the enemy opened his batteries upon the masses of our troops at this point without regard to the presence of his own. Towards the close of the struggle three batteries near the point assaulted, which had lost heavily in men and horses, were withdrawn, and as soon as the affair was over their places filled with fresh ones. Soon the necessary measures had been taken to restore this portion of the line to an effective condition. It required but a few minutes, as the batteries, as fast as withdrawn from any point, were sent to the Artillery Reserve, replenished with ammunition, reorganized, returned to the rear of the line, and there awaited assignment.

The foregoing extracts, together, embrace the main features of this celebrated charge, but Longstreet in his report mentions some incidents in addition, worthy of notice. After describing the preliminary cannonade, he says: "I gave orders for the batteries to refill their ammunition chests and to be prepared to follow up the advance of the infantry, and gave to General Pickett the order to advance to the assault. I found that our supply of ammunition was so short that the batteries could not reopen." The ammunition train had been moved further to the rear on account of Kilpatrick's threatening demonstrations. Longstreet, continuing, says:

> The order for this attack, which I could not favor under better auspices, would have been revoked had I felt that I had the privilege. The advance was made in very handsome style, all the troops keeping their lines accurately, and taking the fire of the batteries with great coolness and deliberation. About half way between our position and that of the enemy, a ravine partially sheltered our troops from the enemy's fire, where a short halt was made for rest. The advance was resumed after a moment's pause, all still in good order. The enemy's batteries soon opened upon our lines with canister, and the left seemed to stagger under it, but the advance was resumed, and with some degree of steadiness. Pickett's troops did not appear to be checked by the batteries, and only halted to deliver a fire when close under musket range. Major General Anderson's division was ordered forward to support and assist the wavering columns of Pettigrew and [Major General Isaac R.] Trimble. Pickett's troops, after delivering fire, advanced to the charge, and entered the enemy's lines, capturing some of his bat-teries. About the same moment, the troops that had before hesitated, broke their ranks and fell back in great disorder, many more falling under the enemy's fire retiring than while they were attacking. This gave the enemy time to throw his entire force upon Pickett, with a strong prospect of being able to break up his lines or destroy him before Anderson's division could reach him, which would, in its turn, have greatly exposed Anderson. He was, therefore, ordered to halt. In a few moments the enemy, marching against both

flanks and the front of Pickett's division, overpowered it and drove it back, capturing about half of those of it who were not killed or wounded.

Pettigrew's command came under the fire of a good many of the guns on Cemetery Hill, in addition to those posted on the Second Corps' front, and it was this shattering fire of artillery that caused it to waver and break as described by Longstreet. It scarcely came within effective musket range before it fell back in disorder. Alex Hays, who commanded the division of the Second Corps opposite Pettigrew, says his troops fired but one volley before the break occurred. Many of the enemy, appreciating rightly the danger of retiring through such a fire as they had just passed threw down their arms, and making signs of surrender, rushed into the Federal lines as prisoners. Pettigrew and Pender were both desperately wounded and nearly all their brigade and regimental commanders either killed or wounded. The change of commanders incident to this, at a crisis so appalling, was unfavorable to the steadiness of the troops. The two brigades of Pender's division, marching directly behind Pettigrew's lines, did a little better; they got within easy musket range before breaking.

The distance from the edge of the woods from which the assaulting lines or columns emerged to the Federal line on Cemetery Ridge was about three-fourths of a mile, and with the exception of a few clumps of trees and bushes the entire intervening space was open, cultivated fields, but somewhat obstructed by stone and wooden fences. From Seminary Ridge the ground gently slopes for a few hundred yards and then as gently rises again to an almost imperceptible ridge along which the Emmitsburg road runs. It then descends again, and again ascends in a longer slope to Cemetery Ridge. The assaulting line was in view during its entire march over this distance and was consequently exposed all the while to the fire of the Federal batteries, and during the last half of the transit to the musketry also of a strong line of infantry, a large portion of which was sheltered in some degree behind stone fences or slight breastworks made of rails. When still nearer, the assaulting line was exposed to canister fire from the artillery. Notwithstanding all this, Pickett's portion of the line moved steadily forward. The gaps made in it by the artillery fire were filled up by closing in from the right flank. Although the movement was steadily forward, the troops seemed to shrink from a direct advance and constantly inclined to their left. The guns on Little Round Top enfiladed their lines and for their number did fearful execution, while those on the right and left of the point aimed at by the enemy had a cross fire upon them. Their march across the fields was marked by the killed and wounded who fell in such numbers as greatly to reduce the strength of those still pressing forward.

Pickett, upon leaving the woods on Seminary Ridge, directed his course obliquely to the left, towards a small knoll on Cemetery Ridge occupied by Gibbon's division of the Second Corps. The left of Webb's and right of Hall's brigades of this division rested on this knoll, and these were the commands struck by that part of Pickett's command that succeeded in reaching the Federal line, and these too were the brigades most directly instrumental in repelling the blow.

The batteries of the Second Corps had the brunt of the assault. These were stationed between the infantry brigades and from right to left as follows: Lieutenant George A. Woodruff's "I," 1st U.S. Artillery Regiment; Captain William A. Arnold's "A," 1st Rhode Island Light Artillery Regiment; Lieutenant Alonzo H. Cushing's "A," 4th U.S. Artillery Regiment; Brown's "B," 1st Rhode Island Light Artillery Regiment; and Rorty's "B," 14th New York Independent Light Artillery Battery. Of these battery commanders, Woodruff, Cushing and Rorty were killed in the engagement. Other officers of all these batteries were wounded, several of them mortally, while the loss in men was proportionately great. So much were these batteries cut up that after the engagement they were consolidated, making three out of the five. All of these batteries fought as batteries have seldom fought, and their officers acted heroically. Hall, commanding one of the brigades just mentioned, says: "Lieutenant Cushing challenged the admiration of all who saw him. Three of his limbers were blown up, and changed with the caisson limbers under fire. Several wheels were shot off his guns and replaced, till at last, severely wounded himself, his officers all killed or wounded, and with but cannoneers enough to man a section, he pushed his gun to the fence in front, and was killed while serving his last canister into the ranks of the advancing enemy." All other reports corroborate this of Cushing, and also of the high order of bravery exhibited by the other batteries, officers and enlisted men alike.

As before stated, Pickett directed his attack on Webb's and Hall's brigades, the two right brigades of Gibbon's division, the front of which was covered by stone fences or such temporary breastworks as could be hastily constructed without tools, from rails, stones, and earth. This line reserved its fire until the enemy was within 200 yards, when it was delivered with a withering effect, as was also canister from the batteries. But, notwithstanding, the enemy pressed ahead and were led over the stone wall by General Armistead, the commander of Pickett's leading brigade; and here ensued for near half an hour the fight that occupies such a prominent place in every account of the battle of Gettysburg. Armistead, who had so bravely led his men, was killed at this time.

While the brigades of Webb and Hall were engaged with the enemy in front, Brigadier General William Harrow's brigade of the same division on the left of Hall, and Alex Hays' division on the right of Webb, were pouring in an oblique fire. Still further to the left, beyond Harrow, Stannard, commanding a brigade of the First Corps, swung around two of his regiments, thus securing a direct fire into the right flank of the enemy. The battle in and around this point now became a melee. The enemy concentrating at this one point gained a few rods beyond the stone wall, but the farther he advanced the more desperate became his situation. Troops from every direction closed in upon him until further resistance became unavailing. As if by one impulse, the troops that had so gallantly crossed the stone wall threw down their arms and submitted as prisoners to their equally brave adversaries.

The breach that Pickett made in the Federal line was of no value without the means of holding and enlarging it. More than half of the troops that originally started were those of Pettigrew and Pender, and these, as we have seen, fell back withered by the artillery fire; and without this support the force left to Pickett, after the losses sustained by him in crossing the plain, was entirely inadequate to effect a permanent break in Meade's line. The effective work done by the artillery in driving back Pettigrew and Pender was, therefore, the primary cause of the repulse of the entire attack. When Pettigrew and Pender began to waver, Longstreet sent Anderson's division to brace them up, but when they broke to the rear he recalled Anderson, because as he intimates in his report, the more he sent forward the more went to slaughter or captivity.

Pickett's division consisted of the brigades of brigadier generals Richard B. Garnett, James L. Kemper, and Armistead. The first two were in the front line, while the latter constituted a second line in support. Garnett and Armistead were killed and Kemper wounded. Nearly all the field officers were struck down. Major Charles S. Peyton, who succeeded to the command of Garnett's brigade, describing the conflict in his report, says:

> From the point where we first encountered the enemy's skirmishers, the brigade moved rapidly forward towards the stone fence, under a galling fire both of artillery and infantry, the artillery using canister and grape. We were now within about seventy-five paces of the wall, unsupported on the right and left, General Kemper being some fifty or sixty yards behind and to the right, and General Armistead coming up in our

rear. . . . Our line, much shattered, still kept up the advance until within about twenty paces of the wall, when, for a moment, it recoiled under the terrific fire that poured into our ranks both from the batteries and from their sheltered infantry. At this moment General Kemper came up on the right and General Armistead in rear, when the three lines, joining in concert, rushed forward with unyielding determination and an apparent spirit of laudable rivalry to plant the Southern banner on the walls of the enemy. His strongest and last line was instantly gained; the Confederate battle flag waved over his defenses, and the fighting over the wall became hand to hand, and of the most desperate character; but more than half having already fallen, our line was found too weak to rout the enemy. We hoped for support on the left (which had started simultaneously with ourselves), but hoped in vain. Yet a small remnant remained in desperate struggle, receiving a fire in front, on the right, and on the left, many even climbing over the wall, and fighting the enemy in his own trenches until entirely surrounded; and those who were not killed or wounded were captured, with the exception of about 300 who came off slowly, but greatly scattered, the identity of every regiment being entirely lost, and every regimental commander killed or wounded.

Other Confederate reports, although not so circumstantial, corroborate the foregoing.

The Sixth Corps and the remnant of the Third Corps after the fight of the previous day were coming up and near at hand when the enemy gave up the contest, and fresh batteries from the Reserve were also in readiness to take the place of those exhausted; so that, although, had Pickett been followed by his supports, it is not probable any permanent lodgment could have been effected within the Federal line upon Cemetery

Ridge. The death rate among the assailants was awful and the wounded in proportion. About 5,500 prisoners, including the wounded, were captured.

The discomfited enemy, or at least those who escaped death or capture, took refuge behind their line of batteries which showed such a formidable front together with the masses of infantry known to be in support of them, as to make it extremely hazardous to attempt to follow up the fugitives. It would in fact have been a repetition of the enemy's experiment, but from the other side. Although the artillery ammunition of the enemy had run low at a critical moment of the battle, the batteries were now sufficiently replenished to have made a stout fight, and they were relied upon to repel any countercharge.

Nothing has yet been said of another assault attempted upon the Federal line some distance to the left of that part of it struck by Pickett. Although this was intended to have been a part of Pickett's charge, it was as it turned out an entirely distinct affair. The attempt referred to was that of two brigades of Hill's corps under Brigadier General Cadmus M. Wilcox.

Wilcox says in his report that he received the order to advance to the support of Pickett some 20 or 30 minutes after the latter had started, and that as he advanced he was unable to see a man of those he was sent to support, although he marched partly over the same ground. He was, as it were, lost, and this arose from the fact that although starting from nearly the same point, Pickett inclined to his left while Wilcox inclined to his right with a considerable angle between. When Wilcox arrived at the swell of ground along which runs the Emmitsburg road, he says: "All of the enemy's terrible artillery that could bear on them was concentrated upon them from both flanks and directly in front, and more than on the evening previous; but on my men went down the slope until they came near the hill upon which were the enemy's batteries and intrenchments. Here they were exposed to a close and terrible fire of artillery. Two lines of the enemy's infantry were seen moving by the flank towards the rear of my left." The infantry just referred to by Wilcox were two regiments of Stannard's brigade swinging around to take Wilcox in flank, as two others had but a few minutes before done to Pickett. The "terrible fire of artillery" mentioned by him came chiefly from a battalion of nine batteries and parts of batteries, the latter fragments of the battle of the previous day, of the Artillery Reserve under Lieutenant Colonel McGilvery of the Maine artillery. Mention has already been made of the active service of this gallant officer in the battle of the previous day. He received a wound at Gettysburg from which he soon afterwards died. These batteries, unlike those of the Second Corps, were united in one mass and covered to a slight degree by a hastily constructed epaulment. Between the right of this large battery and those of the Second Corps were four other batteries from the Reserve commanded by Captain Robert H. Fitzhugh. All of these batteries, both of McGilvery and Fitzhugh, had had an oblique fire upon Pickett's lines as he advanced. Fitzhugh now had an oblique fire upon Wilcox, while McGilvery had a direct fire. It was directly towards his position that Wilcox was directing his course.

Notwithstanding the "terrible artillery fire" to which his troops were exposed, Wilcox managed to reach the bottom of the valley, or rather the low ground lying between the swell over which he had advanced and Cemetery Ridge upon which McGilvery's battery was located. This ground was marshy, rocky and somewhat covered by bushes, among which Wilcox's men screened themselves and took shelter as much as possible behind the rocks. They, however, soon fell back in rout from this place, leaving many behind who, dreading the "terrible artillery fire" mentioned by Wilcox, gave themselves up in preference to returning over the ground by which they had come. In this way Stannard's command secured almost an entire regiment, colors and all. In this affair there was but little musketry fire, the repulse was accomplished by the artillery fire alone. It is, however, almost to be regretted that Wilcox was not allowed to force his way, as did Pickett, into the Federal lines, where his entire command would almost inevitably have been captured or destroyed by the infantry.

Mention has already been made of the shortness of supply of artillery ammunition arising from the fact that the corps had sent back to Westminster with the impedimenta a large part of that intended for their batteries, and of the great concern that this led to among those who were aware of it. When the enemy commenced his cannonade preliminary to his infantry advance, General Hunt, well knowing what was coming, gave strict instructions that as little firing as possible should be indulged in by the batteries, that they should husband their ammunition for the crisis certain to follow. This was strictly adhered to by McGilvery's batteries, with the exception of three of them, which opened fire by direction of Hancock. This firing was, however, soon discontinued by direction of Hunt, and all of the batteries had an ample supply with which to meet the crisis. The batteries on the Second Corps front being more immediately under Hancock's control expended most of their ammunition, except canister, before Pickett commenced his advance, and therefore had none with which to break up his formations while crossing the fields and get beyond musketry and canister range. These circumstances led to an angry controversy between Hancock, commanding a corps, and Hunt, chief of artillery, as to the extent of authority of each over artillery matters.

The repulse of Wilcox ended the battle of Gettysburg. Lee, in his report says: "The severe loss sustained by the army and the reduction of its ammunition, rendered another attempt to dislodge the enemy inadvisable, and it was therefore determined to withdraw." On the following morning, July 4th, Lee started his trains with such of the wounded as could bear transportation for the Potomac, taking the roads leading through the Cashtown and Fairfield passes into the valley leading by Hagerstown to Williamsport. His troops retained their position until dark when they too were put in motion by the same route, and marching day and night to avoid pursuit, soon reached the Potomac where his army strongly entrenched itself in a line covering the fords at Williamsport and Falling Waters. Meade harassed Lee's retreat with cavalry and on the 12th confronted him with his entire army, but finding him so strongly entrenched, desisted from immediate attack. During the night of the 13th Lee crossed the river with his entire command, partly by fording and partly by a temporary pontoon bridge, and this ended the Gettysburg campaign, the second one of invasion that Lee had undertaken.

Public opinion severely criticized Meade, as it had done McClellan at Antietam, for not annihilating the rebel army. These adverse criticisms were materially modified before the war ended.

The losses in this campaign, nearly all of which occurred on the field of Gettysburg, were for the Federals, 2,834 killed, 13,709 wounded and 6,643 missing, for a total of 23,186. The Confederates suffered 2,665 killed, 12,599 wounded, and 7,464 missing, for a total of 22,728. Among the killed on the Confederate side were generals Armistead, Barksdale, Garnett, Pender, Pettigrew and Paul J. Semmes; on the Federal side, generals Reynolds, Farnsworth, Weed and Samuel K. Zook.

In this battle the Federal artillery lost six pieces by capture. None were captured from the Confederates, although several pieces were picked up by the pursuing cavalry, and two were captured in an engagement near Falling Waters. The loss in horses, killed and disabled, and of material, was unusually heavy on both sides.

It will be seen from the foregoing that the artillery of Meade's army performed no insignificant part at the battle of Gettysburg and was always at the right place at the right time, a fact clearly attributable to the new organization that had been given it. At each crisis of the battle, and there were several of them, it turned the trembling scale in favor of the Union cause.

Resting a few days after crossing the Potomac, Lee continued his march up the Shenandoah Valley, and crossing the Blue Ridge at the passes near Luray, continued down the south side of the Rappahannock to the neighborhood of Culpeper. Meade, crossing the Potomac at and below Harper's Ferry, marched his army parallel with that of his adversary, but on the eastern side of the Blue Ridge, and arrived near the Rappahannock at about the same time. Here he was directed to take up a threatening position, but not to advance against Lee.

Lee had a strong strategic position behind the Rappahannock in which he securely entrenched his army, and this enabled him to detach Pickett's division to the south side of the James River, threatening Suffolk, and to send Longstreet with Hood's and McLaws' divisions to assist General Bragg in the impending battle of Chickamauga. This latter fact having become known to the War Department, the Eleventh and Twelfth Corps were detached from the Army of the Potomac, and under Hooker hastened to the reinforcement of Major General William S. Rosecrans, but reached him too late for the battle of Chickamauga.

Lee's invasion of Pennsylvania emboldened the copperhead element of the North and led to the draft riots of New York City, to suppress which required the detachment of a large force from the Army of the Potomac, and this was not returned to it until about the middle of October. In the meanwhile, the corps of the Army of the Potomac had their depleted ranks replenished by the accession of many recruits from the enforcement of the draft and from volunteering.

In the first part of October, Lee made an excursion towards Warrenton which resulted in a brisk affair at Bristoe Station between the Second Corps, temporarily under Warren, and Hill's corps, in which the latter was worsted. On the 7th of November Meade advanced across the Rappahannock, and routing Lee from his entrenchments at Rappahannock Station and other points, forced him to retire behind the Rapidan where he secured himself behind strong entrenchments at Mine Run. Meade, advancing, established his army about Brandy Station, and in these positions the two armies remained, confronting each other until the opening of the memorable Wilderness-Petersburg campaign of the following spring; just before the opening of which the First and Third Corps of the Army of the Potomac were consolidated with the Second, Fifth and Sixth, commanded respectively by Hancock, Warren and Sedgwick. This consolidation gave to the army an efficiency it never before possessed, and gave to the artillery brigade of each corps about 12 batteries each. These brigades were each placed under a colonel with other field officers as assistants, together with a proper staff and complete supply departments. The artillery was at last upon its legs and from this on moved along without any hindrance, except occasional interference from those commanders not yet educated up to the progress of events and who still hankered to control it.

Captain Andrew Cowan's 1st New York Independent Battery Light Artillery within the Confederate words on the Petersburg, Virginia, line, April 1865. (*Library of Congress*)

SEVEN

PETERSBURG

I T WAS NOT UNTIL JUST BEFORE the opening of the spring campaign of 1864 that the new system–that of corps brigades of batteries–was thoroughly completed. At this time the infantry corps were consolidated, reducing their number to three, viz., the Second commanded by Winfield Scott Hancock; the Fifth, by Governeur K. Warren; and the Sixth by John Sedgwick. This was a vast improvement. The army consisting approximately of 100,000 men present, was capable of giving to each corps upwards of 30,000 men, without counting in the cavalry corps, which remained as before. The artillery brigades of each of these corps consisted of 12 batteries of 72 guns.

The Army of the Potomac thus organized, started on its famous campaign from the Rapidan River to Petersburg (May 6 to June 17th) almost a continuous battle of 42 days. Not a day passed without its battle or engagement, and the losses in killed and wounded attest the intensity of the fighting. According to the best authority these losses, killed and wounded, were but little short of 75,000 men. These immense losses were replaced by drafts from the troops garrisoning the defenses of Washington and from every other available source.

Ulysses S. Grant, present in person, was in general command, and as his instructions from Washington compelled him to "fight it out on this line"–the overland route from Washington to Richmond. He adopted the "hammering out" method of reducing Robert E. Lee's army. To this end there was no sacrifice too costly; but costly as it proved to be it was perhaps the most economical in the end; for the grinding to pieces of the Army of Northern Virginia led directly and immediately to the collapse of the Southern Confederacy.

The new system that had been inaugurated by Congress to have a military head to command the army instead of the Secretary of War, enabled Grant, now Lieutenant General, to operate the campaigns of the various armies simultaneously and in concert, thus depriving the enemy of the advantage of concentrating first upon one army and then on another, and with a greatly inferior aggregate force generally to have at the points of actual contact superior numbers. While Grant was making his Virginia campaign, William T. Sherman was marching upon Atlanta; Edward R. S. Canby was conducting an active campaign on the Gulf, and Nathaniel P. Banks by operations on the Red River, was holding the attention of the Confederate Trans-Mississippi army; thus rendering it impossible for Lee to draw reinforcements from any quarter. Every man that he lost was one gained by Grant who meanwhile had his losses replenished by drafts on the troops garrisoning Washington, and from other sources. When he approached the James River, the Army of the Potomac was joined by Major General Benjamin F. Butler's army of the James, making Grant's total force exceed that which it was when starting out, notwithstanding his very great losses in battle.

The campaign from the Rapidan to Petersburg included the sanguinary battle of the Wilderness; those around Spottsylvania, at Tolopotomy, at Cold Harbor, as well as those at Petersburg prior to June 18, at which time the army settled down to siege operations before that place. In addition to the abovementioned battles were a large number of others of less magnitude, but nevertheless very severe as engagements.

In many ways the country embraced by the campaign was a difficult one. Numerous unfordable rivers had to be crossed; roads were few and of inferior quality, the country was very much wooded and in some large areas nothing but a mere wilderness. All of these things were as favorable to the defense as they were unfavorable to the Union Army and Lee availed himself of every advantage in the most skillful manner, particularly as to forcing his adversary to make battle in dense woods where Grant's artillery was in a measure neutralized, and where the Northern infantry was at a disadvantage as compared with their Southern antagonists. The strenuousness of this campaign tested to an exhaustive degree the efficiency of the organization that had been adopted for the artillery, the result being that there was nothing material to be suggested by way of improvement.

This is perhaps a proper place to note that in this campaign mortars were for the first time introduced in the Army of the Potomac for field service. This occurred at a point where the enemy held a position on the farther side of a river over which it was desirable for the Union forces to construct a bridge. So strongly was he entrenched that no amount of ordinary firing could dislodge him, and it was not until a battery of Coehorns were brought up from the Artillery Reserve that a vertical fire could be brought to reach his position behind breastworks. This kind of fire, so strange to him, soon made him abandon the position. From this time on mortars were in constant use. As the entrenched lines of the contending armies were always in close proximity—generally within easy range of the Coehorns—these pieces, portable by hand, were found very effective for work in the trenches.

After the battle at Cold Harbor, Grant seeing that he could not get to Richmond by "fighting it out on that line," adopted McClellan's plan of changing base to the James River and approaching the Confederate capital by that line. The object of his operations on the south side of the James was to get possession of the railroads leading to Richmond from that direction. Several of these uniting at Petersburg made that place a most desirable objective point, hence the siege of Petersburg, lasting from June 18, 1864, to April 2, 1865. In no sense, however, was the town invested. When Grant approached the place, after crossing the James, he found the enemy in force strongly entrenched on one side of the town. For several days desperate fighting took place, but in vain, to force the enemy back. The later erected more breastworks until in a little while these grew into formidable ramparts stoutly armed with artillery. Grant's troops entrenched in the same manner, and at every available place batteries were put in. From this time on, the entrenchments grew to great strength but without much regard to form or comeliness.

Along these lines, at intervals of six to eight hundred yards, were constructed earthen forts, some of which were laid out with engineering skill, but most of them, especially those that had grown up during the early period of the siege, were without any regularity of trace, merely strong enclosures to keep out the enemy should he come that way. Some of them were quite large, covering several acres of ground and capable of sheltering two or three thousand men. In these the men constructed "gopher holes" to protect themselves from the shells of the enemy and the rigors of the winter.

In appropriate places between the forts, emplacements called batteries were constructed for artillery, sometimes siege pieces, sometimes mortars, but most often field batteries. Artillery was also placed in the forts. The object of having forts along the line was to prevent the enemy, in case he should break the line at any point, from extending the breach beyond the forts to the right and left; as was illustrated when the Confederates broke through at Fort Stedman.

Guns of field batteries when on the line became in fact guns of position, the pieces alone with a good supply of ammunition being at the epaulment. The remaining part of

Union artillery at Petersburg sketched by Alfred R. Waud. Note the coehorn mortar on the right. (*Library of Congress*)

the battery was encamped in some sheltered place near at hand where it was kept in readiness for any emergency. Batteries not having their guns on the line were also held in like readiness. At the time of the attack on Fort Stedman such batteries came in very opportunely, being the main element in repulsing the enemy.

The firing lines being very close to each other, the utmost vigilance was exercised, day and night, to prevent surprise. In this condition of tension it was not unusual for spells of firing to break forth unexpectedly, arousing the entire line. Starting with the pickets it frequently extended to the artillery, bringing on an artillery duel approximating (in noise and smoke at least) to a battle. The "Mine" assault and the assault that closed the siege, April 2, 1865, were the only heavy assaults made by the Federals; and that upon Fort Stedman, March 25, 1865, was the only serious one made by the Confederates.

The Mine assault took place, July 30, 1864, by which time the contending armies had settled themselves firmly behind strong entrenchments. The object of the mine was, by the discharge of several tons of gunpowder under the works of the enemy, to destroy enough of his line to open a way through it for a large storming column to pass and thus secure a lodgment beyond. If fully successful this breach was to lead through the outskirts of the city to the South Side Railroad, the chief goal aimed for, and only about a mile distant.

Preparations for the attack were made by assembling as much artillery as possible along that part of the Federal line confronting the position of the mine. The object of this artillery was by following up the explosion with a powerful fire, to sweep all the field adjacent to the mine so effectively as to prevent the enemy from sending reinforcements to meet their adversary issuing through the breach caused by the explosion. The Second Corps had been massed in reserve, a short distance away, to give support to the corps holding the line confronting the mine position, and in case of success to drive home the attack to the railroad; the corps in reserve had its batteries in readiness to accompany the movement.

The explosion of the mine destroyed about 100 yards of the Confederate line, including within this space, a battery of several field pieces. The Federal artillery opened with vigor, and did its work well. The assaulting column, consisting of a division and some other troops of the Ninth Corps, was thrown into much confusion by having to pass over very broken ground before reaching the crater made by the explosion, and being but feebly led failed to get beyond the crater. The plan was that, once in the breach, the troops would turn to the right and left and thus gain more of the line before the enemy could bring up reinforcements. This part of the plan failed entirely. The troops of the storming column pushed forward until the crater, a huge hole of broken masses of earth intermingled with the fragments of the battery that had been blown up with the parapet, was filled with a disorganized mass of men. In the meanwhile the Confederates were making their way to the rim of the crater from whence they were pouring a pitiless fire upon the squirming mass within. In this manner the crater became a veritable slaughter pen. The enemy found sheltered way to the edge of the crater by means of trenches, already there, leading up from the rear to the position lately occupied by his battery, and were thus secure from the artillery fire now sweeping over the field. Seeing the utter failure of the enterprise, the troops of the assaulting column were recalled from their perilous position, and thus ended the mine assault.

The Confederate assault upon Fort Stedman is supposed to have been, in fact was, part of a deep laid scheme formed by Lee to escape from Grant at Petersburg, and then by rapid marching, endeavor to unite with "Joe" Johnston then confronting Sherman in North Carolina. The two armies thus united were to wipe Sherman out and afterwards to prolong the conflict by turning upon Grant. Lee entrusted the assault upon Fort Stedman to one of his enterprising officers, Major General John B. Gordon, who, with a strong force, was to break through the Federal lines and, by making his way to the rear, so threaten the grand depot at City Point as to cause Grant to withdraw for its defense troops from the extreme left of the line, thus leaving a free passage open for the escape of Lee and his troops.

In execution of his part of this scheme Gordon had massed his troops in a ravine behind that part of the Confederate line confronting Fort Stedman. At this point the lines were little more than 100 yards apart, so near in fact that ordinary picketing was done from the main line of works, a fact which made it less difficult to affect a surprise such as that now attempted by Gordon.

For various reasons the lines of both sides were unusually strong in this vicinity. On the Union side batteries were emplaced so as to cover with their fire every foot of approach, while other batteries, not in position, were so conveniently at hand as to bring their fire to bear in like manner. Altogether there were some 50 field pieces thus arranged, in addition to which there were a dozen or more siege guns emplaced in batteries or small forts forming a line about half a mile in rear of Fort Stedman. This supporting line had been constructed to meet just such an emergency as now confronted Stedman. Gordon, moving from his concealment in the ravine with about 5,000 men, made his assault at early dawn, piercing the Federal line before the troops holding it were fully aroused to a condition of resistance. But as his troops turned to the right and left to gain possession of more of the line, resistance accumulated against them until they were finally checked in both directions. A good deal of this checking was the result of fire from the forts next adjoining Stedman, to the right and left, illustrating the wisdom of having entrenched lines well studded with redoubts. The infantry of adjoining commands, now fully aroused to the gravity of the situation, sprang to their work with boldness, and for a time there was fierce fighting.

A reserve division of infantry [Third Division, Ninth Corps], Brigadier General John F. Hartranft's, was encamped a short distance back, but although prompt in moving, it did not arrive in time to take an active part in the battle. Up to this time in the morning the haziness of the atmosphere had prevented the Federal artillery from firing, fearing that it might injure friend and foe alike; but when the mist lifted, the batteries opened from every direction, delivering their fire so as to cross it in front of Stedman. This fire was so vigorous as to make it extremely hazardous for anyone to attempt crossing the narrow strip separating the two lines of works. Several hundred Federal prisoners had been taken in the assault, but guards conducting them to the Confederate line shrank back before the terrible fire and captors and captives alike took refuge in the "gopher holes" of the fort. Gordon, there in person, urged his troops forward, but soon becoming convinced of the hopelessness of his task ceased all aggressive movements and interested himself only in getting his men back to their lines. He himself got back, but 1,900 and odd of his men remained captive, in addition to which were about 500 killed and wounded. The Federal loss in killed and wounded was not so large, while that in prisoners was comparatively crippling.

As the haze of the morning began to disappear, Gordon from his position at Stedman saw on the side of the hill before him many batteries and on the crest of the ridge a long line which he took to be a heavy line of infantry, but which in reality was a harmless mass of spectators attracted there by such unusual commotion. It was the sight of this line dimly seen by him that made Gordon falter more than anything else at a time when success seemed most assured to him.

Directly behind the crest of the hill upon which the line of spectators stood ran Grant's railroad, a line hastily constructed to carry supplies from the depot at City Point to the farther extremity of the line at Hatcher's Run, a distance of some 20 miles. The point on the hill referred to was known as Meade's Station, around which was an unusual accumulation of sutlers' and photographers' shanties, teamsters' camps and the like, but most of all quite a settlement of the Christian Commission, which had made it a center from which to do its good work. A little farther beyond was a large hospital camp full of convalescents and attendants, which, when the time came, gave forth a good quota of sightseers. Aroused by the sound of battle at that unusual hour this motley mass rushed to the crest of the hill to see what might be seen; and it was these people that Gordon had mistaken for a heavy line of battle ready to receive him.

The physical part of his defeat was due, however, to the artillery fire encountered by him. Without such fire he would have had plain sailing notwithstanding the stout opposition put up against him by the infantry. The foregoing brief account of the assault on Fort Stedman has been introduced to illustrate the use made of field artillery in siege operations like those at Petersburg.

Gordon's failure proved to Lee the helplessness of his situation at Petersburg and Richmond. Grant, however, frustrated any further attempt at escape by assaulting his lines at Petersburg, thus bringing about a hasty evacuation, resulting in Lee's surrender at Appomattox.

One army corps sufficed for the occupancy of that part of the line adjacent to Petersburg; the other three prolonged the line about 12 miles in the direction of Five Forks. The object of thus extending it was to endeavor to reach around the right of the enemy and thus gain the South Side Railroad, his chief line of communication in this direction. This extension of lines was made by successive steps, resulting in hard fighting and several severe battles, among which may be mentioned Ream's Station and Hatcher's Run. Throughout this entire distance the lines of both contestants became strongly entrenched and many stout earthen forts were erected for the reception of field batteries. In the other direction, that is towards Richmond, a similar line crossing the Appomattox River, included Bermuda Hundred, and crossing the James; swung around to the southward of Richmond to Fair Oaks, a distance altogether, from Hatcher's Run to Fair Oaks, of about 35 miles of continuous line of earthworks; a veritable Torres Vedras in extent.

During all these operations the field batteries played no idle part. They shared in all the marches, in the fighting, and in the wearisome vigils of the trenches. Under whatever condition, the system of organization under which they were acting proved most satisfactory. Not being attached either to divisions or brigades they were more systematically cared for and their tours of duty in the trenches more uniformly equalized.

Harmonious cooperation existed between the artillery and infantry commanders on the line; a condition due largely to the fact that local commanders on the line, having been relieved from the care and responsibilities of batteries, did not feel it incumbent on themselves to assume directions in matters of technical administration. The artillery brigade organization for each corps still continued without change, and the officers commanding these brigades, and their assistants, made it their business to see that batteries were properly posted along the line of entrenchments. In this way the maximum of efficiency was secured.

The final assault on the Confederate lines took place April 2, 1865, causing Lee to withdraw from both Petersburg and Richmond, and endeavor to escape from Grant by forced marches southward. The Federal army took up immediately the pursuit, the batteries upon the lines hitching up and moving out as though nothing had happened during their eleven months of siege work. The campaign from Petersburg to Appomattox was a chase intermingled with some good sharp fighting in all of which the artillery had its share; and this closed the war so far as the Army of the Potomac and the Confederate Army of Northern Virginia were concerned.

Union artillery behind infantry lines firing at Confederate troops on the far right during the battle at Stones River, Murfreesboro, Tennesee, December 31, 1862. The original caption states, "The enemy while advancing at the overcoats, supposing them to be Union Soldiers lying down; they were allowed to advance to the point represented, when the artillery and musketry opened upon them and they were repulsed with heavy loss. Representing General Palmer's Division, and General Rousseau's Division; as seen from the position of the 15th an 19th Regulars while supporting Guenther's and Loomis' Batteries. (*Library of Congress*)

EIGHT

STONES RIVER

THE ORGANIZATION OF THE two principal western armies, that of the Ohio under Major General Don Carlos Buell, and that of the Tennessee under Grant, was effected about the same time as that of the Army of the Potomac under McClellan, a sketch of which has been given previously. The Army of the Ohio, or as it was subsequently called, the Army of the Cumberland, constituted the center, while the Army of the Potomac and the Army of the Tennessee were the left and right, respectively, of the grand army that stretched across the northern border of the rebellious states from the Atlantic to the Mississippi. This central army, called into existence at and about Louisville, Kentucky, consisted, as first organized, of seven divisions of infantry, each of three brigades. Some had four, but three was the established rule. To each brigade was attached a field battery. In each division one of the battery commanders was designated as chief of artillery, but his functions were, as in the Army of the Potomac, merely nominal, and those of the chief of artillery of the army were simply administrative, not those of actual command. The organization of the artillery, therefore, ascended no higher than the individual battery, the scope of service of which was limited to that of a small body of infantry. There was not, as in the Army of the Potomac, an artillery reserve or any other body of batteries to compensate for the defects arising from the dispersion of batteries to brigades.

The artillery of this army consisted at first, and for a long period afterwards, of every variety of gun known to the service, and for want of proper adjustment of these the batteries were of mixed calibers and kind. Some even had three kinds of pieces, while most of them had two kinds, smooth-bores and rifles, or smooth-bores and howitzers, intermixed. But few had pieces all of one kind, and this made great confusion and difficulty in the supply of ammunition and other stores.

Buell's army, as thus organized, consisted of 79,334 infantry and 28 light and two siege batteries, together with 12 regiments of cavalry numbering 11,496 men, making a total of 94,765 men. The batteries, as a rule, had six pieces each. A few had but four pieces. At first there were no horse batteries, regularly designated and equipped as such. These gradually grew into existence as the cavalry developed and necessity called for their service.

Buell designated four of his divisions, commanded respectively by major generals George H. Thomas, Alexander "Aleck" McDowell McCook, William Nelson, and John J. Crittenden, to constitute a movable army under his personal supervision, and which, after the capture of Forts Henry and Donelson, by the Army of the Tennessee under Grant, was to unite with the latter army, the whole under Halleck, for a projected campaign against the enemy's position at Corinth, Mississippi. This mobilized portion of the Army of the Ohio, with its cavalry and artillery, made an effective force of 37,000 troops. The remainder, about 36,000 effectives, were assigned to the duty of maintaining his long lines of communication and to guarding avenues of approach through Tennessee and Kentucky to Cincinnati and Louisville. The 20,000 men belonging to the army not included in the above, comprised the sick and non-effectives and the recruits, many not yet armed, in camps about Cincinnati and Louisville.

Meanwhile, Grant had organized the Army of the Tennessee and established it in camps at Shiloh, on the Tennessee River, awaiting the arrival of Buell's army and of Halleck to take command of both in the campaign against Corinth, Mississippi, distant about 25 miles. On the 6th of April (1862) the enemy, under General Albert S. Johnston, making an unexpected attack on Grant, threw his army into confusion and forced it back upon the landing at the river, where it found shelter for the night behind a line of artillery hastily formed from the remnants of batteries that had been driven back with the infantry, together with some siege guns which happened most opportunely to be at that place.

Buell, hastening forward, crossed the river with three of his divisions, and uniting with Grant, drove the enemy from the field on the following morning and regained the camping ground of the previous day. In this battle the batteries with Buell took an active part, some of them a heroic part, but there was nothing in the engagement to indicate whether the organization adopted for the artillery of the Army of the Ohio was on the whole good or bad.

Halleck arrived on the 11th, and assuming command, cautiously moved upon the enemy at Corinth, where he arrived on the 30th of the following month. The enemy evacuated the place, part of his troops under Major General Pierre G. T. Beauregard remaining in Mississippi, while the larger part under Bragg, moved eastward to secure possession of the important strategic position of Chattanooga, from which to operate through the states of Tennessee and Kentucky to the Ohio River. Buell was detached with his army to operate against Bragg's movements, but in doing this he was handicapped by Halleck's instructions to repair and keep open the Memphis and Charleston railroad, running parallel to the enemy's front, and easily destroyed by him as fast as rebuilt. These conditions enabled Bragg to reach Chattanooga in advance of Buell, and screened by the ridges of the Alleghenies, he pushed his way rapidly through eastern Tennessee into Kentucky, and was heading directly for Cincinnati and Louisville.

Buell, abandoning Halleck's impracticable railroad project, hastened to intercept Bragg's movements, which he finally did when the latter was upon the threshold of the cities above mentioned, and brought him to bay at Perryville, a village about 60 miles southeast of Louisville. Here, on the 8th of October 1862, a sharp battle was fought by part of the troops of each army, and proved sufficiently decisive to cause Bragg to continue his retrograde movement out of Kentucky into Tennessee, where he put his army into winter cantonment at Murfreesboro, a village on Stones River, 30 miles south of Nashville.

After the battle of Perryville, Buell began to concentrate his army at Nashville, a point which to the end of the war continued to be of great strategic value. But this action not being approved by Halleck, now acting as general-in-chief at Washington, Buell was relieved from command and Rosecrans assigned to it in his place. The latter, seeing the wisdom of Buell's plans, continued them, notwithstanding the strong and persistent opposition of Halleck.

The order of the War Department making this change of commanders designated this army as the Fourteenth Army Corps, a designation which it held until after the battle of Stones River, a couple of months after, when it was changed to that of the Army of the Cumberland, an honored name which it bore to the end. Rosecrans organized it while it was the Fourteenth Corps into the "Right Wing," the "Center," and the "Left Wing," commanded respectively by "Aleck" McCook, Thomas, and Crittenden, with five divisions in the "Center" and three in each of the wings. The organization of divisions remained as before and the batteries continued assigned to the infantry brigades. Rosecrans had as chief of artillery Colonel James Barnett of the 1st Ohio Light Artillery

Regiment, who exercised functions confined entirely to administrative matters, with scarcely the shadow of actual command. Each division had a nominal chief, only one of whom was a field officer, a major, who had over him a captain as chief of artillery of the "Wing." Colonel Barnett and this major were the only field officers of artillery in this entire army. The senior battery commander in each division, with one exception, acted, or was supposed to act, as its chief of artillery in addition to commanding his own battery. The individual batteries, being assigned to brigades, were under direct control of the brigade commander, or in fact of any one superior in rank to their own commanders, who chose to give them orders. They were, as it were, orphans without any of their own kin to care for them.

General Buell, while he showed marked talent and capacity as an organizer and disciplinarian, and gave to the army which he organized an impress which it never lost, failed entirely to grasp the role to be performed by artillery since the introduction of the rifled musket and artillery of greater range and precision. He was a close student, but failed to observe the changes that had taken place since the books which he studied were written. As assistant adjutant general and military adviser of Secretary of War John B. Floyd, just before the war, he was the parent of the blunders in reference to artillery matters so pointedly referred to by General Hunt in his paper in the *Journal of the Military Service Institution.*

Rosecrans, in taking command of the army, continued with vigor the work which Buell had commenced of repairing the road from Nashville back to Louisville, a distance of 185 miles. This important road had been so thoroughly destroyed by Bragg during his advance into Kentucky that it was not reopened until the latter part of November. During the following month every effort was made to supply the troops with greatly needed clothing, rations, and ammunition, and also to accumulate such quantity of all supplies as to provide against future interruptions. Bragg, appreciative of the importance of this line to Rosecrans, organized large cavalry commands, which he sent under brigadier generals John H. Morgan and Joseph Wheeler, to break it up. With this knowledge, Rosecrans, on the 26th of December, put his army in motion to attack the enemy at Murfreesboro. Bragg's outlying troops in the direction of Nashville, falling back, resisted by brisk skirmishing the advance of Rosecrans, until on the afternoon of the 30th, the latter having pushed close up to the main line of the enemy at Murfreesboro, the resistance approximated the magnitude of a battle.

Murfreesboro, a country village near the center of the State of Tennessee, has no military importance of its own, except that it stands across the Louisville and Chattanooga railroad, the line of approach for Rosecrans to the latter place, the great strategic point aimed for. It is also the center from which radiate numerous roads through a fertile and abundant country from which the Confederate army drew many supplies. About a mile to the northwest of the town, flowing northward, is Stones River, an inconsiderable tributary of the Cumberland River. Directly west of the town its course is northward, soon to trend to the northwest. It was within this bend that was fought the principal part of the battle of Stones River, or as the Confederates designate it, of Murfreesboro. In ordinary seasons this river is but an insignificant stream, fordable at almost any point by infantry, and with numerous fords everywhere for artillery. The Nashville railroad, crossing this stream at the town, pursues a straight course almost due northwest. The Nashville turnpike, after crossing the stream at nearly the same point, crosses the railroad at an acute angle and then pursues its course on the west side of the railroad and approximately parallel with it. This turnpike, being Rosecrans' line of communication with his base at Nashville, was of the utmost importance to him. It was furthermore the line upon which he formed his broken troops and therefore constitutes an important feature of the battlefield. Upon the approach of Rosecrans, Bragg formed his army directly across this road,

STONES RIVER ★ 241

about two miles from the town, and with the exception of Major General John C. Breckenridge's division, the whole of his line was beyond the river from the town. His troops were in two lines on an undulating eminence in the edge of the woods with open fields in front. The first line was strongly entrenched. The second was about 600 yards in rear of the first. On the opposite side of the open fields, also in the edge of the woods and on an undulating eminence, Rosecrans established his line of battle almost parallel with that of his antagonist. The two lines had an average distance apart of about 1,200 yards.

Breckenridge's division, the extreme right of Bragg's army, was on the east side of the river, with its right retired so as to cover that flank and the Lebanon road reaching the town from that direction. On the left of Breckenridge came the division of Major General Jones M. Withers, with its right resting on the river. To the left of Withers came the divisions of major generals Benjamin F. Cheatham, Patrick R. Cleburne and John P. McCown, in the order mentioned. The right wing was commanded by Lieutenant General Leonidas Polk, and the left by Lieutenant General William J. Hardee. The extreme right of the line, beyond Breckenridge, was guarded by Wheeler's cavalry, while upon the left was that of Brigadier General John A. Wharton, both exceedingly enterprising in cutting off everything not lying close behind Rosecrans' main line. The lines of each army, exclusive of the cavalry, were about three miles long.

The Federal army was disposed entirely on the west side of the river. The "Left Wing," under Crittenden, consisted of the divisions of brigadier generals Thomas J. Wood, Horatio P. Van Cleve, and John M. Palmer. The first two massed near the river preparatory to the attack contemplated by Rosecrans on the following morning. Palmer was in line with his left resting on the river and his right extending beyond the railroad and turnpike near their point of intersection. This point became interesting as the scene of some of the most desperate fighting of the battle. Palmer was joined upon his right by Brigadier General James S. Negley's division of Thomas' command, the "Center." The other division of Major General Lovell H. Rousseau, together with Colonel Moses B. Walker's brigade, was in reserve behind Negley. The remainder of Thomas' command had been left behind to guard Nashville and the railroad back to Louisville.

Next upon the right of Negley came the divisions of brigadier generals Philip H. Sheridan, Jefferson C. Davis and Richard W. Johnson, all of McCook's "Right Wing." Each of the divisions on the line had one of its three brigades in reserve as a support to the two on the line. The batteries were with the brigades to which they were attached and each brigade commander exercised control over his own battery. Rosecrans' line thus consisted of 10 brigades and the same number of batteries, in line, together with five brigades and a like number of batteries in immediate support. In addition to these, the divisions of Wood and Van Cleve were held in mass with the batteries to cross the river on the following morning for the purpose of attacking Breckenridge.

The ground occupied by the Federal troops was slightly undulating, rocky, and with but few exceptions, covered with a dense thicket of cedars, forming a good covering for the movements of infantry, but impracticable for batteries except where roads were cut through. Towards the left and rear, along the turnpike and railroad, the country was more open, and it was here that Rosecrans formed his final line when driven from the first position. The batteries, scattered along the line as just described, were posted according to the individual notions of the respective brigade commanders as to the functions of artillery in a general engagement. Generally, each battery was kept intact, but sometimes they were broken, with their sections separated. The sequel will show how this arrangement of the artillery turned out.

Rosecrans' army, as it thus stood confronting the enemy, consisted of 117 regiments of infantry, 18 regiments of cavalry, and 32 batteries of 185 guns. Bragg's army consisted of 107 regiments of infantry, 18 of cavalry, (not counting those of the brigades of Morgan and Nathan B. Forrest, absent raiding the railroad) and 24 batteries of about 120 guns. As a rule, the Confederate regiments were stronger than those of the Federal army, and it is therefore probable that the infantry and cavalry of the two opposing forces on this occasion were about equal, while superiority in artillery was greatly in favor of Rosecrans.

In numbers, Rosecrans' returns for December 30th, the day preceding the battle, give his strength as 41,421 infantry, 2,223 artillery, and 3,296 cavalry, making a total present of 46,940, or an effective for line of battle of about 43,400. In actual fighting force the two opposing forces were as nearly equal, as to numbers, as it is practicable for armies to be, and in organization they were almost identical. Bragg, like Rosecrans, had his batteries attached to brigades, and neither had any reserve artillery.

Rosecrans proposed to himself to take the initiative, and his plan of battle was to occupy the attention of Bragg's left wing under Hardee by demonstrations with McCook's right wing, while Wood's and Van Cleve's divisions of Crittenden's left wing crossed the river to attack Breckenridge and drive him from the high ground which he occupied, and upon which batteries were to be established to take in flank and rear of the main line of the Confederates on the other side of the river. At the same time the divisions of Palmer and Negley were to move forward to the attack. The whole right of the enemy, thus assaulted in flank and front, was expected to give way, and being doubled back on the left, the entire army was to be driven off to the westward and from its lines of communication, with a view to its utter destruction as a military force.

The only condition deemed necessary for the entire success of this plan was that McCook should hold fast his position on the right for three hours. This McCook assured Rosecrans he was fully able to do. The extreme right was held by two brigades, brigadier generals August Willich's and Edward M. Kirk's, of Johnson's division, which for the purpose of covering the flank, were retired almost at right angles with the line of Davis' division, the one next on the left. Johnson had his headquarters a mile and more in rear, through the cedar brake, and here he had his reserve brigade with its battery. Willich and Kirk had their batteries with them, but not in position to guard against surprise. McCook had no chief of artillery to give even a nominal supervision over the batteries of his wing; neither did Johnson have a chief. Everything was left to brigade commanders to be managed in their own way. Captain Warren P. Edgarton, commanding Battery E, 1st Ohio Light Artillery Regiment, attached to Kirk's brigade, says in his report: "General Kirk pointed out a spot about 100 yards in the rear of the position I then occupied, sheltered by a heavy growth of timber, and ordered me to bivouac there for the night. I represented to him that I could not place my guns 'in battery' there, or defend myself if assaulted. He replied that I should be protected, and that ample notice should be given when I was expected to take a position in line of battle. After I had brought my guns into park, the right of the brigade was thrown across the muzzles in front." This was a fair sample of the posting of batteries along the whole line. When the surprise came, this captain managed to get in a few shots, but was soon overrun by the enemy and he and all his guns captured.

The right flank of McCook's wing, held by Johnson's division, rested on no natural obstacle and no artificial one was created for it, it was virtually in the air. Rosecrans had no reserve artillery with which to strengthen any weak point; but even had Johnson's three batteries been properly posted and united, and the infantry supporting them entrenched and on the alert, Hardee could not have overrun this flank as he did, and McCook could probably have held the position for the appointed three hours. Rosecrans did not personally inspect this part of his line nor send any competent person to do it for him. He left it all to McCook, who seems to have left it to Johnson, who had his camp beyond reach of the direct supervision of his troops.

During the night of the 30th, Bragg formed his plan of battle, almost an identical counterpart of that of Rosecrans. Hardee, on the left, was to advance McCown's and Cleburne's divisions against Rosecrans' right, held, as we have seen, by McCook's wing, which being broken and thrust back, Polk was to advance Withers' and Cheatham's divisions and force back the center; the whole movement to be made by a steady wheel of the entire line on Polk's right as a pivot. By this plan McCook's "Right Wing" was to be driven back and upon the center and left, and the whole line finally driven from its communication with Nashville and to utter defeat.

Rosecrans' order was to commence the movement at seven in the morning; Bragg's to attack at daylight, which gave him a start of about a half hour of his adversary, and this start gave Bragg the initiative and was decisive of the events that followed. Promptly at the appointed hour Wood and Van Cleve started with their divisions, and were partly across the river when the sound of battle announced an attack by the enemy upon the extreme right. Soon Rosecrans received intelligence that his right wing was broken and fast crumbling to pieces to the rear. This at once threw him upon the defensive and it was necessary to arrest further movement on the left. The half hour's start of his adversary that Bragg got changed every phase of Rosecrans' plans. Wood's and Van Cleve's divisions were immediately recalled and hastened towards the right and rear to assist in checking and repelling the enemy, now gaining such alarming headway in that direction.

At half-past six o'clock Hardee commenced to swing the divisions of McCown and Cleburne around to envelop McCook's right flank. While the ground was quite unknown to the Federals, it was entirely familiar to their opponents, a circumstance giving great advantage on a field so intricate with woods and thickets. Mention has already been made of the defenseless condition of McCook's right. Although pickets guarded the front and flank a short distance out, there was otherwise but little vigilance or preparation, as if in a state of expectancy. Willich had gone to see his division commander a mile and more to the rear and the battery horses had been sent to water. The pickets were driven in by the steady rush of the enemy who swept through the brigades of Willich and Kirk like a tornado. Two of the guns attached to Willich's brigade were "in battery" guarding a road from the westward; the other four were in park in rear of the infantry. A few discharges of canister were fired from most of these pieces, but soon three of them fell into the hands of the enemy. Two others stampeded with the infantry through the cedars, while the remaining one, under the battery commander, fell back and from time to time joined in attempts made to check the enemy. The battery with Kirk's brigade came "in battery," and as soon as its front was cleared of the stampeding infantry, fired a few rounds of canister and then fell into the hands of the enemy, captured entire. Its captain, one of its lieutenants, and many of its men were wounded and captured at their pieces, while a number were killed.

The battery attached to Johnson's reserve brigade encamped in the woods far to the rear, hastened forward as soon as possible, and met the enemy in hot pursuit of the other two brigades. After a gallant fight, during which its infantry support fell back, it too was forced to retire with the loss of two pieces and many men and horses disabled.

Everything considered, these three batteries did all that could be expected of them under such disadvantageous circumstances. It is easily imagined, and not improbable, that if the 18 guns of these batteries had been united in one mass, and well supported by infantry strongly entrenched, McCook's right would not have been routed incontinently as it was. Bragg's active cavalry and scouts had discovered the loose condition of things on the extreme right and his attack was made with the confidence of assured success. In every

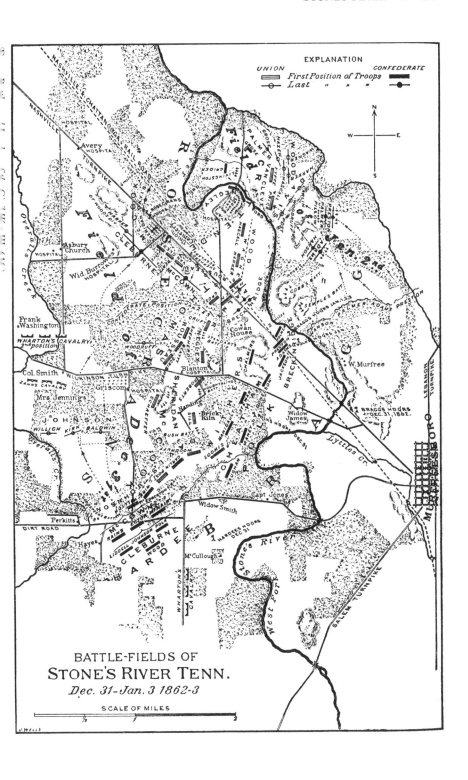

BATTLE-FIELDS OF
STONE'S RIVER TENN.
Dec. 31-Jan. 3 1862-3

SCALE OF MILES

essential respect the break of this wing was similar to the rout of the Eleventh Corps at Chancellorsville.

Johnson's division being driven from its position on the line uncovered that of Davis, the right brigade of which, Colonel Philip S. Post's, joined on to Johnson's left brigade. Colonel William E. Woodruff's brigade was on the left of Post, while Colonel William P. Carlin's was in reserve. As soon as possible, Post's brigade was swung back to face the enemy, now approaching from that direction. Captain Oscar F. Pinney's 5th Wisconsin Independent Light Artillery Battery, attached to this brigade, changed its front to conform to this movement and came "in battery " in a cornfield where it opened a spirited fire upon the enemy, exultant over the hasty rout of Johnson's division, but now temporarily checked by this fire and that of the infantry. Soon, however, the infantry began to melt away and the battery was compelled to retire, leaving its captain and a number of wounded men in the hands of the enemy. Owing to the disabling of many horses one of the pieces had to be abandoned while the remainder were hauled off chiefly by hand.

Captain William A. Hotchkiss' 2nd Minnesota Independent Light Artillery Battery was attached to the reserve brigade, but during the night had an advanced position from which it was withdrawn just before daylight. When the attack fell upon this brigade, forcing it to fall back across an open field to the edge of the woods where it made a momentary stand, the battery was enabled to fire a few rounds. The brigade then retired about a mile and made another brief stand in the edge of a cedar thicket from which it again soon retired to the final position near the Nashville turnpike. This battery lost no guns.

Captain Stephen J. Carpenter's 8th Wisconsin Independent Light Artillery Battery was attached to Woodruff's brigade, which connected with the right of Brigadier General Joshua W. Sill's brigade of Sheridan's division. The brigade commander had this battery divided into half batteries, but with only one piece in position. The brigade made a determined resistance for a few minutes and the battery was enabled to do some good work before being forced to retire. The captain and a number of men were killed and a number of men and horses disabled, but no guns were lost. Here was another block of three batteries rendered almost useless by the manner in which they were dispersed along the line.

Davis' division made a stubborn resistance, but its position in line brought it in front of Cheatham's division, which now made an assault upon it in front while the divisions of McCown and Cleburne, having swept Johnson away, were attacking it in flank and working around to its rear. The enemy speaks of this as being one of the hotly contested points of the battle, but Davis was unable to withstand this overwhelming attack upon his front and flank, and being forced back, uncovered Sheridan's right. Sheridan up to this time had been hotly engaged with the enemy in front, but was compelled now to change front to meet the new danger upon his flank. Before making this change of front his three batteries had been posted with their brigades in the usual way and were actively engaged. But in making the change of front, which was a difficult maneuver through the thickets and under the assaults of the enemy, the batteries became shaken loose from their brigades and naturally gravitated together and towards some open space at the angle formed by Sheridan's division in its new position and that of Negley still on the original line and next on Sheridan's left. It so happened that two of Negley's batteries, not able to find positions with their brigades on the line by reason of the density of the cedars, were on this flank at the open space, now the angle, making in all a battery of 30 pieces, which for nearly four hours resisted the most desperate efforts of the enemy.

The Confederate General Polk, referring in his report to this position, says: "His batteries, which occupied commanding positions, and enabled him to sweep the open field in his front, were served with admirable skill and vigor, and were well supported." He then describes the terrible effect of their fire, and goes on to say: "Nothing but a charge could meet the demands of the occasion. Orders were given to take the batteries at all hazards, and it was done. The batteries, two in number, were carried in gallant style. Artillerists were captured at their pieces, a large number of whom and of their infantry support were killed upon the spot."

Withers, commanding one of Polk's divisions, says of the same thing: "Opposite there were three batteries strongly supported by infantry. The capture of the batteries and rout of the supports was a necessity. Anderson was, therefore, directed to take the batteries at any cost." He then describes how he reinforced Anderson, and the fire to which his troops were exposed, how they were repulsed several times, but finally succeeded in driving the infantry supports and capturing six guns of one battery and two of another. He mentions his losses in doing this as something phenomenal.

Sheridan, after describing his change of front, says: "In this position I was immediately attacked, when one of the most sanguinary contests of the day occurred." After describing the advance of the enemy over the open ground with his lines and masses of infantry and three batteries of artillery, he again says: "The contest became terrible. The enemy made three attacks, and were three times repulsed, the artillery range of the respective batteries being not over 200 yards."

The charge of the enemy that captured the eight guns broke the angle held by the artillery, and the loss of this caused Sheridan's whole line to fall back through the thicket to the new line now forming along the turnpike. The stubborn tenacity with which Sheridan had held his position, it was now about 11:00 A.M., enabled Rosecrans to make such disposition of his available troops as to establish a new line along the Nashville turnpike. Upon this line the scattered fragments of Johnson's and Davis' divisions were now being rallied, and it was to this that Sheridan's division retired, but not entirely unmolested by Hardee's divisions which, by this time, had worked their way well around in Sheridan's rear.

The divisions of Davis and Sheridan were of about equal strength and composed of the same kind of troops. They were, in fact, approximately identical, and fought with equal skill by their gallant commanders, but with vastly different results. The former was forced to yield the ground after a brief, but brave struggle. The latter held on against even greater odds for nearly four hours, and then was forced to give way only because the position held by his artillery was broken and some of his guns captured. The only reason apparent for this difference is, and it is certainly a logical one, that by a fortuitous circumstance Sheridan's batteries were shaken loose from the brigades to which they were attached and by still greater good fortune were united at a point where their massed fire held the enemy in check until their position was carried by successive assaults of the enemy. Davis' batteries remained scattered, and gave in consequence but little support either to each other or to the infantry; nor could they deal upon the enemy the stunning blows of guns in mass.

This was a momentous crisis in the events of the battle. It was of vital moment that the break in the right wing should not extend itself to the center and left until a new line could be established to stay the further progress of the enemy. This was done by the batteries that had so fortunately come together at the angle between Sheridan and Negley. They were captains Charles Houghtaling's Battery C, 1st Illinois Light Artillery Regiment, Asahel K. Bush's 4th Independent Indiana Light Artillery Battery, and Henry Hescock's Battery G, 1st Missouri Light Artillery Regiment, of Sheridan's division, and Lieutenant Alexander Marshall's Battery G and Captain Frederick Shultz's Battery M of Negley's division, both of the 1st Ohio Light Artillery Regiment. Houghtaling, after losing his battery, joined his remaining men to batteries that were short-handed and did further noble work in the fight.

While Sheridan was so stoutly holding on in the manner just related, Rousseau, whose division of Thomas' command, held as a reserve, was sent through the cedar brake to the right and rear of Sheridan to check the progress of the enemy now following closely upon the broken divisions of Johnson and Davis. Rousseau had but two batteries with him at this time, Captain Cyrus O. Loomis' Battery A, 1st Michigan Light Artillery Regiment, and Lieutenant Francis L. Guenther's Battery H, 5th U.S. Artillery Regiment, both attached to brigades; the other battery being absent with Colonel John C. Starkweather's brigade, guarding a ford several miles down the river. Rousseau, deploying the two brigades with him, advanced into the cedar thicket. The batteries endeavored to follow their brigades, but found it impossible to do so, on account of the density of the growth. Guenther, attached to Lieutenant Colonel Oliver L. Shepherd's brigade of regulars, pointing out this fact to Thomas, who was present with Rousseau, was directed by him to take position, together with Loomis, in the open field, where their batteries would be of service in the event of the repulse of their brigades, a thing that did soon happen, and most bloodily, too.

These two brigades encountered a large part of Hardee's wing, and besides being vastly outnumbered, were at a still greater disadvantage on account of the dense growth of small trees or shrubs covering the field. The Confederate troops, from habits of life, being accustomed to the brakes, jungles, and hummocks of the South, were more at home in such a situation than those of the North, and man to man were superior to them in such thickets as those in which this fight took place.

The brigades were forced back out of the thicket closely followed by the enemy. As soon as the fronts of the batteries were cleared of their friends, the guns opened with canister, causing the enemy to retire hastily to the concealment of the thicket. This enabled the infantry to rally and form line upon the batteries. Of this Rousseau says: "As the enemy emerged from the woods in great force, shouting and cheering, the batteries of Guenther and Loomis, doubled-shotted with canister, opened upon them. They moved straight ahead for awhile, but were finally driven back with immense loss. In a little while they rallied again, and, as it seemed, with fresh troops, and assailed our position, and were again, after a fierce struggle, driven back. Four deliberate and fiercely sustained assaults were made upon our position and repulsed."

Not only did Loomis' and Guenther's batteries check and repulse the enemy at this crisis, but they formed the nucleus of a line upon which other batteries and troops formed, until the position proved impregnable to the enemy. This was the second line and owed its existence largely, if not entirely, to the seemingly trifling circumstance that Guenther was direct-ed by Thomas to put his battery in a certain position with ref-erence to the thicket into which the brigades penetrated. The ordinary course would have been for Guenther and Loomis to have struggled as best they could after their brigades into the brake with their batteries, where, unable to do any service, they would inevitably have been captured. But Thomas, him-self a veteran artillerist and a thoughtful man, directed differ-ently, and the result was most fortunate for the Federal army.

So urgent was the demand for troops to check the enemy, now seemingly upon the verge of breaking Rosecrans' army to atoms, that Captain James St. Clair Morton was sent with his engineer brigade to join Rousseau's brigades on the right. Attached to Morton's brigade was Captain James H. Stokes' Illinois Light Artillery Battery, which wisely abstaining from entangling itself in the thicket, took position on the right of Loomis and Guenther. At the same time the two brigades of Van Cleve's division, lately recalled from the other side of the river, were also hastened to the right next to the engineer brigade. One of the two batteries of these brigades, Captain George R. Swallow's 7th Indiana Independent Light Artillery Battery, followed its brigade as far as possible into the thicket, where, fortunately finding some open ground, it was enabled to do some good firing, though ineffectual in checking the enemy. When his brigade was driven back, Swallow, by great effort and good fortune saved his battery, which he then placed upon Guenther's line. Lieutenant Alanson J. Stevens, commanding Pennsylvania Independent Light Artillery Battery B, with the other brigade, referring in his report to this part of the battle, says: "We found everything there in confusion, and it impossible to follow our brigade, and the battery nearly in the lines of the enemy. You then gave me permission to fight on my own hook and do the best in my power." With this, he too placed his battery on Guenther's line.

Colonel Charles G. Harker's brigade of Wood's division came up with its battery on the right of Van Cleve's brigades. Harker thus describes the situation as he then found it: "On approaching the right, much confusion was visible; troops marching in every direction; stragglers to be seen in great numbers, and teamsters in great consternation endeavoring to drive their teams they knew not whither. My progress was impeded by the confusion, while the enemy was pouring shot and shell upon us from at least three different directions." Extricating his brigade from this confusion, he passed on and took position on the extreme right, where he immediately deployed his brigade, and moving to the front, soon encountered the enemy in great force. These he promptly engaged, and sending his battery to as favorable a position as he could find, resolutely baffled the enemy in every effort to get further around on that flank, until by the falling back of Van Cleve's brigades, he too was forced to withdraw, in doing which his battery, Captain Cullen Bradley's 6th Ohio Independent Light Artillery Battery, lost temporarily two of its guns. They were immediately retaken by a gallant charge of the 13th Michigan Infantry Regiment. Bradley then established his battery on Guenther's line. This was decidedly the most critical period of the battle, and had it not been for the thoughtful circumstance of withholding Guenther and Loomis from following their brigades into the entanglements of the thicket, and posting them on ground favorable for their fire, which they were able to hold until other batteries and troops formed upon them, the whole of Rosecrans' army would have been routed.

Although the line thus formed was, so to speak, an accidental line, it was the best that could have been taken under the circumstances, even after a most careful selection. It covered, still, the turnpike, Rosecrans' communication with Nashville, and was upon ground more open and favorable for the artillery, which soon proved to be his chief reliance. The broken divisions of Johnson and Davis were collected here, and what artillery they had remaining was added to that already in position, making altogether a battery so formidable as to resist every assault of the enemy.

The Confederate commanders give due credit for the obstinate resistance they met with before reaching this point, but it was here and by these batteries that they first met with a check that arrested them entirely. Hardee, after describing how he collected and reformed his troops and replenished their ammunition, says: "It was now past 3 o'clock. In moving through the open ground to drive the enemy from the last positions they held, near the railroad, a fierce and destructive enfilading fire of artillery was poured upon the right of Cleburne's division from batteries massed near the railroad embankments. At this critical moment the enemy brought up a fresh line to oppose our wearied troops." This line was in reality the new line formed as just described. Hardee then goes on to describe how he was repulsed, and returning twice, was again each time repulsed, until he finally abandoned further attempt to carry this part of the Federal position. He says: "The enemy lay beyond the range of our guns, securely sheltered behind the strong defense of the railroad embankment, with wide, open fields intervening, which were swept by their superior artillery. It would have been folly, not valor, to assail them in this position." This closed the fighting on the right, for this day, December 31st.

Hardee, in his report claims that in woods and brush the Confederate infantry is superior to Federal infantry, but concedes that in open ground, where artillery can have full effect, its superiority gives the latter a decided advantage. The same view was held by all Confederate commanders who, whenever practicable, endeavored to secure the advantage of woods in which to fight.

When Sheridan was forced back and the batteries at the angle between his division and that of Negley were driven from their position, as previously described, the right of Negley was, in its turn, exposed to the onward push of the enemy. His and Palmer's divisions, the only two now remaining on the original line, were assailed by every available man and gun of Polk's wing, and the most persistent efforts were made to crush in this remainder of the Federal line. Palmer's batteries were scattered in the usual way with their brigades, and although most gallantly served, failed to deliver such telling blows as fell from Sheridan's group of batteries. Negley fell back almost immediately after Sheridan, and Palmer soon followed, both taking position on the new line along and in front of the Nashville turnpike.

Rosecrans' entire army had now changed position. From being across and at right-angles with the Nashville pike it was now parallel with it. The left still rested on Stones River, near its former position, while, upon this as a pivot, the whole line had swung back through a quarter circle. The new line, situated on comparatively open ground somewhat elevated and undulating, was hastily entrenched, and the troops occupied it relatively almost as before; that is, McCook on the right, Thomas in the center, and Crittenden on the left.

Rosecrans had lost during the early part of the day 28 pieces of artillery, which falling into the hands of the enemy with a considerable quantity of ammunition about equalized the artillery strength of the opposing forces. His remaining 157 pieces, or a majority of them, were now in position on the new line. For the management of this artillery there were but two field officers, the colonel and major before mentioned, neither of whom had had much experience in this branch of the service, nor on this occasion exercised much authority in directing it. Happily, however, Crittenden's chief of artillery,

John E. Mendenhall, although but a captain, rose to the occasion and assumed command of the batteries on the left, which he managed in such manner as to derive from them the greatest efficiency.

Polk still continued his utmost endeavors to crush and roll back the left of Rosecrans' new line. Breckenridge's division was brought from beyond the river to assist in this, "but the time lost," says Polk, "enabled the enemy to recover his self-possession, to mass a number of heavy batteries, and concentrate a strong infantry force on the position, and thus make a successful attack very difficult." He, however, made several desperate assaults, all of which were repulsed with great slaughter on both sides. The Confederate reports agree that these repulses were due to the concentration of artillery fire upon their masses. Bragg says: "We succeeded in driving him from every position except the strong one held by his extreme left flank, resting on Stones River, and covered by a concentration of artillery of superior range and caliber, which seemed to bid us defiance." It was in reality the very same artillery that he had met earlier in the day and which he had driven back with the infantry to the position he was now endeavoring to take; the only difference being that in the disasters of the forenoon, the batteries to a great extent had become shaken loose from their brigades and thus became able to act as batteries should. They were now in hand and ready for concentrated action.

The contracted line now occupied by Rosecrans necessarily concentrated the batteries and gave to their fire the effect of artillery in mass. It was this that repelled the enemy. The subtle influence of moral effect came in to reassure the infantry, which now stood in equal readiness to meet the enemy.

The ammunition trains had fortunately escaped the swoop of the enemy's cavalry, and taking refuge behind the new line were in convenient positions for replenishing the exhausted boxes of the infantry and the chests of the artillery. The batteries that had been scattered or damaged were brought together and put in condition for further service as rapidly as possible. Mendenhall, taking chief charge of those upon the right, posted them to the best advantage. The captains of those upon the left, being without any specific head, did, each for himself, the best that he could. It will be remembered that there was no organization of the artillery higher than that of the single battery and that all these were scattered to brigades from which most of them had become separated during the operations of the day among the cedar brakes. As might be supposed, battery commanders were subjected to orders and counter-orders from almost any one who chose to give them. This idea is expressed in the report of Charles C. Parsons, one of the battery commanders, who had been ordered to occupy a certain position. He says: "During the night and on the next morning I was ordered by different officers to resume my previous position. I was obliged to decline obeying these orders, owing to those I had received from Captain Mendenhall, directing me to await his own. The position in which I was placed by this conflict of orders was exceedingly painful, but I found myself justified by subsequent events." These events were those attending the final attack made by the enemy for the purpose of establishing batteries on the high ground on the further side of the river for the purpose of enfilading the Federal position, which object was frustrated by this officer and others whose batteries were thus posted for this purpose. Almost every battery commander will recognize in this incident like perplexities in his own experience.

Captain Mendenhall, chief of artillery of the left wing, soon got 43 pieces into position on the elevated ground overlooking the river and covering the left flank. These guns were added to from other corps until they numbered, in all, 58 pieces.

Hardee having failed to force the right of the new line, Polk now redoubled his efforts against the left, the key point of which was a wooded knoll known as the "Round Forest" situated in the acute angle formed by the crossing of the railroad and turnpike. Around this position the fighting was desperate. In addition to his masses of infantry the enemy brought to bear upon it all of his available artillery, but to no purpose, except to add to the slaughter. The brigades of William B. Hazen, Brigadier General Charles Cruft, Brigadier General Milo O. Hascall and others, stood resolutely to their work and gave ample support to the batteries cooperating with them. The enemy made several distinct assaults, each one of which was signally repulsed. How this was done is best stated in the words of Bragg, who says: "Upon this flank, their strongest defensive position, resting on the river bank, the enemy had concentrated not less than twenty pieces of his heaviest artillery [there were in reality more than double this number], masked almost entirely from view, but covering an open space in front of several hundred yards. Supported right, left, and rear by heavy masses of infantry, this position proved impracticable, and after two unsuccessful efforts the attempt to carry it by infantry was abandoned. Our heaviest batteries of artillery and rifled guns of long range were now concentrated in front of, and their fire opened on, this position. After a cannonade of some time the enemy's fire slackened, and finally ceased near nightfall," he might have added, because his batteries were driven away.

This closed the battle for this day. Bragg established his troops in a line parallel with that of the new position occupied by Rosecrans and strongly entrenched it. Breckenridge's division was returned to the further side of the river to prevent the Federals from making any movement in that direction. During the night Rosecrans had all of his reserve ammunition issued, and finding that he had still enough for another day's fighting, resolutely determined to hold his position and await results.

Bragg's batteries, although actively handled and well served, failed to accomplish the work due from them. Like those in Rosecrans' army, they were attached to brigades and thus dispersed without proper command; could act but feebly.

No fortuitous circumstances brought them together in groups whereby their fire could be more effective. Bragg was quick to perceive this defect and before the opening of the next campaign adopted the battalion system of Lee's army at Northern Virginia.

The battle was not renewed as a general engagement on the following day, January 1st, but instead the enemy made close reconnaissance of the Federal position. Each time, however, that he showed himself in any considerable force in front of the cedar thicket in which he was screened, the Federal batteries forced him to retire hastily. In the afternoon Van Cleve's division of Crittenden's corps was sent across the river to occupy the high ground that dominated the left of Rosecrans' line, and which in possession of the enemy would afford him means of enfilading the whole of Rosecrans' line. The other divisions of this corps were moved up near the river in support of Van Cleve, who deployed his brigades at right angles with the river along a low ridge, the summit and sides of which were somewhat open fields.

At daylight on the morning of the 2nd, Bragg gave orders to his corps commanders to feel the Federal position and ascertain the disposition thereon of the troops. Accordingly, a number of batteries were advanced at several places, supported by large bodies of infantry. But these were all speedily driven back to their cover by the Federal batteries in readiness and ever on the alert against any movement of the enemy.

The position on the further side of the river, held by Van Cleve, was menacing to Polk's flank, and Breckenridge was directed to dislodge him and crown the ridge with artillery for the double purpose of saving Polk's flank and of enfilading the Federal line; and for this purpose 10 Napoleon guns were sent him in addition to his own batteries. Breckenridge formed his troops for the attack in two lines, about 200 yards apart, with the artillery between. Captain Felix H. Robertson, in charge of the 10 Napoleons, remonstrated against this arrangement for the artillery, arguing that it could do no good in such a position; that, while it would embarrass the movements of infantry, it would itself be powerless to act because of being covered by the front line. He was, however, overruled in this, and the batteries took the position indicated. In this order the force advanced and soon struck Van Cleve's right brigade resting on the river. This brigade offered stout resistance for a few minutes, but the numbers against it being too great, it fell back in confusion, followed by the other two brigades, all in consternation, across the river. When Breckenridge's troops showed themselves on the ridge, exultingly following Van Cleve, it looked as though Rosecrans' left was doomed to destruction and that his entire line would again be forced from its position, and this time probably to dispersion. But, at this critical moment, Mendenhall's 52 guns opened with an effect thus described by Crittenden in his official report. He says: "They [Breckenridge's troops] cannot be said to have been checked in their advance–from a rapid advance they broke at once into a rapid retreat." Here was presented the strange spectacle of two large bodies of armed men running from each other in the utmost consternation. The left of Breckenridge's lines moving to the attack among the trees along the river bank came under the fire of the infantry on the opposite side and were slaughtered unmercifully. Other troops crossed over to take the place of Van Cleve's division and pursued the flying enemy until dark.

Breckenridge failed to get his artillery into position. Captain Robertson states that the batteries were overrun by the fleeing infantry before they could be placed "in battery," and in addition were so exposed to the artillery fire from the opposite side of the river that they were forced to leave the ground as rapidly as possible, leaving behind them three pieces. The batteries halted on the edge of a wood, hoping to establish a line upon which the infantry would rally, but the latter abandoned the field in spite of every effort to restrain them. The batteries now drew all the fire and they too had to retire still further; and finally after dark, drew off altogether.

Robertson says: "The contagion of flight had spread to the artillery, and it was with great difficulty that several pieces were brought away, owing to the drivers being frightened. . . . There was no organization that I could see or hear of until after the enemy had been checked, [drew off from pursuit, he should have said] save in the artillery. I have never seen troops so completely broken in my military experience." The unwilling testimony of other Confederate witnesses confirms this lurid picture, showing the effect that Mendenhall's guns had when massed upon these troops, the flower of the Confederate army. Breckenridge, after describing how he routed Van Cleve's division, goes on to say:

> It now appeared that the ground we had won was commanded by the enemy's batteries, within easy range, on better ground, on the opposite side of the river. I know not how many guns he had. He had enough to sweep the whole position from the front, the left, and the right, and to render it wholly untenable by our force present of artillery and infantry. . . . We lost three guns, nearly all the horses being killed, and not having the time or men to draw them off by hand. One was lost because there was but one boy left (Private Wright of Captain E. E. Wright's battery) to limber the piece, and his strength was unequal to it.

The repulse of Breckenridge was the well defined effect of artillery in mass. There was no infantry or cavalry combined with it. It was all artillery, pure and simple, and differed essentially from the occurrences of the first day's battle in the right wing, where the batteries, being scattered with brigades, were able to afford but feeble resistance, and all infantry and artillery were swept away.

After the repulse of Breckenridge, Rosecrans hurried across the river a strong force, consisting partly of Crittenden's and McCook's troops, and made a permanent lodgment on the ground from which Van Cleve had been driven. These troops hastily entrenched themselves, and Bragg, realizing their threatening attitude, sent Hardee across with reinforcements for Breckenridge, but Hardee desisted from any serious attack.

To prevent troops being sent to assist Van Cleve against Breckenridge's attack, Polk made heavy demonstrations, in fact a formidable attack, upon the Union right on the opposite side of the river. Seven of his batteries were moved forward to a rise of ground near "Round Forest," and while Mendenhall's batteries were engaged in dispersing Breckenridge, succeeded in gaining a lodgment for their infantry in the "Round Forest," but were unable to gain further ground. The fighting of the infantry at this point was of the most determined and sanguinary nature.

During the following day, January 3rd, but little more than picket firing was indulged in by either side, but this was close and searching. The Federal batteries were kept on the alert and each time any considerable body of the enemy showed itself in front of the thicket it was pelted back. Neither commander felt himself in condition to renew the battle, and during the night of the 3rd, Bragg silently withdrew, taking the road to Tullahoma, another point on the railroad about 30 miles nearer Chattanooga.

This action on the part of Bragg gave to Rosecrans the prestige of victory, which up to this time was decidedly in favor of the Confederates. Bragg gave as his reason for it that he was led to believe from the reports of his cavalry commanders, operating in Rosecrans' rear, that heavy reinforcements for the latter were near at hand, and that these would make him so strong as to enable him to resist all attacks, and that he could not await an attack from Rosecrans because of the low state of his supplies and the care necessary for his sick and wounded. Most of the latter were, however, left behind and had to be cared for by the Federals.

Rosecrans, on account of his exhausted supplies, was unable to give pursuit. Every step he took in that direction carried him still further from his base, communication with which was constantly infested by Bragg's overwhelming force of cavalry. He accordingly cantoned his army for the winter at Murfreesborough, where he remained until the 23rd of the following June, when he resumed his movements against Bragg who had his army strongly entrenched at Tullahoma.

Such was the battle of Stones River, a battle which presents to the military critic some interesting and remarkable features, among which may be mentioned the fact that the numbers of the contestants was as nearly balanced as it is practicable to have opposing armies, neither of which was so situated as to receive assistance beyond his own immediate lines. In this respect it was a square fight in which every division, brigade, regiment and battery of both sides participated. Every organization was represented in the list of losses, and these in the aggregate were about equal and represent a percentage, about 25 percent, seldom reached in European battles, and but rarely excelled in any of the great battles of the Civil War.

The most remarkable features of the battle were the fortuitous circumstances attending the service performed by the artillery of the Federal Army, whereby it was enabled at each crisis to turn what seemed to be inevitable disaster into final victory. A recapitulation of the foregoing account will more fully elucidate this fact. When the two armies were drawn up facing each other for battle, the commander of each formed a plan of battle almost the counterpart of the other. Each was to make a vigorous attack with his left wing, with a view to breaking his opponent's right, which was to be rolled back upon the left and eventually to utter rout and disaster. Both commanders commenced to move at about the same time in the morning, but Bragg struck first, and thus gaining the initiative, at once threw his opponent upon the defensive and upset all of his hopeful plans. Rosecrans' extreme right, taken culpably unawares, made but slight resistance, and this, exposing the right, enabled the enemy to push his way to the right and rear of the line still remaining intact. To meet this flank attack, Sheridan swung back his division, thus making an angle with Negley's division of the original line. Sheridan's three batteries had been arranged in the usual way with his three brigades, but in the change of front became detached in consequence of the cedar thickets, and by a fortunate circumstance gravitated towards the angle before mentioned, where they united with two batteries of Negley's division which happened to be at that position because they too, could not follow their brigades by reason of the thickets. This formed a battery of 30 pieces, which notwithstanding the most desperate efforts of the enemy, held him in check for near four hours, and until another fortuitous circumstance brought other batteries into position to check the enemy effectually at the moment when Bragg's plan for breaking up the Federal Army was in full tide of success. This was the turning point of the battle. The seemingly insignificant circumstance that prevented Guenther's and Loomis' batteries from following their brigades into the thickets, instead of which they posted themselves by Thomas' direction in the open field and thus formed a nucleus for other batteries, prevented in like manner from accompanying their brigades into the wood, was the culminating point of the contest. The enemy, following closely upon the Federal brigades into the open field, got no further than the effective canister range of these guns. The infantry, reassured by this, reformed and gave much needed support to the batteries. Thus a new line sprang into existence at a moment when all was seemingly lost. By sheer accident these batteries were cut loose from their brigades where they could do little or no good and instinctively took position where they did the most eminent service. These were the main features of the battle of the first day, in which it is easy to perceive the very important part enacted by the artillery.

The high ground on the opposite side of the river was an object of much concern to both commanders. Rosecrans sent Van Cleve's division to occupy it. Bragg sent Breckenridge to dislodge Van Cleve and to crown the eminence with artillery. Van Cleve's brigades retired in haste before Breckinridge, but when the troops of the latter came into view and under the fire of Mendenhall's guns they retired in still greater confusion and haste. It was these guns and nothing else that prevented Breckenridge from carrying out his designs and planting his batteries where they would have been disastrous to the Federal line. Polk, to assist Breckenridge and prevent troops from being sent to the assistance of Van Cleve, made the most desperate assaults possible with all the troops at his disposal to break the Federal left at and about "Round Forest," all of which were repulsed by the combined efforts of the infantry and artillery. These were the principal events of the second day's battle, which was the end of the fighting, and here again it will be observed that the artillery did most conspicuous service.

There was perhaps no general battle during the entire war in which the infantry, as a whole, performed its part better than at Stones River, and it is no detraction from its superb conduct to claim for the artillery the credit so justly due the latter. The Federal batteries were handicapped at the start by their dispersion to brigades. So soon, however, as disaster had destroyed this faulty arrangement and given them freedom from such unnatural restraint, they naturally united for the common good, with the results just stated.

Soon after this battle the three grand divisions of the Army of the Cumberland, designated in the battle as the "Center," the "Right" and the "Left" wings, were constituted the Fourteenth, Twentieth, and Twenty-first Army Corps, com-manded respectively by Thomas, "Aleck" McCook, and Crittenden. A fourth, or provisional corps under Major General Gordon Granger was organized, which soon after-wards took the permanent designation of the Fourth Corps, into which the Twentieth and Twenty-first were subsequent-ly merged. The original Fourth Corps of the Army of the Potomac, commanded by Erasmus Keyes, was discontinued and its troops transferred to other organizations.

The artillery of this army continued attached to brigades, as before. Nothing in the way of better arrangement or organization seems to have been suggested for it by the striking events of Stones River. It was not until after the events of Chickamauga that any change was made looking to a more efficient organization.

Alfred R. Waud's drawing of the Confederate line advancing through the woods toward Union troops at Chickamauga, September 19, 1863. (*Library of Congress*)

NINE

CHICKAMAUGA

(FIRST DAY)

As STATED, THE CONFEDERATE ARMY under Bragg withdrew after the battle of Stones River, leaving the Federal army under Rosecrans in possession of the field. Bragg withdrew behind Duck River, some 37 miles distant, and entrenched his army among the rugged hills and defiles around Tullahoma.

Rosecrans continued at Murfreesboro until the 22nd of the following June (1863), when he commenced a series of movements which caused Bragg to leave his strong position and fall back 82 miles across the mountains to Chattanooga. In these operations there was considerable sharp skirmishing and some combats, but nothing approaching a general engagement. Arrived at Chattanooga, Bragg strongly entrenched his position and awaited the development of Rosecrans' plans. The latter immediately commenced preparations for an advance upon Chattanooga, now become his objective; to reach which he had to cross, not only the Tennessee River, in itself a great obstacle, in the presence of an enemy, but several exceedingly rugged ridges of the Cumberland Mountains.

On the 16th of August he commenced his movements, and by a system of strategy and logistics rarely equaled in campaigning, so threatened Bragg's lines of communication as to cause the latter to withdraw from his chosen stronghold, which some of Rosecrans' troops entered as he was leaving. This was effected by the 9th of September, and by Rosecrans crossing his army at several points below the town, but at distances so widely separated as to make his flanks no less than 45 miles apart.

Bragg, upon withdrawing from the town, retired to La Fayette, about 25 miles nearly due south from Chattanooga and nearly opposite the center of Rosecrans' extended line. Between the two opposing armies stretched four ridges of mountains; first, Racoon Mountain; next, the river; then Lookout Mountain and Missionary Ridge; and then Pigeon Mountain. In order to concentrate his army, it was necessary for Rosecrans to cross these ridges at several passes, and while doing so Bragg endeavored to meet the separate columns as they emerged therefrom and defeat them in detail. But this plan failing, through want of promptness in some of his subordinates, he hastened to attack his enemy while in the act of concentrating.

It therefore became of vital importance to the Federal commander to get his disunited corps together as quickly as possible. But Rosecrans, mistaking the character of Bragg's movement, and thinking him in full retreat towards the interior of Georgia, instead of concentrating at once, hastened forward Crittenden's corps from his extreme left and McCook's from his extreme right in pursuit, thus still further separating his scattered forces, and this by an intervening country exceedingly rough, and with but few roads, and those of the poorest kind.

When it was ascertained that Bragg was not, as supposed, on the retreat, but was holding his army at La Fayette, preparing to strike the scattered forces of his opponent, intense anxiety was felt by Rosecrans and his subordinate commanders. But by strenuous exertions a concentration was effected before Bragg gave his contemplated blow.

This concentration was effected in the valley of the Chickamauga, lying between Missionary Ridge and Pigeon Mountain. The corps of McCook and Thomas were closed in to their left upon that of Crittenden, which had been recalled from Ringgold where it had been sent as before stated in pursuit of Bragg. The latter had made efforts to prevent the concentration, but the tardiness and want of energy of some of his subordinate commanders thwarted his purposes. Heavy reinforcements having arrived from Lee's army in Virginia, and Johnston's army of the Mississippi, he now determined to attack and crush the Federal army as a whole. His attack was to have been made on the 18th, but owing to the bad roads, small bridges, difficult fords and dense forests, his operations were delayed until early morning of the following day.

The Chickamauga is a large creek flowing northeastwardly between Missionary Ridge on the west and Pigeon Mountain on the east, emptying into the Tennessee River three miles above the town of Chattanooga. From crest to crest of the two ridges just mentioned the average distance is only about seven miles. The included valley is undulating, rough, full of ravines and with edges much broken by projecting spurs of the ridges. Being but sparsely settled it was chiefly covered with forest, thick with underbrush. The State Road leaving Chattanooga, and running almost due south through La Fayette, crosses Missionary Ridge at Rossville Gap, three miles, from Chattanooga, then skirting along the easterly flank of the ridge, crosses Chickamauga Creek at Lee and Gordon's mill, distant from Chickamauga 15 miles. It was along this road between Rossville Gap and Lee and Gordon's mill that the Federal army found itself concentrated on the morning of the 19th, when Bragg made his attack.

These are the general features of the country about Chickamauga, but as the special topography of the field had an unusual influence on the events of the battle, especially as to the employment of artillery, it is necessary to particularize certain features of it to obtain a full understanding of the conflict. The ground upon which this took place lies between Missionary Ridge on the westward and Chickamauga Creek on the eastward, both of which have a northeasterly and southwesterly direction, and are distant from each other, that is from the crest of the ridge to the creek, about four miles. The State Road bisecting the ground upon which the battle was fought may be taken as the axis of the field, and along it are several points which, although they had no influence *per se*, upon the military operations, are nevertheless important as points of reference. The first of these is the McDaniel house and fields, about three miles from Rossville. Near this house was the Federal left. About a mile further south is the Kelly house and fields; this was the center of Thomas' position and was the scene of the most constant, persistent and sanguinary struggle of the battle. About half a mile further on is the Brotherton place, the point struck by Longstreet's column of attack which swept away the entire right wing of the Federal army. About a mile further on is another house and fields, known as the Vineyard, near which rested the federal right on the morning of the first day. This does not, of course, include the fields of operations of the cavalry, which generally were on the flanks of the main force.

West of the State Road and almost parallel to it runs the Crawfish Spring road, from which diverges the Dry Valley road at the Glenn house, about a half mile in rear of the Vineyard. The Dry Valley road winds up a canyon and crosses Missionary Ridge at McFarland's Gap, and thence on by way of Rossville to Chattanooga. From McFarland's Gap to Rossville Gap, along the crest of the ridge, is about three miles. Spurs of the ridge extend down almost to the State Road, the most important one, and one which figured largely in the battle, being the Snodgrass Hill, more especial mention of which will be made further on.

From the State Road eastward to the Chickamauga, an average distance of about two miles, the land is rolling and covered with primeval forest and thick undergrowth, but here and there are small clearings and fields, not sufficient, however, to have had much influence in a military point of view.

In this forest took place the battle of the 19th, as also part of the battle of the 20th. A large part of the fighting of the second day took place along the line of the road and upon the slope of Missionary Ridge, where the field was also greatly obstructed by woods and underbrush. Farther up the slope of the ridge, the ground, being more cultivated, was less obstructed.

From several bridges and fords across the Chickamauga, country roads ran through the forest to the State Road, affording the Confederates means of approach from the further side of the creek, while the space between the latter and the State Road afforded him ample room for deploying his columns, screened from view by the density of the forest.

Rosecrans' army consisted of the same three corps with which he had fought the battle of Stones River. These were as follows: The Fourteenth, commanded by Thomas, consisted of the divisions of Brigadier General Absalom Baird, Negley, Brannan, and Major General Joseph J. Reynolds. The Twentieth, commanded by Alex. McD. McCook, consisted of the divisions of Davis, R. W. Johnson, and Sheridan. The Twenty-first, commanded by Crittenden, consisted of the divisions of T. J. Wood, Palmer, and Van Cleve.

Each of these 10 divisions had three brigades, to each of which was attached a battery. The cavalry corps, commanded by Brigadier General Robert B. Mitchell, consisted of five small brigades and one battery. Colonel John T. Wilder's brigade of infantry of Reynolds' division was mounted and served as cavalry. In addition to the foregoing was a provisional or reserve corps commanded by Gordon Granger. Only three brigades ever were present, and these were posted at or near Rossville Gap to hold that important position against the enemy.

The other three corps extended along or near the State Road, from about six miles south of Rossville Gap, to Lee and

Gordon's mill about five miles farther on. On the evening of the 18th they stood: McCook's on the extreme right, Crittenden on the extreme left, and Thomas in the center. Brigadier General George D. Wagner's brigade of Wood's division of Crittenden's corps had been left behind as a guard at Chattanooga and was the only organization in the entire army not upon the field. The divisions of Brannan and Reynolds, with their six batteries, absent from the battle of Stones River, had now rejoined Thomas' corps. In all, there was an addition to Rosecrans' force since Stones River of 37 regiments of infantry and nine batteries of 48 guns. The cavalry had received but little augmentation.

Bragg's army as it stood confronting Rosecrans' consisted of the corps of Polk, major generals William H. T. Walker, Simon B. Buckner, and D. H. Hill, together with a provisional corps under Hood. The right wing was under Polk, and the left under Longstreet, who had just arrived with two divisions of his corps from in front of the Army of the Potomac in Virginia. Buckner, who had been guarding eastern Tennessee with his corps, was brought from Knoxville, while several brigades had arrived from Johnston's army recently operating in rear of Grant while the latter was besieging Vicksburg.

Bragg's army, actually in the field and engaged in the fight, consisted of 184 regiments of infantry, 28 of cavalry, and 43 batteries of about 190 pieces. Against this force, Rosecrans opposed 142 regiments of infantry, 18 of cavalry, and 34 batteries of about 195 guns. Longstreet did not have his batteries from Virginia with him, which accounts for Bragg's greater percentage of infantry. According to the best data available, Rosecrans' army numbered about 65,000 of all arms, while that of his adversary was about 85,000, which is about the proportion given by the number of regiments in the two armies.

Of Bragg's 35 brigade commanders of infantry, all but four had their appropriate rank, that is they were brigadier generals; while with Rosecrans, 19 out of his 32 brigade command-

ers were colonels. An examination of the rosters of other armies shows about the same status; and this notwithstanding the fact that the proportion of general officers in the Federal service was greater than in the Confederate. To the thoughtful this has a deep military significance.

This absenteeism was not, however, so much through the fault or delinquency of the officers themselves as from causes generally beyond their control. Many were "shelved," chiefly in the first part of the war because they had not fulfilled the highly wrought popular expectations of the times. Many were mere political appointments, or appointments representing certain foreign elements who, when tested by actual command in the field, were found wanting and had to be "shelved "or put upon other duty. Others were in attendance as witnesses before the "Committee on the conduct of the War," where some of them were either grinding their own axes or dulling those of others. These were some of the causes producing the evil of absenteeism referred to. The straitened circumstances of the Southern Confederacy admitted of no such loose practices. As against the foregoing class of "dead heads" in the Federal service, was another class composed of those who were habitually with their commands in the field, and whether good or bad as generals, were attending to their duties faithfully.

While quite a number of promotions in other branches of the service justly followed the Stones River campaign, none, not even one, was vouchsafed to the artillery, and this, notwithstanding the distinguished services of some of the officers of that branch. Battery commanders still remained battery commanders. The organization of this branch of service, especially in the Army of the Cumberland up to this time, had no use for any higher grades than that of battery commander, hence such officers were doomed to serve without the soldierly hope of advancement.

Profiting by the lessons of Stones River, Bragg reorganized his artillery by uniting the batteries of each division into a battalion, to which was assigned an actual commander, a field officer of appropriate rank. In addition, each corps had its battalion of corps batteries, besides all of which there was an army reserve of several battalions.

Rosecrans, on the other hand, left his batteries still attached to his diminutive infantry brigades, trusting apparently that should another disaster happen, his artillery would notwithstanding rise to the occasion and again enable him to hold the field. But what was done at Stones River was fated not to be repeated at Chickamauga.

Following the ordinary regimental organization of artillery, the 36 batteries that Rosecrans had should have had 15 field officers. There were in reality but two, and these had no actual command over the batteries, only a mild species of administrative function as staff officers. Eighteen of Rosecrans' batteries were "Independents" without regimental organization, and therefore not entitled to field officers.

Bragg issued his orders for an attack to commence at daylight on the morning of the 19th. His plan was to cross his troops over the Chickamauga during the night. Hood's corps upon the right was to strike the extreme left of the Federal line, supposed to be Crittenden's corps, and doubling it up, was to sweep down the line, while the other corps in succession were to take up the assault from right to left and complete the victory.

Polk, commanding the right wing, was dilatory and not in readiness to commence the attack until long after the appointed time. In the meanwhile, some changes had taken place in the Federal line which modified considerably the expectations of Bragg.

Through the activity of his cavalry, Rosecrans became aware that the enemy were moving northward down the Chickamauga, thus threatening to cut off his communication with Chattanooga by the Rossville Gap. To extend his line in that direction, he directed Thomas to move his corps in rear of that of Crittenden and come into line on the left of the latter. McCook was to move his corps to the left, filling the space vacated by Thomas and connecting with Crittenden's right. Thomas pushed forward uninterruptedly during the night and at daylight on the morning of the 19th the head of his column had reached Kelly's house on the State Road, where Baird's division was posted. Brannan's division followed and was posted on Baird's left. Thomas' other two divisions, those of Reynolds and Negley, were delayed and before they could get up, the battle was opened, and they never did get into their proper position.

This "on the right into line" movement was a maneuver of inversion more appropriate for the drill ground than to the field of battle. In this instance it destroyed the solidarity of every corps, not one of which was left intact in its organization; and this led to the dismemberment of divisions also, until, as the battle progressed, scarcely one of these was left intact. A plain and simple movement, simultaneously, of the entire line along the State Road, upon or near which it was then posted, would have effected the object arrived at without the disorganization resulting from the method adopted. And the movement should not have been arrested at Kelly's house, but should have been continued on to connect with Granger at Rossville Gap, thus resting the left flank on Missionary Bridge and securing it from being turned. As it was, both flanks of Rosecrans' army were in the air and both were turned, but not successfully.

It will be seen, as this account progresses, that this great battle of two days was one essentially of brigades. This arose primarily from the wooded character of the country and secondarily from the tactical inversions just mentioned, the nature of the enemy attacks and to various other causes. The brigades as they moved from place to place were followed each by its battery, as best it could in such a wooded and broken country. Under such circumstances the batteries were not only an encumbrance to their brigades, but had their opportunities for usefulness reduced to a minimum while their exposure to capture and loss was a maximum. Some of them, becoming entangled in the forest in their desperate attempts to preserve connection with their brigades, were captured without firing a shot, while but few got opportunity of doing such work as they were capable of had they been properly organized.

An analysis of the official reports shows that the chief loss in guns and other artillery material occurred, not when the batteries were in firing positions, but when entangled in positions to which they had been led by their brigades. General Willich, an educated and veteran soldier whose brigade was conspicuously efficient throughout the battle, says in his report:

> The ground being wooded and hilly, it would not allow free manoeuvre for artillery, and I gave Captain [Wilbur F.] Goodspeed instructions to keep his battery [Battery A, 1st Ohio Light Artillery Regiment] out of musket range, and in rear of the infantry until further orders, . . . during most of the time, and during the most trying circumstances, I could give him very little advice, partly on account of the formation of the ground, partly on account of the character of the battle, the enemy charging on us alternately from all directions of the compass.

This is a fair picture of the operations of most of the batteries, and in a measure explains why so little real service was permitted to fall to the artillery. The reports of other brigade commanders are in monotonous harmony with that of Willich, and taken in the aggregate, show that solicitude for their batteries occupied much of their time and attention; often too, when the exigencies of battle demanded the whole of both for their brigades. That the artillery was capable of doing much valuable service, will appear in that part of the narrative where, at a most critical period, a number of batteries became shaken loose from their brigades, and uniting, checked the enemy when he had broken the line of battle.

Owing to the topography of the field, as just described, it was difficult, often impossible, for commanders to exercise personal supervision and control over their commands. Regiments even frequently became broken and their parts separated, but as a rule brigades managed to preserve a fair degree of integrity. Above this there was but little unity. The battle was therefore almost entirely a conflict of brigades and can be understood only by following the operations of each, which makes an account of it unusually long and full of details; and as the batteries almost invariably followed or attempted to follow their brigades, the operations of the artillery are inseparable from those of the brigades.

Soon after Thomas got the divisions of Brannan and Baird into position near the Kelly house, he received information that a brigade of the enemy was in his front near the Chickamauga, and that it had become isolated by having the bridge behind it destroyed. He was led to believe that it could be captured entire without great difficulty. He accordingly directed Brannan to send forward a brigade, supported by his other two, to perform this service. Colonel John T. Croxton's brigade, the first sent forward, advanced through the woods about a mile when it came in contact with the enemy, not however as an isolated brigade, but in force. He soon became hotly engaged and the brigades of colonels Ferdinand Van Derveer and John M. Connell were sent to his assistance. It soon became apparent that these brigades were getting the worst of the fight and that the enemy was in heavy force. Thomas directed Baird to support Brannan with his division, consisting of the brigades of Colonel Benjamin F. Scribner, Brigadier General Starkweather and Brigadier General John H. King; the latter was the regular brigade and had with it a regular battery, "H" 5th U.S. Artillery Regiment.

Each of the brigades as they went in attacked or were attacked with fury, and although fighting most resolutely, were driven back about half a mile, taking position finally upon a slight ridge about three-fourths of a mile east of the

State Road. This was resolutely held until the close of the day, when the troops were withdrawn a few hundred yards to another ridge, which became part of the line of battle of the next day.

Croxton's brigade, the first sent forward, was accompanied by Battery C, 1st Ohio Light Artillery Regiment, commanded by Lieutenant Marco B. Gary, which however was unable to come into position for firing until after the brigade commenced to retire. Gary says he then received orders from his brigade commander to fall back and take position on a ridge to the right and rear. "From this position, I threw a few shells at a high elevation, and over the heads of the infantry, for effect only. Three successive times during the day I was ordered by Colonel Croxton to a position in the face of the enemy, and each time the infantry was driven back so rapidly that I was again ordered to the rear as soon as I had obtained a position bearing on the enemy." His losses during this day were slight, but on the succeeding day he lost a number of men killed and wounded, together with many horses, one gun and some other parts of his battery.

Van Derveer's brigade of the same division moved forward into the woods about a mile-and-a-half and considerably to the left of Croxton's brigade. Here it encountered the enemy endeavoring to push his way around to get in position to strike him in flank. The fight soon became hot and stubborn, but the brigade was forced to give ground. It was accompanied by Lieutenant Frank G. Smith's Battery I of the 4th U.S. Artillery Regiment, of four Napoleon guns. The two sections of this battery, commanded by lieutenants George B. Rodney and John M. Stephenson, were so judiciously handled as to do some excellent work, particularly with canister at close quarters. As the brigade fell back from one position to another the battery took up successive positions, changing front to fire to the right, left or front, to meet each fresh attack of the enemy. Smith met with considerable loss in men and horses, but lost no guns. On the following day this battery, as will be more

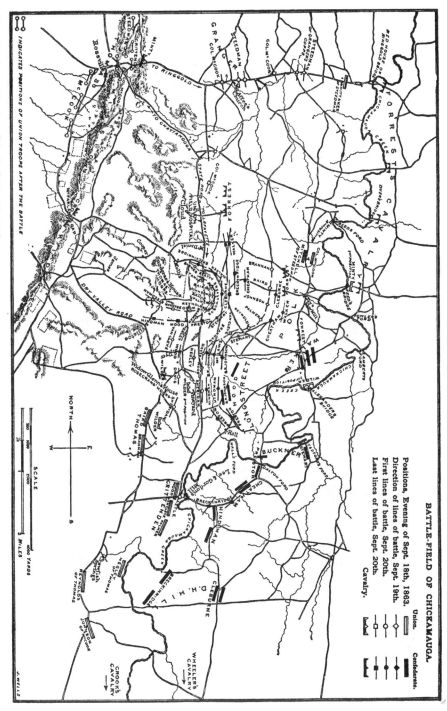

particularly mentioned, took position on Snodgrass Hill and was the heroic battery of the battle.

Connell's brigade was accompanied to the front by Josiah W. Church's Battery D, 1st Michigan Light Artillery Regiment. This brigade became united in the fight with Van Derveer's, and the battery, cooperating with Smith's, had the same experience as the latter, and did equally as good service, but in retiring had the misfortune to lose one of its guns. On the following day Church's battery, although moving about attempting to follow its brigade, was enabled to do some good work; but finally, being caught in the disaster which befell the left wing of the army, was swept away, saving but one of its six guns.

After checking the advance of the enemy on the extreme left, Brannan's division was moved back and around towards the center to assist in repulsing attacks in that quarter. When it became evident to Thomas that Brannan's division was not equal to the task before it, the division of Baird was sent in to his assistance on his right. Baird's division, as above stated, consisted of the brigades of Scribner, Starkweather and King, each with a battery. King, being upon the left, next to Brannan, was the first to advance. His battery, "H" of the 5th U.S. Artillery Regiment, the same that under Guenther had done such good service at Stones River, was now under Lieutenant Howard M. Burnham. King advanced through the woods until near Brannan's position, and while hotly engaged was forced to change front to meet an attack from heavy masses approaching on his right. Only one regiment and the battery had time to get into the new position before the blow was struck, and this scattered the entire brigade to the rear. The same blow struck and sent to the rear Scribner's brigade which had come up on the right of King.

Lieutenant Joshua A. Fessenden, who upon the fall of the other two officers succeeded to the command of the battery, says:

During the morning the battery was ordered forward by Brigadier General King, and came upon the enemy about 12 M. in a dense wood. The battery was hardly in position before the troops on the right giving way, it was exposed to a most terrific fire of musketry from the front and flank. General King ordered the battery to limber to the rear, but it was impossible to execute the order, since many of the cannoneers were killed and wounded and the horses shot at the limbers. At the first fire Lieutenant Burnham fell mortally wounded; Lieutenant [Israel] Ludlow was also wounded, and myself slightly struck on the right side. The battery was taken by the enemy.

The enemy soon after being forced to retire temporarily, the battery was recovered, but so crippled in men and horses as to be of no further service during the battle. The caissons with all the ammunition had to be abandoned for want of horses to haul them off. At the same time the gun lost by Church was retaken.

The enemy in his reports made great triumph over the rout of King's brigade of regulars and the capture of the battery. All who were on that part of the field claimed the honor of it, but the distinction seems to be justly due to Brigadier General St. John Richardson Liddell's division of Walker's corps.

Scribner's brigade, the next on the right of King's, was attacked with equal vehemence, and with like result. It too, was forced to change front, and with it the 1st Michigan Light Artillery Regiment, Battery A, under Lieutenant George W. Van Pelt, who was killed at his guns. When the brigade gave way, five of the guns of this battery fell into the hands of the enemy; one got off safely, and one was subsequently recaptured.

The other brigade of Baird's division, Starkweather's, was marched around in rear of the other brigades to relieve Croxton's brigade, now out of ammunition. Here the 4th

Indiana Independent Light Artillery Battery, attached to this brigade, met with an experience similar to that of the batteries of King's' and Scribner's brigades. Upon the first advance of the enemy, the brigade gave way and the battery was able to fire only a half dozen rounds before being overrun. Lieutenant David Flansburg, commanding it, was wounded and captured, as were also many of the enlisted men. Five of the guns were captured, but subsequently retaken, and from the wreck a battery of four pieces was organized which did good service later in the day, and were the only guns out of the entire 18 belonging to this division that were again brought into action, either on this or the following day.

The density of the woods in which the battle took place enabled the heavy masses of the enemy to approach unseen. The Federal brigades, moving to the front successively, were invariably driven back and the batteries allowed no time for limbering up. In the case of those that fell into the hands of the enemy, the loss of horses made it impossible for them to withdraw even though time had been afforded them for limbering.

The batteries being tied down to the movements of the brigades to which they were severally attached, were unable to select and occupy positions (such as there were) where they could act with greater effectiveness. Burnham's battery, with King's brigade, fired but 16 shots; Van Pelt's, of Scribner's brigade, but 64; and Lieutenant David Flansburg's, of Starkweather's, only about half a dozen, before being overrun by the enemy; and the same thing happened to other batteries not yet mentioned. General Baird seems to have been aware of the impropriety of handling artillery in this manner, but gives as a reason for so doing, that the batteries "could not be left behind for want of protection, and were therefore directed to follow closely the brigades, making their way through the trees." A battalion organization for his batteries, with an appropriate commander, would have relieved him from this embarrassment and at the same time afforded the batteries an opportunity of availing themselves of such advantages for efficient service as the field afforded.

Brannan's and Baird's divisions, although driven back from the positions where their brigades first encountered the enemy, turned several times as they retired and drove back their assailants, again, themselves, to be driven. The troops first encountered by Brannan and Baird were those of Brigadier General John Pegram's division of Brigadier General Nathan Bedford Forrest's cavalry corps, which the night before had crossed the Chickamauga at Reed's bridge, and were now at Jay's steam sawmill, about half a mile in front of the brigade. The cavalry was dismounted to fight as infantry, but it soon became apparent to Forrest that they were unable, alone, to hold the ground. He therefore called for reinforcements of infantry and Colonel Cladius C. Wilson's brigade of Walker's division of William H.T. Walker's corps was hastened to his assistance, soon followed by Brigadier General Matthew D. Ector's brigade of the same division, and these shortly afterwards by the brigades of Brigadier General Edward C. Walthall and Colonel Daniel E. Govan of Liddell's division of the same corps.

The presence of Thomas so far to the left of Crittenden disarranged Bragg's plan. To meet this unexpected phase of affairs, he too had to resort to some movements of inversion. Walker's corps was to have gone in on the left of Hood; now he, and all the troops that followed him, were on Hood's right, and were going in successively by divisions or brigades. Hood's attack was essentially made against the point originally intended, but instead of its being against the extreme Federal left, it fell, owing to the leftward movement of Rosecrans' troops, much nearer the right of the Federal position.

Walker, finding himself unable to hold his own, called for reinforcements. Cheatham's division of five brigades, of Polk's corps, was the first to arrive. According to his account, he advanced his line of battle about noon and soon encountered the Federal troops advancing rapidly in pursuit of Walker's troops. These he succeeded in checking and driving back for some distance when his own troops were checked, and in a short time forced to retire and await reinforcements. Cheatham seems to have had the same experience with artillery as had the Federals, for he reports losing one entire battery and part of another. But he adds: "The pieces and caissons were, however, subsequently recaptured."

These incidents are thus particularized to show the swaying back and forth nature of the struggle that took place in this dense forest. That which has thus far been related was but the commencement of the first day's battle.

When, as has been related, Brannan's and Baird's divisions arrived at the Kelly farm and faced towards the enemy there was considerable interval between Baird's right and the left of Crittenden's corps. To fill this gap, Johnson's division of McCook's corps was transferred from the right, arriving about noon, or some two hours after the battle had been in progress. Johnson immediately pushed his brigade into the woods on Baird's right and at once became hotly engaged.

Palmer's division of Crittenden's corps closed to the left on Johnson. After Palmer, came, in the order named, the divisions of Reynolds, of Thomas' corps; Van Cleve, of Crittenden's; Davis, of McCook's; Wood, of Crittenden's, and finally Sheridan, of McCook's corps. Negley's division of Thomas' corps was held in reserve in rear of the center of the line to give service wherever it might be needed. It will be observed that with the exception of Brannan's and Baird's divisions, no two adjoining each other belonged to the same corps; one of the fruits of the unfortunate tactical inversion heretofore animadverted upon. Brannan and Baird did not long continue together.

While these movements were in progress on the Federal side, similar movements were taking place with the Confederates. After the combined forces of Walker and Cheatham had been checked, as heretofore stated, Polk, commanding the Confederate right wing, was ordered to send Breckenridge's division of his corps across the Chickamauga and to proceed in person to direct matters on the right. Cleburne's division of Hill's corps was sent to report to Polk and was hastened up to assist Walker and Cheatham to hold their ground. It came into the fight on Cheatham's left. [Alexander P.] Stewart's division of Buckner's corps was moved up from the second line and went in on the left of Cleburne and right of Hood.

The impetuosity of Stewart's attack, assisted by other troops, temporarily broke the Federal center. Some of Hood's brigades were veterans of Longstreet's corps from the Army of Virginia. Other of Longstreet's brigades did not arrive in time to take part in the battle of the first day, and Longstreet himself did not arrive until late at night on that day.

Johnson's division arrived at an opportune moment to check the enemy, who but a short time before had broken the brigades of King and Scribner of Baird's division. His division consisted of the brigades of Willich and colonels Philemon P. Baldwin and Joseph B. Dodge. The first two started into the fight together, but soon became separated. Dodge's was sent towards the right to assist Hazen's brigade of Palmer's division, which had been closed in to aid Johnson. The brigades of Willich and Baldwin, moving forward, inclined to their left, enabling them to attack with vigor the flank of the enemy pursuing Baird's broken troops. At the same time, Brannan attacking in front, the enemy was driven back, permitting Baird to rally his troops and reestablish his line.

Goodspeed's Ohio battery followed closely Willich's brigade, but found opportunity for firing only a few rounds. It, however, rendered good service by furnishing horses to haul off five pieces which the brigade gallantly captured. Captain Peter Simonson, commanding an Indiana battery [5th Independent Light Artillery Battery] attached to Baldwin's brigade, fired about 130 rounds, but while retiring before the enemy, lost one of his guns. Captain Edward Grosskopff, commanding an Ohio battery [20th Independent Light Artillery Battery] accompanying Dodge's brigade, was unable to fire at all until after the brigade had fallen back, at dark, to where the final stand was made, and then he fired only a few rounds. He did little or nothing the following day and altogether proved himself an exception to the general rule of efficiency governing other battery commanders.

While Johnson's brigades were thus engaged, Palmer s division of Crittenden's corps came into the fight on Johnson's right. This division consisted of the brigades of Hazen, Cruft, and Colonel William Grose, each with a battery. In fact the latter had two batteries, "H" and "M" of the 4th U.S. Artillery Regiment, each of four guns, commanded respectively, by lieutenants Harry C. Cushing and Francis L.D. Russell.

Palmer's brigades started in echelon from an open field near State Road, but soon after entering the woods they became separated. Arriving abreast of Johnson they immediately became engaged in the terrific contest then going on at that part of the line. The enemy was pushed back a considerable distance, but fresh divisions coming up, Palmer's brigades were in turn forced back, and took position on a slight ridge which was held for some two hours, until the enemy, concentrating on that part of the field, swept everything before him back behind the State Road. In the meanwhile, the batteries had had opportunity of doing some good work as the ground here, being less wooded, was slightly more favorable for artillery than other parts of the field.

Hazen's brigade, running short of ammunition, was relieved by Brigadier General John B. Turchin's, and retiring beyond the State Road, had just completed replenishing its boxes when it found itself in position to assist in repulsing the assault of the enemy which broke the line in front of this point. Turchin's brigade belonged to Reynolds' division of Thomas' corps, which, together with Colonel Edward A. King's brigade, Reynolds was conducting to the left to join Thomas. The other brigade, Wilder's, of this division, was acting as mounted infantry and not immediately present. The necessity appearing urgent to Reynolds, he arrested his further movement to the left and pushed in his two brigades to the assistance of Palmer's.

When Turchin went to the relief of Hazen, he was accompanied by Captain William A. Andrew's 21st Indiana Independent Light Artillery Battery, of which he says: "The position on this day was so bad and so wooded that my battery could fire only three shots during the day's fighting, and these were fired at the rebel stragglers after we had made the charge." Captain Samuel J. Harris' 19th Indiana Independent Light Artillery Battery, of E.A. King's brigade, accompanying the latter into the woods, was able to fire a few rounds to assist its brigade in its severe contest, but had finally to fall back with it, minus one Napoleon gun.

Reynolds had been preceded by the two brigades of Van Cleve's division of Crittenden's corps. The third brigade had been left behind to guard the crossing at Lee and Gordon's mills. Arriving opposite Palmer's right, Van Cleve boldly pushed his two brigades into the woods where they soon met the enemy, which they drove some distance, capturing four guns. But the enemy, rallying, recaptured the pieces and drove back the brigades some distance. Van Cleve, then rallying, forced back the enemy, capturing four other pieces, which he succeeded in bringing off. Again he was driven back, but again rallying, drove the enemy until overwhelmed by his masses. His brigades were broken and driven far to the rear. It was at this point that the enemy had concentrated his greatest efforts and this was the supreme moment of peril during the battle of the first day. Here, the enemy driving everything before him, penetrated the Federal line and was upon the point of breaking the army in twain when arrested in a manner soon to be related.

Captain Alanson Stevens' Pennsylvania battery accompanied one of Van Cleve's brigades into the fight and was enabled to do a small amount of firing, but lost four of its pieces in the final attack. These were, however, made good by adopting some of the guns captured from the enemy.

Swallow's Indiana battery did not accompany its brigade to the front, but remained near the road. General Reynolds seeing it idle, placed it in position to form a nucleus for a new line should the front line be broken. To this he added Harris' battery when it came back from the front with the fragments of E.A. King's brigade, as likewise two pieces of Captain Eli Lilly's 18th Indiana Independent Light Artillery Battery, belonging to Wilder's mounted brigade, which happened to be near by. The four remaining guns of this battery were a short distance to the right where they had an oblique fire upon the enemy towards their left. Almost adjoining Harris' battery on the left were Cushing's and Russell's batteries of the 4th U.S. Artillery Regiment and Lieutenant Giles J. Cockrill's Battery F, 1st Ohio Light Artillery Regiment, which came back from the front and were gathered together and placed in position by Hazen. In addition, there were several other guns, parts of other batteries, making altogether upwards of 30 pieces.

When the front line began to give way, as just related, the enemy followed up the success with great impetuosity. Reynolds says:

> I met our retiring regiments in person, pointed them to 14 guns in position (those which he had stationed) as evidence that the enemy must be thrown back, and by great exertion succeeded in reforming several regiments in rear of the batteries. . . . These batteries fired with terrible effect upon the enemy, his progress was checked, and our line for a time prevented from yielding any further. The enemy now shifted further to the right where there was evidently an opportunity in our line, and coming in on the flank our regiments again became disheartened and began to retire. The batteries following the regiments changed front and fired to the right, and the line was reformed along a fence

nearly perpendicular to its former position, with the batteries in the edge of the woods."

Soon after this the enemy was entirely repulsed and the line reestablished, this time along or near the road.

Hazen, who as before stated, was near this position with his brigade replenishing his ammunition, seeing the break, advanced his brigade, but was unable to withstand the enemy who were pressing forward in mass. He says:

> I found myself the only general officer upon that part of the field, and as to check the further advance of the enemy was of the utmost importance, I hastily gathered and placed in position all the artillery then in reach (the batteries before mentioned), in all about 20 pieces, and with the aid of all the mounted officers and soldiers I could find, succeeded in checking and rallying a sufficient number of straggling infantry to form a fair line in support of the artillery. My brigade could not be brought into position in time, there being but about two minutes to make these dispositions before the blow came, when the simultaneous opening of all the artillery with canister checked and put to rout the confronting columns of the enemy. It is due Lieutenants [Norman A.] Baldwin, . . Cockerill, . . Cushing and Russell, . . commanding batteries, to state that for accuracy in manoeuvring and firing their guns in the immediate presence of the enemy on this occasion, the army and country are placed under lasting obligations.

The Confederate reports touching on this part of the battle are in harmony with the foregoing, establishing the fact that it was the firmness of these batteries that prevented them from reaping the advantages of victory on this occasion.

Most of the troops that caused this break were of Hood's division, which had arrived from Virginia in advance of its artillery. From this and other causes the Confederates had but few guns to reply to those just mentioned. Owing to the change of position of the contending forces, the attack of Hood, intended originally to have been the first, became in reality the last.

Towards the Federal left the breach did not go beyond a portion of Palmer's division, while on the right it included the divisions of Davis, Wood and all other troops as far as Sheridan's division, which latter held the extreme right. Davis' division of McCook's corps followed pretty shortly after Van Cleve, and immediately went forward into battle on the right of the latter. One of his brigades, that of Post, with its battery, was absent guarding trains, leaving him but two, those of [Brigadier General William P.] Carlin and Colonel Hans C. Heg, for the fight. In passing Rosecrans' headquarters the battery of Heg's brigade was left as a guard; that of Carlin's brigade, Hotchkiss' Minnesota, secured a favorable position in a small field on the right of the brigade, where it together with four pieces of Lilly's battery of Wilder's mounted brigade, did good service until forced to retire with the infantry. Davis' brigade fell back in confusion, but in due time was rallied behind the batteries established by Reynolds and Hazen. Hotchkiss' battery took position here also and contributed its share in repulsing the enemy and restoring the broken center.

About 3:00 P.M. Wood's division of Crittenden's corps and Colonel Sidney M. Barnes' brigade of Van Cleve's division, both of which had been guarding the crossing at Lee and Gordon's mills, were ordered to hasten down the road to join in the fight. Barnes was leading, and when opposite the right of Davis, formed line and pushed through the jungle until he struck the enemy, when he too was forced to give way. His battery, the 3rd Wisconsin Independent Light Artillery, commanded by Lieutenant Cortland Livingston, following closely, came into battery in the open field with Hotchkiss' battery; and with the latter fell back with the infantry, and taking position on the further side of the road, did good service. The brigade was rallied on the batteries.

Wood, following close after Barnes, sent one of his brigades, Harker's, into the woods to support Heg's of Davis' division, which was now giving way. Harker, deeming his battery useless in such a position, directed it to remain behind where there was some open ground. Harker resolutely held his position and did splendid service, until, like those before him, he too was forced back. In the meanwhile, Captain Bradley, commanding his battery, the 6th Ohio, "with," says Harker, "the eye of a true soldier, selecting the best ground in his vicinity, opened with telling effect upon the enemy, inspiring our own troops with confidence and causing dismay among the enemy. As our troops fell back the battery retired with prolonges [heavy ropes carried on the gun carriage to pull the cannon] fixed until it got a good position in the woods to the rear, where it was supported by our own troops. It here did great execution in repulsing the enemy, and remained in this position until I rejoined it."

Wood's other brigade, that of Colonel George P. Buell, was scarcely formed to advance into the forest, "when," says Wood, "it was struck by a crowd of fugitives and swept away in the general *mélange*. The whole brigade was carried off its feet. It was necessary for it to fall back across the narrow field on the Western side of the road to the edge of the woods, under the cover of which it rallied." Buell's battery, the 8th Indiana Independent Light Artillery, of Captain George Estep, took position near the road. "A moment after this," says Estep, "and the battery was filled with men falling back in great confusion. I was compelled to cease firing till our men passed from my front. I thought I would then be able to deal a destructive fire on the advancing line of the enemy, but he was pressing so closely upon our line, delivering his fire as he advanced, his shots taking effect on my horses, I was compelled to retire my battery." In doing this he lost, temporarily, one of his pieces. The other five he moved back across the field to the edge of the wood into which his brigade had retired. Here, he again opened fire, and with the other batteries before mentioned, checked the enemy who did not attempt pursuit over the open field.

"Order being restored," says Wood, "and a sufficiently solid formation acquired to warrant an advance, I led the brigade back in person, and reoccupied the ground from which it had been forced–the site on which it had been originally formed." [He continued:]

> In this advance a portion of Carlin's Brigade participated, led, by [Brigadier] General Carlin. Estep's battery, attached to Buell's Brigade, accompanied the advance. Scarcely had the lost ground been repossessed than the enemy emerged from the woods on the eastern side of the cornfield, and commenced to cross it. He was formed in two lines, and advanced firing. The appearance of his force was large. Fortunately, reinforcements were at hand. A compact brigade of Sheridan's Division, not hitherto engaged, was at this moment crossing the field in rear of the position then occupied by Buell's brigade and the portion of Carlin's. This fresh brigade advanced handsomely into action, and joining its fire to that of the other troops, most materially aided in repelling a most dangerous attack. But this was not done until considerable loss had been inflicted on us. The enemy advanced near enough to cut down so many horses in Estep's battery that he could not bring off his guns; but as our infantry held its ground, they did not fall into the hands of the enemy.

Estep, recovering his guns, restored his battery during the night to a fighting condition for the battle of the next day in which he lost everything he had. Wood's other brigade, Wagner's, together with its battery was occupying Chattanooga, and consequently not engaged in the battle of either day.

The brigade of Sheridan's division which Wood mentions as coming in so opportunely, was that of Colonel Luther P. Bradley, which having formed on the road, "moved steadily forward across a piece of open level ground and ascended a gentle slope when the enemy opened with a most withering fire of musketry, which cut down Colonel Bradley and his adjutant at the outset." This fire was replied to with such firmness as to cause the enemy to withdraw hastily, leaving behind Estep's battery, which he had captured. Captain Mark H. Prescott's Battery C, 1st Illinois Light Artillery Regiment, attached to Bradley's brigade, had no opportunity of becoming engaged, nor did those of the other two brigades of Sheridan's division.

At the time when the divisions of the left center were giving way, that of Brannan, which had been so heavily engaged during the forenoon, but was now comparatively idle, was hurried from its position on the extreme left to the assistance of the center, and did some good service. During the night it took position in line between Reynolds on its left and Negley on its right. When it was withdrawn from the left of the line, Dodge's brigade of Johnson's division was moved around to the left of Baird to take its place. In the movement of divisions from right to left, as has just been described, Negley's division of Thomas' corps had been left behind to cover the right flank of Rosecrans' position and the withdrawal of the trains by the roads leading through gaps in Missionary Ridge.

Some Federal cavalry was in observation still farther to the right and rear. During the forenoon Negley had some sharp fighting. Late in the afternoon, being relieved by the cavalry, he moved his three brigades rapidly to the left, but was too late to become much engaged. By that time the enemy had been stayed and the broken line repaired. He now took position in line near the right of Reynolds, but during the night Brannan moved his division up between them. His batteries were with their brigades.

It was now becoming dark. The enemy, after his repulse before the center, did not renew his attack in this quarter. Thomas had selected an advantageous position (that is, as advantageous as circumstances would admit of) for his wing on a slight crest a few hundred yards in rear of the position then occupied by his troops. As the latter were withdrawing to it, the enemy made a furious onslaught upon them, but were repulsed with heavy loss. This closed the battle for the day. The troops, exhausted by day and night marching and the severe fighting, rested during the first part of the night, but towards morning began to cover themselves with such breastworks as they could improvise; that is Thomas' wing did so. Those of the right wing were moved back and forth, without either getting into position or constructing entrenchments. McCook, Crittenden and Rosecrans himself were all on this part of the line, each giving orders, often conflicting.

Thomas' part of the line was a flattened crescent with its convexity towards the enemy. The extremities of the crescent rested on, or very near, the State Road. It thus ran around the Kelly farm and was established from 50 to 100 yards within the woods that skirted the Kelly field, which lay along the road for half a mile, and was a quarter of a mile wide. The enemy was busy during the night constructing breastworks, evidently fearful of unexpected attacks or repulses in their attacks next morning.

During the day all of Rosecrans' troops had been hotly engaged except Negley's division and two brigades of Sheridan's division, and even these had had their skirmishes. This does not of course include Granger's three brigades at or near Rossville Gap. According to Confederate accounts, all of Bragg's troops were engaged except Breckenridge's division and six brigades of other divisions. The carnage, as may well be supposed from such stubborn fighting, was very great, and the Confederates claimed the victory because they held the ground over which the fighting had taken place. But, while this was the fact, the events that took place on Thomas' front the next day showed that every pace to the rear had but strengthened his position. The only substantial advantage the enemy gained was a nearer approach to the State Road towards Rossville Gap, which if permanently in the hands of the enemy, would have proved truly a disaster to Rosecrans. The events of the following day will show that the whole of the Federal right wing should have been transferred during the night to the left of Thomas.

Although Bragg had failed in his plan to crush the Federal left and double the line back upon itself, his troops were now more in hand and more numerous than before for another attempt. Rosecrans made no effort during the night to secure a better position. Both his flanks continued in the air. The most prominent features of the battle of the first day were purely accidental. Bragg's plan was to attack the Federal left at daylight, but the troops designated for this purpose did not get into position until long after this time, and were moving to do so when met by Croxton's brigade, which under a misapprehension had been sent into the forest to investigate that part of the field. Croxton at once became engaged and other brigades had to be sent to his assistance, and others, in succession to these, until the entire army was drawn into battle. Each brigade as it moved to the front struck the enemy and attacked vigorously, thus converting a defensive battle into one of attack. The enemy meanwhile, was moving to the attack also, and this accounts for the peculiar direction assumed by the line of battle. The first brigades of the Federal left moved into the forest about a mile-and-a-half, those that followed had successively less distance to go before coming upon the enemy, for he too was moving to the encounter, until finally the brigades on the extreme right did not have to move forward at all. Thus was given to the Federal line, along which the conflict raged, a position to the front of and oblique to that upon which it was intended to receive attacks of the enemy.

While the Federal troops fought almost exclusively as distinct brigades, the Confederates engaged theirs more by divisions, but the density of the woods was such as to break these up more or less into separate brigades and to convert the battle on their side also into one of brigades. The peculiar surging back and forth nature of the conflict was due to a combination of the foregoing causes.

The supreme crisis of the day happened when the center was broken, and a fatal disaster was averted only by the batteries placed in position by Generals Reynolds and Hazen. Through the shaking up that the brigades got at this time, the batteries were freed from the brigades to which they were attached and were therefore available to be massed to meet the emergency. What they then did forcibly illustrates two very important features in the use of field batteries; one of which is that they should be kept together in groups as much as possible so that their combined fire may have, as it had in this case, a telling effect wherever delivered; the other is that batteries thus grouped, constitute a firm basis upon which broken troops may be rallied.

It was, however, a sad commentary upon the system of organization or method adopted for the artillery of that army that a division and a brigade commander had to leave their own important functions at such a time to attend to duty which under a proper system would have been performed by an artillery commander. As soon as the crisis was over the batteries rejoined their brigades to continue to follow them through the vicissitudes of the battle of the following day, but without a like opportunity of giving evidence of their capabilities.

The brigades to which the batteries were attached averaged only about 1,460 muskets on the line of battle. Brigade commanders, whenever practicable, placed their batteries in the center of this short line, but often the batteries were broken by having regiments posted between their sections. Not only was the effectiveness of the artillery fire impaired by this system, but the solidity of the infantry line destroyed, a fact substantiated by the reports of division, brigade and regimental commanders. The reports of these commanders are curious as showing the extraordinary manner in which their commands became broken into detachments and intermingled, artillery and infantry, each in the way of the other, to the confusion and hindrance of both. Under such circumstances it was impossible for batteries to do much really valuable work, or more than was done on this day.

Owing to the density of the woods and the scarcity of roads leading through it, the enemy was able to bring into action only a limited number of his batteries. But these, owing to the battalion system adopted by Bragg, were at least kept from impairing the efficiency of his infantry. The   Federal right wing, after repulsing the enemy that had pushed it back across the State Road, was not again brought forward into line with the left wing under Thomas, but bivouacked for the night to the westward of the road. Thomas' right rested on the road, from which it bowed in a compact line around to the eastward, until it almost reached the same road again to the northward of the Kelly house and fields.

The headquarters of Maj. Gen. George H. Thomas on Snodgrass Hill at Chickamauga photographed in 1902. (*Library of Congress*)

TEN

CHICKAMAUGA

(Second Day)

W HEN Brannan's division was withdrawn from the left
of Baird's, as heretofore stated, Dodge's brigade of
Johnson's division was sent to replace it. This brigade now
constituted the extreme left of the Federal line, and from this
around to the extreme right the divisions stood in the following order: Baird's, Johnson's, Palmer's, Reynolds', Brannan's,
Negley's, Davis', and Sheridan's; those of Van Cleve and
Wood were in reserve in rear of the right center. The first five
constituted the left wing under Thomas, the remainder the
right wing, nominally under McCook.

Opposite this line, in the woods that had been fought over
during the previous day, lay the enemy about half a mile distant. His line, from right to left, consisted of the following divisions: Breckinridge's and Cleburne's of D.H. Hill's corps;
Brigadier General States R. Gist's and Liddell's of Walker's
corps; and Cheatham's of Polk's corps. These constituted the
right wing under Lieutenant General Polk. The left wing
under Longstreet consisted of Stewart's and Brigadier General
William Preston's divisions of Buckner's corps, Brigadier
General Bushrod R. Johnson's and Hood's of Hood's provisional corps, followed by McLaws' of Longstreet's corps, and

by Major General Thomas C. Hindman's of Polk's corps on the extreme left.

In addition to the foregoing, Forrest had his corps of cavalry, consisting of two divisions, on the right, where during the battle of both days, he was exceedingly active and enterprising. Dismounting his men to fight on foot, they became efficient infantry, and were in fact the only troops that Brannan and Baird had to contend with for a considerable period on the forenoon of the first day. The Federal cavalry was on the right and left doing good service in guarding the flanks.

Bragg adopted the same plan of battle for the second day that he had tried for the first. General Polk, commanding the right wing, was ordered to assault the Federal extreme left at dawn and to take up the attack in succession rapidly to the left. The left wing under Longstreet was to await the attack of the right, take it up promptly when made, and then the whole line was to be pushed vigorously and persistently against the enemy throughout its whole extent. Polk was not himself present, nor did he have his troops in readiness for the attack until long after the appointed time, in fact, not until about half past eight o'clock. Meanwhile, the Confederates made a reconnaissance around the Federal left and across the State Road "proving the important fact," says Bragg, "that this greatly desired position was open to our possession."

General Thomas, fearing for the weakness of his left, made a request early in the morning for Negley's division to take post on the left of Baird. Rosecrans ordered that Negley's place in line should be filled by Wood's division. Through delays most unaccountable, this was not done until about 9:00 A.M., but about an hour before this time one of Negley's brigades, that of Brigadier General John Beatty, had been dispatched in all haste, and arrived just as the enemy was moving to the assault. He at once became hotly engaged, and this was the commencement of the momentous battle of the second day.

The addition of Breckinridge's division to the right of Cleburne's greatly outflanked Thomas' left, now held by

Beatty, whose brigade was greatly attenuated to cover as much ground as possible. Still further on, Forrest, with a division of dismounted cavalry, was working his way around to Beatty's rear. This overwhelming force soon broke and scattered Beatty's regiments and captured two of the guns of Captain Lyman Bridges' independent Illinois battery, attached to that brigade. William Bishop, the lieutenant commanding them was killed.

After Beatty was broken the attack fell upon Baird's division, throwing King's brigade of regulars into disorder, which extended to the adjoining brigade of Scribner. It will be remembered that in the battle of the previous day Baird's batteries had suffered so severely that he had but four pieces for the whole of his line. These were placed at that point where his line began to come back towards the State Road. The troops on the remainder of his line were therefore without either the physical or moral support of artillery.

By this time the tardy movements on the right had permitted Negley to send another of his brigades, that of Colonel Timmothy R. Stanley, to the assistance of Beatty, who had succeeded in rallying some of his regiments. Notwithstanding the great inferiority of their numbers, these troops checked the enemy. Meanwhile Grose's brigade of Palmer's division, Van Derveer's of Brannan's, and Colonel George F. Dick's and Barnes' of Van Cleve's division, were hurried to the left, and joining in the fight effectually repulsed Breckinridge and Forrest.

The brigades sent to the left, or at least some of them, were those lying in support of divisions on the line and were thus in a measure available. As a rule, each division had two brigades in line and one in support. There was no reserve division; the reinforcing of any part of the line, therefore, meant the weakening of some other part.

Grose's brigade was accompanied by Cushing's battery "H," 4th U.S. Artillery Regiment, which, as usual, did splendid service until the ammunition in its limbers was expended.

When being relieved by Russell's, "M" of the same regiment, it withdrew to replenish from its caissons. After this, Cushing was ordered to take position with other batteries on Dyer's Hill, an eminence directly in rear of that part of the Federal line struck by Longstreet's charge, which swept everything before it. Here Cushing lost one of his pieces by the disabling of his horses. The battery of Van Derveer's brigade, Smith's "I," 4th U.S. Artillery Regiment, did not accompany its brigade, being about that time sent to Snodgrass Hill where it took position and continued to the close of the battle doing most effective work.

Dick's brigade was accompanied by Swallow's battery, but before reaching its destination it was recalled and placed on Dyer's Hill, where it also lost one piece. Dick's brigade, upon meeting the enemy, was broken in two; one portion retired to Snodgrass Hill where it did good service, the remainder joined a body of troops that Negley collected and conducted from the field.

When Barnes started for the left, his battery, Livingston's Wisconsin, being unable to follow him directly, on account of the woods and other difficulties, was sent to Dyer's Hill where five of his pieces fell into the hands of the enemy. This brigade continued on the left during the remainder of the day.

Captain Frederick Schultz's Battery M, 1st Ohio Light Artillery Regiment, which had attempted to accompany Stanley's brigade, became separated from it and did not rejoin it during the day. It became one of those subsequently conducted ingloriously from the field by Negley, as will be mentioned further on.

Negley's third brigade, Colonel William Sirwell's, arrived too late to assist in the repulse of Breckinridge. Together with most of the regiments of Beatty's brigade, it, with the exception of one regiment, was gathered up by Negley and marched from the field. Captain Marshall's Ohio battery, attached to Sirwell's brigade, had the same experience as had Schultz's. Both of these batteries however managed to get in

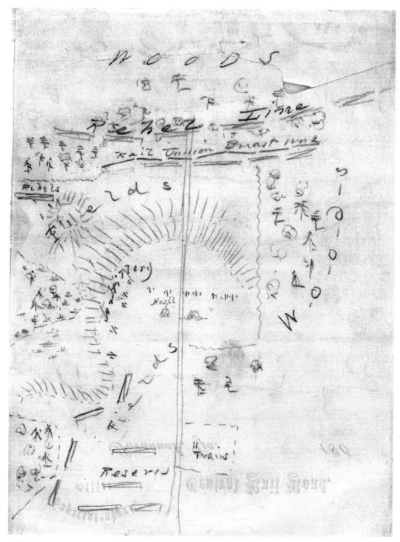

Alfred R. Wauld's map of the action around Snodgrass Hill (center). (*Library of Congress*)

a few shots, which no doubt contributed towards the repulse of Breckinridge and Forrest.

Thomas, perceiving the imminent danger of his left and rear, being himself an old artillerist and knowing the value and proper use of that arm in strengthening an unprotected flank, directed General Negley, who had now himself arrived on that part of the field, to "mass as much artillery on the slopes of Missionary Ridge, west of the State Road, as he could conveniently spare from his lines, supported strongly by infantry, so as to sweep the ground to the left and rear of Baird's position." Negley set to work most energetically and soon had collected seven full batteries and some parts of others, in all 52 pieces; but mistaking the purport of the instructions given by Thomas, took them, together with such infantry as he could collect, in a direction directly opposite to that intended and posted them on Snodgrass Hill, a prominent spur of Missionary Ridge extending down in rear of the right of Thomas' wing. Thomas had no officer of artillery to whom he could entrust the duty for which he thus took a division commander, and as the latter himself had none, he had to neglect his brigades to attend to the work in person; a direct result of the artillery system, or want of system, that prevailed in that army. What became of the infantry and batteries collected by Negley will appear further on.

It was only by the most determined fighting that the bold attacks of Forrest and Breckinridge were repulsed, but the repulse was decisive and followed up until the enemy were beyond the position from which they started in the morning. While being forced back, the brigades of the enemy would turn and, for a time, drive back their adversaries. In this way the ground was fought over, back and forth, several times.

Following soon after the repulse of Breckinridge, came the furious assault of Cleburne's division. This fell principally on Johnson's division and the right brigade of Baird's division; all behind breastworks and well supported by artillery. The repulse that ensued was very sanguinary to the assailants, who were followed up by skirmishes from the main line.

Upon the repulse of Cleburne, the divisions of Gist and Liddell of Walker's corps were pushed into the fight, but they too failed to break the Federal line. At the same time,

Cheatham's powerful division of 24 regiments took up the fight on the left of Walker, his assault falling principally on Johnson and Palmer, whose troops, sheltered behind their extemporized breastworks, received the assaults with coolness and delivered their fire with deadly accuracy.

Meanwhile, Breckinridge had rallied and swinging still further around to his right was coming squarely up on the rear of the Federal line. Just at this critical moment Van Derveer arrived with his brigade and scattered the enemy to the rear, following him up until entirely clear of the field. Grose's brigade followed soon after Van Derveer's and drove back a portion of Walker's troops that had got temporary lodgment on the left of Baird's position.

While these things were transpiring on the left of Rosecrans' line, other events to be more particularly noticed hereafter, were happening on his right. Longstreet's first movements against this wing were eminently successful, but after this his operations were a series of assaults upon a new line formed on Snodgrass Hill. To relieve him as much as possible, Polk was ordered at 3:00 P.M. to make another attack along his whole line. This chief attack was to be another turning movement around Thomas' left, which was now greatly weakened by the loss of the troops conducted away from it by Negley. Here he massed the divisions of Breckinridge and Liddell, and Brigadier General Frank C. Armstrong's division of dismounted cavalry, with a number of batteries of artillery. The remainder of Polk's troops were formed to assault the breastworks occupied by Baird, Johnson and Palmer, and with these were brought up as many batteries as the wooded nature of the country would permit.

Liddell's division struck Baird's line behind breastworks and was repulsed, but Breckinridge, sweeping farther around to his right, was rapidly gaining Baird's rear. At this moment it seemed as though Bragg's plan of breaking the Federal left and rolling it back upon the center and right was upon the point of success. But most opportunely aid came from

Johnson's division on the right of Baird. Willich's brigade of this division was lying in support near the Kelley house, and with it was Goodspeed's battery. These at once changed front and engaged the enemy. The fire of the battery was especially good and temporarily checked the enemy. Other troops uniting with Willich, Breckinridge was again repulsed.

The artillery of the enemy did good firing, but was invariably driven back by its opponents. One of the Confederate commanders, Colonel Benjamin J. Hill, speaking of these efforts, says: "This artillery did noble service in helping dislodge the enemy from his first line of fortifications, dealing out destruction at every discharge. They did noble service until they exhausted their ammunition. During the progress of this artillery duel, my negro boy having failed to bring up my sword, I took a pole or club and with this drove up officers and men of my own command who were shielding themselves behind trees, as well as those on the left of the left regiment of Jackson's Brigade." After several repulses it became impossible for even the most desperate of the Confederate commanders to bring their troops up to confront the breastworks.

The whole of Polk's wing was now repulsed for the second time, but immediately commenced to brace up for another advance, which took place just at twilight when Thomas' troops were vacating their lines. Barnes' brigade remained near Baird's position, as did also Van Derveer's until about 4:00 P.M., when the latter went to Brannan's assistance on Snodgrass Hill. Grose's brigade rejoined its division, Palmer's, on the line; the other detached brigades followed Negley. The Confederate commanders who were repulsed attributed their want of success to lack of generalship on the part of Polk, who caused the attacks to be made in succession and without reserves to strengthen weak places, or follow up success.

Polk's methods lacked generalship; they were almost imbecile. Instead of massing his troops in a solid column of attack to fall with irresistible weight upon Rosecrans' exposed flank, he stretched his line out until its strength and offensive power were lost by attenuation, and as its end swung around to envelop the Federal flank it became itself a flank in the air. Had his troops been massed, as were those of Longstreet, to strike Thomas squarely in flank, that wing would inevitably have been broken and the whole of Rosecrans' line rolled back upon itself, to the destruction of his entire army.

The front of Thomas' position with a short returning flank was covered with temporary breastworks which the enemy reached around. Here he was met, not by a solid division, but by detached brigades hurried from other parts of the line. These brigades had no common commander, but each fought independently. Negley, a division commander who was to have commanded, mistaking his orders, appeared among them only to conduct a portion of them away. The success attending this part of the battle was, upon the part of the Federals, simply phenomenal. The comparatively small loss among the troops, who were sheltered by breastworks, as against the terrible slaughter of their assailants, attests the value of such works for a defensive position.

While these events were in progress on the left of the Federal army, other and still more momentous events were transpiring on the right. The operations, as to their plan and execution on both the Federal and Confederate side, were of a character almost diametrically opposite, as were also their results. Polk's efforts were, as we have seen, a succession of attacks, each in itself insufficient to make a decisive impression; at the close of the contest Thomas' lines were as intact as at the beginning.

Longstreet, on the contrary, formed a powerful column of attack, flanked on each side by a heavy division, the whole of which he pushed forward simultaneously. He swept the Federal right wing from the field of battle.

In Thomas' wing every division, brigade and battery was in its proper position ready for the attack. In the right wing nothing was in readiness. During the night the divisions of Sheridan and Davis had been moved off to the right and rear, each separated from the other and both from those of the main line. The divisions of Wood and Van Cleve, of Crittenden's corps, were massed together some distance from the line. That of Negley was, in fact, the only one in line. Immediately after daylight Rosecrans gave orders to have these errors and omissions corrected, but everything moved slowly. Negley was withdrawn, as before stated, to assist Thomas on the extreme left, and Wood took his place in line, but so tardily that it was not until the turning movement of Breckinridge had well progressed that his brigades reached that critical point. Two brigades of Van Cleve's division were sent upon the same duty. Davis had got his two brigades in line and was closing in to fill up a gap on his left when the crash came. Sheridan, now a considerable distance from Davis, had just received orders to hasten with two of his brigades to the extreme left of Thomas' wing, and had barely started when he had to wheel into line to meet the attack of Longstreet.

Rosecrans was at this point of the line giving personal attention to many details and urging promptness on all those about him. McCook and Crittenden were there also giving directions. Notwithstanding so many commanders, there was great delay in preparing for the blow which every one could see might come at any minute. Fortunately, Polk's tardiness in making his attack on the right delayed Longstreet who, before making his attack, was to wait for Polk to commence his movements. Even after this delay of over four hours the troops of Rosecrans' right were unprepared.

The amount of marching that was done during that night and early morning by the right wing would have placed it boldly on the left of Thomas, thus covering the ground to Rossville Gap, that most desired by the enemy. Thomas' right would then have rested on Snodgrass Hill, as it did after the right wing had been swept away. Bragg's plans would have been disarranged and the condition of things with Rosecrans so much improved as almost to assure him of success.

The command of Longstreet consisted of the divisions of Stewart, Preston, Bushrod Johnson, Hood, McLaws and Hindman, containing, actually present, 17 brigades of 84 regiments, and 21 batteries of about 84 guns. Opposed to these were the divisions of Reynolds, Brannan, Wood, Davis and Sheridan, and one brigade of Van Cleve's; making in all 12 brigades of 49 regiments, and 12 batteries of about 60 guns.

Longstreet arrived late in the night of the 19th. Soon after daylight next morning he started to see his command, which he at once set about putting in shape for the work of the day. This he did by forming in his center a powerful column of attack under Hood, his reliable lieutenant, consisting of three divisions, each behind the other in line of battle. The first line consisted of Bushrod Johnson's division of three brigades and two batteries; the second of Hood's division of three brigades under Law. This division had just arrived from Virginia and its batteries were not yet up. The third line consisted of the two brigades of McLaws' division, then commanded by Brigadier General Joseph B. Kershaw, also from Lee's army, and without batteries.

It will be observed that these formations took place only a few hundred yards in front of the Federal line, but so screened from it by dense woods and the hilliness of the ground as not to be observable from it. Indeed, when going into position many of the brigades of Hood's divisions did not themselves realize the formation of which they were being made a part. A thick line of skirmishers kept back the Federal skirmishers and prevented them from finding out what was going on. In this connection it may be remarked that a great deal, in fact, most of the fighting of this battle, was done, so to speak, in the dark. Neither contestant could see much of the other, but usually burst most unexpectedly out of the woods upon his opponent.

On the right of the leading division of Hood's column was Stewart's division of Buckner's corps, consisting of three brigades and four batteries, while on the left of the column was Hindman's division of Polk's corps, of three brigades and three batteries. The divisions were formed with two brigades in the front line and one supporting where there were three brigades. Preston's division of Buckner's corps of three brigades and three batteries was held in reserve in rear of Stewart.

Longstreet, fresh from Gettysburg, where he had witnessed Lee's mistake in sending a small force to do the work of a much larger one, seemed not disposed to leave anything to chance, but to make the assaulting column irresistible. His superiority in numbers enabled him to do this. In addition to the batteries accompanying divisions, Longstreet had two battalions of reserve batteries, all of which were brought into requisition during the day, so far as the wooded and broken nature of the country would permit.

Bragg's plan of battle had not progressed as anticipated. Polk's attack upon Thomas' wing was signally repulsed and Longstreet was directed to attack without delay. It was now 11:00 o'clock Longstreet started forward his entire line; Stewart's division on the right, Hindman's on the left, with Hood's powerful column in the center. The center of the leading division of the column struck the Federal line at the right of Wood's position, or rather of the position which he had just left, for it so happened that at the moment Hood started forward Wood received an order from Rosecrans to "close up on Reynolds as fast as possible." As Brannan was between Wood and Reynolds this could not be executed literally; and only constructively by Wood's withdrawal from the line and passing to the rear of Brannan. This Wood did, thus leaving a gap in the line, and through it Hood's column passed with but little opposition. Striking this opening by the enemy was a mere coincidence. The enemy knew nothing of Wood's movement or of the opening until he emerged from the woods into the narrow field in front of it.

Davis, seeing the interval thus left by Wood, was closing in to his left when he was struck. Sheridan, who was in the act of starting to join Thomas, had barely time to reform line before he too was struck. In addition to the gap which Davis was in the act of closing up on his left, there was an interval of several hundred yards between him and Sheridan; on the right of Sheridan was nothing, therefore he and Davis were both detached outposts, as it were.

Davis' division, consisting of only two brigades present, happened to be behind a slight breastwork constructed by some other command, in a strip of woods in front of which there some small fields surrounding the Brotherton house, situated on the State Road. Behind this strip of woods were open fields interspersed with patches and strips of wood, covering the hills on each side of a by road leading back from the Brotherton house to the road leading to Chattanooga by the McFarland Gap. This was the road taken by Davis' command after it became broken.

The two brigades of Davis' division met the enemy with such a deadly fire as to stun him for a moment and cause some confusion in his ranks. Recovering from this, General Johnson, commanding the leading division of Hood's column, says: "my whole line, Gregg's Brigade in rear, supported by Hood's division under Law in a third line, swept forward with great force and rapidity, and carried the breastworks, from which the foe precipitately retreated under a heavy fire, particularly directed to the left from my left brigade." A few hundred yards brought Davis' disorganized men into the open fields in rear of the woods from which they had been driven. Here they were exposed to the full effect of the fire of the pursuing enemy. Ineffectual attempts were made by brigade and regimental commanders to reform their lines on a rocky ridge in the open field a few hundred yards to the rear, but the heavy loss of officers made the attempt only partly successful. It was, however, sufficient to check for a moment the advance of the enemy. But Johnson, straightening up his line, again rapidly advanced, driving everything before him. It was at this time that Hood received the wound which caused him the loss of a leg. The command of the column then devolved on Kershaw, the next officer in rank.

Owing to the movements of Davis' brigades his two batteries were unable to get into position with their brigades before Hood struck the blow. They were then ordered at once to the rear, and neither of them fired over half a dozen shots during the day.

Davis' brigades, failing to rally, fell back to the Dry Valley Road, which they followed to the more open ground beyond McFarland's Gap, where the men were gathered together and dispositions made to resist the enemy should he follow. Here the batteries rejoined their brigades. They had become inextricably involved among the trains of wagons, ambulances and artillery carriages crowding and hurrying along that narrow and tortuous defile.

It will be remembered that Sheridan had formed two of his brigades into columns to march as a reinforcement to Thomas. His remaining brigade of Colonel Bernard Laiboldt was favorably posted on a hill to the rear and right of Davis for the support of the latter. From this hill it made a bold advance to check the enemy now breaking Davis' line. In this advance the brigade was accompanied by its battery, "G," First Missouri Light Artillery Regiment, which endeavored to come into battery under a heavy fire of musketry from the enemy. But before it could do any firing, or extricate itself, its captain, Henry Hescock, and three of the pieces fell into the hands of the enemy.

Sheridan's other two brigades were moved along the ridge to the support of Laiboldt and advanced down the hill with it. Brigadier General William H. Lytle, commanding one of the brigades, posted his battery, Captain Arnold Sutermeister's 11th Indiana Independent Light Artillery Battery, near the base of the hill. Here it was enabled to get in a few rounds of canister before being obliged to withdraw. But owing to the loss of horses the captain was obliged to abandon two of his pieces. The other four escaped and coming into battery on the hill in rear did some firing before being finally driven from the field. General Lytle was killed at this time.

Bradley's brigade and its battery had the same experience as the other two. The battery did some valuable firing, but owing to the loss of horses had to abandon three of its pieces. All of these brigades held their ground as long as it was possible to do so, but they had to fight in an isolated position against the whole of Hindman's division, as well as part of Hood's column.

The whole of Sheridan's division fell back in disorder to the Dry Valley Road, but here the brigades were rallied and conducted by Sheridan over Missionary Ridge and past McFarland's Gap to the Rossville Gap, where, taking the State Road, he came in on the extreme left to the assistance of Thomas. The latter, however, had commenced to withdraw before his arrival and he had no opportunity of entering the fight on that part of the field.

The divisions of Sheridan and Davis did some gallant and stubborn fighting before giving way. Longstreet bears gruesome testimony to this in his report, saying: "The enemy's dead at this point marked well his line of battle."

This flank of Rosecrans' army, as well as the one from which Breckinridge was repulsed, was entirely in the air, but Longstreet, confident in his numbers, resorted to no turning movement. He simply aimed to pulverize it by one blow. Sheridan and Davis had between them 30 guns. Had these been massed on one or two of the eminences on that flank they undoubtedly would have held the enemy in check and afforded the infantry opportunity for rallying. As it was the batteries stuck close to their brigades and were enabled to do but little service, in fact no service at all.

During the night after the battle of the first day, Crittenden was ordered to hold Wood's and Van Cleve's divisions of his corps in reserve to assist either wing of the army in case of need. For this purpose he selected a hill 500 or 600 yards in rear of the main line and directly in rear of the opening subsequently left by the withdrawal of Wood. In front of this hill were open fields, in one of which stood the Dyer house. As a matter of convenience the hill has been called by the same name.

The batteries of the two divisions, some six in number, were posted on the hill, and the divisions massed near by. But soon after daylight on the 20th Wood was sent to replace Negley on the front line and two brigades of Van Cleve's division were hurried to the left to assist Thomas. One or two of the batteries were left on the hill, and about the time of Longstreet's attack were joined by others until there were in all 26 guns. The withdrawal of the infantry had left them entirely without support and when struck by the enemy they were speedily dispersed. It was expected by Captain Mendenhall, Crittenden's chief of artillery, when sending the batteries there, that the infantry now breaking on the front line would rally on these batteries and form a new line. In this he was, however, disappointed. The divisions of Sheridan and Davis belonged to another corps, were some considerable distance off to the right, and knowing nothing of this line of guns, or of the lay of the land on that part of the field, fell back by the Dry Valley Road, thus passing around the right of the position occupied by the batteries. The other troops that were broken, or at least most of them, were rallied on a new line connecting the intact part of the original line with Snodgrass Hill, which was several hundred yards to the left, or north, of Dyer's Hill.

It will be remembered that when Wood withdrew to "close up on Reynolds," he passed by a flank movement in rear of Brannan's division, which continued to hold its place in line. When Hood struck his blow Wood's division was directly behind that of Brannan, and close behind him was Brigadier General Samuel Beatty's brigade of Van Cleve's division, then upon the point of starting for Thomas' left. These three commands, Brannan's, Wood's and Beatty's, formed the right jamb of the opening through which Hood thrust his column. But the opening was not wide enough and Hood's right brigades struck each of these commands and thrust them aside.

Brannan's right brigade, that of Connell, was badly broken up. A portion of it, under its commander, joined the troops Negley was then collecting on Snodgrass Hill, and which were so ingloriously led from the field. The other portion rallied with other troops under Brannan and did brave service in the fighting yet to come. The battery with this brigade, Church's Michigan, managed to get in a few shots, but lost three of its pieces; the other three, escaping, joined the batteries on Dyer's Hill, where two of these also were captured.

The falling away of Connell's brigade exposed the flank of the next brigade on its left, which was Croxton's, and which, while endeavoring to change front to fire to the right, became broken in two, one half joining, or rather remaining in contact with Reynolds' division, still intact on its left, while the other half was rallied on Snodgrass Hill and gallantly assisted in the desperate fighting that took place there. The battery with this brigade, Lieutenant Gary's Ohio, after firing a few shots, extricated itself from the melee with the loss of one gun, and joining Negley was marched from the field.

Brannan rallied such men as he could of his own division on Snodgrass Hill and, perceiving the vital importance of the position, prepared to hold it to the last extremity. Negley had by this time succeeded in collecting together eight batteries and parts of batteries, numbering altogether 52 guns, together with quite a large infantry force, all of which he organized into a marching column, and then quietly conducted the whole from the field and joined the mass of fugitives hurrying along the Dry Valley Road to McFarland's Gap. Fortunately, Smith's regular battery remained, and this Brannan supported with the handful of troops he succeeded in rallying. The latter were subsequently joined by fragments from Wood's and Van Cleve's divisions, together with some from Negley's division arriving too late to be marched away by him. He was also strengthened by several regiments loaned him by Palmer and Reynolds. Altogether, he had about 2,500 men with which he bravely held the hill until the timely arrival of Brigadier

General James B. Steedman's division of Granger's corps and Van Derveer's brigade late in the afternoon.

It will be borne in mind that Wood's division was directly in rear of Brannan's when the enemy struck his blow. His right brigade, that of Buell, was carried away bodily. Buell succeeded in rallying one or two regiments which he placed on Brannan's right, on Snodgrass Hill, where they did splendid service. The other regiments, scattered and broken, found their way back to the Dry Valley Road and thence to McFarland's Gap. The battery of this brigade, Estep's Indiana, was on Dyer's hill and fell bodily into the hands of the enemy.

Wood's other brigade, that of Harker, changed front to meet the enemy on its flank and bravely stood its ground. Samuel Beatty's brigade, which, it will be remembered, was directly behind Wood, was overrun by the troops breaking in front of it and was thrown into utter confusion. It was, however, rallied in separate portions, and joining Brannan on Snodgrass Hill bravely assisted in holding that vital position. Swallow's Indiana battery, belonging to this brigade, was in position on Dyer's Hill, from which it fired a few shots before being driven away by the enemy. It lost one piece.

Snodgrass Hill, so frequently mentioned, was a prominent spur of Missionary Ridge, extending down from the latter in an oblique direction in rear of the right of Thomas' wing. On the opposite side of the hill from Thomas' position is the Dry Valley, along which a road runs to McFarland's Gap. The ground to the southward of the Snodgrass spur is very much broken by hills and ridges, one of which is the Dyer Hill or ridge, upon which the batteries so often mentioned were stationed. On the opposite side of Dry Valley, which is a mere canada, are other spurs of Missionary Ridge, along the slopes of which Hindman's division, the extreme left of Bragg's army, followed the broken troops of Rosecrans' right wing, and then crossing over, joined in the attack on Snodgrass Hill. The crest of this hill has a crescent shape, with the concavity towards the southward or Dry Valley side, forming somewhat of a cove, sometimes called the "Horseshoe." This particular point became the scene of the most bloody strife. Around the rim of this cove or "Horseshoe" Brannan posted the troops he had rallied. A short distance to his right, were the troops, including 52 guns, which Negley had collected. Smith's battery of the 4th U.S. Artillery Regiment, belonging to Van Derveer's brigade, then on the extreme left, was included among these guns. This battery was next to Brannan's position and was left behind when Negley moved away. It then attached itself to Brannan's command.

On the left of Brannan's position were the troops rallied by Wood. These extended down the slope and across a narrow valley at the foot of the Snodgrass spur. The line thus formed was perpendicular to the one held previous to Longstreet's assault. Its left connected with Reynolds' division, which had not been moved from its position and was still a part of Thomas' compact line. Between Reynolds and Wood was an interval, or thin part of the line; later in the day this was filled, or strengthened, by Hazen's brigade, brought over from Palmer's position, which was on the left of Reynolds. The line thus formed was continuous and reasonably compact from Brannan on Snodgrass Hill, around to the left of Baird on the State Road, where Breckinridge and Forrest had made their attacks earlier in the day. It was an irregular semicircle with a diameter of about half a mile.

On this line Thomas had all that remained intact of Rosecrans' original line of battle, from which had been swept away the divisions of Davis and Sheridan, and part of Van Cleve's division. Negley took away about 3,500 men, and in addition there were a miscellaneous lot of stragglers from Wood's, Brannan's and other divisions, estimated at about 1,500. Roughly stated, Thomas had about two-thirds of Rosecrans' infantry force. In artillery he was not so fortunate. Five batteries had been swept from the field with the divisions of Sheridan and Davis, and five more from Dyer's Hill. Negley took away seven batteries and parts of other batteries, leaving for Thomas only 10, and most of these had suffered more or less in the fight of the day before; so that he had in reality but 51 pieces. Thomas was the sole commander, Rosecrans, McCook and Crittenden had all been carried to the rear in the break on the right.

On his way to Chattanooga, Rosecrans dispatched Brigadier General James A. Garfield, his chief of staff, to Thomas, informing him of what had happened to the right wing, and directing him to assume command of everything remaining on the field, left it to his judgment when and how to retire to Rossville, there to take up a fresh position for resisting the further advance of the enemy. Rosecrans proceeded on to Chattanooga to make arrangements for the disposition of his army when it should fall back to that place. Garfield reached Thomas about 4:00 P.M. On his way through Rossville Gap he found that Granger had gone with Steedman's division to the assistance of Thomas.

At this time, although there was no fighting going on, on the left, the battle was raging furiously from the center around to the right. Thomas' only hope therefore was by resolute fighting to hold his ground until night should afford him more favorable opportunity of withdrawing. Until the arrival of Granger on the right of Brannan, Smith's battery was the only one on the new line of Snodgrass Hill. On the other or old part of his line, the batteries remained as before, distributed with their brigades along the line of temporary breastworks.

The position now held by Thomas was the strongest yet occupied by Rosecrans' army, and the resistance that he was capable of making to the most desperate efforts of the enemy indicates plainly the ground which Rosecrans should have taken up in the first place for a defensive battle. Here, his right would have rested on Snodgrass Hill and his left on Missionary Ridge at Rossville Gap. The chances of success would then have been decidedly in his favor and the result would doubtless have settled all question as to which side won the battle.

Returning now to Hood's column of assault; Bushrod Johnson, commanding the leading division, straightened up his line which had become somewhat disarranged by the first shocks, and then started forward again. He says: "Our lines now emerged from the forest into open ground on the border of long, open fields, over which the enemy were retreating under cover of several batteries, which were arrayed along the crest of a ridge (Dyer's Hill) on our right and front running up to the corner of a stubble field, and of one battery (one of Sheridan's) on our left and front posted on an elevation in the edge of the woods, just at the corner of a field near a peach orchard, and southwest of Dyer's house."

As previously mentioned, the batteries on Dyer's Hill had been left entirely without infantry support. Crittenden, Van Cleve and other officers made unsuccessful attempts to rally fugitives to their support. As soon as the fronts of the batteries were clear of the fugitives some of them opened fire and for a brief period retarded the advance of the enemy. But the latter, throwing out a cloud of skirmishers, gradually worked around through the ravines and brush and gained positions on their flanks and partly in rear. What now occurred is best told in the language of Captain Estep, one of the battery commanders, who says:

I immediately cautioned my lieutenants about holding fire till ordered (until our own men got out of the woods in front), but a few moments elapsed, however, till the enemy came up in splendid style in heavy lines to the right of my front. I ordered firing to commence with shell and canister. I am confident that we wounded hundreds of them as they came up. Other batteries were in the same line with mine and dealing perhaps equal destruction to the enemy, but just then when I supposed that we were going to drive them back, we received a galling fire from the enemy who had got position in force on our right flank and rear;

but a moment more and the enemy was charging us from the right. My horses were killed and disabled and I could do nothing but leave the battery in his possession.

The other batteries had a similar experience; they were all crippled by the loss of horses, and out of 26 guns, 15 fell into the hands of the enemy. In withdrawing what they could save under such heavy pressure, the batteries had no other direction to follow except to the Dry Valley, where they took the road to McFarland's Gap, near which place they eventually joined their respective brigades.

Notwithstanding this loss of so much of the artillery force from the field, the time gained was of the utmost importance. It enabled Thomas' troops to get into position on Snodgrass Hill, now the key point. It also enabled the divisions of Sheridan and Davis to pass by on the Dry Valley Road before being intercepted by Hood's column. It will be remembered that these divisions did not break and scatter to the rear when first struck by the enemy, but rallied and turned at several points, thus consuming the time which would have enabled Hood's troops to reach the road in advance of their passage had it not been for this delay.

It was now about mid-day. Johnson, after capturing the guns on Dyer's Hill, pressed forward his line through a narrow strip of woods and across open fields to another ridge about 600 yards from Dyer's Hill. From the crest of this ridge the ground descends abruptly to Dry Valley, in which, at the upper extremity of Snodgrass Hill, is a small cove in which stands Villeto's house and fields. The road along this narrow valley was a confused mass of wagons, ambulances, guns and caissons, quite a number of which were captured by the enemy near the Villeto place. Some of the wagons were loaded with infantry ammunition, which gave a timely supply to the enemy, while Thomas' troops, defending Snodgrass Hill, became so exhausted of it that the boxes of the dead and wounded were searched for a last round.

After gaining possession of the last ridge referred to, Johnson halted for short time to reform his line and reestablish connection with other commands from which he had now become quite separated, being considerably in advance of them. The division commanded by Law, following immediately after Johnson, had scarcely passed beyond the line which had recently been occupied by the Federal troops when it received such a fire upon its right flank as to cause it to stampede, under the impression that it was being flanked by Thomas' troops. Law's three brigades were not again brought into the battle.

Kershaw's division, composed of his own and Brigadier General Benjamin G. Humphreys' brigades and forming the third line of Hood's column, changed front to the right and moved along the valley that lies between the foot of Snodgrass Hill and the State Road. This movement, if successful, would have taken the main part of Thomas' line in reverse. From the extremity of Snodgrass Hill there extends to near the State Road a narrow ridge, the abruptness of whose sides gives to it the quality almost of a natural parapet. Troops holding it could load behind it out of reach of the enemy's fire and then advance to the crest of it to deliver a plunging fire on the advancing foe. These were still the days of the muzzle loader, requiring considerable time for the soldier to charge his piece. The troops holding the ridge had, in addition, the moral effect inspired by the command which it had over those below. Wood, perceiving the advantage of this ridge, placed Harker's brigade and a part of Buell's behind the crest. Later in the day Hazen's brigade took position alongside of Harker. Neither of these had with them their batteries. That of Harker had fallen into the hands of Negley, and that of Hazen had been left in position on the line from whence the brigade had moved. Thomas had no reserve with which to strengthen a weak point, and had but a single line, a break at any point of which meant a break of the whole.

While Kershaw was swinging around his division, in the manner stated, Bushrod Johnson changed his front also to the right so as to attack Snodgrass Hill, and Hindman, crossing over Dry Valley, brought his division up on the left of Johnson. Johnson had four batteries, two of which stuck close to his division throughout the day and were exceedingly active in taking positions from which they gave great annoyance to the Federal troops. These batteries were now brought up to dislodge Smith; but the latter held his ground, and with his lieutenant, Rodney, fought his guns until dark put an end to the conflict, when, with the rest of the troops, he withdrew, having but six rounds remaining in his chests.

About 2:00 P.M. Johnson, with his own three brigades and one of Hindman's, made an impetuous charge against the hill, but was signally repulsed and forced back to the ground from whence he had started, where he reformed his command and waited for the arrival of Hindman's other two brigades. The ground in front of Snodgrass Hill over which the enemy had to maneuver to make these attacks was greatly broken into hills and ravines, thickly covered with woods and underbrush. The crests of the hills or ridges were each a little higher as Snodgrass Hill was approached, which latter had an elevation of about 200 feet above the general level of the ground at the base of the hills or ridges. Snodgrass Hill was wooded, but beyond it were fields in which stood the Snodgrass house, now used as a field hospital. Towards its upper extremity the hill was cut through by a ravine which the enemy took advantage of to get in rear of Brannan's right. The Federal troops holding the hill were without even the semblance of rifle pits or breastworks.

Johnson being now joined on his left by Hindman's two absent brigades, and all in readiness with his batteries so disposed as to assist in the assault or take advantage of any success, the whole line moved forward over the broken hills and gulches to the second assault upon this part of Snodgrass Hill. Hindman's brigades extended beyond that part of the hill held by Brannan and were rapidly gaining his rear through the cut, or ravine, just referred to.

At this most critical moment of the battle Granger made his appearance with Steedman's division of two brigades and two batteries. Granger, guarding the approaches to Rossville Gap, had heard the sound of the battle four miles off to his right, and judging from the way it had been moving that something was wrong, with true soldierly instinct deemed it his duty to go to the assistance of his comrades, although without orders to do so. On his way he had met some of Forrest's dismounted cavalry and some of Breckinridge's troops who attempted to intercept him or cause delay. Detaching Colonel Dan McCook's brigade to attend to these, he hastened on with Steedman's two brigades.

Following close upon Granger was Van Derveer with his brigade, which it will be remembered had been sent in the forenoon to assist in repulsing Breckinridge from the extreme left. Smith's battery, belonging to this brigade, was already and had been for hours on the ground doing distinguished service. Granger came up directly in front of the gap through which the enemy was making his way and occupied the ground lately vacated by Negley. Van Derveer took position on his left and on the right of Brannan.

Granger did not wait for the enemy, but advanced to meet him, and here took place one of the most obstinate struggles of the day, resulting in the repulse of the enemy who was pursued and driven back behind the ridge from whence he came. So badly was the enemy broken up that Hindman's three brigades, says Johnson, "did not again enter the fight. . . . The retreat on this hill was precipitate, and called for all the exertions I could command to prevent many of the troops from abandoning it. The officers, however, joined with every energy and zeal in the effort to stay the retreat, and by appeals, commands, and physical efforts, all save a few who persisted in skulking behind trees or lying idly on the ground, were brought up to our lines in support of the artillery." These were

among the choice troops of the Confederacy and their demoralization but shows the spirit of the attack by which they were
repulsed. The slaughter that took place in this assault and
repulse was upon both sides unprecedented. With such troops
as Johnson could bring to the scratch he made several attacks,
each feebler than the foregoing, until near sundown, when
another general advance was made.

Almost of as much importance as the troops themselves
was the ammunition brought by Granger's brigades. Thomas
was cut off from his ammunition trains, and Brannan's troops
had expended their last rounds and were searching the boxes
of dead comrades for a few more cartridges, when Granger
appeared with a fresh supply.

The two batteries accompanying the brigades of
Steedman's division did their full share of the work of repuls-
ing the enemy. These were the 18th Ohio Independent Light
Artillery Battery under Captain Charles C. Aleshire, and
Battery "M," 1st Illinois Light Artillery Regiment, under
Lieutenant Thomas Burton.

Kershaw's division followed that of Johnson until it arrived
where the Federal line had been before being swept away by
Johnson. Here, it changed front to the right, which occupied
considerable time, and then commenced to move northward
parallel to the State Road, which brought his brigades fronting
the position held by Wood with Harker's brigade and a few
regiments from other brigades. After a little preliminary skirmishing, Wood fell back to the narrow ridge terminating the
lower extremity of Snodgrass Hill and which has already been
mentioned as a natural parapet across the narrow valley
between the base of the hill and the State Road. The left of
Kershaw's division covered also a portion of Snodgrass Hill.
From this point the line was continued to the left by the divisions of Johnson and Hindman.

About 1:00 P.M. Kershaw made his first attack with his
own and Humphreys' brigades. This was handsomely
repulsed "after," as Kershaw says, "one of the most gallant

struggles I have ever witnessed." About 3:00 P.M., being reinforced by Anderson's brigade of Hindman's division, he made
another assault in conjunction with the troops on his left. This
attack likewise was repulsed. Longstreet now ordered forward
Preston's division, the one held in reserve, for a final effort;
this was made about 4:00 o'clock, but with no better result
than the former. It was the one which Granger and Van
Derveer took part in repulsing. The most experienced soldiers
declared it to be the severest battle of musketry they had ever
witnessed. Until Granger arrived with the two batteries of
Steedman's division, Smith's was the only battery on that line.
But it was heroic, and the enemy are free in stating the damage it caused them.

This virtually closed the contest on the right flank of
Thomas' position. Longstreet applied to Bragg for assistance
from Polk's wing, "but was informed," says Longstreet, "that
his troops had been beaten back so badly that they could be
of no service to me."

Stewart's division, a part of Longstreet's command flanking
Hood's column of assault on the right, moved forward with
the column, but striking Reynolds' two brigades behind their
breastworks of logs was so badly repulsed that it had to retire
to its first position to reform. Stewart, who was a veteran of
experience, describing his assault, says: "For several hundred
yards both lines pressed on under the most terrible fire it has
ever been my fortune to witness, . . new batteries being
opened by the enemy on our front and flank, heavily supported by infantry, it became necessary to retire. . . . During this
charge, which was truly heroic, our loss was severe."

Thomas had now repulsed every corps, division, and
brigade of infantry in Bragg's army, as well as some of his dismounted cavalry. All of these had been brought up twice to
the assault, most of them three, and some of them four times,
until there was no more assault left in them for that day. For
anything that the enemy was capable of doing to the contrary,
he could apparently have held his position indefinitely, had it

not been for lack of ammunition. His trains had been cut off from him and were beyond Missionary Ridge. He, however, managed to get up a small supply with which to insure his safe withdrawal. His troops were suffering also for food and water. Under these circumstances he determined to hold on until nightfall, and then withdrawing, fall back to Rossville Gap, and there take up a position to hold the enemy in check until the scattered troops of the right wing could be collected for a new defensive line at Chattanooga.

The movement was commenced by Reynolds' division at 6:00 o'clock, which on that day of the year was the hour of sunset. Reynolds was to post his division so as to cover the withdrawal of the other troops, but soon after leaving his line a body of the enemy was seen approaching the left flank behind Baird. This proved to be a part of Breckinridge's division, again feeling its way around that flank. A sudden dash of one of Reynolds' brigades drove these back, after which Reynolds' brigades, together with that of Willich, took commanding positions to cover the withdrawal of the other troops. Baird, Johnson and Palmer followed, but the enemy, having gathered himself together, for a final effort, now advanced and attacked with fury these divisions as they were in the act of leaving their breastworks. This resulted in some confusion and considerable loss in killed and wounded and a few prisoners, but after regaining the shelter of the woods beyond the Kelley fields the brigades were reformed and taking the "Ridge Road" reached Rossville without being pursued. Wood and Steedman retired from Snodgrass Hill without molestation. By some oversight Brannan had not been notified that his right was uncovered. The enemy, on the alert, perceiving this, pushed through the ravine on the right of where Steedman had been and was forming in rear of Wood's position, when Van Derveer and some other of Wood's troops turned upon them, and after a brief but severe conflict drove them back, thus securing the safe withdrawal of the whole.

The enemy made great capital out of these last attacks, claiming that they had driven Thomas from his position. Immediately after the withdrawal of the latter the enemy occupied his lines, but advanced no further. Thomas brought with him from the field all of his artillery, save two pieces with broken carriages; and all ambulances and wagons, leaving nothing for the enemy but the unfortunates too badly wounded to be removed, and these were gathered into field hospitals and left with medical supplies and attending surgeons.

Frequent mention has been made of General Negley's strange conduct on this day, and, as his withdrawal from the field occasioned the loss to Thomas of 48 pieces of artillery, leaving him but 51 with which to maintain his position, it is pertinent to be more explicit on this point. It has already been stated that to strengthen his left flank against the dangers then threatening it, Thomas instructed Negley "to mass as much artillery on the slopes of Missionary Ridge, west of the State Road, as he could conveniently spare from his lines, supported strongly by infantry so as to sweep the ground to the left and rear of Baird's position." Under these instructions Negley soon collected batteries and parts of batteries to the number of 52 pieces. But, misapprehending the purport of Thomas' order, instead of posting them so as to protect the left flank, he sent them to Snodgrass Hill in a direction directly opposite from that intended. Here, supporting them with one of his brigades intact and such parts of other brigades as he could pick up, he placed some of the batteries in positions from which they did some long-range firing upon Longstreet's force, which by this time was driving the right wing up the Dry Valley Road. His position on the hill or ridge was to the right of Brannan, and about the place where Steedman afterwards met the enemy.

At this time the fighting was very heavy on the left at the point where Negley should have posted his batteries, and in fact also it was heavy all around to Brannan's position. Stragglers were numerous from both the right and left. These seem to have given Negley the impression that the day was lost, and being overwhelmed by the responsibility of so much artillery on his hands, he formed it into column with the infantry he had collected and, marching by a wood road to his right and rear, reached the Dry Valley Road which he followed through McFarland's Gap. Here he halted and with his organized regiments was energetic in collecting stragglers and organizing them so as to resist the enemy should he reach the gap. He left Snodgrass Hill but a short time before Hindman's and Johnson's divisions made the furious assault before mentioned. Had he remained a few minutes longer, he could not have withdrawn by that route and would have been compelled to fight. His whole idea seems to have been to save his artillery, not to use it. In the meanwhile, the infantry brigades on the left, that he should have been attending to and which were battling to keep the enemy from crushing that flank, were allowed to take care of themselves.

The infantry conducted away has been variously estimated from 700 up to 3,500. Negley claims the first figure, but the latter more nearly represents the number who left the field consequent upon his action. He withdrew without orders and without being driven off, and while his comrades were hotly engaged holding by the skin of their teeth the ground upon which they fought, and who were in dire need of the guns and men he was taking from them. A Court of Inquiry, after a rather perfunctory examination of the case, accepting his views, namely that it was his first duty to save his artillery, not to use it, exonerated him from all blame.

In the open ground beyond McFarland's Gap, he collected stragglers which he organized, and with the troops he already had, made a force of about 5,000 men. Davis soon arrived with the remnants of his division and in a short time thereafter Sheridan, with his division well in hand. It was then learned that Thomas was still holding his ground, and a consultation was held when it was determined that Davis should remain to guard McFarland's Gap while Sheridan should proceed on to hold Rossville Gap. Negley was to take position between the two to give assistance to either. The batteries had now joined their brigades from which they had become separated. Arriving at Rossville Gap, Sheridan found that Granger had gone to the assistance of Thomas, whither he too, at once proceeded.

This was the state of affairs when Thomas fell back from the position he had so skillfully and bravely defended. By midnight he had established a line along Missionary Ridge covering both gaps, and with strong reserves in rear, using for this purpose all troops within reach. The troops were in good condition, except from the great fatigue of two days' hard fighting. Only a few had straggled back to Chattanooga or beyond recall. Thomas, in the absence of Rosecrans, commanded the whole and held the position until after nightfall of the following day when he withdrew each corps, division and brigade going direct to the position assigned it on the new line near the town.

During the 21st Bragg made threatening demonstrations on Thomas' line and there was some sharp skirmishing, but the former deemed it prudent not to make any general attack. Rosecrans lost in the battle of both days 1,637 killed and 9,756 wounded, for a total of 11,413. He lost also 4,757 missing, most of whom were either killed or wounded, but not being otherwise accounted for, were reported as missing, making a grand total of 16,170.

Bragg's losses, as compiled from the "Records of the Rebellion," aggregated 17,804, or 1,634 more than his opponent. He probably did not have quite so many captured as his adversary. Rosecrans reports that he captured from him 2,005. The loss in the two armies was about in proportion to their relative strengths in killed and wounded, not counting the missing; it was about 18 percent. In some of the Federal subdivisions it reached the terrible figure of 50 percent. In Steedman's division the loss was 1,178 out of 3,700.

The intensity of the fighting in this battle will be better comprehended when it is observed that in the Franco-Prussian War in 1870, the average loss at the battles of Woerth, Spicheren, Mars-la-Tour, Gravelotte and Sedan was 12 per-cent. At Magenta, and Solferino, in 1859, the average loss of both armies was less than nine per cent. At the great battles of Marengo and Austerlitz, sanguinary as they were, Napoleon lost an average of less than 14.5 percent. The loss of Wellington at Waterloo was less than 12 percent.

Rosecrans represented the number of guns lost as 36. Bragg claimed 51, but this included 15 captured from his troops and left on the field for want of horses to draw them off.

As Bragg's army slept on the field, it was claimed that he had won the battle, and great was the rejoicing over it throughout the South and among their sympathizers in the North. For a time appearances certainly favored this view; the enemy, following up Rosecrans, closely besieged his army in Chattanooga, and cutting his lines of communication, reduced it to starvation. A large number of artillery horses perished for want of forage and the remainder became so reduced in strength as to be unserviceable. This state of things continued about a month, until the first troops to arrive and open com-munication and give relief to the beleagured army were the Eleventh and Twelfth Corps, under Hooker, from the Army of the Potomac. These corps, after a severe and successful engagement with Longstreet's troops at Wanhatchie, took possession of Lookout Valley and opened communication with Rosecrans' army some days previous to the arrival of Sherman with part of the Army of the Tennessee.

But, however, it may have been with the battle, whether a tactical defeat or victory, it is certain that Rosecrans had gained the objective of the campaign, which was the capture of Chattanooga, the strategic center of the middle zone of the Confederacy and the gateway to its vitals. Bragg had been maneuvered out of it by Rosecrans' masterly strategy, and being heavily reinforced, attempted to regain it by crushing the Federal army. In this he failed, and hence the victory rested with his adversary. Chattanooga was never regained by the enemy, but became a few months afterwards the base from which Sherman started on his memorable march to cut the Confederacy in twain. That Bragg, with his superior numbers and the tactical advantages given him by Rosecrans, did not crush the Federal army was due to the inferior generalship of Polk, opposed to the sturdy repellant blows of Thomas.

In this battle the Federal artillery had to contend with every disadvantage possible, except one, which was that the individual batteries were good and well commanded. But the wooded character of the country, taken in connection with the restriction imposed upon them by being tied down to diminutive brigades, neutralized this, a fact clearly and forcibly expressed by Colonel Harker, one of the brigade commanders, who in his report says:

I have already stated that I had directed Captain [Cullen] Bradley [commanding the battery attached to his brigade] to keep well to the rear, but to conform his movements to my own. I did this partly from prudential considerations and partly from what I conceived a proper appreciation of the artillery arm of the service. While I have no disposition to criticize the conduct of others, and particularly my superiors, I nevertheless consider it my duty to state that I believe in many instances batteries in the late engagement were placed in positions where artillery could not be effectively used, and, from the nature of the country, could not easily be extricated. I believe that it was in this way that most of our artillery was lost in the late engagement. In other instances, from a want of judgment and knowledge of our lines, some of our artillery injured many of our own men. I submit this question as one of such great importance in the science of battles as to merit the serious consideration of the general commanding, the department.

It may be asserted that, although Chickamauga was the most difficult possible field for artillery, it was nevertheless not entirely destitute of favorable positions; among these may be mentioned the flanks of the line of battle, both of which rested entirely in the air and invitingly vulnerable to assaults from the enemy. Following well established military rules, these flanks should have been strengthened by massing on each a strong artillery force. As it was, each was exposed to heavy assaults; that upon the right crumbling to pieces the entire right wing, and that upon the left failing only through the inferior generalship of the commander of the Confederate right wing. Failure by Rosecrans to thus strengthen his flanks is most surprising occurring as it did so soon after his experience at Stones River, where his right flank for want of proper precautions, was swept away like that of Hooker at Chancellorsville.

Then too, when it became necessary or seemed to be necessary to move the line of battle, already established along the State Road, forward to meet the enemy in the depths of the forest, the batteries, instead of following, should have been massed at points on the State Road, along which was more or less of cleared and open ground. Here they would have been within supporting distance of the line fighting in front, and in readiness to meet and repulse the enemy in case he should succeed in breaking through the fighting line. Just such a thing did happen on the afternoon of the first day; but by good luck, a mere accident it was, some 30 pieces were available to be put in position to repel the enemy and restore the broken line.

The events of this battle, to say nothing of that of Stones River, opened the eyes of Rosecrans to the glaring defects of the organization and command of his artillery, and it was not many days before he adopted remedial measures. The batteries were taken from infantry brigades; two were allowed to each division, while the other seven of each corps were organized into a brigade (battalion) and placed under the direct command of a field officer of artillery, and the whole artillery of the army under Brigadier General Brannan, who had so ably commanded an infantry division in the preceding campaigns, and was furthermore an experienced artillery officer. From this on there was an efficient service of artillery in the Army of the Cumberland, and while the effective work done by it was increased there was no further loss of guns by the score.

At the same time that the artillery was reorganized the infantry received a better organization. The two corps that had been commanded by McCook and Crittenden were consolidated into one, which received the designation of the Fourth, in place of the old Fourth of the Army of the Potomac, which had become extinct. This was placed under Gordon Granger.

Shortly after the battle of Chickamauga the Eleventh and Twelfth Corps were hastened from the Army of the Potomac to assist in opening the blockade of Chattanooga. These were soon after merged into one, the Twentieth, under Hooker, and from this on constituted a part of the Army of the Cumberland. In this reorganization of the infantry, the numerical strength of brigades was greatly increased, giving heavier divisions with increased efficiency.

About the last of October Rosecrans was superseded in command of the Army of the Cumberland by Thomas. Grant was assigned to the command of the whole Military Division of the Mississippi, which was made to embrace the Army of the Cumberland under Thomas, of the Tennessee under Sherman, and of the Ohio under John Schofield, together with other troops not immediately connected with the military operations from Chattanooga to Atlanta.

Rosecrans had been in command of the Army of the Cumberland just one year, during which time he had fought the battles of Stones River and Chickamauga, and had thrust the enemy back from Nashville to beyond Chattanooga, thus recovering all the ground that had been lost by Halleck's disposition of troops while in command, in the field, during a few weeks after the battle of Shiloh.

A short time after the arrival of Sherman with the Army of the Tennessee to the relief of the beleaguered Army of the Cumberland at Chattanooga, that is, on the 23rd to the 25th of November, was fought the battle of Missionary Ridge, which forced Bragg back to Dalton, about 25 miles further south, where his army rested during the winter. Meanwhile, Grant was created lieutenant general and placed in command of all the Federal armies, and making his headquarters with the Army of the Potomac, turned over his western command to Sherman, who, during the winter, prepared the Armies of the Cumberland, Tennessee and Ohio for the Atlanta Campaign of the following spring. Brigadier General Barry was assigned to him as chief of artillery, and with characteristic energy soon brought about many improvements, chief among which may be mentioned the simplification of the calibers of pieces, which up to this time had been greatly mixed in the batteries of the western armies, thereby causing great difficulty and confusion in the supply of ammunition and stores. From 12, the number of calibers was reduced to four. The proportion of guns was likewise reduced from three to two per 1,000 men. The surplus guns were sent to the rear to serve as guns of position at the various fortified places necessary to maintain so long a line of communication through a hostile country. The entire artillery force that took the field with the three armies just mentioned consisted of 50 batteries of 254 guns, 167 officers and 6,125 men; for the command of all of which there were besides Barry, as chief of artillery of the whole, one brigadier general, one colonel and one lieutenant colonel, chiefs of artillery of each army respectively, and the ridiculously small number of five majors for the command of brigades and battalions of batteries. Captains had to be detached from their batteries to perform the duties of field officers. It has frequently been mentioned that it was the policy of the Government to have as few field officers of artillery as possible. Starting out blindly with this policy, it was adhered to even after its folly had been fully demonstrated and army commanders were making exertions to get more.

For Sherman's three combined armies an Artillery Reserve of 18 additional batteries was organized, but owing to the nature of the campaign, this reserve did not follow the movements of the active force, but was left at Nashville where it acted as a feeder to supply the batteries at the front, thus keeping the latter always in the highest state of efficiency. No regularly equipped horse batteries, such as those of the Army of the Potomac, served with the Western armies, but suitable mounted batteries, equipped as lightly as possible, were selected for service with the cavalry and did efficient service.

On the 6th of May 1864, Sherman having concentrated his army in the vicinity of Chattanooga, commenced his Atlanta campaign. His active army then consisted of 98,797 men of all arms and 254 guns, opposed to which was the Confederate army, entrenched at Dalton, consisting of 60,000 men in round numbers, with a proportional amount of field artillery. In his fortifications at Atlanta the enemy had 20 pieces of heavy artillery. This army was now commanded by "Joe" Johnston, who had superseded Bragg. But before the capture of Atlanta, Johnston himself was superseded by Hood, who continued in command until his army was broken and scattered by Thomas on the 15th of the following December at the battle of Nashville and the pursuit that followed.

As Sherman advanced, Johnston was forced to fall back from one point to another, entrenching at every eligible position and making desperate resistance everywhere. In this way occurred a series of hard fought battles in which the artillery was conspicuously efficient.

On July 20th the Federal army closed in upon Atlanta, which was strongly fortified and well armed. From this time to September 1st was a series of desperate battles, in all of which the artillery took a most prominent part. On the night of the date last mentioned the enemy evacuated this stronghold, which virtually terminated that part of these operations known as the Atlanta campaign. But there were other operations yet to follow.

About this time the Confederate States President Davis visited Hood's army and projected for it a campaign in which, by a circuitous march of some 300 miles, it was again to invade Tennessee, and thus cause Sherman to withdraw. The movement for the execution of this project was commenced by Hood during the last week of September. To meet it Sherman detached Thomas with the Fourth Corps under Stanley, and the Twenty-third under Schofield, with instructions to gather up the various detachments guarding the lines of communication back to Nashville, and all other troops he could lay his hands on, and drive Hood back. This resulted, as before stated, in the utter destruction of Hood's army as an organized force.

Besides the large numbers that were killed and wounded, Thomas captured upwards of 13,000 prisoners, including eight general officers. A large proportion of those still remaining turned off at every crossroad and by-path to their homes. A few, and but very few, were held together to join other armies. Thomas captured 72 pieces of artillery and nearly all of Hood's remaining ammunition.

Thus passed out of existence the most formidable rebel army of the West, the one to which the Army of the Cumberland had been constantly opposed. It was originally part of the force with which General Albert Sydney Johnston assailed Grant at Shiloh on April 6, 1862, the object of which battle was, by defeating Grant, to open the way for an invasion to the Ohio River through Tennessee and Kentucky. Failing at Shiloh, Bragg marched the greater part of the Confederate force to Chattanooga, which he made his *point d'appui* for operations looking to the same end. Buell, who had joined Grant at Shiloh, was sent with his army to capture Chattanooga, but owing to the long lines of railroads he was obliged to keep open to maintain his supplies, Bragg was enabled to secure a firm hold not only of Chattanooga, but upon the mountains eastward, to Knoxville, the ranges of which formed screens from behind which he suddenly burst, turning Buell's left and threatening his line of communication. On the first day of September commenced that memorable race for the Ohio River. Buell outmaneuvered his adversary and finally on the 7th of October, brought him to bay at Perryville, Kentucky, where for the first time as distinct forces, these two armies, that of Buell, now called the Army of the Ohio, but subsequently the Army of the Cumberland, and that of Bragg, known to the Confederates as the Army of the Tennessee, grappled in battle.

Following this, occurred the battles of Stones River, Chickamauga, Missionary Ridge, those on the Atlanta campaign, and finally that of Nashville, which closed the career of the Confederate Army of Tennessee. With the exception of the Army of the Potomac and Lee's Army of Northern Virginia, no other two armies during the Rebellion had so long and so desperate a struggle.

A late nineteenth-century painting of the Union artillery firing on the advancing Confederate line during the Battle of Shiloh. (*Library of Congress*)

ELEVEN

SHILOH

(First Day)

H AVING NARRATED THE OPERATIONS of the artillery in
some of the principal campaigns of the armies of the
Potomac and Cumberland, a like attention will now be given
to the Army of the Tennessee. To the three divisions, those of
major generals Charles F. Smith, John A. McClernand, and
Lew Wallace, with which General Grant had captured Fort
Donelson, were added three others, those of brigadier generals William T. Sherman, Stephen A. Hurlbut and Benjamin M.
Prentiss, the whole receiving the name of the Army of the
Tennessee, and constituting the right of the Federal grand
army stretching from the Mississippi to the Atlantic, a distance of about 1,000 miles. The left of this grand army was the
Army of the Potomac, then under McClellan, operating on
the waters of Chesapeake Bay against Richmond, the capital
of the Southern Confederacy. The center was the Army of the
Cumberland (then called the Army of the Ohio) under Buell,
operating southward through Kentucky and Tennessee.

Each of these armies had its special mission to perform;
that of the Tennessee was to open the Mississippi River, a
work which it virtually accomplished by the reduction of
Vicksburg, the capitulation of which took place on July 4th,

1863. In the meanwhile, it fought many battles, the first of which was that of Shiloh, April 6th and 7th, 1862. It is to the operations of the artillery in this battle, where it performed a remarkable and distinguished part, which this section is to be directed.

The fall of forts Henry and Donelson had caused the Confederates to abandon the whole of Kentucky and the greater part of Tennessee, and on the Mississippi, to fall back from Columbus to Island Number Ten and New Madrid and take up the line of the Charleston and Memphis railroad in northern Alabama and Mississippi, a line running east and west parallel to the front they now proposed to defend. This line was of the utmost importance to the Confederate cause and all available troops were concentrated for its maintenance. The most vital point on it was Corinth, a village in the northern part of Mississippi at the intersection of the Mobile and Ohio railroad with the road just mentioned. Here were assembled, under General Albert S. Johnston, the three corps of Bragg, Polk, and Hardee, with a provisional corps under Breckinridge. Beauregard was second in command, but had no specific assignment. The village of Corinth is situated 21 miles southwest of Pittsburg Landing on the Tennessee River, a place of steamboat freighting and debarkation for Corinth and other villages on the neighboring railroads.

The object of the campaign now undertaken by the Federal forces was to gain possession of Corinth, and thus by breaking the Confederate line, shake him loose from his hold on the Mississippi. The Tennessee River, making a long sweep through the northern part of Alabama and Mississippi and thence northward to the Ohio, afforded transportation for Grant's army to Pittsburg Landing. The movement was commenced during the first week of March. A depot was established at Savannah Landing, on the opposite side of the river, nine miles below. On the 14th Pittsburg Landing was occupied, and soon the whole army was transferred to it, except the depot still at Savannah. Buell's Army of the Ohio, then at or near Nashville, was to march overland, and uniting with the Army of the Tennessee, was to cooperate in the movement on Corinth. When everything should be in readiness, General Halleck was to leave his headquarters at St. Louis and personally assume command of the whole.

The 5th of April was the time set by Buell for his junction with Grant. He was, however, notified that he need not hurry his march, as transportation to cross the river would not be ready for him before the 8th. Nelson's division, however, arrived at Savannah on the evening of the 5th, and the other divisions of Buell's army were, under the direction of that energetic leader, making their way forward as rapidly as the miry nature of the roads would permit.

Johnston, fully informed by spies, and the officiousness of disloyal citizens, of every movement of the Federal armies, determined to strike Grant's army before the arrival of Buell and set the morning of the 5th as the time for his assault. But owing to the bad condition of the roads and heavy rains on the 5th, his army did not get into position for the blow until the following morning. It then consisted of the following troops actually present:

	Div.	Brig.	Reg.	Bat.	Guns
Polk's Corps	2	4	16	4	10,399
Bragg's Corps	2	6	28	6	19,564
Hardee's Corps	1	3	18	6	5,750
Breckenridge's Corps, provisional	1	3	17	5	7,846
Artillery					2,353
Cavalry					2,932
Aggregate present for duty	6	16	79	21	48,844

The cavalry was attached to corps; the batteries to brigades, one to each brigade; a few had two.

Opposed to this force Grant had present for duty:

Division Name	Div.	Brig.	Reg.	Bat.	Guns
McClernand's	3	12	4	24	7,029
W.H.L. Wallace's					
(Smith's)	3	15	4	24	8,708
Lew Wallace's	3	11	2	12	7,564
Hurlburt's	3	12	3	18	7,302
Sherman's	4	12	3	16	8,830
Prentiss's	2	10	2	12	5,463
Unattached		2	4	22	
Aggregate present					
for duty	18	74	22	128	44,896

While Johnston had 3,948 more men than Grant, the latter was superior to him in artillery by 10 pieces. Grant had about an equal number of cavalry. The two armies were therefore very nearly equal in fighting capacity.

The Confederate system of returns embraced a column showing the *effective* for the line of battle. This gave the actual fighting strength of his commands. The Federals, on the contrary, had no such system, but under the heading of *present for duty* embraced every man, whether *effective* for the fight or not. This included teamsters, musicians, hospital attendants, cooks, and a host of others absent from the actual fighting line. This has always led to great confusion in stating the relative strength of the opposing forces of the Federal and Confederate armies. Generally, the effective of the latter has been taken as synonymous with the present for duty of the former, thus making the Confederate force always appear the weaker, even when actually greater. The regiments of the two services being about equal in strength their numbers always afford a very close approximation to the relative strength of opposing forces on any occasion. In this instance Johnston had 79 and Grant 74; but Lew Wallace's division of 11 regiments being absent from the battle of the first day left Grant with but 63 regiments against his opponent's 79. This therefore was the relative strength of the fighting force of the two armies at Shiloh on the first day, the day when most of the fighting was done.

Ten of Grant's guns were heavy pieces standing on the bluff near the landing. The two batteries serving them had not yet received their horses. The other two unattached batteries were new arrivals, simply awaiting assignment, but were brought forward and attached to divisions during the battle. There was no artillery reserve.

The Federal cavalry, slightly less in number than the Confederate, was attached by regiments or squadrons to the divisions. This arrangement accounted in no small degree for the almost total ignorance of the enemy's movements up to the time when he came in contact with the Federal outposts.

The Army of the Tennessee was purely an army of volunteers, only two small companies of cavalry being regulars. It was furthermore essentially a western army, there being in it not a single organization from east of the Ohio River. All of the general officers were western men. The regiments were brigaded by States as far as practicable. In this connection it may be mentioned that Buell's army possessed most of these characteristics also.

Majors Ezra Taylor, 1st Illinois Light Artillery Regiment, and John S. Cavender, 1st Missouri Light Artillery Regiment, were chiefs of artillery respectively of Sherman's and Brigadier General William H.L. Wallace's divisions. In the other four divisions the senior battery commander was the nominal chief for his division. Practically, he was simply captain of his own battery and nothing more.

Colonel Joseph D. Webster of the 1st Illinois Light Artillery Regiment, in addition to his duties as Grant's chief of staff, performed those of chief of artillery for the army. For some 15 years prior to 1854 he had been an officer of the Corps of Topographical Engineers and was therefore presumably somewhat familiar with artillery matters. Nevertheless, the batteries were of a very mixed character as regards caliber. In other respects they were in good condition, composed of excellent men, and as a rule, well officered. Some of them had seen service at the battles of Fort Donelson, but generally they were unseasoned as to fighting. The three field officers just mentioned were the only field officers of artillery present in that army. Eight of the 22 batteries were independent batteries and were therefore not entitled to be represented by field officers; one of the evils attending this system of bringing batteries into service.

The country from Corinth to Pittsburg Landing is undulating, broken into hills and ravines, and wooded for the most part with oak and occasional patches of undergrowth. Cultivated clearings seldom break the continuity of the forest. The Landing is on the left bank of the river. The bluffs at this point are some 100 feet above ordinary watermark and are cloven by a series of ravines, through one of which runs the main road to Corinth. Beyond the bluffs of the bank stretches back a kind of tableland, rolling and with ridges, cleared near the crest of the acclivity, but wooded and rough further from the river, with here and there a small cleared field. At the date of the battle two log cabins formed the only buildings in the immediate vicinity of the Landing, but about three miles out, on the Corinth road, stood a rude log chapel called Shiloh Church, which gave name to the battle.

A short distance beyond the church rise, not far from each other, two small brooks, Owl Creek, a tributary of Snake Creek, and Lick Creek, which, thence diverging, run windingly into the Tennessee River, five miles apart, on either side of the Landing. On this plateau, encompassed by the river and its two tributaries, lay encamped on the night of April 5th, 1862, five divisions of the Army of the Tennessee, with a sixth, that of Lew Wallace, at Crump's Landing, five miles down the river on the same side.

Sherman's division was the most advanced. Two of his brigades, those of colonels Ralph P. Buckland and Jesse Hildebrand, were slightly in front of Shiloh Church, covering the main road to Corinth. His right brigade, that of

McDowell, was detached a few hundred yards to the right, covering the Purdy road at its crossing of Owl Creek, while his other brigade, that of Colonel David Stuart, was detached a mile or more to the left, covering the road to Hamburg, a landing about four miles above Pittsburg. Stuart occupied a hill overlooking Lick Creek, not far from its confluence with the river. Sherman's division was therefore spread out to cover the entire front, from Lick Creek on the left to Owl Creek on the right, a distance of about three miles. Subsequently Prentiss' division of two brigades took position between Stuart and Sherman at Shiloh, but leaving an unoccupied interval of about a mile on its right. Prentiss' division covered the Ridge road to Corinth.

Captain Frederick Behr's 6th Indiana Independent Light Artillery Battery was with McDowell's brigade on the right, with one piece detached at the crossing of Owl Creek. Captain Samuel E. Barrett's battery, B, 1st Illinois Light Artillery Regiment, was with Buckland's brigade on the right of the church, while Captain Allen C. Waterhouse's Battery E of the same regiment was with Hildebrand's brigade on the left of the church, the Corinth road running between the camps of the two brigades. One section of Waterhouse's battery was posted with a portion of Hildebrand's brigade in advance, beyond a ravine formed by one of the branches of Owl Creek. Stuart's brigade was without a battery. Prentiss had with his division Captain Emil D. Munch's 1st Minnesota Independent Light Artillery Battery and Captain Andrew Hickenlooper's 5th Ohio Independent Light Artillery Battery, the last named having arrived only the day before.

The troops just mentioned, namely, the four brigades of Sherman's division and the two of Prentiss', with their five batteries, constituted the front line of encampments. It cannot be called a line of battle since, although covering the main roads leading towards the enemy, there was no connection between the parts or any of the other features characterizing such a line. Not a rifle pit was dug or a spade full of earth thrown up to cover the troops, nor a tree felled to obstruct the approach of an enemy. At this period of the war troops had not learned the art of entrenching. It was, in fact, looked upon with disfavor, as savoring of timidity, as though afraid to meet the enemy openly in the field.

There was no system whatever in the positions of the other three divisions. McClernand had the camps of his three brigades about half a mile in rear of Sherman's position at the church, and with him were three batteries, those of Captain Jerome B. Burrows, 14th Ohio Independent Light Artillery Battery; Captain Edward McAllister, Battery D, 1st Illinois Light Artillery Regiment; and Lieutenant George L. Nispel, Battery E, 2nd Illinois Light Artillery Regiment.

About a mile in front of the Landing and the same distance in rear of McClernand, were the camps of W.H.L. Wallace's division, with Captain Charles M. Willard's Battery A, 1st Illinois Light Artillery Regiment; Captain Henry Richardson's Battery D, 1st Missouri Light Artillery Regiment; and Captain Frederick Welker's Battery H, 1st Illinois Light Artillery Regiment. Some distance to the left of Wallace was Hurlbut's division, with Captain John B. Myers' 13th Ohio Independent Light Artillery Battery; Captain William H. Ross' Battery B, 1st Michigan Light Artillery Regiment; and Captain Charles Mann's Battery C, 1st Missouri Light Artillery Regiment. Between the camps of the two divisions just named and McClernand's camp, is Brier Creek, a tributary of Snake Creek, flowing in a deep marshy ravine with broken and wooded bluffs on each side. This ravine played an important part in the last act of the battle of the first day, as behind it the entire army took refuge and was protected from further advance of the enemy by the artillery hastily gathered there for that purpose.

The four unattached batteries were encamped at various places not far from the Landing. These were the batteries of captains Lewis Margraff [8th Ohio Independent Light Artillery Battery], Edward Bouton [Battery I, 1st Illinois Light

Artillery Regiment], and Jasper M. Dresser [Battery E, 2nd Illinois Light Artillery Regiment], which, during the battle, were brought forward and served with McClernand and Sherman. Captain John W. Powell's Battery F, 2nd Illinois Light Artillery Regiment went, in like manner, to Prentiss, leaving Captain Relly Madison's Battery F, 2nd Illinois Light Artillery Regiment, and Captain Axel Silversparre's Battery H, 1st Illinois Light Artillery Regiment (without horses) with their heavy guns on the bluffs near the Landing.

From the foregoing it will readily be seen that the divisions of this fine army were not encamped with a view to defense against apprehended attack. But they did fulfill Halleck's instructions to prepare for his contemplated campaign against Corinth. The work of organizing brigades and divisions was continuous and drilling was unceasing. Everything indicated preparation only for a deliberate forward movement, not for a possible attack by the enemy. Grant had his headquarters still at Savannah, nine miles distant and on the opposite side of the river. The infantry outposts lay within a mile of the front divisions. The cavalry, broken into detachments and scattered among the divisions, was incapable of extended reconnaissance. Sherman, it is true, ever vigilant, kept his little battalion on the go and frequently made reconnoitering expeditions some miles to the front, often encountering parties of hostile cavalry. Occasionally a regiment or even a brigade of infantry was sent out, but the positive orders of Halleck not to be drawn into a fight with any considerable force of the enemy that might bring on a general engagement, prevented any possibility of ascertaining the dispositions and intentions of the enemy.

On the 3rd Sherman sent out Buckland's brigade about three miles. Two companies were sent still further, both of which encountered hostile cavalry. These were the pickets of Hardee's corps, which on that afternoon had reached this point. Next day a cavalry dash on Sherman's picket line swooped off a lieutenant and seven men. Cavalry and infantry were sent out in pursuit, which proceeded until they came in sight of a large body of the enemy's infantry and with it some artillery. Quite a brisk skirmish marked this enterprise. All of this was duly reported to Grant, but it was thought to be only a close reconnaissance by the enemy.

On the following day, the 5th, the outposts observed many signs of the presence of the enemy, but on this day, as misfortune would have it, Sherman had no cavalry to send out. The regiment that he had, had gone to exchange with another, which latter had not yet arrived. He, however, strengthened his outposts and enjoined renewed vigilance on the part of the pickets. On the same day Colonel James B. McPherson, Grant's engineer officer, made a reconnaissance towards Hamburg and Lew Wallace sent one towards Purdy from Crump's Landing, both of which discovered the enemy in activity. Thus, in every direction, the enemy was found approaching, yet from some strange fatality Grant did not become convinced that he contemplated any serious attack. Such was the military situation in the Federal camp on the evening of April 5th.

Turning now to the Confederate position at Corinth, we find that Johnston, instigated by Beauregard, had been quietly but earnestly preparing for an advance upon the position at Shiloh, and had waited until the last minute for the arrival of all possible reinforcements. As the attack was to be one of surprise, every precaution was taken to cover up the preparations necessary for the movement. Suddenly, on the afternoon of the 3rd, Johnston put his corps in motion, with Hardee in advance, followed by Bragg, Polk, and finally by Breckinridge. Hardee encamped for the night about five miles from the Federal position and here is where he was discovered by Sherman's reconnaissance, as heretofore stated.

Johnston's original program was to deploy his columns at daybreak on the 5th and attack at 10:00 o'clock, but owing to the bad condition of the roads his columns did not all get into position until late in the afternoon of that day. Hardee, however, deployed at the proper time, but as his three brigades were not sufficient to extend from Owl Creek to Lick Creek, Brigadier General Adley H. Gladden's brigade of Withers' division of Bragg's corps was added to Hardee's right. Bragg deployed the remainder of his corps about 500 yards in rear of Hardee's line, and Polk his corps about 800 yards in rear of Bragg, while Breckinridge deployed forward upon the right of Polk. The two rear lines were to act as feeders to the first, and scarcely had the battle opened before portions of each were hurried forward to fill up gaps here and there, wherever Hardee required assistance. Very soon the three corps had become so confusedly intermingled that commanders were at a loss to know what to command. This was a new departure in battle tactics, and so faulty as to weaken greatly the Confederate assault.

About three o'clock, when the battle was at its hottest, Johnston was killed, devolving the command upon Beauregard. Just previous to this it had been arranged among the corps commanders themselves that Bragg should have charge of the right, Polk the center and Hardee the left, independent of the commands to which the troops belonged. Breckinridge's division had been brought around to the extreme right of the Confederate line.

So far as the Confederates had a tactical plan, it was to break the Federal left, and then, sweeping across the hills and ravines towards the Landing, drive everything down to the *cul de sac* between the river and the back waters of the overflowing Snake Creek. The plan, if successful, would have terminated then and there the field service of Grant's army, as well as the military career of that great chieftain himself.

But while the chief effort was made against the Federal left, assaults were most determinedly made all along the line, and when the battle became fully opened no troops on either side were idle, except, of course, those of both armies who, becoming dismayed at the first onslaught, sought safety by straggling, the Confederates to the woods in their rear, and the Federals to the bluffs near the river.

The attack was intended to be a surprise, and every movement was directed to that end. The Federal troops, thus taken unawares, could do nothing but strike back when the enemy struck, and soon the field became a series of bloody conflicts, so irregular as to be impossible to follow, except in a general way.

Returning now to the Federal troops, we find that about three o'clock in the morning of the 6th, three companies were sent out under Major James E. Powell, from Everett Peabody's brigade of Prentiss' division, for the purpose of picking up some of the parties of the enemy seen the evening before hovering about in the woods. These companies, moving forward a couple of miles to the right and front, encountered the outposts of the enemy with whom they had a brisk skirmish, lasting perhaps an hour. In the meanwhile Colonel David Moore of the 21st Missouri Infantry Regiment, also of Peabody's brigade, was sent out with his regiment to support Powell and the outposts. He advanced but a short distance beyond where Powell had his skirmish before encountering a brigade of the enemy, which he repulsed. The enemy, coming up in stronger force, drove back Moore's command and followed it up with his entire line of battle, encountering the Federal outposts, which fell back fighting to the main line, and here the battle soon opened with fury.

The first shots between Powell and the enemy were fired at a quarter after five. As soon as the firing swelled into volume indicating a serious attack Prentiss formed his brigades in line and advanced a few hundred yards in front of their camps. His two batteries, those of Munch and Hickenlooper, took position on commanding ground, the former between the brigades and the latter on the right of the right brigade.

Sherman's two brigades at the church also formed line and advanced to the brow of the ravine of Owl Creek in front of his camps. Barrett's battery, better known as Ezra Taylor's battery, took position on rising ground in front of Shiloh Church. Four guns of Waterhouse's battery were a short distance to the left, between two regiments of Hildebrand's brigade. The other two guns of Waterhouse's battery had been occupying an advanced position beyond the ravine. These with the regiment with them, fell back before an approaching skirmish line and took position with the battery.

Sherman, seeing that the enemy was advancing in force, sent word to Prentiss, notifying him of the fact, to McClernand asking for support to his left, and to Hurlbut, asking him to support Prentiss. McClernand sent three regiments of Colonel Julius Raith's brigade, which took position on Sherman's left, next to Waterhouse's battery. Hurlbut sent Colonel James C. Veatch's brigade of four regiments, which after great delay, took position towards Prentiss' right. These seven regiments did not fill a tithe of the interval between Sherman and Prentiss, an interval greatly broken by the ravines of Owl Creek and dense with wooded entanglements; a place of all others most congenial to the enemy, and of which he took ample advantage to gain the flank of both Sherman and Prentiss.

The direction of the enemy's advance was such as to bring him first in contact with Sherman's left and Prentiss' right. The resistance made by the outposts of these two divisions delayed the front line of the enemy until the other two closed up on it, taking position in it wherever intervals were to be found. Thus, the four brigades of Sherman and Prentiss, together with the two sent to their assistance, in all six, were confronted by 10 of the enemy. The enemy was active in bringing forward his batteries, which in number of guns was quite as disproportionate as was the infantry.

It was seven o'clock when the hostile lines became fairly engaged. From now on until seven in the afternoon the battle raged without intermission, first upon one part of the field, then upon another, and at times, at all points; in all of which the batteries had their full share, and as a rule did well their parts.

McClernand, learning that Sherman was hard pressed, moved forward his other two brigades, which he formed in line on the left of Raith, already connecting with Sherman's left. The batteries of Captain Jerome B. Burrows, 14th Ohio Independent Light Artillery Battery; Captain Edward McAllister, Battery D, 1st Illinois Light Artillery Regiment, and Nispel moved up with these brigades. Still more of the enemy's brigades concentrated in front of this point, and the fight became extremely fierce. McClernand was finally, about 9:00 A.M., compelled to give way, in which movement Burrows, having lost seventy of his horses, himself and two of his lieutenants being wounded, was obliged to abandon his battery. This giving way of McClernand uncovered Sherman's left, which was now exposed to a flank fire from the enemy, under the effect of which Sherman's left brigade, Hildebrand's, broke, and becoming scattered, did not again come together as an organization during the battle. Portions of it, however, attached themselves to other commands and did valuable work. Hildebrand himself, being without command, gave personal assistance to Sherman and McClernand. When this brigade gave way, four pieces of Waterhouse's battery fell into the hands of the enemy; Waterhouse was wounded.

Meanwhile, Buckland's brigade, Sherman's other brigade at the church, and Barrett's battery were withstanding assaults from several brigades of the enemy, the chief of which was from Cleburne's brigade of six regiments and its two batteries of Hardee's corps. The batteries were posted on the opposite side of the ravine of Owl Creek, through the tangled morass of which the brigade struggled and endeavored to climb the wooded ascent beyond, only to be driven back again with great slaughter. Barrett's battery was conspicuous from the skill with which it was handled. The giving way of Hildebrand exposed Buckland to an enfilade fire, and about 10:00 A.M. Sherman withdrew him to form a new line along the Purely Road, about a mile in rear of his former position.

McDowell's brigade, off towards the right guarding the crossing of Owl Creek by the Purdy Road, had not yet been attacked. Sherman moved it back along the road to connect on the right with Buckland's brigade. Captain Behr, commanding the battery with McDowell's brigade, was killed while bringing his guns in battery, and several of the men being struck at the same time, all the rest stampeded, fleeing from the field with the caissons.

Sherman being obliged to fall back still further, three guns of this battery thus abandoned, fell into the hands of the enemy. The gun of this battery which had been detached on outpost at the bridge was saved and did good service in assisting the outpost companies in cutting their way through to regain the brigade.

McClernand, rallying his brigades, formed them on Sherman's left. Barrett's battery, moving back by the Corinth road, came into position with McClernand's division. In addition to McAllister's and Nispel's batteries belonging to McClernand, Captain James P. Timony's unattached Battery B, 2nd Illinois Light Artillery Regiment's 20-pounder Parrotts were brought up from the rear. Major Ezra Taylor, Sherman's energetic chief of artillery, brought up the unattached batteries of Margraff and Bouton, which he posted on Sherman's line.

The enemy now gathered his brigades for a fresh assault upon Sherman and McClernand, and from now until about 4:00 P.M. the struggle was fierce and sanguinary on this part of the field. In general features it was a succession of attacks by brigades, sometimes several brigades at a time. These being repulsed the Federal troops would follow up until they in turn were driven back. At one time McClernand's brigades surged forward half a mile or more, but meeting fresh brigades were again forced to retire. In one of these operations Timony lost his 20-pounder battery and Nispel two of his pieces. The general result of the battle was, however, a gradual retrograde movement of the Federal line, until finally, about 4:00 P.M.,

Sherman and McClernand took position behind the ravine of Brier Creek. After this Sherman had no more fighting for this day. McClernand was vigorously assaulted by Preston Pond Jr.'s brigade of Bragg's corps, which he repulsed with little loss to himself but considerable to the enemy. This ended the fighting on this part of the field.

A good portion of McClernand's command had become scattered and had "disappeared." Of Sherman's division one entire brigade had "disappeared," except some fragments which had attached themselves to other organizations. His three remaining brigades were also greatly broken. Sherman's division was composed entirely of raw troops. "None of them," he says, "had ever been under such a fire before, or beheld heavy columns of an enemy bearing down on them, as they did on the first day of the battle. They knew nothing of the value of combination and organization. When individual fears seized them the first impulse was to get away;" a volume in a few words expressive of the difference between veterans and raw troops. The new line taken up by Sherman and McClernand covered the bridge near the mouth of Owl Creek, over which it was momentarily expected that Lew Wallace would arrive with his division from Crump's Landing.

Grant had passed the night of the 5th at Savannah, intending to move his headquarters to Pittsburg Landing permanently on the morning of the 6th. Upon learning at 6:30 A.M. of the cannonading heard in the direction of Shiloh, he immediately started by steamer for that point. In passing Crump's Landing he gave orders to Wallace to have his command in readiness to move instantly upon receipt of orders to that effect.

Soon after arriving at Pittsburg, Grant dispatched an officer to Wallace with instructions to march without delay. But by some misapprehension as to the direction, Wallace took a road which, if pursued, would have brought him far without the Federal lines. Impatient at the delay, Grant sent another officer to hasten Wallace. The latter was informed of the prop-

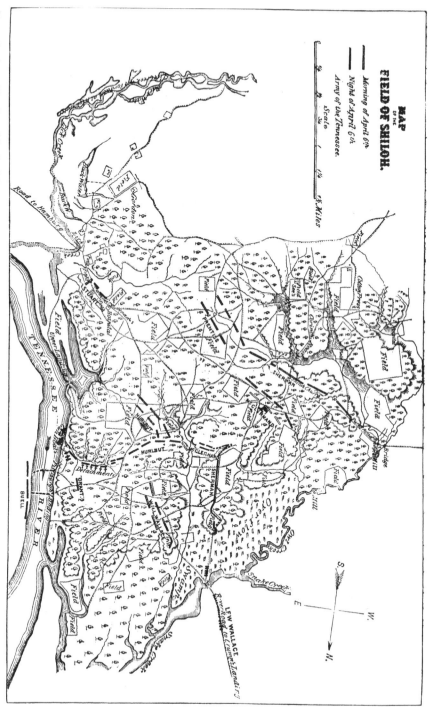

er road, but in regaining it, had to countermarch his division and make a march altogether of about 12 miles. He did not arrive at Pittsburg until after dark, some time after the close of the battle for the day.

Grant arrived on the field between eight and nine o'clock. Previous to this no one had exercised control. Each division commander acted as he thought best, which in every case was to do everything possible to beat back the enemy. But the most critical part of the battle was fought without a commanding officer, causing more or less of uncertainty and delay in getting the rear divisions to the points where most needed in front.

Before leaving Savannah, Grant gave orders to Nelson, of Buell's army, to march his division up the river until opposite Pittsburg. Upon arriving at the Landing, Grant, taking in the situation at a glance, gave instructions to hasten an abundance of ammunition to the front. The bluffs about the Landing were already thronged with fugitives from the front. These he gave instructions to have collected and organized to return to the fight, after which he proceeded to the front, and inspecting the field, gave such instructions as seemed necessary, the general tenor of which were to hold on and fight to the bitter end. This was about 10:00 A.M.

Turning now to the left wing, we find, as has already been stated, that the battle was opened by a portion of Peabody's brigade of Prentiss' division, which, very early in the morning, had been sent on reconnaissance beyond the outposts. Prentiss promptly formed line of battle with his two brigades about a quarter of a mile in front of their camps. Peabody had moved his brigade to the front to the assistance of his detachment, but being heavily pressed by greatly superior numbers was forced back into line with the left brigade. Hickenlooper's battery was on the extreme right, while Powell had his battery near the center between the brigades.

In this position Prentiss was attacked about 7:30 A.M. by the brigades of Colonel Robert G. Shaver, Gladden, and

Brigadier General James R. Chalmers, composed of regiments double in number to those of his command. After a gallant struggle his division, about nine o'clock, gave way and fell back through his camps, leaving behind Powell's guns and caissons and two of Hickenlooper's guns, all the horses of Hickenlooper's two guns being killed or disabled.

Hurlbut, notified by Prentiss that he required assistance, was by this time moving up with the brigades of Colonel Nelson G. Williams and Brigadier General Jacob G. Lauman, his other brigade, Veatch's, having been sent forward earlier, and Prentiss' regiments, drifting through Hurlbut's command, were, many of them, rallied, and were here joined by a fresh regiment just arrived by boat. With these Prentiss took position along an old sunken washed out road, which the men used at first as a sort of rifle trench. Hickenlooper's remaining four guns were stationed on an elevated position to the right of this line. Prentiss was directed by Grant to hold this position at all hazards. Hurlbut formed his two brigades in line on the left of Prentiss, posting Ross' battery on the left, and Myers' on the right and somewhat advanced, so as to concentrate its fire upon some open ground in front. Mann's battery, sent at first towards the position occupied by Stuart's brigade was withdrawn and placed in the interval between the two brigades. Thus formed, Hurlbut awaited attack, which was not long in coming.

The division of W.H.L. Wallace was encamped at the other extremity of the field from Prentiss, not far from the crossing of Snake Creek, by the Crump's Landing road. About half past eight the division started to join Prentiss, leaving two regiments of Brigadier General John McArthur's brigade to guard the bridge over Snake Creek (one of his regiments had already been sent to Sherman). McArthur, with his other two regiments and Wood's battery, went to the assistance of Stuart, of Sherman's division, whose brigade occupied, it will be remembered, an isolated position on the extreme left covering the Hamburg crossing of a tributary of Lick Creek. Two 20-

pounder Parrotts of Welker's battery also followed in this direction. Wallace led his other two brigades to the right of Prentiss, forming a line oblique to that of the latter, and with an interval of about 200 yards between. In the salient angle thus formed were Hickenlooper's four guns. The interval was subsequently filled by the 8th Iowa Infantry Regiment. Richardson's battery was at first posted between Wallace's brigades, but subsequently changed to the right, where was also Captain Peter P. Wood's Battery A, 1st Illinois Light Artillery Regiment. Welker's battery of 20-pounder Parrotts, except the two pieces near McArthur, was posted near the left and center of Wallace's line. The right of Wallace's line was but a short distance from McClernand's left, while there was but little interval between Hurlbut's left and McArthur's regiments operating on the right of Stuart, whose position was next the river and slightly to the left and rear of Hurlbut.

All of Grant's five divisions present were now in line, extending in an irregular form around from Owl Creek on the right, where the right of Sherman rested, to Lick Creek on the left, where Stuart's brigade was posted. The ground was rolling and wooded, but quite free from underbrush, except in the ravines, many of which intersected the field in various directions. Interspersed here and there were fields, while country roads traversed the country from one place to another, but all trending more or less to the Landing. The enemy had possession of the camps of Sherman, McClernand and Prentiss, and being somewhat demoralized by their success, gave opportunity, though brief, for the formations just described.

As it was important to the enemy that the brigades of Stuart and McArthur should be got out of the way, so as to open a passage along the river towards the Landing, a strong force consisting of Brigadier General John K. Jackson's and Chalmers' brigades, with their batteries, together with some other troops, were sent against this position. It was now about ten o'clock and a brisk contest ensued, which lasted nearly two hours. Several times the enemy were repulsed, but returning, made fresh assaults, with the result that the Federal regiments, being driven back from one position to another, were finally forced to fall back to the Landing; this uncovered Hurlbut's left.

In the meanwhile, a heavy attack was in progress against Hurlbut, Prentiss and Wallace, opened by the fire of several batteries; a shot from one of which blew up a caisson of Myers' battery, which, as has been stated, had been placed in an advanced position. This so stampeded the battery officers and men alike that they most shamefully fled, leaving everything behind. Some men from another battery spiked the guns and cut loose many of the horses. The officers of this battery were dismissed and the enlisted men transferred to other organizations, leaving the name of the battery, the 13th Ohio, a blank in the army list of that State, which furnished so many distinguished generals and gallant troops. So far as known this was the only instance during the entire war where abject cowardice was charged to any battery.

Scarcely had Wallace formed his line before the enemy, at ten o'clock, assaulted Prentiss, and almost simultaneously, Hurlbut and Wallace. The salient in which was Hickenlooper's battery became, for a time, the chief point of attack. The enemy brought up a number of batteries to face this position, all of which were replied to most vigorously by Hickenlooper, and such other batteries as could bring their fire to bear. From this time on until 5:30 P.M. the battle raged against some part or other of the position held by Wallace, Prentiss, and Hurlbut. It was a succession of assaults by the enemy, at first by single brigades entirely inadequate in strength to the task, afterwards by many brigades combined, which accomplished the work and eventually carried the field.

The first of these assaults was by Gladden's brigade of Wither's division against Prentiss. This was repulsed. Simultaneously with this Brigadier General Alexander P. Stewart's brigade of Brigadier General Charles Clark's division was led against Wallace's front; which, being repulsed, rallied and twice again returned, until exhausted, it withdrew from the fight. Bragg, who was commanding on this part of the field, now ordered Colonel Randall L. Gibson with his brigade of Brigadier General Daniel Ruggles' division to carry the position. This fresh brigade charged gallantly, but the deadly fire of musketry in front and enfilading fire from batteries, cut the ranks to pieces, and the brigade fell back discomfited. Gibson made another attempt, but with even more disastrous results.

Gladden's brigade, having recovered after its repulse before Prentiss, now essayed an assault upon Hurlbut. This was met by Lauman's brigade with such a fire of musketry as to send it back. Three times it rallied and returned to the assault, but was finally put out of condition for further combat. Two brigades, Brigadier General John S. Bowen's and Colonel Winfield Statham's, of Breckinridge's division, were now pushed forward. After a series of efforts by these, Hurlbut's regiments began gradually to retire, a portion of them turning upon Statham, broke his brigade and caused it to fall back. In endeavoring to rally and bring back one of Statham's regiments, Johnston, the Confederate commander, received a fatal shot. The command of his army now devolved upon Beauregard, who was at this time superintending operations against McClernand and Sherman.

Bragg now assumed entire charge of the troops on this wing, which consisted in most part of two brigades of Wither's division of his own corps, two of Cheatham's division of Polk's corps, and two of Breckinridge's reserve corps, together with some eleven batteries. These he assembled for a general advance. Hurlbut, seeing these preparations, made dispositions accordingly. Wood's battery, which had been with McArthur, was posted on the Hamburg road, and nearby were two 20-pounder Parrotts of Welker's battery. About half past three Bragg moved forward. The artillery, aided by the infantry fire of Hurlbut's division, checked the first impulse and brought Bragg's line to a halt. Hurlbut, deeming further effort to hold his position useless, now gave orders to retire; first giving notice to Prentiss. About half a mile to the rear he attempted to make another stand, but the attempt was ineffectual. He fell back beyond his camp to the bluffs near the Landing. In this retrograde movement one of the 20-pounders before mentioned was abandoned, but recovered shortly afterwards. Ross, in passing a marshy ravine, lost his entire battery.

Hurlbut out of the way, Bragg now directed his force against the flank and rear of Prentiss. While all of this was transpiring on the Confederate right, Beauregard, Polk and Hardee were giving their attention to McClernand and Sherman on the Federal right. It has already been stated that by 4:30 P.M. McClernand and Sherman had been forced back across the ravine of Brier Creek to the plateau near the Landing. Some of the troops that had been operating against them were now available for service against Wallace and Prentiss, who with their four greatly depleted brigades were still holding their ground. The brigades of Colonel Robert M. Russell, Colonel Robert P. Trabue, and Brigadier General Bushrod R. Johnson, together with such other troops as could be collected from Polk's corps, were now brought against Wallace's flank and rear, and presently united with those of Bragg from the other direction, thus completely surrounding Prentiss and a portion of Wallace's command. Prentiss had swung back until his line was almost parallel to that of Wallace. Thus, they were back to back about 150 yards apart, fighting in opposite directions. Wallace now gave the order for his regiments to cut their way out. Colonel James M. Tuttle's brigade, facing to the rear, led the way, but several regiments, while covering the withdrawal of the batteries, became so hemmed in that it was impossible to escape. All of the batteries got out without much loss. Hickenlooper joined Sherman on the extreme right. About this time Wallace was killed, and what was left of his command devolved on Tuttle. Groups and squads of Prentiss' men succeeded in making their way out before the circle was closed. Prentiss, with the remaining fragments of the two divisions, made a desperate struggle, but further resistance being hopeless and useless, he surrendered himself and about 2,200 men. This was about 5:30 P.M.

The troops that got away lost no time in getting back to the bluffs at the Landing where Grant's entire army was now forced into a space little greater than one square mile, with an un-bridged river in rear and a victorious and exultant enemy in front. Lew Wallace's division had not arrived from Crump's Landing. Nelson's division was still on the opposite side of the river on its way up from Savannah, and the other divisions of Buell's army back miles away on the miry road behind it. The stragglers seeking shelter about the bluffs along the river constituted a large percentage of Grant's army. These were variously estimated at from 7,000 to 10,000; no more, however, than those of Beauregard's army, in which, according to Confederate accounts, the straggling was even greater; the difference between the two cases being that Grant's fighting line was driven back upon its stragglers, enclosed by the river, where they were more noticeable, while those from Beauregard's line drifted back out of sight in the forest and had no demoralizing influence over the enthusiasm of his more resolute troops.

The divisions of Prentiss and W.H.L. Wallace were so broken and scattered that not a brigade of either remained intact in organization. One of Sherman's brigades was dispersed entirely, while two others were greatly scattered. Hurlbut's and McClernand's divisions were the only two out of the whole five that were holding together in anything like entire organization, and these too were fearfully depleted by the casualties of battle and by straggling. To even the most sanguine the situation appeared almost hopeless. But here, when scarcely a ray of hope was left, one factor of battle developed to save the day.

It has before been mentioned that standing on the bluffs near the Landing were a number of heavy guns intended for

Union troops hastily retreating to Pittsburg Landing in the face of a relentless Confederate attack. (*Library of Congress*)

the siege of Corinth. Ten of these were in charge of the companies of Madison and Silversparre, but were without horses. Colonel Joseph D. Webster, Grant's chief of staff and acting chief of artillery, had the presence of mind to cause these to be placed in a firing position on commanding ground a half mile or so from the Landing.

These batteries formed the nucleus for a line of artillery that closed across the entire front of the position into which the army was now being huddled. As batteries and parts of batteries came back from the front they took position on this new line.

Immediately above the Landing a wide and deep ravine opens from the river. For some distance back from the river its bottom was filled with backwater and was impassable. Half a mile back it was still deep, abrupt, and marshy, though passable for infantry. Here the heavy guns were posted. Further around were the ravines of Brier Creek, which empties into Snake Creek. Behind these ravines the other batteries took position, thus covering the entire front with a line of artillery of some 80 pieces. Nelson, of Buell's army, arriving at this time, says: "I found, a semicircle of artillery, totally unsupported by infantry, whose fire was the only check to the audacious approach of the enemy." Grant, however, had about 15,000 organized men behind this line which, if necessity had demanded, would have given it ample support.

When Sherman and McClernand first retired behind Briar Creek the enemy made some vigorous attempts to reach them, but were easily repulsed. After that most of their assailants were moved to their right to assist in giving the *coup de grace* to Wallace, Prentiss, and Hurlbut. This having been accomplished Bragg pushed forward the divisions of Ruggles and Withers, and such other troops as were available or at hand, with a view to further crushing the left and thus completing the victory.

Bragg says: "The prisoners," meaning those captured with Prentiss,

> were dispatched to the rear, under proper guard, all else being left on the field that we might press our advantage. The enemy had fallen back in much confusion, and was crowded in unorganized masses on the river bank, vainly striving to cross. They were covered by a battery of heavy guns, well served, and their two gunboats, which now poured a heavy fire upon our supposed positions, for they were entirely hid by the forest. Their fire, though terrific in sound and producing some consternation at first, did us no damage, as the shells all passed over and exploded far beyond our position.

Polk, who cooperated with Bragg in the operations that led to the capture of Prentiss, and joined with him in the further advance upon Grant's left, says:

> The field was now clear; the rest of the forces of the enemy were driven to the river and under its bank. We

had one hour or more of daylight still left; were within from 150 to 400 yards of the enemy's position, and nothing seemed wanting to complete the most brilliant victory of the war but to press forward and make a vigorous assault on the demoralized remnant of his force.

At this juncture his gunboats dropped down the river, near the Landing, where his troops were collected, and opened a tremendous cannonade of shot and shell over the bank in the direction from where our forces were approaching. The height of the plain on which we were, above the level of the water, was about 100 feet, so that it was necessary to give great elevation to his guns to enable him to fire over the bank. The consequence was that the shot could take effect only at points remote from the river's edge. They were comparatively harmless to our troops nearest the bank, and became increasingly so as we drew nearer the enemy and placed him between us and his boats.

Some of the Confederate brigade commanders near the river, however, mentioned in their reports that the fire of the gunboats did prove annoying to their men, who were caused to shelter themselves in ravines to avoid accident. But as Bragg's brigades arrived in front of the batteries posted by Webster, they were met by such a fire as to cause them to recoil. The batteries they brought up were no match for the heavier pieces opposed to them. Hurlbut, who had collected what he could of his own division, together with fragments from other commands, to the number of some 4,500 men, and posted them in support of the batteries, says: "In a short time the enemy appeared on the crest of the ridge, but were cut to pieces by the steady, murderous fire of the artillery. Generals Sherman's and McClernand's artillery was rapidly engaged, and after an artillery contest of some duration the enemy fell back."

Beauregard, made aware of this formidable line of artillery, gave orders for his troops to draw off. In his report he does not, however, admit his inability to have carried Grant's last position. He adroitly seeks for explanation elsewhere, chief among which was that his troops were exhausted and hungry. A few paragraphs before he boasted of the abundance they had found in the captured camps. He gives as a further reason that Grant's army had taken shelter under the fire of the gunboats, which at that period of the war was the great Confederate bugbear, and sufficient, as Beauregard evidently thought, to cover up his true reason for withdrawing. He knew, as well as Bragg and Polk did, of their inability under the circumstances to inflict damage on his troops had he continued the assault. The truth is Beauregard saw in this well posted line of artillery an obstacle so formidable that he was not willing to jeopardize the prestige of victory already gained by an attack which must almost inevitably prove disastrous.

Whether he intended simply to withdraw for the night or for final retreat, matters not; time was gained for the arrival of Buell, and this turned the scale in favor of Grant. It was quite dark before the whole of Beauregard's troops could be withdrawn, and he left it to the discretion of his different commanders to select places of bivouac for their troops for the night; and they generally dropped down where it was most convenient. A large portion of them found shelter from the pouring rain that set in during the night in the camps they had captured during the day. Johnston's faulty method of forming his three corps into lines, one in rear of the other, the front one to be fed by detachments from the two in rear, had produced inextricable confusion, and commingling of commands. Beauregard therefore had no line of battle and was little prepared for the serious work thrust upon him early the following morning.

Grant's army passed the rainy and uncomfortable night in bivouac behind the ravines of Briar Creek and the line of artillery. Sherman was on the extreme right, resting on Snake

Creek. McClernand was next to him, and Hurlbut next to McClernand, resting his left near the heavy guns. The fragments of the divisions of W. H. L. Wallace and Prentiss were scattered promiscuously. Wallace had been killed and Prentice captured, leaving their commands to the senior colonels not yet familiar with the surroundings.

Lew Wallace arrived from Crump's Landing as dark was setting in and posted his division in rear of Sherman. Just as the battle was closing in front of the heavy guns, the leading regiment of Nelson's division of Buell's army disembarked at the Landing, and pushing out to the front, exchanged several volleys with the enemy. But neither the arrival of Nelson's division, which until the next day Beauregard thought to be two days' march distant, nor that of Lew Wallace, which he thought had been in the fight and was part of the troops driven back, had anything to do with Beauregard's withdrawal. It was due to that judiciously established line of artillery and to nothing else. When all seemed lost, this line arose as a shield against further disaster.

In studying the official reports of this battle we cannot avoid admiring the enterprising manner in which the batteries of the enemy were brought into action, often with the utmost audacity, and the skill with which they were served. These were met by the Federal batteries, equally well served, and as skillfully handled.

A large portion of the Federal infantry was unseasoned to battle, nevertheless there was scarcely a battle of the war where as a whole it exhibited better fighting qualities, and this notwithstanding the many disadvantages that led to an undue amount of straggling, which, however, was no greater than that of the Confederates. The battle was fought under many disadvantages to the Federal troops, chief among which was the want of a line of battle at the time of attack. The enemy deployed his line almost within musket shot the day before and had nothing to do but to march forward and attack in overwhelming numbers Sherman and Prentiss, occupying detached positions in front of the other three divisions. During the entire day there was no connected line of battle. The enemy, having 30 percent more men on the field, was enabled to concentrate a superior force, first against the Federal right wing and then against the left, using many of the same troops in both cases.

The Confederate corps organization was a great advantage, as affording commanders for both wings and the center. Grant, having no such organization, the divisions of his wings fought without any common commander to direct their movements and efforts, and thus secure that degree of cooperation so essential on a field of this nature.

It is worthy of note that in Johnston's army, both he and his successor, Beauregard, had been educated to the military profession, as had likewise his three corps commanders, Polk, Bragg and Hardee, together with several of his division and brigade commanders; while in Grant's army there was but one besides himself above the rank of colonel who had been so educated. The exception referred to was Sherman, his second ranking division commander, who by his personal bravery, stubborn resistance, and intuitive skill, soon became the central figure on that hotly contested field.

Until the arrival of Grant, about 9:00 A.M., there was no one on the field exercising command of the whole, and by that time the battle had gained such headway that nothing could be done further than to strike back when struck. At all times the Confederates held the initiative and derived full advantage from it.

The losses during this day were heavy, something like 6,000 killed and wounded and 3,000 missing (including the 2,200 captured with Prentiss) many of whom were either killed or wounded. The Confederate loss was equally as great in killed and wounded, but not so heavy in prisoners. The Federals lost 33 pieces of artillery, most of which were recovered on the following day. No hostile movement was made by either army during the night, but each lay, chilled and comfortless, in the pouring rain, awaiting the events of the morning.

Union Generals Ulysses S. Grant and William T. Sherman established a last line of defense at Shiloh that included these 24-pounder siege guns. (*U.S. Army Military History Institute*)

TWELVE

SHILOH

(Second Day)

IT WILL BE REMEMBERED THAT the leading brigade of Nelson's division of Buell's army arrived just at the close of the battle on the evening of the 6th. The other two brigades arrived soon afterwards, all having to be ferried in steamers across from the opposite side of the river. Crittenden's division of two brigades arrived during the night, and early in the morning McCook's, of three brigades, began to arrive. The last brigade did not reach the landing until about 10:00 o'clock.

Accompanying Crittenden's division were the batteries of Captain Joseph Bartlett, "G," 1st Ohio Light Artillery Regiment, and Mendenhall, "H and M," 4th U.S. Artillery Regiment. With McCook was Terrill's battery, "H," 5th U.S. Artillery Regiment. The remainder of Buell's batteries, as likewise his cavalry, had to be left behind for want of transportation. That portion of Buell's army present to take part in the battle consisted of 29 regiments and the three batteries just mentioned, and may be estimated very closely at 17,000 men in line. Lew Wallace's division, which had arrived fresh from Crump's Landing, contained about 5,000 effectives. Of those that had been in the battle of the day before, about 15,000 were organized and in condition to renew the fight. In all, Grant had about 37,000 effective men against the remnant of Beauregard's army, which now could not have been much over 20,000 men for battle.

Grant, appreciating the advantage of the initiative in battle, had determined to attack his adversary at daylight on the following morning, and in consultation with Buell and Sherman that evening, decided that Buell with his army should attack on the left, and Grant's immediate command the right. Immediately after daylight the troops moved out. Nelson's division, the extreme left, took position across the Hamburg road towards the river, then followed towards the right the divisions of Crittenden, McCook, McClernand, Sherman and Lew Wallace; the latter rested on Owl Creek. Hurlbut's division was in support in rear of McClernand, while the fragments of Prentiss' and W. H. L. Wallace's divisions were posted by regiments or brigades as supports at various places along the line. The batteries were with their divisions.

Nelson moved forward soon after daylight and his skirmishers, striking those of the enemy, notified Beauregard that an attack was impending. Soon after this he learned that a part at least of Buell's army had arrived. He had not anticipated this, for he had been informed the day before, through his detective agents, that Buell's troops were still two days' march in rear. His scattered troops were got together as quickly as possible. The attack was entirely unexpected to him and he was in nowise prepared for it. On his right were parts of five brigades which Withers hastily put together, and adding Chalmers' brigade and three batteries, boldly confronted Nelson. A halt of an hour or so that the latter had to make to allow Crittenden and the rest of the line to come forward was valuable time, improved by the enemy in getting into position.

When Nelson again advanced, he came upon Withers' heterogeneous force, which was driven back. Nelson, being without artillery applied to Buell, who sent him Mendenhall. The latter placed his battery in the interval between Nelson and Crittenden and at once engaged the batteries of the enemy. After about half an hour the latter ceased firing, but soon after reopened, accompanied by musketry. "I immediately answered," says Mendenhall, "and in a very short time his fire again ceased." Presently the enemy reopened from the battery towards Mendenhall's left and also from the one towards his right. Separating slightly his sections, he replied to them both, the fire from which soon ceased, but only for a short period, when it was again resumed and again silenced. Half an hour later the enemy opened with a battery on Mendenhall's right, to meet which, he changed front and opened with case shot and canister on infantry advancing from the same directions. The infantry was repulsed, and falling back, the enemy's battery again opened. The enemy now advanced on his, the enemy's right, and for a period Mendenhall was exposed to an enfilade as well as a direct fire. He now changed the direction of his fire and opened with canister on the infantry approaching on the left. The latter being repulsed, he again directed his attention to the battery in his front, the fire of which he soon silenced.

In the meanwhile, Hazen's brigade, advancing, captured the central battery which Mendenhall had silenced. But Hazen, not being supported either on the right or left, was exposed to a terrific fire on both flanks and front, and was forced to retire with a loss of more than half of Nelson's division during the entire day. By this time Crittenden was greatly retarded in his forward movement by a battery in his front. Mendenhall, being sent for, soon so crippled this battery that it was not able to get away when the infantry advanced. He then moved forward, and occupying its position, continued firing upon the enemy until the latter disappeared from the field. Nelson, in his report, states that Mendenhall's battery gave his division "most refreshing relief." There were but few instances during the war where any battery was more efficiently handled than this by Mendenhall.

Hazen's brigade being knocked to pieces, Brigadier General Jacob Ammen's, the one on its left, was unsupported on both flanks, and being heavily pressed was in danger of being broken. Nelson again applied for artillery, and Buell sent him Terrill's Battery H, 5th U.S. Artillery Regiment, which at that time, 9:00 o'clock, had just landed. Hurrying to the support of Ammen, the enemy was repulsed. Following the retreating enemy in company with Ammen's skirmish line, Terrill took position on a ridge in front from which he could obtain a better fire on the enemy's batteries to the right. The enemy, being reinforced, now advanced, driving back the skirmish line, and Terrill was obliged to fall back, firing with prolonge fixed. In this manner he kept back the advancing line of the enemy until Colonel Tuttle brought around to the assistance of Ammen a portion of what was left of W.H.L. Wallace's division from the battle of the day before. Tuttle sent forward a couple of regiments to the support of Terrill and the Confederate line retired to its former position in the timber. Ammen's line, which had fallen back under the galling fire evoked by Terrill's battery, now returned and occupied the ridge with Terrill.

It was now nearly two o'clock, and the enemy having withdrawn from Nelson's front, Terrill advanced his battery until he got an enfilading fire on the enemy with whom Crittenden's and McCook's divisions were heavily engaged. He gave special attention to a couple of the enemy's batteries retarding McCook's advance. Sending one section still further ahead, he obtained a reverse fire which soon caused the opposing batteries to retire. Thus relieved, McCook, advancing, drove the enemy.

Nelson, in his report, speaking of Terrill, says: "This battery was a host in itself." Other commanders being likewise profuse in their praise, Terrill was rewarded with a brigadier generalcy, not, however, to command artillery, for which he had proved himself so well qualified, but to command a brigade of infantry, at the head of which he was killed a few months afterwards.

General officers were not considered necessary for the command and management of artillery. Scarcely were field officers so considered until towards the close of the war. This point has been animadverted upon previously.

Bartlett's battery, belonging to Crittenden's division, took position with the latter in rear of an open field surrounded by thick woods held by the enemy. Here he did good service until about noon, when he withdrew to replenish his ammunition. When he returned the battle was ended.

About one o'clock Beauregard gave orders to withdraw. His line of retreat was necessarily by the main Corinth road, past Shiloh Church. Across this Beauregard established his strongest line and made his stoutest resistance, holding it as long as possible to enable his troops from the right and left to withdraw safely. Here, in front of McCook, McClernand and Sherman, took place the heaviest fighting of the day. McCook having no artillery, Bouton's battery was sent to him from Sherman, and those of McClernand immediately on his right gave him assistance. Lew Wallace's division had swept up Owl Creek on the right of Sherman and using his batteries freely had driven in towards the center all of that flank of the enemy. The fighting about Shiloh Church became intense. The enemy had here the divisions or parts of the divisions of Clark, Cheatham and Ruggles, together with numerous odd brigades, and was well supplied with batteries. These were engaged by the batteries of Bouton, McAllister, Wood, Captain Noah S. Thompson [9th Indiana Independent Light Artillery Battery] and Lieutenant Charles H. Thurber [Battery I, 1st Missouri Light Artillery Regiment].

Beauregard was fighting to secure his retreat, and maintaining the struggle as long as possible, was finally about 3:00 P.M., obliged to fall back. He established a battery and a brigade on the rising ground south of Owl Creek, commanding the ground about Shiloh Church, and withdrew his troops behind them. Two miles beyond this, a rear guard took position again. At Mickey's farmhouse, some two miles further,

Breckinridge was stationed and continued there for several days. The rest of the army passed on to Monterey, and by the end of the week all were back again in their works surrounding Corinth.

There was no pursuit of the retreating army beyond the last position taken up by him on the high ground beyond Owl Creek. The cavalry, dispersed as it was to divisions, was not organized for efficient work, and the infantry was so thoroughly fagged out by two days of incessant fighting, with an intermediate night of drenching rain, that it was contented to drop to rest in the position it held when the last shot was fired. The enemy, barely able to drag himself away, was trembling with fear lest a pursuit might be made. Bragg, on the following day, when about half way back to Corinth, reported to Beauregard: "Our condition is horrible. Troops utterly disorganized and demoralized. Roads almost impassable. . . . It is lamentable to see the state of affairs, but I am powerless and almost exhausted. Our artillery is being left all along the road by its officers; indeed I find but few officers with their men." Others report a similar condition of affairs. Cavalry horses were sent back and recovered most of the abandoned artillery, and as fast as wagons got back to Corinth, their teams returned to assist others through the miry roads, which in consequence of constant rains had become almost, if not entirely, impracticable, and the troops, suffering from want of food and exhaustion, were unable to repair them. The rout and demoralization of this army, which less than a week before had set out with high spirits, as Beauregard boastingly asserted, to drive Grant's army into the Tennessee River, was not excelled even by Bull Run, between which and it there were in reality many points of resemblance.

On the following day, Sherman, with as much cavalry as was at hand, and two brigades of infantry, advanced two or three miles and drove back the rear guard of the enemy, which made a brief stand, after which he returned. He could not take artillery with him on account of the impassable condition of the roads. Grant was prohibited by Halleck, still at St. Louis, from advancing any part of his command in pursuit beyond a distance from which it could not return the same day, and this virtually prevented any pursuit whatever. Everywhere Sherman saw evidences of hasty and disorganized retreat, especially in artillery material, left for want of means to drag it through the miry roads.

The divisions of McClernand, Sherman, Hurlbut and W. H. L. Wallace, reoccupied their old camps, which having been in the enemy's possession for 24 hours were thoroughly despoiled. Buell, now joined by Wood's division, distributed his divisions along the front where they had fought, and thus the battle ended. Halleck arrived on the 11th, and taking charge in person, began in a methodical way to make preparations for an advance on Corinth. This was in accordance with his original plan, so rudely interfered with by the battle just described.

Beauregard expected an immediate and energetic advance, and with great promptness and spirit got up Earl Van Dorn's and Sterling Price's troops from the Mississippi, those of Sam B. Maxey and Danville Leadbetter from Tennessee, and called in detachments from everywhere. Jefferson Davis urged the governors of adjacent states to raise as many troops as possible and send them to Beauregard without delay. In this way the muster rolls of his army soon swelled to about 112,000 men. In reality he did not at any time have much over one-third this number present.

Meanwhile, that is, on April 21st, Halleck's army was reinforced by Pope's Army of the Mississippi, summoned from the operations just begun before Fort Pillow. Thomas' division of Buell's army arrived soon after the battle. These reinforcements together with some other detachments, gave Halleck an effective force of about 100,000 men.

The aggregate Federal loss for both days was 1,735 killed, 7,882 wounded and 3,956 captured, making a total of 13,573. Of these, 236 killed and 1,728 wounded belonged to Buell's army, which army had almost none captured. The aggregate Confederate loss for the entire battle was 1,728 killed, 8,012 wounded and something over 1,000 captured. Many of the captured on both sides were wounded. Although the fighting was at times very intense on the second day, the chief loss occurred on the first day, in which the number of the killed and wounded in Grant's army was a fraction over 25 percent of those engaged. In Beauregard's army the loss in killed and wounded was a fraction over 24 percent.

The loss in artillery on each side was about equal. Grant lost 33 pieces on the first day, most of which were recaptured on the second; for those that were not, an equal number were captured from the enemy.

The battle of the first day was in favor of the Confederates, but the victory was prevented from being made decisive by the circle of artillery before mentioned. This gave time for the arrival of Buell's army, after which there was scarcely a ray of hope left for Beauregard. What would have been the fate of Grant's army had Buell not arrived so opportunely is a matter of conjecture, but the probabilities are that Grant would have repulsed any attack that Beauregard could have made on him.

Halleck organized his army into the right wing, center, left wing, and reserve. The right wing comprised all of the Army of the Tennessee (except the divisions of McClernand and Lew Wallace), together with the division of Thomas from Buell's Army of the Ohio, and was commanded by Thomas. The center, composed of the Army of the Ohio, except Thomas' division, was commanded by Buell. The left wing, the Army of the Mississippi, to which Gordon Granger's division of cavalry was still attached, was commanded by Pope. The reserve, under McClernand, comprised his division and that of Lew Wallace. Grant was appointed second in command, but without any specific command or duty. No change was made affecting materially the artillery arm.

Halleck did not get ready for the march until the last day of April, and then he moved with such precaution that although but slightly opposed, it required 30 days to make the 15 miles intervening between his position at Shiloh and that of the enemy at Corinth. His entire army was entrenched at every halt, and all subordinate commanders were forbidden to do anything that might bring on a general engagement. The enemy's cavalry kept close in front of Halleck's army and as he drew nearer to Corinth the enemy offered stouter resistance to his advance. Sharp skirmishes took place, but nothing amounting to an engagement. In the meanwhile, Beauregard, having sent away all valuable stores, the sick and his heavy artillery, issued detailed instructions for the evacuation to take place at three o'clock on the morning of the 30th. At six o'clock explosions and clouds of smoke notified Halleck that Beauregard was leaving, and by eight some of the Federal troops entered the place. Pope, with a portion of his own army and a couple of divisions from the Army of the Tennessee pursued some 30 miles discovering that Beauregard had taken position a few miles further on in an inaccessible locality behind swamp and jungle. Upon the approach of Pope, Beauregard continued his retreat to Tupelo and the pursuing force returned to Corinth.

Several days before reaching Corinth, Halleck had dispatched Colonel Washington L. Elliot with two regiments of cavalry to make a circuit around Corinth and strike the railroad 40 miles in its rear, doing all practicable destruction to it. This expedition was eminently successful. Elliot, striking the road at Boonville before daylight on the 30th, destroyed a train loaded with ordnance stores, artillery and ammunition, besides so thoroughly destroying the road as to prevent its being of further use in the evacuation. Sheridan commanded one of these cavalry regiments, having been assigned to it the day before, and it was upon this occasion that he received his first lesson in bold cavalry raiding.

The possession of Corinth by the Federal troops was of great strategic importance, but the victory was barren in every other particular. It was nearly bloodless. A fine opportunity was lost for giving the enemy a stunning blow. Halleck at once began to break up his fine army, sending it by detachments to guard and repair railroads. Pope, being called to the East to commence his Virginia campaign against Lee, his Army of the Mississippi was distributed to Grant and Buell. Thomas' division was returned to Buell, and that entire army was turned eastward along the Memphis and Charleston railroad to march to Chattanooga. Buell had instructions to repair and keep open the road as he proceeded, a work which caused such delay that Bragg was enabled, by sending his troops by rail around by the way of Mobile, to reach Chattanooga before him. From this point Bragg boldly assumed the offensive, moving straight for Nashville and Louisville and compelling Buell to fall back to the Ohio River at Louisville, where he arrived ahead of his antagonist, and here commenced the campaign embracing the two important battles of Stones River and Chickamauga, treated previously.

Halleck was called to Washington to assume the duties of General-in-chief. Grant was restored to command, but it was some time before he could recollect his scattered army, the Army of the Tennessee, for effective work.

Bragg had succeeded Beauregard, who was sent East. Upon starting for Chattanooga Bragg left Van Dorn, who being joined by Price from west of the Mississippi, had an active force of about 40,000 infantry, amply supplied with an enterprising cavalry, constantly interrupting Grant's lines of communication.

The Army of the Tennessee was not again brought together as a whole until the Vicksburg campaign of the following year, by which time it was organized into four army corps, the 13th, 15th, 16th and 17th, commanded respectively by McClernand, Sherman, Cadwallader C. Washburn, and McPherson. It then consisted of 14 divisions and 40 batteries, with a good supply of cavalry. The batteries were still attached to divisions. Incredible as it may seem there were but three field officers, majors, with all of this artillery. None of those of the artillery who had fought so gallantly at Shiloh and other places had been promoted. In the meanwhile, promotion among their comrades in other branches had been active.

The great work assigned to the Army of the Tennessee was the opening of the Mississippi, that it might run unvexed to the sea. This work it accomplished by the capture of Vicksburg, which capitulated on the 4th of July of the following year, 1863. After this a portion of it was sent to the relief of the Army of the Cumberland, now, after the battle of Chickamauga, beleaguered by Bragg in Chattanooga.

In the spring of the following year, 1864, the Army of the Tennessee, now commanded by McPherson, was united with that of the Cumberland, now under Thomas, and the small Army of the Ohio under Schofield, for the Atlanta campaign by Sherman. General Barry was appointed Chief of Artillery for these combined armies, to the artillery of each of which he gave a battalion organization. The batteries of each corps were united into a brigade as a distinct command, in place of the division and brigade assignments heretofore existing in these armies. Thus organized, a greater degree of efficiency was secured, and a less amount of artillery required, to perform the same amount of effective work. Soon after the capture of Atlanta, September 2, 1864, Sherman, sending Thomas, with the Army of the Ohio and part of that of the Cumberland, to destroy Hood, now in his rear, organized the remainder of his force, consisting chiefly of the Army of the Tennessee, for his "March to the Sea." Having accomplished this march, Sherman turned from Savannah northward in pursuit of an army that "Joe" Johnston had collected to retard his movements. This army he forced to capitulate at Durham, North Carolina, April 26, 1865, being one of the closing acts of the Great Rebellion. From Durham the Army of the Tennessee was marched to Washington where it was mustered out of service. A large portion of the artillery with which it had made the Atlanta and other campaigns accompanied it in these marches through Georgia and the Carolinas. The

Army of the Tennessee is remarkable for having been the chief factor in the capture of three Confederate armies, at Fort Donelson, Vicksburg, and lastly the one just mentioned at Durham.

COMMENTS

THE CHARACTERISTIC FEATURES of the battle of Shiloh, so far as artillery was concerned, were so very similar to those of Chickamauga, already remarked upon, it is not necessary to repeat. At both battles the artillery had no higher organization that that of the single battery and in both the Federal army was almost destitute of field officers of artillery, ignoring entirely the fact that the greater the difficulties of the field, the greater is the necessity of having good organization and the proper class of officers to execute it.

In both battles the batteries simply followed brigades into action without regard to finding eligible positions for using their guns. To get their batteries through the intricacies of the forest and keep in touch with their brigades, was, in fact, as much as could be expected of battery commanders without obliging them to look the field over for suitable firing position. Thus deprived of the means requisite for securing good firing positions, the batteries generally fell into the very places least suited to them for the use of their guns, and in a sense became mere encumbrances to the field.

At Shiloh as at Chickamauga, good firing positions were scarce; nevertheless, there were some, and these should have been sought for and utilized. The enemy, managing better, did this, and was greatly assisted by it in their attacks; especially at Shiloh when he concentrated batteries on his right wing to assault the Federal left.

Shiloh forcibly illustrates the fact that guns are most frequently lost when the troops with whom they are serving are
forced to retire. Then it is, when the fighting is most intense,
the batteries have to extricate themselves, not only from the
fight, but the wooded entanglement surrounding them; and
this generally with depleted teams, and in all the confusion
attending such occasions.

The aggressive nature of the Confederate attacks made the
field of Shiloh one of retrograde movement to the Federals
from the beginning to the end of the first day; and this
accounts for the enormous percentage of the loss of artillery.
And this occurred all over the field, wherever batteries happened to be with their brigades.

At no point on this field were batteries grouped to gain
advantage in firing position or to strengthen a point that might
be weak. The only guide to batteries was to follow brigades,
apparently regardless of any advantage that might offer by
going elsewhere for better opportunity for using their guns.

At Shiloh the Federals had two batteries–12 pieces–of 20-
pounder Parrot guns. These unwieldy pieces accompanied
their brigades to the front, where seven of them soon fell into
the hands of the enemy. The organization, or rather want of
organization, of the artillery provided no class of officers
whose business it was to direct in such matters–matters pertaining to the appropriate use of different kinds of batteries–
and so the captains had nothing to do but to blindly follow
their brigades.

The captains of these batteries could not have failed to note
the inappropriateness of this method of employing their batteries; but to protest or even suggest opposition at such a time
would have been a delicate matter. A system that throws the
duty of making objections to going into battle, upon a captain,
because of the unsuitableness of his guns for the work, is not
only a bad one but a wicked one.

Many battles of the Civil war had similar incidents.

The battle of Shiloh, like Chickamauga, was one essentially of brigades–the brigades of one army against those of its opponent–and as the operations of batteries were confined to the narrow zone of action of their respective brigades, the ability of batteries to do effective work was curtailed to a minimum. The defectiveness of this system of thus distributing batteries was illustrated in many battles of the Civil War.

The inspiration for the formation of that line of guns which, when all seemed lost, checked the enemy and saved Grant's army from destruction, seems to have come from Colonel Webster, who in addition to being Grant's chief of staff, acted also as his chief of artillery, and who, seeing the 10 siege guns standing idle on the river bluff, had them run by hand to a good firing position further out, whence they were able to sweep with their powerful fire the ground over which the enemy must pass to reach the discomfited infantry now forced into the *cul de sac* embraced by the river and its overflowing bayou, Snake Creek. This peninsula, all that was left of the field to Grant's army, did not exceed a square mile of firm ground. The marshy and entangled ravine of Brier Creek extended nearly across the neck of the peninsula, and behind the creek Sherman and McClernand, formed a line of guns extending to the siege pieces already mentioned, thus forming a compact line of not less than 80 pieces. The enemy, approaching in strong force, were confident of speedy victory. But the sight of this line together with the fire experienced from the guns, caused him to desist from further attack and to withdraw for the night, thus making possible another – a "second day" for Shiloh, and this second day gave the victory to Grant.

In this respect the operations of the artillery at Shiloh were similar to those at Stones River, when the Army of the Cumberland, broken and driven back through a dense cedar thicket, rallied under the shelter of a line of batteries which, had become shaken loose from their brigades while in the thicket, had gravitated together on open ground beyond the forest, and there formed a line of guns that checked the further progress of the pursuing enemy; thus enabling the broken infantry to reform and there make successful resistance to the enemy, not only on this but on the following day – a "second day" for Stones River. The morning of the third day found the enemy in full retreat from Murfreesboro never to return again to occupy that battlefield.

Stones River and Shiloh are two conspicuous instances where the fire of an artillery line save the day and won the battle when all hope had vanished. In both instances the formation of the line of guns was due to the fact that the batteries had been forced for the time being from attachment to infantry units and were available for concentration in mass.

The happy ending of both these hotly contested battles seems to have allayed all apprehension that the artillery of the two winning armies – the Army of the Cumberland and the Army of Tennessee – required a more efficient and modern organization. But the disaster of Chickamauga, following a few months after Stones River, forced the subject to the front in the Army of the Cumberland, resulting in immediate reformation.

The Army of the Tennessee, meeting with no such disasters as that at Chickamauga, adhered to its antiquated methods until its junction with the Army of the Cumberland and Ohio to form part of the army led by Sherman against Atlanta. Then, it was given a system of artillery organization following the lines of those of the Army of the Potomac.

The battles of Shiloh, Chickamauga, and Chancellorsville together with many others of the Civil War not mentioned in the foregoing analysis, all go to show that the more difficult the field, the greater is the necessity for having batteries free from restraint caused by being attached to small units of infantry. This, not only for the greater efficiency of the artillery, but of those of the infantry as well. Furthermore, these battles representing the three great Federal armies of the Civil War go to show that with the artillery like causes in each produced like effects, and were not mere traits belonging to any particular one of them.

REPORTS OF BATTLES, SKIRMISHES, MARCHES, ETC.

During the Civil War, no system was observed in the methods of making up and sending reports of operations in the field, the consequence being that great confusion exists as to the actual occurrences of that important period. The comparatively insignificant military operations of this country preceding that epoch had not been sufficient to bring much knowledge of this subject to the front or to make its importance felt. No systematic methods of education had been in vogue in the regular service prior to that date and nothing had been done in way of preparation for the emergency then at hand; and, strange to say, no systematic method was devised or adopted during the war to meet the occasion and preserve to history a faithful account of the great events then transpiring.

While it is true that a vast mass of official reports found lodgment in the War Office, the publication of them develops important omissions and incongruities, showing the lack of system that then existed. For want of such a system, and knowledge of its application, the armies of the Civil War were sadly off. Officers did not know what was essential to report, and thinking it necessary to mention only glowing deeds of valor, often indulged in very figurative language. As imperfect as this publication is, it has retrieved from oblivion much that was valuable of the history of that period and as it is the only thing of the kind that approximates to accuracy it is extremely valuable, and emphasizes strongly the necessity for the most perfect system possible.

Owing to the fact that during the greater period of the war batteries were attached to brigades, or at most to divisions, to which their commanders made their reports, these reports were peculiarly liable to fail in being transmitted to higher sources. While battery commanders were, as a rule, punctual in making reports it is a well known fact that but comparatively few appear, even by reference in other reports, in the "Records"; from which it may be inferred that the majority of them fell by the wayside.

From this cause alone most of the war history of the artillery has passed into oblivion. The descendants of those who served with it and who assisted in no small degree in making the war history of that period, will search the records, many times in vain, for even mention of the honorable deeds of their ancestors.

ARTILLERY ON THE MARCH

Owing to the fact that artillery was, during the greater part of the Civil War, attached to either divisions or brigades, the management of it on the march was very defective. Thus attached, the batteries were generally disposed of along the infantry column in a manner violative of one of the first principles of good marching; viz., that bodies of horse and foot should not be mingled together on the march; this for the reason that having different gaits they are mutually fatiguing to each other. So it was, batteries alternated with brigades or at best with divisons, to the great detriment of both, especially the batteries. The two arms having different paces caused a succession of short halts, from which starts were very wearying to the horses of the batteries. Theoretically a column of infantry marching upon a road of uniform quality moves at a uniform rate. Such in reality is far from being the case. Short halts will inevitably happen, each causing a lengthening out of the column in spite of every effort to the contrary.

Artillery, when mixed in with infantry, is forced to partake of this stopping and starting motion, making it necessary for the teams to overcome the inertia of a heavy load at every start, thus causing an unnecessary expenditure of animal vitality at every halt. This waste of vitality, small as it may be for an individual horse, becomes a very great wastage in the aggregate. Strange as it may seem, these halts and starts most frequently occur at points most disadvantageous to the artillery.

When, later on in the war, the system of consolidating the batteries of each corps into a brigade was introduced, the batteries were kept more together on the march, experiencing less of this kind of disadvantage and less waste of horse flesh, harness, etc. At the same greater efficiency was secured in many ways, especially in being more available for service in case of collision with the enemy. Under the dispersed system, when batteries were attached to brigades or even to divisions, great delay was often experienced in getting them into firing positions at times of emergency, that is, when the attitude of the enemy called for a deployment of the column, making it desirable to bring forward batteries promptly to suitable firing positions. While the infantry was capable of deployment in any direction, through woods and brush, and over ground impracticable to batteries, the latter were forced to find some circuitous route, often to the great disadvantage of other troops crossing the same ground. On very difficult ground batteries frequently became stragglers and for a time lost, as was the case at Chickamauga; and this possibly at a time when their services were sorely needed on the firing line. Even when getting into line with the commands to which attached they frequently found themselves in positions where they were unable to use their guns by reason of the topographical conditions of their immediate surroundings. A greater number of batteries were therefore required for the same amount of work performed, a fact much sooner appreciated by the Confederates than the Federals. The former did away with the dispersed system and introduced the battalion system much in advance of the latter, and greatly to their advantage, as a study of many of the battles will show.

The batteries of each corps being concentrated, and organized into a command under officers whose business it is to be informed of all the surroundings, not only marched their commands more advantageously, but brought their guns into action with greater promptness and efficiency than did the division or brigade commanders of the discarded system.

Here is not an inappropriate place to mention that during the early period of the Civil War, when batteries were attached to divisions and brigades, and the art of marching troops was less well known, the artillery was subjected to great inconvenience and the service to loss, through a custom always prevailing with fresh troops, of causing batteries to be hitched up, ready for the march, long before the time appointed for starting. This pernicious practice came from an idea, always prevailing with the inexperienced, that because batteries are more complicated in their makeup than other troops, they require more time to prepare for the road. This is altogether an erroneous idea. While it is true that there is a multiplicity of matters to be attended to in preparing for the march, each man has his specific duties to perform, and he alone attends to it, doing things in their sequence and at the appointed time. This is organization; instruction gives the balance, insuring promptness and punctuality, qualities that make it possible for batteries with all their multifarious outfits to prepare for the road as quickly as troops of any other branch of the service. The tedious waiting, generally before daybreak, and often in most inclement weather, following a too early hitching up, is wearing alike upon the men and horses, and when long practiced conduces to dilitory and slovenly methods in the battery.

Batteries organized into brigades or battalions, are not liable to this species of demoralization for the reason that the management of such matters are in the hands of those familiar with the internal economy of batteries. A great improvement in this respect was observable after the reorganization of the artillery.

Top, officers of the 1st New York Light Artillery photographed in 1862. Bottom left, an unidentified Union soldier wearing a Hardee hat with artillery insignia and armed with a pistol; right, an artillery soldier holding the original regulation saber while carrying a pistol in his belt. (*Library of Congress*)

PERSONAL ARMAMENT OF BATTERIES

THE WHOLE MATTER OF WHAT SHOULD be the personal armament of the men of a battery received serious consideration
from a board of battery commanders who but a short time
previous to the outbreak of the Civil War, prepared the drill
regulations of that period. These officers, all veterans of the
Mexican War, and some of them with more recent experience
with the Utah Expedition, were imbued with the idea that
batteries should be able to take care of themselves under any
and all conditions, and although divided in opinion as to the
kind of arm for the men of a battery, they finally compromised
on the saber, which proved to be entirely useless.

Battery drill regulations prescribed a saber for all men of a
battery—noncommissioned officers, drivers, and cannoneers,
alike; but this saber was a heavy, clumsy affair, exceedingly
inconvenient to the soldier at all times, but particularly so at
such times as required most activity. When volunteer batteries came into service, they, too, adopted the saber; but as campaigning progressed this weapon was cast aside by both volunteers and regulars, except only in some or most instances,
when it was retained for the use of noncommissioned officers.
A very little active field service proved it to be entirely useless
as a weapon, and while being thus useless it was so cumbersome as to greatly interfere with the performance of duty
required of artillery soldiers. So thoroughly was it superfluous
that no attempt was made to improve it, either in weight or

model. With such qualities it soon became relegated to innocuous disuse, not, however, by any form of official order, but by simple disappearance. On the march it soon found its way, with other trash of its kind, to the caissons or carriages of the pieces, where battered, broken and rusty, it was carried along as trash until such time as it could be brought before a duly authorized inspector for formal condemnation to be "dropped" from property returns of the battery; or, more frequently, it was eliminated from the returns by the remark "lost in action."

The sabers retained for noncommissioned officers were used more as badges of authority than as veritable weapons. Noncommissioned officers not thus armed were supplied with revolvers, certainly a very great improvement on the saber.

The first battery to be equipped as horse artillery discarded entirely the saber and adopted the revolver for all the men. Other batteries, following as horse batteries, adopted the same custom. But it was soon discovered that revolvers were of no practical use for men of a battery, even for horse batteries, and in a little while they too fell out of use except for noncommissioned officers, who still retained them more as badges of authority than for actual use as weapons.

The fundamental idea of suggesting that the men of field batteries be individually armed arises from the supposition that the battery may be caught without the protecting support of other arms of the service and thus fall easy prey to the enemy. All of which might possibly occur with a carelessly conducted expedition, or even with an army corps marching in the country of an enemy without ordinary precautions. But where such conditions exist, no amount of personal armament will suffice to correct the evil. When batteries fall under incompetent commanders, whether of army corps or of small expeditions, they must take their chances and that is all that can be said about it.

Batteries do not operate in the field without the support of other troops. In a general sense, all the troops about them, whether a single battalion or an army corps, become their supports, and reciprocally, they are the supports to such troops. They each do their proper share of the battle with their own specific arms, using them in such manner as to be most effective. When their supports are hard pressed by the enemy, then is the time for batteries to put in their greatest efforts, not however by resorting to the use of hand weapons, always of little value at such times, but by standing to their guns with strenuous energy.

In spite of everything to the contrary, batteries will sometimes be lost in battle, even by the victorious party. But to attempt to prevent it by resorting to puerile methods, such as the use of sabers or revolvers, is to tempt Providence.

It is furthermore sometimes supposed that batteries require arms for the use of their camp guards. Nothing is more fallacious. A driver's whip in the hand of a sentinel at the picket line is far better in preserving order among the horses than a saber or revolver, and as to sentinels over the battery park, their functions, as mere watchmen, are performed quite as well without as with arms. To the eye of the amateur soldier these suggestions may seem highly unmilitary; but it must be remembered that in time of war all that is not actually useful should be discarded.

APPENDIX A

The following is an edited extract from Henry J. Hunt, "Our Experience in Artillery Administration," *Journal of the Military Service Institution*, March 1891, 214-223.

Whilst the South had at the beginning of the war a better raw material for infantry and cavalry, the North had the best for artillery. It has been well said that "a battery carries with it all that goes to make up civilization." It requires many mechanics with their tools and stores, and also what are called "handy men," intelligent and self-reliant, for no two men at a gun do the same work. No country furnishes better men for the artillery proper than our own northern, and particularly our New England states, and if, as in other armies, the best fitted for this service were assigned to it, we would lead the world in this arm.

In nearly all modern armies a distinct organization called the "Train," formerly furnished drivers to all branches of the military service. A company of the train and one of cannoneers were united to form a battery, which, being the largest artillery force that could be controlled by a single voice, was the artillery unit, and the tactical equivalent of the squadron of cavalry, or battalion of infantry. Our own service, through necessity, improved this system. Having no organized "train" a company of artillery when mounted and converted into a battery had to furnish drivers from its own members. Frequent mounting and dismounting caused one of the artillery captains to devise a simpler system of instruction, adapted to our actual condition and arranged in progressive lessons, for the use of beginners. Omitting prescribed infantry and cavalry exercises it made the duties of cannoneers and drivers interchangeable. The system was adopted by the War Department just in time to meet the demands of our volunteer army, and enabled the batteries to take the field as soon as the infantry.

In 1857 the Ordnance Department prepared four gun-howitzers, of the new system devised by the Emperor Napoleon III, to replace all other field pieces, and issued them to one of the light batteries. This gun weighed 1200 pounds, was sufficient for either shell or shot, and greatly simplified the munitions, instruction, and service. It was an improvement in the material, analogous to that in the personnel, and they together made the battery homogeneous.

The battery was on the extreme left at Bull Run, where the artillery, mainly by the canister fire of the Napoleon guns and unaided by infantry, repulsed the Confederate attack under circumstances that stopped the pursuit of our defeated right at Cub Run. [Major] General [John A.] Logan therefore claims that Bull Run was a drawn battle. Without going so far as this, we may safely claim that two or three batteries, a dozen guns, repulsed the attack of the enemy's right, disconcerted the operations of his whole army, and probably saved our own from destruction.

Our disorganized troops returned to Washington, and [Major General George B.] McClellan was immediately summoned from West Virginia.

One of his first acts was to appoint Major W.F. Barry his chief of artillery. A better choice could not have been made.... He was chief of artillery of the Army of the Potomac in its Peninsular campaign, and occupied the same position in [Major General William T.] Sherman's campaign of 1864-65, being Inspector General of Artillery between these periods for all the armies, with his headquarters in Washington.

Charged with the artillery defenses south of the Potomac after Bull Run, I soon learned that, with the exception of the light 12-pdr. battery and a few rifled batteries, all our field artillery must be created.

Unfortunately we adopted a rifle gun of 3-inch caliber, the feeblest in the world; and our ammunition, of which there was no fixed system, was not good. With uninstructed gunners the best material is wasted; with poor ammunition the best gunners are at fault. Then the complication from which the Napoleon gun had relieved us,–a great variety of ammunition,–was brought back with the rifle-gun, for which different systems of projectiles, Parrott's, Schenkl, Hotchkiss and Ordnance, were supplied, which gave different ranges with the same charge of powder. These systems would get mixed in the same battery, and affect its efficiency. There was amongst the younger artillery officers a demand for the rifle-gun as the latest improvement, and it was urged by the Ordnance, but General McClellan wisely took the opinion of the older officers and directed that half the batteries should be light 12-pdrs. This gun held its own to the end of the war, and at the request of General [John] Buford several of these batteries were equipped as horse artillery, because of their superiority at close range. With six horses to the piece they answered the purpose.

There was another matter that injuriously affected the artillery. It is admitted in all modern armies that it requires more time and instruction to prepare a man for artillery duties than for those of infantry or cavalry, but artillery demands for recruits were generally neglected until those of the other arms were supplied. Hence they were not furnished in sufficient numbers, nor in time to receive proper instruction, before the opening of a campaign, and the batteries were often dependent on the troops to which they were attached for temporary details to aid in serving the guns in battle. Yet with all the drawbacks, the batteries–I refer specially to those of the Army of the Potomac,–were pronounced by foreign officers, as well as by our own, to be "decidedly good." This was due to the zeal and devotion of the battery officers and men, and the simplified system of instruction. Whilst few if any of them reached the high standard of the old batteries that served in Mexico, they did not lack other fine qualities that distinguished the latter. Whenever opportunity offered they exhibited equal courage, daring and dash. They were just as ready to sacrifice themselves and often did sacrifice themselves, for the benefit of the other arms. It is unnecessary to cite instances, the history of the war abounds in them, and Confederate official reports, and non-unofficial writings, had given a generous and manly need of praise to this arm of the Federal service.

But the conditions were very different in the Mexican and Civil wars. In the former the artillery acted almost invariably by single batteries attached to brigades, or small divisions. The commanding general, communicated his plans, or orders, to his battery captain, and left him to execute his part of the work, in his own way, with the same freedom of action that other commanders possessed. The results were excellent....

In the Civil War, the artillery commands were composed of masses, a single army corps sometimes had more field artillery than served in the Mexican War. The disproportion of the artillery of an army corps to a single battery, was as great as that of a division of infantry to a regiment. It therefore required higher organization, higher grades of officers, with appropriate staffs, and more of them, then did the other arms. But the War Department wholly ignored the artillery, and left commanding generals to their own devices as to its organization. Nearly all the surviving artillery officers of the Mexican War, and many of the field officers of the arm, were assigned to other duties. The legal organization of the volunteer regiments provided for field officers, and the supply of generals for the large commands was left to the laws providing general officers for the whole army.

Let us now see what came of all this. General Barry told me that when at the War Department, he stated that General McClellan asked in the beginning for but two artillery generals, one as chief, the other to command the reserve, leaving the selection of brigadiers to command the corps artillery until field service indicated the proper selections; the Adjutant General [Brigadier General Lorenzo Thomas] objected that the law always allowed one brigadier for four regiments, forty companies, and that sixty artillery companies in his army would not warrant the appointment of two generals. General Barry replied that a battery was not the equivalent of a company, but of a battalion; but the Adjutant-General's opinion as usual prevailed. The next year [Major] General [Henry W.] Halleck held that a battery was equal to a regiment of infantry, that it was commanded by a captain, therefore could not need field officers, and it was directed in general orders that artillery should be taken into service by single batteries, "thus rendering the field and staff unnecessary." One cannot but feel a sympathy for the Department. It had really a hard question to decide. Here were the General-in-Chief and the Adjutant-General of the Army, the two highest military authorities, at issue; both were graduates of the Military Academy, and each was strong in his faith. Coin was out of circulation, so they could not "toss up" and settle the matter by "heads and tails," and it did not seem to occur to the Secretary to decide by drawing lots. So both principles were adopted, and to the end of the war the artillery was deprived of general officers, because the batteries were companies, and of field officers, because batteries were regiments. Of course, all promotions ceased in the artillery, and many accepted it elsewhere.

It followed, from the lack of both general and field officers with competent staffs for making their control effective over such extensive spaces as were covered by artillery masses, that there was difficulty in organizing and directing artillery commands. It is always an evil when bodies of troops, whose commanders are of equal rank, are placed as a whole under the command of one of them. The chief should always be of higher rank than those under his orders, and not merely the first among equals. It gives him weight and consideration everywhere, and doubles his value. "The king's name is a tower of strength." Now, as the few artillery field officers, at first mustered into service, disappeared by promotion, or casualties, the senior captain succeeded as such, and had to control other captains whose batteries were serving with his own, and as from time to time still other batteries joined whose captains had precedence of commission, the command of the whole body changed frequently, and instability was added to the other evils.

You have now amongst you an honored citizen, one of those who, as a captain, subject to all these drawbacks, admirably managed the artillery of his army corps, refused high promotion in other arms, and at the close of the war was given the barren brevet, not of major general, which he had earned, but of brigadier, the effective rank, to which, now the actual discharge of its duties, he had been entitled for years.

Every effort was made to remedy this state of things, but in vain. The War Department and the army administration turned a deaf ear to all representations, official and unofficial. Yet there was one easy way by which most of the evils could have been avoided. Immediately after the Battle of Fredericksburg, I asked [Major] General [Ambrose E.] Burnside to see President Lincoln and ask him to confer the artillery brevets recommended for the Peninsula and Antietam campaigns, and to assign the officers to me for duty according to their brevet rank; that this was asked not for the gratification of these officers, but because the good of the public service demanded it; that it would enable me to provide the corps and division artillery with chiefs of competent rank for their duties. General Burnside informed me on his return to the army that he had done so, that the president acquiesced at once, saying that when at Antietam he had promised General McClellan that he would do this; and requested that when General Burnside saw the Secretary, he would ask him to have the commissions made out, which Mr. [Edwin M.] Stanton promised to do. But, unfortunately, General Burnside mentioned the circumstance to General Halleck that evening, who said it must not be done, and had it stopped.

We may now illustrate by incidents in our Civil War how [the time had come for the employment of artillery in large masses, as a separate arm, as well as an auxiliary for special purposes], notwithstanding the failure of our "Grand Staff" to recognize it, or in any way to provide the means to secure its benefit.

At a conference of General Burnside with his grand division commanders to determine as to a battle at Fredericksburg, and how it should be fought, I undertook to put the army across the river on certain conditions, one of which was that all the Napoleon guns of the divisions should be placed at my disposal for the purpose, to rejoin their divisions as they crossed the bridges. This created so much dissatisfaction and even remonstrance on the part of division commanders, who did not probably understand that all artillery of an army is to be employed, when required for army purposes, under the general of artillery, that General Burnside at once abandoned an intention he had already formed on their suggestion, to break up the artillery reserve as soon as the battle was over, and distribute the batteries to the divisions. He now had the proofs before him that a strong artillery reserve, under the immediate command of the chief of artillery, was indispensable; for he could not rely on a prompt or cheerful acquiescence in calls on the divisions to supply its place when needed. The necessity in this case was absolute, because all the reserve artillery and the core reserves were required on a long line of nearly five miles, in order to command the whole ground in front of us, including the town, and to control the movements of the troops on the plain.

After the bridges were thrown the army passed over, and each division as it entered the town took its batteries with it, although not more than half a dozen could be employed there. The plan of battle was changed without my knowledge, and an attack ordered on the extreme right of the enemy, with only two divisions–[Brigadier General George] Meade's supported by [Brigadier General John] Gibbon's. The attack was resolute and for a time Meade was successful, but the supports were not sufficient; the enemy rallied and drove back both divisions, with heavy loss, Gibbon being wounded. Had I been informed in advance I could easily have drawn a hundred idle and useless guns from the town, where they blocked the streets, joined them to those on the plain, and supported by two of [Major General Joseph] Hooker's divisions, then on the spot, left both of [Major General William B.] Franklin's corps free for the assault. I have little doubt that Franklin would have succeeded, and if so, it would have been a disastrous day for [General Robert E.] Lee's army. It appears to be settled that General Lee abstained from taking the offensive after this and the bloody repulses at Marye's Heights, partly from the belief that Burnside would renew his assault, but mainly because of our artillery force on Stafford Heights on the north side of the river.

Whilst this goes to show that the development of the Federal artillery accomplished its purpose, there is room to regret it. [Lieutenant General Thomas J.] Stonewall Jackson, it appears, desired to take the offensive and "drive the Yankees into the river." Lee had a much larger force here than at Chancellorsville, but we had crossed in order to bring him to battle and would have welcomed such an attack–it probably would have resulted in a Federal victory.

Malvern Hill affords another instance of the power of artillery when acting in a mass, and of the importance of a large reserve, available for all exigencies that may arise. General D.H. Hill, in a recently published paper in the *Century*, says: "Our loss was double that of the Federals at Malvern Hill. Not only did the fourteen brigades which were engaged suffer, but the inactive troops, and those brought up as reserves too late to be of any use, met many casualties from the fearful artillery fire, which reached all parts of the woods for miles around. Hence more than half the casualties were from the Federal field pieces, an unprecedented thing in warfare."

All the disposable batteries of the reserve were here thrown in to reinforce the corps artillery, and we may remark that the forming of this powerful reserve by General McClellan had been much criticized. The night of this battle I was asked by a prominent officer of the War Department staff if it was true that all the batteries of the reserve had been engaged that day. On being informed that on average, each battery had been sent out twice, and always more artillery than that belonging to the troops was urgently needed, he expressed his surprise, and said that his opposition to the reserve would cease, for that day had proved the soundness of General McClellan's judgment. I may add that, with one third of the guns in the army, the reserve suffered in the peninsula half the losses of the artillery and killed and wounded.

I have failed in my purpose, if I have not made it clear that with proper organization and administration our artillery in the Civil War, good as it was, might have been more serviceable and produced greater results; that the War Department cannot manage it, and that its pressing need was, as it still is, a responsible chief for the whole arm, with a competent staff, military and administrative. The extent to which this would be centralizing and simplifying its administration may be illustrated by the condition of a single battery under the present system. In all that pertains to its personnel it is dependent on the Adjutant General's Department; as to its guns, carriages, ammunition and harness, on the Ordinance; for its horses, forage and means of transport, on the Quartermaster's Department. The artillery driver, seated in an ordnance saddle, rides a quartermaster's horse, his bridles are ordnance, and he urges his off horse with an ordinance whip, his horseshoes are ordnance, the smith who sets them a quartermaster's man. I have known batteries to go unshod at distant posts, whilst the two departments were settling in Washington their respective responsibilities in the matter. Thus since it has no head of its own, the artillery remains dependent not only on the various headquarters and the War Department, but upon the concurrence of all these bureaus, failure in any one of which nullifies the work of the others; and among them all the battery suffers, sometimes breaks down.

That this still continues is a disgrace to our army administration. During the whole War, the principal evils and their causes were repeatedly called to the attention of the War Department, but in vain, and I will close now by repeating the concluding paragraph of my last official report as commander of the artillery of the Army of the Potomac. "I do not hesitate to say that the field artillery of this army, although not inferior to that of any other in our service, has been from one third to one half less efficient than it ought to have been, whilst it cost from one third to one half more money than there was necessity for. This has been due principally to want of proper organization, which has deprived it of the experienced officers required for its proper command, management and supervision; and it is in no respect the fault of the artillery itself."

APPENDIX B

The following is an extract from John C. Tidball, "Remarks Upon the Organization, Command, and Employment of Field Artillery During War: Based on Experiences of the Civil War, 1861-1865," (1905), 36-37.

When, in April, 1862, the Army of the Potomac took up its march for the Peninsula . . . Yorktown was the first place at which the enemy was encountered, and so strong was his position then, aided as it was by many conditions adverse to the attacking force, it was deemed expedient to reduce the place by regular siege operations. In these the Artillery Reserve took an important share of the work, furnishing officers to assist the engineers in constructing batteries and other entrenchments; but most particularly was the Artillery Reserve useful in supplying teams, men and officers to transport siege pieces and other heavy ordnance to their places of emplacement; difficult work that had to be done only at night.

Those in charge of this part of the work found it more advantageous to call upon the Artillery Reserve for assistance than to go to the divisions and meet the remonstrances of division commanders. Thus at the very outset it was found that the Artillery Reserve was a very handy thing to call upon to do work of a general nature. It brought to the front the fact that in the Artillery Reserve the commanding general had at hand, a well organized artillery force ready for duty anywhere without interfering with the arrangements of either corps or division commanders.

INDEX

(Page numbers followed by *f* refer to illustrations.)